The Government & Politics of
IRELAND

THE POLITICS OF THE SMALLER EUROPEAN DEMOCRACIES

Editors

Hans Daalder   Val R. Lorwin

Robert A. Dahl   Stein Rokkan

The Government & Politics of
IRELAND

Basil Chubb

WITH A HISTORICAL INTRODUCTION BY
DAVID THORNLEY

Stanford University Press, Stanford, California
London: Oxford University Press
1970

Stanford University Press
Stanford, California
London: Oxford University Press
© 1970 by the Board of Trustees of the
Leland Stanford Junior University
Printed in the United States of America
Stanford ISBN 0-8047-0708-1
Oxford ISBN 0 19 690385 8
LC 77-93493

Preface

This book is intended primarily for students of Irish politics—for my students, in fact, and others like them who have lacked an up-to-date general work on the government and politics of the country. Before I began it, I was uneasily aware that little research had been done on Irish politics and, in particular, that there was virtually nothing on the political sociology of the Irish. It would be difficult, I thought, to write a satisfactory book. The finished work certainly demonstrates this fact, and no one is more conscious of it than I.

As I began this book, I was fortunately invited to join an international project supported by the Ford Foundation to study the politics of the smaller European democracies. The aim of the project is to produce a series of works on a number of the small countries of Western Europe, together with one or more works of comparative analysis. By participating in the meetings of the American and European scholars engaged in it, I have been able to benefit from the help and advice of the editors of the series—Professors Val Lorwin, University of Oregon; Hans Daalder, University of Leiden; Robert Dahl, Yale University; and Stein Rokkan, University of Bergen. This volume is the first of the series. If it remains insular, it is in spite of the editors.

Because so little political research has been done in Ireland, I have had to rely heavily upon personal inquiries. I am indebted to far more people than I can mention here—public servants, deputies and senators, officers of the Oireachtas, party officials, county managers, the secretaries and other officers of many associations, newspaper editors and journalists, executives and others in radio and television. To the many in all these categories who have helped me and whose willingness to assist I have sometimes exploited, I wish to express my thanks. The Yeats passages on pp. 33 and 42 are quoted from pp. 337 and 309 of *The Collected*

Poems of W. B. Yeats (The Definitive Edition, © 1956) with the kind permission of Mr. M. B. Yeats, Macmillan & Co. (London), and The Macmillan Company (New York).

In no country more than Ireland is a knowledge of the past, even the distant past, essential to an understanding of the present. I am, therefore, particularly grateful to my colleague, Professor David Thornley, for contributing a historical introduction. He is much better equipped than I am to do so. I acknowledge with thanks the help I had from my colleague Patrick Lyons, M.A., M.Litt., Lecturer in Economics, in the preparation of statistical material. Brian Farrell, M.A., Lecturer in Politics in University College, Dublin, and John Whyte, M.A., Lecturer in Political Science at The Queen's University, Belfast, read the manuscript, and I thank them for their comments and suggestions.

Throughout the preparation of the book I have been aided by Miss Geraldine Counahan, B.A., and I take this opportunity to acknowledge her assistance. In particular, she is responsible for the compilation of many of the tables and the preparation of material on Irish elections and elected representatives, both national and local.

As Arthur Young finished writing a preface to *A Tour in Ireland* on January 24, 1780, he added a note addressed to his Irish readers which I can do no better than to reproduce, changing only the address:

TO THE IRISH READER

In case of any errors or omissions being discovered in the following papers, by readers whose situation enables them to ascertain the truth, the author will be particularly obliged by a communication directed to him [at Trinity College, Dublin]; and if the work should hereafter be reprinted, due attention shall be paid to such corrections.

B.C.

Contents

Tables

Illustrations

Glossary of Irish Terms

Some, but by no means all, Irish political institutions are commonly called by their Irish names even when speaking in English. For the convenience of non-Irish readers a list of such terms used frequently in this book is given here.

Bunreacht na hEireann. The Constitution of Ireland. This term is usually applied only to the Constitution enacted in 1937 and still in force.

Dáil (full title, *Dáil Eireann*). House of Commons, Chamber of Deputies.

Eire. Ireland. The Constitution (Article 4) says that the name of the State is *Eire* or in the English language *Ireland*. The name Eire is often used outside Ireland to denote the present state, which comprises de facto only part, though the largest part, of the island of Ireland.

Fianna Fáil (literally Soldiers of Destiny). The title of the major party, founded by Eamon de Valera in 1926.

Fine Gael (literally Tribe of Gaels). The successor of Cumann na nGaedheal (literally League of Gaels), the pro-Treaty party. At present the second largest party.

Gaeltacht. The name given to the Irish-speaking areas. These are mostly situated on the western seaboard, in Donegal, Mayo, Galway, and Kerry.

Garda Síochána. The Civic Guards, Police.

Oireachtas. Parliament.

Seanad (full title, *Seanad Eireann*). Senate.

Sinn Féin (literally We Ourselves). Originally a nationalist political movement founded by Arthur Griffith in 1905. In 1917 a number of separatist groups coalesced under the title of Sinn Féin, pledged to the achievement of an independent republic. The movement split over the terms of the Treaty with the United Kingdom (December 1921). The movement has continued in existence ever since.

Taoiseach. Prime Minister.

Teachta Dála. Member of Parliament (literally messenger or delegate of the Dáil). Abbreviated to TD.

The Government & Politics of
IRELAND

ULSTER

CONNACHT

LEINSTER

MUNSTER

Londonderry

DONEGAL

BELFAST

Donegal Bay

Sligo

MONAGHAN

SLIGO

LEITRIM

CAVAN

Dundalk

MAYO

ROSCOMMON

LONGFORD

LOUTH

Westport

WESTMEATH

MEATH

Drogheda

IRISH SEA

Athlone

DUBLIN

GALWAY

OFFALY

DUBLIN

Galway

Dun Laoghaire

Galway Bay

KILDARE

R. Shannon

WICKLOW

LAOIGHIS

ATLANTIC
OCEAN

CLARE

TIPPERARY

Carlow

CARLOW

Kilkenny

Limerick

WEXFORD

LIMERICK

Tipperary

KILKENNY

Clonmel

Waterford

Wexford

Tralee

KERRY

WATERFORD

St. George's Channel

Killarney

CORK

Cork

50 Miles

Bantry

Historical Introduction

DAVID THORNLEY

Two basic factors, one economic and one geographic, have for long cast their shadow over the politics of Ireland. The first is that the island possesses no abundance of mineral resources and, consequently, no tradition of industrial development. This means that Ireland has been dependent for its national wealth upon agricultural production, and upon importation for the bulk of the artifacts that sustain industrial civilization. Today and for the foreseeable future, Ireland is, therefore, defined by economic circumstance as essentially an exporter of primary agricultural produce, notably cattle, and an importer of heavy industrial equipment and consumer goods. For these reasons the Irish people have for centuries been condemned to the proportionately low standard of living that is often the concomitant of agricultural production; it has also made Irish economics, and therefore Irish politics, abnormally sensitive to external forces over which the political state of Ireland can have no control.

The second determinant factor is the proximity of Ireland to the larger and wealthier island that is Great Britain. The role of Britain as the main market for Irish exports and for Irish emigrant labor, and as the main purveyor of Irish imports of manufactured goods, is one that has survived unchanged the violent fluctuations in the political relationship between the two islands. Over one million Irishmen emigrated to Britain in the first forty years after their country had won political separation from the neighboring island. Today, approximately 70 per cent of Irish exports go to Great Britain and over 50 per cent of Irish imports come from there. Inevitably, the political fortunes of the two islands have been intertwined. Ireland was for almost seven hundred years a subordinate part of the British political system; six of the island's 32 counties, containing roughly one-third of its people and of its total wealth, remain part of the United Kingdom. Irish political debate for centuries has been dominated by the proximity of so large and obvious an influence. Legal, administrative, and electoral developments in Ireland for centuries mirrored those of England and still retain the mark of their origin; a common language serves government and culture. Even negatively, this principle has operated: the development of Irish popular religion was colored by reaction against the political implications of the Anglican settlement, and Irish political nationalism tended, with some exceptions, to express itself through English forms and English metaphors. Duality between the assertion of national identity and economic and for many years political subsumption into the British orbit is, therefore, the most recurrent single facet of the Irish political character.

This duality presents the student of Irish politics, historical or contemporary, with something of a dilemma. Many of the questions he seeks to answer concern British as much as Irish politics. The questions —how was political democracy achieved and how did centralized modern administration develop?—are obvious examples. No historian could hope to comprehend the complexities of Irish politics without a parallel study of those of Britain, and for long periods, most notably the half-century between 1868 and 1922, the converse is equally true. The student may, therefore, be tempted with some justice to treat Ireland as an ex-colonial, recently independent state. In this case, he may well feel that the most useful questions to ask are more like those the student of Indian or Canadian politics would ask than those of the student of Sweden or Holland. Such an approach has much to justify it, especially in administrative terms, and is a useful antidote to the romantic school of Irish historians, who have tended to see Irish history as the record of a continuous struggle for national independence.

II

Valid in part as the study of Irish political development in the context of British imperialism may be, and useful as a corrective, it ignores factors that have been recurrently crucial in the shaping of Irish history. Unlike so many of the emergent African states, Ireland is not a legal unity superimposed arbitrarily upon ethnic and economic diversity by a conqueror. The island in many respects is a natural unit possessing a history of unified development which antedates by centuries the assertion of British dominance over it. After a succession of migratory incursions from neolithic times, the island was subjected to invasion by the Celts in the fourth century B.C. The invaders divided the lands they conquered into petty kingships. The province or "fifth" was the largest effective unit, but a theoretical "high kingship" was later developed in the hands of the family of Ui Neill and based upon Tara in County Meath.

This political unity was often more theoretical than real, and effective power seems normally to have been contained in a balance between the dominant northern and southern tribal kingships, based respectively on Tara and Cashel. But it was buttressed by a genuinely unified tradition of language, culture, religion, law, and social life. Moreover, largely because Ireland escaped the direct influence of Roman imperialism, these were institutions that differed in certain aspects quite strikingly from those of Britain. Pre-Christian Ireland has been described by one scholar as "tribal, rural, hierarchical and familiar,"[1] and these characteristics conquered rather than succumbed to the successive external influences of the period between the fifth and eleventh centuries. A complex of interrelating kingships remained the form of political organization. Class divisions fell rigidly into three main groups: the landed aristocracy, the serfs, and the practitioners of culture, from poets and craftsmen to doctors. All were embedded in a legal framework of privileges and duties none the less rigid because they were essentially customary. Perhaps the feature of this legal tradition that was to conflict most sharply with English law was the conception of property as vested in a familial group rather than in a single individual. Social life was pastoral and agricultural, with the typical unit the homestead. Contact with Roman Britain was maintained up to a point in trade and, in Rome's declining days, in piracy, but without the stimulus of Roman overlordship no urban tradition developed. Christianity came to Ireland through western British missionary influence, but the attempts of St. Patrick, the most famous of the first half-legendary missionaries, to impose a formal diocesan system upon the island never accorded happily with its social characteristics, such as the absence of towns. The monastic tendency took root early, with the monasteries firmly tied to the ruling family in each petty kingdom, and by the end of the sixth century the Irish Church was characteristically monastic in organization. It was to remain so until the Gregorian reforms of the twelfth century.

Irish religion was unusual in yet another way that was to leave its mark upon the development of national consciousness down to modern times. This was its emphasis on learning. The Gaelic-speaking Celts of Ireland already possessed a remarkable oral tradition of pagan sagas. To

[1] D. A. Binchy, "Secular Institutions," in M. Dillon, ed., *Early Irish Society* (Dublin, 1954), p. 54.

this was added, from the seventh century onward, a flowering of Celtic Christian culture which has been described as the "most remarkable spiritual, intellectual and artistic movement of Dark Age Europe."[2] Perhaps the most obvious physical manifestation of this creativity was the way in which the Irish Church dispatched waves of self-exiled missionaries to the recovery for Christianity of much of Western Europe. But culture, artistic and literary, went hand in hand with religious enthusiasm. During the seventh century the poets and storytellers were gradually absorbed into the Church, while the monks contributed the patient skill of manuscript writing and illumination, both sacred and profane, both Latin and vernacular.

This short-lived cultural flowering led to the development of a tradition of Gaelic literature and song, which was to provide a cultural distinguishing mark in the long-drawn battle against English influence that began in the twelfth century. So long as the old tribal kingships held tenuous sway over a shrinking Gaelic Ireland, the old vernacular and the old reverence for Gaelic culture were to survive. With the completion of the English conquest in the seventeenth and eighteenth centuries, the patrons of Gaelic culture withered away, and the last of the Gaelic poets could only lament the passing of an era that for a thousand years had produced a continuous stream of literature. The conquered Gaels finally adopted the language of their conquerors; they diluted it with Anglicized Gaelic constructions to an extent that almost makes Anglo-Irish writing and speech an independent linguistic form, but in the census of 1851 less than 30 per cent of the people were classified as Irish-speaking.

This victory of the English language was never to be reversed. But Gaelic culture was to gain a remarkable second lease on life in the late nineteenth and early twentieth centuries. In literary terms this was to be the work of a school of prose and verse writers, mostly of mixed Anglo-Irish rather than Gaelic blood, and many of whom were Protestants. Their best-known if not most typical figure was the poet and dramatist W. B. Yeats, who turned to Gaelic legend for inspiration. In more popular terms, a similar inspiration was to be seen in the attempt of the Gaelic League, which was founded in 1893, to restore Gaelic (now usually called Irish) to its position as the vernacular of the majority. This attempt was unsuccessful, but it succeeded in engendering a remarkably widespread intellectual identification with Gaelic culture. This identification was almost always synonymous, by then, with po-

2 L. and M. de Paor, *Early Christian Ireland* (London, 1967), p. 64.

litical nationalism. The ideal of Patrick Pearse, a product of the Gaelic League and leader of the revolution of 1916, from which six years later political independence was derived, was to achieve an Ireland "not free merely, but Gaelic as well; not Gaelic merely, but free as well."

It follows, therefore, that the phenomenon of "Gaelic Ireland" can never be discounted by the student of history or twentieth-century Irish politics as irrelevant to his theme. The finest flowering of Gaelic culture was relatively short-lived; it reached its height in the seventh and eighth centuries; by the middle of the ninth century it had begun to wane as a delayed result of the Viking raids which had commenced as Ireland fell into the sphere of Scandinavian expansion at the end of the eighth century. The Vikings brought some considerable benefits, notably the introduction to Ireland of urban life; towns like Dublin and Wexford date from this period. But the Church, once the principal inspirer of art and letters, declined in spirituality and in cultivation, and by the twelfth century it was a subject of reproach to Continental reformers, providing one of the theoretical justifications for papal approval of the English invasion. The structure of authority was correspondingly shaken after the end of the tenth century as the possession of the high kingship was increasingly in dispute, and the warring factions were never able to offer unified resistance to the English invaders, who from the twelfth to the eighteenth century eroded and finally destroyed their power. But despite this failure, Gaelic Ireland was to bequeath a system of law and authority, language, custom, social habit, and arguably even religion, essentially different from their English equivalents. And in the age of political nationalism, the memory of this "differentness" was to give cohesion and confidence to those who sought to rationalize their economic, political, and religious grievances against English rule in the demand for the political separation of the two islands. So the Gaelic ideal bridges a millennium between the Europe of the monasteries and the Europe of Mazzini.

III

The will of Gaelic civilization to survive was abetted by the spasmodic nature of the English conquest. The first Norman arrivals in the second half of the twelfth century were less the spearhead of an "English invasion of Ireland" than royally (and papally) licensed freebooters. They consolidated themselves in what lands they could conquer in the east of the island and sporadically sought to extend them, living in alternate amity and strife with their Gaelic neighbors. Significantly, the most successful of the first Norman leaders symbolized the consolidation of his gains by marrying into the Gaelic aristocracy. After three centuries of this sort of practice, many of these alleged exponents of the power of the English monarchy on its Irish frontiers had become, in a famous phrase, "more Irish than the Irish themselves," thoroughly acclimatized to the use of Gaelic language, dress, and manners, despite largely futile legal proscription of such practices.

In the fourteenth century, the power of this first wave of invaders reached its high water mark territorially, but Ireland remained even then divided into three areas. The first was the "English land," where English law and administration ruled. Its extent fluctuated; it was permanent only in the environs of Dublin, extending north into the eastern seaboard counties of Meath and Louth and west into the neighboring county of Kildare. This area, which became known as the "Pale," was to develop a political and to some extent ethnic distinction which left its mark on Irish politics long after the island had been administratively united under English law. Second, there were the great feudal "liberties," which enjoyed a substantial measure of effective self-government, and third, large areas, especially in the north and west, where Gaelic rule survived largely intact. Few English kings visited Ireland, and fewer still stayed there for long; as one medieval historian has put it, "the persistent flaw in English rule in Ireland was the absence of the monarch himself."[3]

In the fifteenth century, as English power declined, riven by the Yorkist-Lancastrian conflict, the Gaels reasserted themselves and the area of direct English influence shrank. At the same time, the feudal lords, descendants of the original invaders, whom after four centuries one may legitimately describe as "Anglo-Irish," attained their fullest measure of aristocratic home rule. At the end of the century the most powerful man in the island, who "came nearer to being the accepted king of Ireland than any man since the Conquest," was Garret More Fitzgerald, the Great Earl of Kildare, a hibernicized aristocrat under whose auspices as technical "Deputy" to the Crown "Gaelic Chiefs and old English lords allied and intermarried openly."[4] At the end of four centuries the conquest was, therefore, not merely physically incomplete inasmuch as large areas of the island remained under the authority of the Gaels; it had also produced a cultural and almost an ethnic fusion of conquerors and conquered whose aristocracy was the "Anglo-Irish" or, as they were often called on account of their long removal from the land of their ancestral origin, the "old English," a group suspicious of royal power and intermittently successful in ignoring it.

3 E. Curtis, *A History of Ireland* (London, 1966), p. 88.
4 *Ibid.*, p. 156.

This three-part balance was inevitably upset in the sixteenth century when the Tudor family successfully renewed and reasserted the powers of the English monarchy. A combination of political and religious accident and deliberate intent compelled the Tudors to assume the obligation finally to subdue Ireland to the Crown. They did so at first only with considerable reluctance, since aggressive diplomacy was an expensive pursuit and parsimony a Tudor characteristic. This obligation was inherited and completed by the Stuart kings. In practical terms, completion of the conquest involved three main operations: first, the breaking down of Anglo-Irish independence; second, the subjugation of Gaelic Ireland to English law; and third, after 1536, the extension to Ireland of the Protestant Reformation in its Anglican form. By the end of the seventeenth century the relative success of the first two operations and the relative failure of the third had defined the context of what nineteenth-century English statesmen were to call the "Irish question."

The ending of Anglo-Irish home rule was symbolized in military terms by the destruction of the power of the family of Fitzgerald between 1520 and 1540; a generation later a further rebellion in Munster, by then significantly charged with the characteristics of religious war, was defeated after a fifteen-year struggle which devastated much of the southern part of the island. At the same time the Irish Parliament was firmly incorporated into the processes of English rule. The medieval Irish Parliament had been naturally developed by the Crown and the Anglo-Irish aristocracy in a manner broadly derived from English usage. There remained, of course, the essential difference that in England Parliament was an integral part of that feudal hierarchy in which the entire population was set, whereas in Ireland it was irrelevant to Gaelic tradition and to the Gaelic practice that held sway in a large part of the island. Its historic role was, therefore, as the cockpit for the often conflicting needs and ambitions of the Crown and the Anglo-Irish aristocracy. The foundation of the Irish Parliament is usually placed in the year 1297, when Edward I, seeking support for his Scottish wars, authorized the summoning, in addition to the usual council of bishops and peers, of two knights and the sheriff or seneschal from each of the nine counties and five "liberties" which fell within English law. In its gathering of 1376 the Irish Parliament assumed what was to prove its characteristic role. It was never able to impeach the Ministers of the Crown, who remained responsible to England alone. But its right to that most historic of parliamentary powers, the granting of assent to taxation, was established. In the fifteenth century, as the apogee of aristocratic home rule was attained, the independence of the Irish Parliament grew correspondingly, and an act of 1468 stated that English statutes were to be valid in Ireland only if ratified by the Irish Parliament. In this period Parliament was the implement of Fitzgerald ambition and Yorkist intrigue.

Such pretensions were obviously incompatible with the security of the Tudor kingship, and between the end of the fifteenth and the middle of the sixteenth century the Irish Parliament lost its independence. In 1494 the reduction of the position of the Great Earl of Kildare by the new Deputy, Sir Edward Poynings, was ratified in a carefully packed Parliament in Drogheda, and the famous "Poynings' Law" was passed. This act stated that no Parliament was henceforth to meet in Ireland until the royal approval had been granted to its being summoned and to its agenda. The full significance of this law was scarcely perceived then, but it was in fact to nullify the initiative of the Irish Parliament for almost three centuries. The new role of Parliament was most clearly seen in the next century. Under Elizabeth it met only three times. On each occasion it was summoned only to deal with specific business; at other times government proceeded without it.

The subjugation of the Gaels was a longer and more costly proceeding. The tactic of Henry VIII was to bring them peacefully under the rule of English law by the policy of "surrender and regrant." Gaelic chiefs were to be persuaded to surrender their lands, forswear their ancient titles, and accept ennoblement and the regranting of their lands from the hands of the king. The device broke down upon the incompatibility of the English and Gaelic conceptions of property-holding and inheritance. English titles carried little weight in Gaelic Ireland, and the junior members of Gaelic aristocratic families, who had formerly enjoyed some share in the ownership of their lands through the complex familial bonds of Gaelic custom, were loath to accept dispossession of their rights at the hands of a remote English monarch. A direct conflict between the remaining Gaelic rulers and the Crown became virtually inevitable in the second half of the sixteenth century. Excommunication had rendered Elizabeth the legitimate object of Catholic attack, and her ministers had witnessed with alarm the power of the religious issue in the Munster wars, where Anglo-Irish rebellion had been aided by papal and Spanish assistance. They could not afford to tolerate the continued existence of independent Gaelic Catholic principalities on England's western seaboard. The Gaels of Ulster had seen in turn the extension of English law and of Protestantism over the eastern and southern parts of the island; they could not doubt that their downfall was next. At the end of the sixteenth century the Tudor monarchy and Gaelic Ireland reluctantly accepted the costly and final gamble of war. Despite some initial successes, the Gaelic forces slowly succumbed before the superior equipment and the extermination tactics of the royal army. In March 1603, the submission of Hugh O'Neill, Earl of Tyrone, the greatest of the Ulster chieftains, marked the completion of the English conquest and the end of Gaelic Ireland as an independent society with native traditions of law and culture.

But in two respects particularly, the absorption of Ireland into the English political system was quickly shown to be far from complete. A combination of economic pressures at home and the desire to increase the dependably loyal portion of the Irish population as against the suspect Gaels and Anglo-Irish caused the government toward the end of Elizabeth's reign to pursue a course first attempted in the middle of the sixteenth century—the extensive plantation with new English settlers of Irish lands confiscated in the successive wars. In the first major application of the policy, approximately 400,000 acres of Munster lands were offered to speculators who were prepared to undertake to plant them with English families. The scheme was incompetently administered, the lands had been spoliated in war, English families came forward slowly, and the "undertakers" covertly accepted Irish in their place. But the precedents it set were not forgotten either by the government or by the Anglo-Irish. The conclusion of the Ulster wars, and the flight of the Earls of Tyrone and Tyrconnell, provided an opportunity to repeat the experiment upon a much larger scale. The government declared forfeit the whole area now comprising the six modern counties of Armagh, Cavan, Londonderry, Donegal, Fermanagh, and Tyrone, four of which are part of modern Northern Ireland, and proceeded to organize its plantation with English or Scottish settlers.[5] The plantation was not immediately successful; by 1628, there were only about 2,000 English or Scottish families in the six planted counties. But after 1660 the Scottish element came to predominate and to give to Ulster that distinctive ethnic and religious character that has since marked off so many of its inhabitants from those of the rest of the island. By 1641 only 500,000 of the 3,500,000 acres in the six planted counties remained in Catholic hands, and this proportion was further reduced as the century wore on. At the same time, the Scottish immigrants laid the foundation of "the only case of a real democratic, industrial, and labouring colony established in Ireland."[6] So developed the ethnic division that was to gener-

[5] Two of the six counties of modern Northern Ireland, Antrim and Down, were not included in the plantation, though parts of them were granted to settlers of English or Scottish stock, and many immigrants, particularly from Scotland, were brought over by private enterprise.

[6] Curtis, *History of Ireland*, p. 232.

ate the "Ulster question" in the late nineteenth and early twentieth centuries, and, ultimately, the political partition of the island.

The reformed religion never took root among the mass of the population. The Anglican settlement was accepted without much opposition by the great majority of the Irish bishops, and Acts of Uniformity and Supremacy were bulldozed through Elizabeth's month-long Irish Parliament of 1560. But the majority of the old English aristocracy retained their unreformed faith, while no serious attempt was made to convert the Gaelic-speaking majority. In Ulster alone the plantation secured the popular foundations of Protestantism, and even here its Scottish origins ensured that it took Presbyterian rather than Anglican form.

It is, therefore, in this period that we can detect the emergence of many themes that were to become the origin of the Irish question in the period of nationalist agitation, some of which influence Irish politics to the present day. First, the island had been firmly and decisively incorporated into the periphery of English politics and administration. Moreover, whereas in the hybrid Ireland of the fifteenth century the considerable commerce of the south and west had been directed to continental Europe from flourishing ports like Galway and Kinsale, now, with the destruction of Gaelic and Anglo-Irish independence, the axis of communication was established from an eastern center to a western periphery. This shift in emphasis was to prove permanent. Second, this greater economic and political dependence upon the British community became increasingly associated with a "new class," principally though not exclusively distributed in the east and northeast of the island. The loyalty of this class was to Britain, in many cases its place of recent origin and in all cases the guarantor of its political and economic power. Finally, this transference of power was identified in spiritual terms with the reformed religion, imposed by English will and accepted with enthusiasm principally among the newer immigrants, the administrators and planters of the Tudor conquest.

From these three developments grew that convenient identification of political dissent and Roman Catholicism which, overgeneralization though it always was, nevertheless contained sufficient truth to make religious hostility a vital factor in Anglo-Irish politics from the sixteenth to the twentieth century.

IV

If the Tudor conquest was technically successful, it nevertheless bequeathed two of the characteristic problems of Anglo-Irish relations— land and religion. Three classes broadly disputed the possession of the soil of Ireland. First was the Gaelic majority, those people who had been progressively dispossessed and reduced to dependent status for five centuries. Their sense of grievance was to linger in the folk memory until their resurgent victory in the land wars of the late nineteenth century. Second was the "old English" class, originally dispossessors, then often tolerant neighbors of the Gaels, and now finally themselves increasingly dispossessed. Finally, there were the new administrators, planters, and speculators of Tudor and Stuart Ireland, accompanied in Ulster by a large number of tenants, predominantly Scots. In religious terms, the first class was almost exclusively Roman Catholic, the second largely so, and the third exclusively Protestant—either Anglican or Presbyterian.

The most obvious consequence of this realignment in terms of a seventeenth century dominated by English Stuart politics was to impose an appalling dilemma upon the old English in Ireland. Ethnic origin, tradition, and military weakness bound them to the Crown; on the other hand, the fear of economic and religious discrimination had given them grievances in common with the Gaels and a common suspicion of England's Parliament and bureaucracy. Inevitably, in the English revolutions of the 1640's and of 1688, they were driven into a military course of action that was partly an attempted reassertion of Anglo-Irish independence and partly a gambler's fling on the plausible assumption that the Stuarts offered a better prospect of economic and religious leniency than their Protestant adversaries. But in both cases they picked the losing side. The long-term result of the Irish wars of the seventeenth century was virtually to complete the expropriation of both Gaelic and old English Catholics. In 1641, 59 per cent of the land of Ireland remained in Catholic hands; in 1703 the corresponding figure was 14 per cent, and this figure was to be further reduced by the expropriations and the religious conversions induced by the discriminatory religious laws of the late seventeenth and eighteenth centuries. "Protestant ascendancy" over a landless Catholic majority was to be the established pattern of the next two centuries.

Throughout the eighteenth century this conflict found political expression in Protestant dominance of the Dublin Parliament. The remaining upper-class Catholics found virtually their sole political outlet in lobbying for the repeal of the discriminatory laws that excluded them from economic wealth and political power. A sense of economic and religious grievance smoldered among the peasants, which was to find expression in agrarian outrage and the beginnings of proletarian rebellion.

The Irish Parliament remained, of course, the preserve of a Protestant aristocratic minority. It displayed, at least as obviously as the Parliament of the sister kingdom, the contemporary electoral phenomena of rotten boroughs and the buying and selling of seats. Many seats were in the patronage of landlords; in others the votes of the forty-shilling freehold electors were delivered to the poll by the landlords, whose tenants-at-will the voters effectively were. Elections were infrequent, since Parliament might last until dissolved by the Crown; one eighteenth-century Parliament lasted for thirty-three years. Equally, the Irish Parliament remained powerless to control the executive or to exercise legislative initiative. But the physical extension of English law over the island had rendered Parliament at least geographically representative, while its growing assertion of its right to assent to internal taxation forced it to be summoned at least every two years. At the same time it achieved a minor dilution of Poynings' Law by insistence upon its right to debate draft bills for submission to the Lord Lieutenant, the royal representative.

The eighteenth-century Parliament was thus able to become, if not the mouthpiece of Irish popular feeling, at least the debating ground of Irish Protestant grievances against English rule. These fell increasingly under two broad headings. The first was the attempt to assert the independent legislative power of Parliament, especially in respect of fiscal business. The second was a growing economic discontent. The eighteenth-century English policy of restricting Irish manufactures, especially of wool, had the major effect of emphasizing the dependence of Ireland upon agricultural production and the secondary effect of fostering linen production in the northeast of the island. For decades the Irish Parliament demanded the removal of the restrictions upon Anglo-Irish trade. In the course of its campaigns on these two points the Irish Protestant elite acquired some sense of cohesion and identity in opposition to Britain. Their efforts were crowned by success between 1779 and 1782. Most of the restrictions on trade were removed, and the royal power of initiative in respect of Irish legislation was reduced to one of veto over the acts of the Irish Parliament. The victory was more apparent than real; it was reversed eighteen years later in the final legislative union of the two islands under a single Parliament. But while the Irish Parliament of 1782–1800 was ephemeral in history, it gained permanent place in the mythology of nineteenth-century nationalism.

From these parliamentary joustings, the Catholic majority, rich and poor, were firmly excluded. The bulk of the discriminatory laws against Catholics had first passed into desuetude and then been repealed as the eighteenth century progressed. By the end of the century, Catholics might again accumulate wealth and a measure of social status. Both factors, however, frustratingly emphasized that they could neither vote nor sit in Parliament. The Protestant leaders, firm in the defense of their own economic and political rights, were divided on the parallel claims of their Catholic neighbors. Only English tactical pressure secured the granting of the franchise to economically qualified Catholics in 1793, and the Irish Parliament disappeared without having admitted Catholics to its counsels. So religious tension was kept alive as a significant factor even in upper-class Irish politics.

The mass of the population remained excluded from constitutional politics for both religious and economic reasons. The landlords, many of them resident in England, were generally uninterested in agriculture except as a source of profit without involvement; middlemen sublet and sublet again the land of Ireland; the leases of the actual cultivators were generally both short and insecure; tillage was more inefficient and rents higher than in England, and the quicker return offered by sheep farming diminished the area under the plow. The population meanwhile rose to almost five million at the end of the century; it became largely dependent upon the potato crop and a consequent prey to the possibility of famine, of which one in the 1740's was an ominous portent of things to come a century later. Agrarian crime became commonplace in the second half of the century as freer importation of cattle into Britain gave a new incentive to the reduction of tillage. In successive and largely undocumented rural tenant movements, the Irish peasant revolution was born in the south of the island. It found its first outlet in the hamstringing of cattle and, with more political potential, in the murder of their owners' agents.

Late-eighteenth-century Ireland thus possessed in a degree that varied across region, class, and denomination the motives for economic, political, and religious dislike of the system by which it was governed. Into this setting fell the new ideas of Paine and Rousseau, of the American and French revolutions. The Protestant aristocracy formed a paramilitary "volunteer" movement and postured in green uniforms which were symbols half of loyalty and half of independence. The Catholic mass dully contemplated the relationship between its present poverty and second-class citizenship, and the dispossession of its ancestors. The dissident intellectuals, mostly Protestant, imbibed the heady wine of the new republicanism, and in 1791 founded the United Irish Society, dedicated to religious unity with Catholic Ireland and political separation from Britain. Intellectually the Society's greatest strength was, ironically, in Ulster. By the mid-1790's, the Society had decided on rebellion with French aid. In 1798 its plans, such as they were, matured. The rebellion of that year was trivial in military terms. In the southeast alone the peasants, who, being illiterate, had not read Paine, offered serious resistance to the government forces. They paid for their irrational temerity in a series of long-remembered reprisals. But 1798 was nevertheless unique and important. For the first and last time Ulster Presbyterians— who, it must be remembered, were also the victims of religious discrimination by the Anglican state—made common cause with southern Catholics. And the assertion of Irish grievances by armed uprising was made now, not in the context of princely Renaissance politics, but at the dawn of the age of European nationalism.

The results of this rising, ill-planned, ill-led, and savagely repressed, were enormous. In the short term, it sealed the doom of the Irish Parliament, which had lasted for five hundred years. Britain, beset by Napoleon, could not, any more than in the sixteenth century or in 1916, tolerate the survival of a potential enemy to its west. In 1800 a combination of threats, bribes, and promises secured the passing of an Act of Union through both Parliaments. Ireland was henceforth to be represented by four episcopal and twenty-eight secular peers in the English House of Lords, and one hundred Members of Parliament in the Commons. For over a century Irish grievances were to be, in rising crescendo, a theme of the London Parliament. Parnell was Pitt's legacy to Gladstone.

From the long-term point of view, the rebellion of 1798 fashioned the terms of what might be called the "nationalist" (and for our purposes most important) phase of the Anglo-Irish relationship in three ways. In the first place, it made clear to the Irish Protestant landowners that their ascendancy was dependent upon the British connection. It had always been a weakness underlying the gestures of the Dublin Parliament that its members were a minority whose status had been secured by a conquest, in many cases far from remote in time. The year 1798, by showing them the alternative of intellectual republicanism and a Catholic resurgence, wedded most of them firmly and irrevocably to the Crown. Nineteenth-century Irish landlordism was to produce no latterday Earl of Kildare.

Second, the rebellion posed a dilemma for the surviving aristocracy and the rising bourgeoisie of Catholic Ireland. The English government had won them the vote in 1793; it sweetened the pill of the Union with the half-suggested offer of the subsequent removal of their remaining religious disabilities. If the Protestant landlords had found the guarantee of ascendancy in the English Crown, perhaps the wealthier Catholics could pursue its undoing in the English Parliament. It was a more congenial alliance for them than that offered by either intellectual republicanism or peasant violence.

To that last, and ultimately, victorious republican tradition, 1798 bequeathed the first great legend in the creative myth of Irish revolutionary failure. The gallantry of the Wexford pikemen and the savagery of their repression were to pass into the folk memory of those whom Wolfe Tone called "the men of no property," and to give inexhaustible matter to the romantic poets and song writers of middle-class nineteenth-century nationalism. When the men of 1916–22 sang behind the barricades of Dublin and around the campfires of a guerrilla war, many of their most deeply felt songs were of "Ninety-Eight." Equally, the idea that English involvement in Europe was the signal for Irish revolution was also a heritage of 1798; when Patrick Pearse declined to let slip the opportunity of the First World War, this was the precedent he invoked. To that shadowy entity which, with pardonable exaggeration, one Irish revolutionary and historian has called "the underground nation,"[7] the year 1798, with its curious blend of the political republicanism of the intellectuals and the agricultural suffering of the dispossessed, better perhaps than any other date marks the birth of modern Irish nationalism.

v

So far we have endeavored to isolate certain basic strands in the history of Ireland up to 1800 which were to remain the major causal influences in the last century before the gaining of Irish independence. These may be very broadly divided under three headings. The first was the land issue. Throughout the nineteenth century Ireland remained not merely a predominantly agricultural country but one heavily dependent upon the British market. After six centuries of struggle, the original Gaelic stock had largely lost possession of their land, either to landlords who deprived them of ownership and reduced their race to tenant status or, more especially in the northeast, to planters who physically dispossessed them. Already there was developing what was to be the characteristic demographic polarization of the country in the nineteenth century, which still survives in some measure—the division between the west and south, largely poor and overpopulated, and the more wealthy and progressively more industrialized east and northeast. The west and south furthermore showed what was to be their characteristic pattern of a rising small-farm population, excessively dependent upon the production of a single crop, the potato. This class not merely possessed

---

[7] P. S. O'Hegarty, *Ireland under the Union* (London, 1952).

no title of ownership to its land but lacked even security of tenure. It was dependent upon landlords largely English in origin and often domiciled in England, who were concerned more with the profitability of their rents than with the improvement of their lands, still less the improvement of the living standards of their tenants.

Second, as a result partly of the plantations and partly of the effects of the religious penal laws, Irish Catholicism had developed in a particular form. The great bulk of the landed Catholic aristocracy accepted either dispossession or the reformed religion. There was a growing Catholic bourgeoisie whose problems were to assert themselves in the nineteenth century. But no serious effort had ever been made to persuade the peasant community to accept Protestantism. Accordingly, there was a corresponding coincidence by which religious division between Protestantism and Catholicism almost invariably paralleled social division between rich and poor. The result was the growth of a distinctive peasant Catholicism of a special pietistic and unlettered kind, which survives to this day and largely explains the dual role of the priest as spiritual leader and community spokesman.

Finally, there was frustrated nationalist feeling, now increasingly developing in what might be described as a nineteenth-century or modern form. Many factors and many social categories contributed to this political force. There was the rump of the Catholic aristocracy, which had neither cringed into conformity with its social class nor succumbed to the penal laws. There was the slowly growing Catholic bourgeoisie, denied educational opportunity and professional or political outlets in its own country. There were intellectuals of both the northeast and the south like Henry Joy McCracken and Wolfe Tone, both Protestants, whose republicanism was heavily influenced by Continental patterns of thought. Ultimately perhaps most important, there was a suppressed tradition of peasant violence; a tradition that stemmed, above all, from the resentful folk memory of a dispossessed race. This resentment was further fanned by the cultural phenomenon of the Gaelic language and its literary tradition, discouraged, indeed positively suppressed by authority, but by no means dead. In a manner not dissimilar from eighteenth-century Highland Scotland, language became with religion yet another of the stigmata of social isolation and political identity. This association between language and religion was never totally to be lost; to this day the Gaelic Athletic Association, the sporting symbol of one form of Irish identity, employs the Catholic hymn "Faith of Our Fathers" as the ritual prelude to its major spectacles.

If, then, the nineteenth and twentieth centuries were the era of Irish national resurgence, this was the consequence not of one single social revenge theme but of at least three. "The resentment of the common people against their rulers was produced by no question-begging folk myth: it drew its vigour from three great stimuli, at once emotional and practical. Of these a sense of nationality was only one; the others were land and religion. The rivalry of these three great forces at some times paralysed the popular will; their sporadic coincidence produced great cataclysms in the history of Ireland. In their interaction lies the explanation of many of the apparent paradoxes of that story."[8] Finally, the pattern was further complicated by the development of sporadic, minority, and ultimately abortive proletarian socialist movements comparable with those in other Western countries.

VI

The religious issue was the first to assert itself. This was not surprising, since the pressure of the remaining penal laws bore most heavily upon the more educated and articulate section of the Catholic bourgeoisie. This caused for a time a coincidence of Catholic, nationalist, and tenant disgruntlement, but it was a coincidence that was not to last. Toward the end of the eighteenth century the Catholic Church in Ireland had increasingly been placed in an anomalous social position which to some extent it was never to lose. In the context both of European history in this period and of the Irish penal laws, it was ultramontane, conservative, and juridical in form and outlook. Yet it inevitably assumed by default the cultural and often political leadership of a potentially revolutionary sub-nation whose deprivations it shared, at least for the moment. In broad terms the history of nineteenth-century religious conflict is the story of the dissolution of this coincidence of purpose by the steady concession of the demands of bourgeois Catholicism. The removal of the most extreme of the penal restrictions in 1793 had already eased the legal position of the Church, and in 1800 the influence of the Hierarchy was fairly solidly in support of the Union whereas, paradoxically, that of the Ulster Protestant Orange Lodges was the reverse. In return, the offer of "Catholic emancipation"—a euphemism for a process by which the growing Catholic bourgeoisie were conceded full professional and political privileges—was a logical one, although the second half of the bargain was delayed until 1829. Catholic Ireland, as Cardinal Manning and the Vatican were later to point out, could best fulfill its missionary destiny within the mighty empire.

[8] D. Thornley, *Isaac Butt and Home Rule* (London, 1964), p. 13.

And the major Irish seminary, St. Patrick's College, Maynooth, was in this period heavily influenced by refugees from the French Revolution in whom words like liberty and equality evoked no kindly response. After Emancipation, the bond between the Church and the Crown was strengthened by the payment of an annual grant to Maynooth. As R. Lalor Sheil, one of the leaders in the Emancipation movement, put it: "Are not lectures at Maynooth cheaper than state prosecutions?"[9]

The role of the priest as social leader was crystallized by Daniel O'Connell (1775–1847), arguably the first modern politician in Western Europe. O'Connell virtually invented perambulatory demagoguery a half-century before Gladstone's Midlothian campaign. But in Ireland he based it, logically, on the material to hand—the unique literacy and social eminence of the clergy, and the closely knit relationship of the parish unit. The system worked to perfection where mass feeling and clerical interest coincided, as in the Emancipation movement, less effectively where their coincidence could not be taken for granted, as in the land and national struggles. Clerical influence was not uniformly conservative; younger priests, like Fathers O'Shea and O'Keeffe in the Tenant League in the 1850's, braved hierarchical disapproval to espouse quasi-revolutionary movements. This inner division remained a unique feature of Irish Catholicism up to the 1920's and 1930's, when dissident curates could always be found who would absolve republican revolutionaries in the teeth of hierarchical condemnation. But by the time of O'Connell's death the socio-political role of the Catholic clergy was defined, and in the main it was to be exercised against republicanism, socialism, and all manifestations of physical force.

Apart from Emancipation, the main specifically religious issues of the nineteenth century were the tithe and education. In theory a permanent charge upon land for the support of religion in Ireland, the tithe was paid by the Catholic tenant to an alien and unfamiliar clergy in addition to his already usually extortionate rent. Four Anglican archbishops, eighteen bishops, and about 1,400 parish clergy catered for perhaps a tenth of the population, and were maintained by the whole people. Not surprisingly, tithe collection was widely resisted and often had to be enforced by troops. In 1838 a partial solution was adopted; the tithe became a fixed rent charge, and one payable by the landlord, who was to collect it through added rent. One popular grievance was thus removed, but not the fundamental Roman Catholic objection to maintaining the clergy of another denomination. This issue was not

9 Quoted in J. Connolly, *Labour, Nationality and Religion* (Dublin, 1954), p. xiii.

effectively resolved until the disestablishment of the Church of Ireland in 1869.

Perhaps the bitterest religious controversy of the century concerned education. At the primary level blatant Protestant proselytism was the rule. The Kildare Place Society, nominally interdenominational, had been set up in 1811 to counter this tendency, but its efforts carried little popular conviction. Catholic educational demands were at first cautious. A meeting of the clergy in 1826 declared that "the admission of Protestants and Roman Catholics in the same schools may, under existing circumstances, be allowed, provided sufficient care is taken to protect the religion of the Roman Catholic children." Thus, when in 1831 the National Education Board was set up on a basis of "joint secular and separate religious instruction," hopes for its success were high. But the death of the liberal Dr. James Doyle, Bishop of Kildare and Leighlin, left the ultramontane Dr. John MacHale, Bishop of Tuam, the major educational figure in the Hierarchy. In 1837 the Christian Brothers, to this day the mainstay of Catholic primary education in Ireland, withdrew from the Board; in 1850 the bishops forbade Catholic school managers to appoint teachers who had been trained in the interdenominational Model schools, and in 1870 the Powis Commission found that schools were in fact if not in theory denominational. In 1883 denominational training colleges replaced the Model schools. The "managerial" system, in which the local clergyman of appropriate denomination took control of the school as nominal trustee for the parishioners, was effectively established, and survives to this day.

The "University Question" affected fewer people but was comparably bitter. Trinity College, Dublin, the island's sole university, had been opened to Catholics in 1793, but it was not until 1873 that the last religious tests were abolished and the more senior posts opened to "persons of any or no religion"; access to them was in any case beyond the educational resources of most Catholics. In 1838 the report of an educational committee headed by Sir Thomas Wyse proposed the establishing of provincial colleges which should contain either no theological teaching or, alternatively, duplicated faculties, and in 1845 a bill was introduced upon these lines. Nondenominational colleges were opened at Belfast, Cork, and Galway in 1849, and were united in the "Queen's University" the following year, but not before MacHale had obtained papal rescripts denouncing them as dangerous to faith and morals. The denunciations were largely effective; MacHale's demand for "nothing but separate grants for separate education" had become established as the irreducible minimum.

The Hierarchy went ahead with the establishment of a distinctively Catholic University, inviting over the future Cardinal Newman for a brief and uncomfortable spell as its first rector. But it lacked state recognition and, more important, financial aid. In 1879 a characteristically ingenious act of the then Conservative administration set up the "Royal University," a purely examining body, which enabled candidates from the Catholic University to take its degrees, and indirectly provided it with a modest capitation subsidy. Finally, in 1908, the National University was set up, comprising the Cork and Galway Queen's Universities and the Catholic University, the Belfast college becoming the independent Queen's University. Technically nondenominational, the National University was effectively Catholic. The Hierarchy had gained its point, and incidentally a measure of educational partition between Ulster and the rest of Ireland had been determined which anticipated the parallel political solution of 1922.

In sum, the century's religious struggles established, at every social level, a pattern of denominational division, hierarchical conservatism, and clerical community leadership that was to prove one of the decisive legacies to the independent state.

V I I

In historical sequence the issues of land and nationality are even more difficult to separate than those of religion and nationality. From the early years of the nineteenth century onward they were closely linked, and the echoes of their association were to be heard as late as 1931. But since the grievances of the insecure tenantry were relatively satisfied before the termination of the nationalist struggle, and since, in turn, that fact heavily influenced the form taken by the latter conflict between 1916 and 1922, it is perhaps justifiable to consider the land agitation before finally turning to nationalist politics.

The system of landholding that prevailed in Ireland at the beginning of the nineteenth century was not merely based upon the principles of landlord right and tenant insecurity; it was also subject to intense complexity deriving from local custom and successive subletting. So much was this so that one commentator could say in 1830: "Scarcely one profitable acre in Ireland but is subject to a graduated scale of proprietors each being on a previous profit-rent."[10] The process of subdivision and the multiplication of small and ultimately uneconomic holdings was exacerbated by the pressures of rising population and the absence of any

10 A. Flood, *The Poor Laws* (Dublin, 1830).

economic alternative. The increasing profitability of cattle-ranching and the related legislative attempts to restrict subletting proved ineffective to counter it. By 1841, out of a total of 826,000 tenant holdings, 445,750 were under five acres—these were the holdings of cottiers who contracted for a season and, in semifeudal style, paid part of their rent in labor.

But where legislation failed to clear the complex of subletting, the great famine of the late 1840's largely succeeded. The Poor Law of 1847, which forbade relief to anyone who held more than one-quarter of an acre, earned the contemporary description of "the great instrument which was clearing Ireland." The famine also ruined many landlords, particularly the less efficient—and the more humane. But the very complexity of the system of tenure made land sale slow and difficult. The post-famine demand for free trade in land resulted in the Encumbered Estates Act of 1849, under which bankruptcy courts were empowered to sell land on the application either of the legal owner or of the "encumbrancer" or creditor. One of the objects of this Act was ironically evocative of the plantations of two centuries before: it was hoped that thrifty English and Scottish farmers might be tempted to replace improvident and prolific Irish Papists. The hope was vain; by 1857 only 300 such yeomen were among the 7,200 buyers.

The Act did, however, effect a radical change in the system of tenure over much of the country. In the ensuing thirty years almost five million acres, or one-third of the cultivated land of Ireland, was sold under its provisions. The new landlords, anxious to realize a profit on their investment, hastened to the work of clearance; evictions, which from 1847 to 1849 had totaled 25,700, amounted to a further 58,423 between 1849 and 1853. It is unnecessary to stress the physical suffering involved; the consequent demographic changes are more relevant. These, surprisingly, did not necessarily relate to the poor quality of the land. Fertile Leinster, because of its proximity to Britain, was foremost in the changeover to cattle-ranching, with its high profit and low demand for labor. Over the country as a whole, the number of holdings under five acres had fallen by 1851 to 125,811, whereas those over fifteen had risen from 128,000 to 280,000.

In Ulster the tenant had traditionally fared better than his southern equivalent. Although this tradition had no legal sanction, in practice the tenant was considered, broadly speaking, to possess a salable interest in his holding; if the landlord wished to displace him, he was generally obliged either to allow the sale of this interest or to repurchase it himself at its market value. But this complicated custom was progressively eroded by the demands of nineteenth-century utilitarianism.

When, after the famine, the larger tenant farmers of the south began to organize in pursuit of greater legal security, the Ulster farmers had a comparable if less pressing economic motivation to join them. For a time the moderate unified platform became the demand for the universal legalization of the Ulster custom of "compensation for improvements." But the alliance recurrently foundered on the rocks of religious and political division, just as industrial unionism was to divide fifty years later.

The ultimate part practical, part mystical desire of the Irish peasant was not, however, security of tenure, but legally to own the land on which he worked. The unlikely origin of this final process of peasant proprietorship was the Act of 1869, which disestablished the Church of Ireland. As part of its provisions, farming lands formerly held by the Church were offered to its erstwhile tenants with the added inducement of state loan facilities to purchase. By 1880 over 6,000 out of 8,400 tenants had taken the option to purchase. In fostering peasant ownership the 1869 Act was more effective than the actual land reform measure passed by the Liberal Government in the succeeding years; only 877 tenants availed themselves of its highly restricted purchase provisions. This latter Act gave legal force to the "Ulster custom" in those areas where it traditionally existed; elsewhere it introduced a complicated scheme of compensation for improvements and for "disturbance" on eviction. But since it decreed no compensation for eviction on nonpayment of rent and no restriction on rent increases, its provisions were absurdly easy to evade.

The major breakthrough in the establishment of a peasant proprietary came when the agricultural depression of the late 1870's gave birth, first, to the militant Land League of Michael Davitt and, second, to its tactical alliance with the Parliamentary Party of Charles Stuart Parnell. The Land Act, which was passed in 1881, conceded to the tenant what had long been known as the "three F's": fair rent, fixity of tenure, and free sale. In the land courts consequently established, almost 380,000 tenants won rent reductions of around 20 per cent, plus a further 20 per cent reduction for one-third of that number. But the basic claim for ownership remained, ironically, to be conceded by the English Conservative Party, traditionally the instinctive ally of the Irish landlord. The concept of "dual ownership" in the 1881 Act weakened the political influence of the landlord, and a succession of purchase schemes, largely of Conservative origin, completed the process. An Act of 1885, which offered the tenant the loan of the entire purchase price of his holding, was so successful that the original £5 million allotment was quickly doubled. Loans were to be repaid to the government at 4 per cent interest per annum over a period of forty-nine years; with the achievement of Irish independence this obligation was to prove a source of national contention, but for the moment the peasantry were glad to grasp their long-sought security. Further measures of the same kind followed in 1891 and 1896; the Wyndham Act of 1903 encouraged the sale and division of entire estates by offering a 12 per cent bonus to the retiring landlord; later an element of compulsion was added. By 1909 some 270,000 holdings, or about 60 per cent of the country's cultivated land, had been purchased under these provisions. By 1917, out of a total of 572,574 holdings, 367,058 were owner-occupied, and half the remainder were garden plots of less than one acre. When the Free State was established, scarcely 90,000 holdings within its territory were still in landlord hands. The following figures tell the story:[11]

Year	Owners	Tenants	
1870	3.0%	97.0%	(persons)
1906	29.2	70.8	(persons)
1916	63.9	36.1	(persons)
1929	97.4	2.6	(farm area)

The struggle for the land had been bitter, often violent, and charged always with the emotional recollections of the horrific privations of the famine and the evictions that followed it for over a generation. Superficially it ended in a folk victory; the insecure tenant of the 1850's became the peasant proprietor of the twentieth century. In practice his security was often illusory, since his holding, especially in the south and west, was so uneconomically tiny as to render its ownership a doubtful blessing. The folk myth of the nineteenth century is the struggle of the Gael to regain the land; the reality of its conclusion was the establishment over much of Ireland of a small-farm pattern which, since it resisted cooperation, could be sustained only by the safety valve of emigration and by subsidization, first by emigrant remittances and then, in the new state, by doles and transfer payments concealed as agricultural subsidies. This atavistic clinging to uneconomic peasant ownership is perhaps the greatest political influence bequeathed by the nineteenth century to the twentieth, perhaps more decisive even than any issue of nationality or religion. The achievement of successive English reforming administrations, from Gladstone's to Balfour's, was to convert the great bulk of the Irish peasantry from social revolution to social conservatism. In so doing they determined, largely unwittingly, that the

[11] E. Rumpf, *Nationalismus und Sozialismus in Irland* (Meisenheim am Glan, 1959), p. 181.

pattern of the final, national revolution should be socially conservative.

The consequent paradox is, in short, that whereas it is arbitrary for the historian to separate from each other the three issues of land, religion, and nationality, it remains true that the first two were hived off from the third in that they were resolved separately and at earlier dates. Moreover, this separation fundamentally influenced the ultimate conclusion of the national struggle and the form of the twentieth-century state.

VIII

The absence of any necessary association between the three themes was demonstrated as early as the career of O'Connell. The success of the Emancipation campaign in 1829 had rested upon O'Connell's manipulation of a mass movement in which the Catholic clergy, the surviving Catholic aristocracy, the Catholic bourgeoisie, and the peasantry were united behind a single objective. But there was no such unity of purpose behind the principle that the repeal of the Union stood next upon the national agenda. The priorities of the Hierarchy gave precedence to the tithe and to education; they viewed with particular suspicion any aspiration that might be held to bear the smallest trace of Continental republican influence. For the bourgeoisie the doors of Parliament, the bar, and the colonial service were opening at last. Though the peasants could contribute little on their own, even their next priority was, arguably, security of tenure rather than national independence. O'Connell, a convinced advocate of repeal, was consequently compelled to oscillate between a tactical alliance with any reforming British administration and a revival of the emancipation-style mass agitation. He adopted the first tactic in the 1830's, and won from the Liberals minor concessions in such areas as municipal reform, particularly after the appointment of the enlightened Thomas Drummond as Under-Secretary for Ireland in 1835. But the alliance was equivocal and uneasy, and the gains won before Drummond's death in 1840 and the fall of Lord Melbourne's Government in 1841 scarcely justified it.

Accordingly, in 1840 O'Connell, now entering his late sixties, unfurled the flag of repeal and tried to revive the old Emancipation tactics with his National Repeal Association. But his failure was inevitable. Apart from the erosion of bourgeois support already mentioned, he faced one last, insurmountable obstacle: the success of the Emancipation campaign had finally rested upon his capacity to exert moral blackmail upon a British ruling class that was not totally unsympathetic. Irish nationalism, on the other hand, was to be viewed by the bulk of that class, right down to the twentieth century, with the same implacable aversion it was to show toward its own proletarian politics. In the event, the Repeal Association was shown to lack an ultimate threat to British rule, and it dragged out its last years, until, in 1847, the death of O'Connell and the famine between them ended, for the moment, all hope of the development of an effective constitutional nationalistic movement.

O'Connell's growing ineffectiveness, his readiness to temporize with British administrations, and his inexorable aversion to the use in any circumstances of physical force were increasingly irksome to the younger militants in the Repeal Association, in particular a group of intellectuals led by Thomas Davis, William Smith O'Brien, Charles Gavan Duffy, and John Mitchel. Collectively associated in what became known as the "Young Ireland" movement, they maintained a steady criticism of O'Connell's tactics in the *Nation* newspaper (1842–48). Davis, a nationalist writer of enduring influence, died in 1845, but the movement continued, and under the shadow of famine its members finally lost patience with O'Connell and, in 1847, established the rival Irish Confederation. The intellectuals in the Confederation were, however, by no means united in their militancy, and never commanded anything like the popular support enjoyed by O'Connell even in his declining years. Mitchel was a convinced physical-force revolutionary with embryonic socialist leanings, but many of the others were drawing-room patriots. This was shown when the pressure of the famine and the heady examples of Europe in 1848 finally moved them to action. The Irish contribution to the year of revolution petered out in a gentlemanly confrontation between Smith O'Brien and the police in a Tipperary village. There were some impressively rhetorical trials, and a young lawyer named Isaac Butt made a reputation as an advocate which was to prove useful twenty years later. But the adventure left no lasting mark. It did not even leave any lasting martyrs; unlike the peasants of 1798, and the Fenians of 1867, who were shepherded promptly to the gallows or the dungeons, the Young Ireland leaders found their death sentences mitigated by the alternative of transportation to Australia, and most of them lived to comfortable old ages, O'Brien in retirement in his estates, Gavan Duffy ultimately as Prime Minister of Victoria, and Thomas Francis Meagher as a General in the Union Army in the American Civil War.

The 1850's and 1860's were perhaps the most politically barren decades in nineteenth-century Irish politics. The peasantry had been reduced to helpless misery by the famine; O'Connell was dead and the Repeal Association moribund, and the alternative of intellectual republicanism had been easily crushed. The nationalist issue lay fallow for twenty years, and land and religion took precedence over it in a fresh permutation of the three main themes in Irish nineteenth-century politics. The conflicting claims of the land and religious issues to prior consideration rapidly asserted themselves. The Tenant League, founded in 1850 to agitate for greater security of tenure, joined forces with a group of Catholic liberal MP's in the 1852 general election and won a superficially impressive success. Forty-one MP's attended a League conference in Dublin in September 1852, and only one dissented from a resolution that in Parliament these Irish members should hold themselves "independent of, and in opposition to" any government that would not meet their demands for legal security of tenure.

This resolution was notable because it expressed the first serious attempt to form an independent Irish party at Westminster, uncommitted to either the Liberals or the Conservatives; to that extent it foreshadowed the Home Rule Party of 1873–1918. But by the end of the decade it was in ruins. There were many reasons for this: the unrepresentative nature of the electorate and the power of the landlords over it; the absence of suitable candidates from the ranks of the aristocracy and the bourgeoisie; the aversion of mid-nineteenth-century MP's to any form of party pledge or discipline; the subservience to the government, which derived from its possession of administrative patronage; the betrayal of the financier John Sadleir, one of the party leaders, who first took office in defiance of his pledge and then committed suicide, bankrupting many small Irish investors in the process. But not least among the reasons for the collapse of the League and the party was, again, the issue of the competition for priority between land and religion. Dr. Paul Cullen, who was Archbishop of Dublin from 1852 to 1878, was a political conservative whose priorities were quite clear: the faith took precedence, and anything that savored of social or national revolution was anathema. The parish clergy, many of whom had been active in the Tenant League, were instructed to withdraw from politics. The League accordingly lost any remaining chance of maintaining an organizational base on the O'Connellite pattern, and its Catholic parliamentary members were increasingly placed in conflict with their Archbishop. The combination of obstacles was insurmountable, and it was symbolic that Gavan Duffy, the last dogged survivor from the pre-1848 leadership, left Ireland in despair, describing the country as "a corpse upon the dissecting table."

IX

The decade between 1858 and 1868 was the nadir of nineteenth-century Irish constitutional politics. A splintered band of Irish MP's more or less closely affiliated to either of the two major English parties ritually and ineffectively debated the issues of land and religion. But a revival now occurred in the physical-force tradition. Two of the more militant surviving participants in the 1848 debacle, James Stephens and John O'Mahony, were encouraged by the sympathetic response they had found in revolutionary circles in Paris and, more important, in the embittered, anti-British environment of emigrant Irish America to revive the theme of revolution on the twin base of Irish American money plus military expertise, and native peasant support. This time, however, they saw the need for secrecy rather than the flamboyance of 1848. Stephens returned to Ireland in 1858 and established the Fenian Brotherhood, an oath-bound, national organization based on interconnecting circles culminating in a "Supreme Council," the structure of which anticipated the Communist "cell" system. Parallel with this secret activity was a "front" newspaper, the *Irish People*, founded by Stephens in 1863, which disseminated the writings of, among others, such celebrated nationalist romantics as John O'Leary and the novelist Charles Kickham.

The Fenian Brotherhood was perhaps the most ultimately important revolutionary organization in modern Irish history. It represented the first concerted attempt to combine the principle of Irish nationalist revolution with an element of conspiratorial realism. And under its alternative title of the Irish Republican Brotherhood it established a chain of republican leadership whose continuity was never to be totally broken even in the period of its worst reverses. The Brotherhood asserted itself decisively in the final struggle of 1916–22 and the subsequent civil war. It also introduced the association between Irish republicanism and Irish American money that was to endure down to the 1930's. Finally, it used cleverly a tactic later to be employed between 1916 and 1922—to tap the combination of disaffection with England and military skill to be found among the Irish in the lower ranks of the British army.

Despite its long-term influence, the Fenian Brotherhood was, however, little more militarily effective in the 1860's than the Young Irelanders in 1848. Plans for a military rising, heavily dependent on Irish American money, arms, and experience in the Civil War, were laid in the mid-1860's. But the façade of secrecy was penetrated relatively easily by police spies, and the principal Irish leaders, including Stephens, were arrested in 1865 in anticipation of a revolt. Stephens escaped, but proved remarkably hesitant to call his men to arms. When, in March 1867, the decision to do so was taken, the opportunity, if it had ever existed, was past, and the revolt disintegrated in circumstances almost as humiliating as those of 1849. Stephens was permanently discredited, and even suspected of duplicity. The other principal leaders were sentenced to long terms of imprisonment, not in transportation, but in the most hideous confines available within the British prison system, an experience that permanently damaged the health and in some cases the sanity of several of them. Except in America, the chain of command was virtually broken.

Nevertheless, Fenianism left a revolutionary tradition more popularly based and more enduring than any of its predecessors. Its power was quickly shown in three ways. First, it left a "myth" of popular resistance scarcely present in the theories of Young Ireland or the short-lived pragmatism of the Independent Irish Party. Second, it left its quota of martyrs to inspire future generations by the example of their sufferings— men like Jeremiah O'Donovan Rossa, whose privations in Portland Prison, including thirty-five days of torture with his hands manacled behind his back, became a republican legend, and whose funeral in Dublin in August 1915 provided Patrick Pearse, the leader of the 1916 rising, with the opportunity to inspire a great republican demonstration with a dramatic appeal to emulate the sacrifices of the past. In some ways even more celebrated were three men who never took part in the actual rising of March 1867, W. P. Allen, Michael Larkin, and Michael O'Brien, who were hanged in Manchester, after a somewhat dubiously impartial trial, for killing a policeman during the attempted rescue of one of their compatriots. This incident was followed in December by another attempted rescue at Clerkenwell Prison in London in which twenty people were killed in an explosion.

The Fenians, finally, did more than create a new generation of Irish martyrs. They also injected a catalyst into both Irish and British parliamentary politics. The Clerkenwell explosion was the culmination of the process by which William Ewart Gladstone, for some years growingly concerned with the problem of Irish disaffection, became obsessively convinced that it was at the root of British politics. It was an obsession that he was to follow doggedly until his retirement in 1893. In Ireland, Fenianism convinced a growing section of the bourgeoisie that they were caught in a revolutionary situation which the amiable shifts of the 1850's and 1860's were inadequate to palliate. The ultimate irony of the history of Ireland under the Union was that these two exercises in rethinking proved incompatible with each other.

The main English casualty was Gladstone himself. At the time of the 1868 election he was in the first stage of the reconsideration of Irish discontent which was to be the climacteric of his career, but he was not as yet prepared to contemplate even the most limited tampering with the Union between the two islands. Instead he offered a three-point reform program: the disestablishment of the Church of Ireland, the provision of some legal security for the tenantry, and the provision of university education for Catholics. Twenty-five years before, O'Connell would have exulted at such concessions. Now, only the Disestablishment Act of 1869 proved a popular success. The Land Act of 1870 was well-intentioned but complex and feeble, and the University Bill of 1873 satisfied neither the English Liberals, fervently hostile to any form of denominational education, nor the Irish Hierarchy, whose aspiration was state subsidization of a denominational institution effectively run by themselves. The Bill was defeated, and Gladstone's Ministry nearly brought down. The Irish Liberal members, who had in the main faithfully echoed their bishops' views in the division lobbies, were placed in the most hapless position of all. In 1868 Gladstone had seemed about to justify belatedly their timid repetition for twenty years of O'Connell's tactics in the 1830's. Now their justification was gone, and with a marginally larger electorate and, for the first time, a secret ballot, their seats were in imminent danger.

The Unionist reverse provided the necessary fillip for a revival of constitutional nationalism. Like Gladstone's Liberal Unionism, this also stemmed initially from the Fenian catalyst. The lawyer Isaac Butt, a hero of the 1848 trials, had returned to Ireland in 1865 after over a decade in London during which he had dissipated his fortunes and ruined his constitution and his political prospects. A series of accidents won him the brief for the defense of most of the Fenian leaders, and by 1868 he was once again a national figure and, perhaps more important, a Protestant constitutional politician who could command the qualified trust of at least some of those in the Protestant ascendancy, the Catholic liberal bourgeoisie, and the Fenians. In 1870 he founded the tiny, largely upper-class and Dublin-based Home Government Association; in 1873 he expanded it into the Home Rule League, which gratefully accepted Catholic liberal support on its retreat from its Gladstonian honeymoon. And finally, after the 1874 election, he was able to return to the House of Commons as leader of a party of fifty-nine Irish MP's pledged to a measure of self-government for Ireland within a federal United Kingdom, a demand that, in various forms, became known as "Home Rule."

The "Home Rule Party" was to dominate Irish parliamentary politics until 1918. But in practical terms it was, for the moment, little more effective than Gavan Duffy's party twenty years before. There were several reasons for this. The one most usually given is that Butt was an amiable gentleman, unprepared to disturb the even tenor of Westminster. But there were three other reasons of equal importance. Although he was already over sixty years old, his fading energies were further burdened by obligations to creditors. Second, in the five years left to him in Parliament, he had the misfortune to coincide, not with the flexible-minded Gladstone, but with a conservative Administration led by Disraeli, to whom the idea of Irish self-government was a subject for derision. Finally his party, almost as much as Gavan Duffy's, was a party in name only, most of whose members were Liberals prepared to pay lip service to nationalism in order to keep their seats. Not surprisingly, his persuasive powers proved totally vain at Westminster, and by his death in 1879 he had been largely written off by the serious men in his own party and, equally important, by the Fenians in Ireland, England, and America.

Such men were already turning to a possible successor in Charles Stuart Parnell, the youthful MP for Meath. Parnell first attracted militant approval when in 1877, in conjunction with six other Irish MP's, he embarked upon a policy of systematic obstruction of British parliamentary business as a reprisal for England's neglect of Irish grievances. The 1877 struggle reached its climax on July 31 and August 1, when Parnell and six other Irish members kept the House of Commons in continuous session for twenty-one hours. The tactic was provocative rather than constructive, and ultimately was thwarted by the revision of parliamentary procedure, but it served its purpose in contrasting Parnell's insolent determination with Butt's ineffective persuasion.

Parnell's second tactic was to regain at least the benevolent neutrality of the Fenians. He was aided in this by the economic depression of the late 1870's, which produced a major agricultural crisis in Ireland. In the immensely successful Land League, founded in October 1879, he was able to coalesce with the Fenian Socialist Michael Davitt in a mass organization which not merely reunited, for the moment, the themes of land and nationality, but won some kind of cautious approval from the Fenian republicans. This approval Parnell astutely cemented by a fiery tour of Irish strongholds in America, a tactic that was to be employed by future Irish leaders.

Having thus secured his rear, Parnell could turn to the capture of the leadership of an effective parliamentary party. The 1880 election resoundingly demonstrated his popularity; he was returned for three separate constituencies, and by 1881 he was the chairman of the Irish Party.

At once he mounted a twin-pronged assault on the government, now again led by Gladstone, over the land issue. His two tactics were implacable disruption of the parliamentary system in London and mass protest by the Land League in Ireland. His reward was the 1881 Land Act. This Act went a great deal further than that of 1870 to provide security of tenure, but was still far from satisfactory to the left wing of the League. A year of coercion and social tension culminated in Parnell's imprisonment. Leaderless, his popular following became still more inflamed, and violent outrages increased. Parnell, himself a landlord and at heart a social conservative, accordingly made a bargain with the government: his release in return for his support for a somewhat amended Act, and, more important, a semiformal alliance with the Liberal Party.

To Davitt, an exponent of the nationalization of the land, this bargain was a social betrayal, and to many of the Fenians it was an abandonment of the two-tactic strategy by which a constitutional party was buttressed at home by a quasi-revolutionary popular movement. Their view of the bargain was to a great extent correct: "The exclusively constitutional agitation which it foreshadowed was to continue unbroken until the last months of Parnell's life and, indeed, was to hold the centre of the stage until 1916."[12] To that extent it could be argued that the fate of the Parliamentary Party, and the reversion to violence, were determined nine years before it split in 1891.

The dilemma of the Party was now that it must persuade either of the British parties, more probably the Liberals, to endorse Irish Home Rule. Parnell approached this intelligently, biding his time at Westminster while building up a centralized and unprecedentedly disciplined party organization in Ireland. His reward came in the general election of 1885, which sent him back to London as leader of a solid phalanx of eighty-six members, largely middle-class in origin, and pledge-bound to "sit, act, and vote" as a unit.

This election was particularly significant because it was the first held under conditions approximating those of twentieth-century democracy. None of the English franchise reform acts passed between 1832 and 1884 was extended to Ireland without substantial dilution; as late as 1868 the electorate in the twenty-six-county area was as low as 6.5 per cent of the adult population; almost half the thirty-three Irish boroughs had fewer than four hundred voters each, and intimidation and corruption flourished widely. The first major breakthrough was the introduction of the secret ballot in 1872; the second was the 1885 Representation of the People Act, which not only increased the electorate to 26.9 per

---

12 F. S. L. Lyons, *Parnell* (Dublin Historical Association, 1963), p. 12.

cent of the adult population, but was accompanied for the first time by an effective redistribution of seats in accordance with population. The increase in the electorate caused little increase in the number of Home Rule seats, since outside Ulster the Party already effectively controlled the bulk of the constituencies. The new voters were as enthusiastic for Home Rule as the old, and as the electorate continued to grow, the dominance of the Party remained. It was not to collapse until 1918, and its failure then was a function not of mass democracy but of a series of political coincidences.

The immediate result of the 1885 election was another Liberal Government, but one dependent upon Irish support. Although Gladstone had refused to endorse Home Rule before the election, he had been laboriously considering the issue for several years, and he now introduced a bill to give Ireland a subordinate parliament. His party split; the bill was defeated in June 1886, and England's greatest opportunity to settle the Irish question without recourse to violence was lost.

For the next thirty years the Irish Parliamentary Party endeavored again and again to wring Home Rule from successive British governments. But in 1890 Parnell was discredited by his involvement in a divorce case; by 1891 he was dead and the Party was split. It was reunited in 1900 under the leadership of John Redmond, but although it continued to monopolize parliamentary representation in all but northeast Ireland, it was never again the force it had been in 1886. Further Home Rule bills were in fact introduced by Liberal administrations; the first, in 1893, was defeated and the second rendered a dead letter by the war and the 1916 uprising. In respect of the issues of land and religion, major concessions were gained, but the hostility of the Conservative Party and the increasingly well-organized opposition of the Protestant northeast of Ireland toward Home Rule blocked the constitutional road to self-government. The preconditions were accordingly established for the final revival of the revolutionary tradition.

x

The form in which the revolutionary tradition was revived was the combined result of five overlapping movements. These were the renewal of Gaelic culture in the Irish literary revival, the Gaelic League, and the Gaelic Athletic Association; the Sinn Féin movement; the injection of fresh energy into the Irish Republican Brotherhood; the founding of the Irish Volunteers in 1913; and the development of revolutionary socialism by James Connolly in the Irish Citizen Army.

The revival of interest in the Gaelic language and literature was not merely the earliest of these influences; it was also perhaps the most seminal, since it became the symbol of the pursuit of cultural identity. In its purely literary form it was fostered by a generation of Irish writers from Sir Samuel Ferguson to W. B. Yeats, who turned to the Celtic sagas for inspiration and unintentionally sowed more than they knew. As Yeats wrote, over twenty years after the 1916 uprising, in one of his last poems:

> All that I have said and done,
> Now that I am old and ill,
> Turns into a question till
> I lie awake night after night
> And never get the answers right.
> Did that play of mine send out
> Certain men the English shot?

Their initiative inspired an extraordinary popular enthusiasm for the Gaelic language as an inverted badge of serfdom which opened the doorway to the reassuring dominance of prehistory. The Gaelic League was founded in 1893 to reestablish Irish as the national vernacular language; the Gaelic Athletic Association, founded nine years earlier, inspired a popular reversion to historic Irish sports like hurling and handball. Together they were the cradle of almost every revolutionary leader of significance in the final struggle. Douglas Hyde, the first president of the League, and Seán T. O'Kelly, an active member, were to be the first and second Presidents of the State under the 1937 Constitution; Patrick Pearse, Commander in Chief in 1916, began his public career as a League organizer in western Galway; the young men of 1916–22, unable often to purchase rifles, drilled with hurleys and took semi-mythical heroes like Finn and Cuchulainn as their inspiration.

The second initiative was the establishment of a constitutional alternative to the Parliamentary Party, which could repeat the two-tactic alliance with physical force practiced between 1879 and 1881. This was Sinn Féin, which was founded in 1905 but which grew out of the writings of Arthur Griffith in the *United Irishman* from 1898 onward. The ultimate function of Sinn Féin as the political arm of the revolution could, however, scarcely have been predicted at this time. Griffith himself, its first president, was no republican, and was not involved in the 1916 rebellion; he was the exponent of a loose association between Ireland and England centered around the monarchy. And Sinn Féin had no broadly based support; its electoral forays were brushed aside by the Parliamentary Party in a by-election in 1908 and in the general election of 1910. But although neither Redmond nor even Griffith could have anticipated it, the embryonic constitutional alternative of Sinn Féin had only six years to wait before the revolutionary movement provided it with its opportunity.

That this was so was primarily because the Irish Republican Brotherhood was secretly remobilized in the first decade of the century. Still effective and relatively wealthy in America, in Ireland its leaders had become aged and ineffectual. Its transformation followed upon the return to Ireland of Tom Clarke in 1907, and his friendship with younger IRB men like Bulmer Hobson and Seán MacDermott. Clarke was fifty years old, had spent fifteen years in British prisons, often under the most appalling conditions, and had something of the consequent charisma of O'Donovan Rossa. His return and his decision to throw his influence behind the younger IRB men were decisive. By 1911 the Supreme Council of the IRB was in the hands of a small elite wholly committed to early revolution.

Two of the preconditions for revolution were now present: a potential "front" political wing and an oath-bound cadre of militants. There remained the necessity for military organization and training. Two developments provided this. In the northeast the leadership of the anti–Home Rule forces had passed to extremists like Edward Carson, MP for Trinity College, Dublin, who not only were prepared to appeal to the Unionist sentiments of the British army leadership against the Liberal Government, but in the last resort were prepared to defend themselves by force of arms against the imposition of an independent Irish parliament. In 1912 the Ulster Unionists, alarmed by the Home Rule Bill then under debate at Westminster, founded a volunteer force which armed itself and drilled openly. This example was not lost; Patrick Pearse, the Gaelic-speaking schoolteacher, who although probably not yet a member of the IRB was now firmly convinced of the necessity for physical force, remarked drily: "Personally, I think the Orangeman with a rifle a much less ridiculous figure than the Nationalist without a rifle." Eoin MacNeill, a distinguished scholar, a Gaelic enthusiast, and the editor of the Gaelic weekly *An Claidheamh Soluis* (The Sword of Light), in November 1913 wrote an article suggesting the establishment of a parallel nationalist force. The idea was taken up gratefully by the IRB, and the movement was launched on November 25, 1913, at an overflowing mass meeting in Dublin. The aim of the "Irish Volunteers" movement was ostensibly defensive—to guarantee that the Home Rule Bill would not be diluted under the pressure of the Ulster Unionists. However, MacNeill, its president, did not know that the organization was rapidly infiltrated by members of the IRB, whose revolutionary purpose was far clearer, and who took their orders not from their ostensible officers but from the IRB leaders to whom they were oath-bound in allegiance.

The year 1913 also saw the establishment of a second, and in this case proletarian socialist, revolutionary force. At this point it is necessary to look briefly at the development of Irish proletarian politics. These not surprisingly formed a very minor subtheme to the principal issues of land, religion, and nationality. Social grievances were not only predominantly rural but, as we have seen, concerned with moderate claims to either security of tenure or at most peasant ownership. The debates of the 1840's did produce one agrarian socialist in James Fintan Lalor, but he was both untypical and relatively uninfluential. Ireland, indeed, produced only one socialist thinker of eminence before James Connolly in William Thompson, who in the early part of the century in Cork speculated endearingly about vegetarianism and feminism, and even arrived at an early version of the theory of surplus value. But he was even more untypical, and almost unknown until rescued from oblivion by Connolly in *Labour in Irish History* (Dublin, 1917).

The socialism of Michael Davitt has more historical relevance. A convinced socialist of the non-Marxist Independent Labour Party variety, he was unusual in that he brought to the land agitation both the rural hunger of peasant origins and the industrial socialism acquired in his upbringing in the Lancashire cotton industry. These led him to advocate the nationalization of the basic industrial and agricultural resources by the state. But whereas his contribution to the course of the land struggle was unrivaled, his influence upon the form of its solution was negligible. It is in some ways more relevant that Davitt was so vitally committed to Irish Fenianism. This commitment typifies two strands characteristic of the Irish left. The first is the shadowy, but unquestionable, pressure of an element of social militancy in Fenianism which was carried on into the Irish Republican Army. How widespread this "socialist" element inside the republican movement was at any particular stage it is, and may always be, impossible to say. Its presence, however, was unquestionable, and as late as the 1920's and 1930's it produced leaders such as Liam Mellowes and Peadar O'Donnell. But if republican nationalism to some extent at least possessed a socialist orientation, the converse remains true: proletarian socialism was distracted by the pull of nationalism, and whenever a choice of priorities had to be made inside this framework, socialism invariably lost. The price that proletarian republicanism consistently paid for its alliance with the "pure" nationalism of the bourgeoisie was that the social aims of the movement either succumbed to nationalism or were defined in bourgeois terms. So it was in 1881, in 1919, in 1922, and ultimately in the 1930's.

The more formally social movements of the towns were even less effective. In England these took three principal forms: first Chartism; then the slow growth of trade unionism and the largely separate development of small groups of bourgeois socialist thinkers; finally the marriage of the two latter, which produced the Labour Party and placed it in a position to supplant Liberalism inside a two-party system. In Ireland the first was weak, the second generally conservative, the third almost nonexistent, and the conclusion logically very different.

The Chartist movement was briefly effective in the 1840's. It was firmly based in Dublin and Belfast at least; it possessed a gifted leader in Patrick O'Higgins, a Dublin draper who corresponded regularly with his English counterparts and contributed to the *Northern Star*. But unable, like all Irish left-wing movements, either to permeate or to compete effectively with nationalism, it waned in the shadow of O'Connell's hostility and of clerical condemnation. The separation of the more militant Irish Confederation from O'Connell's Repeal Association provided a bourgeois nationalist organization with which Chartism could more naturally sympathize, and through an informal and highly qualified association with the Confederation, Irish Chartism enjoyed its last flourish of optimism between April and July 1848. The price it paid was to share in the general extinction of political militancy which followed on the fiasco of the rising.

Formal trade unions operated quite effectively from early in the century despite the hostility of the employers; according to Sidney and Beatrice Webb, the Dublin unions were the strongest in the United Kingdom in the 1820's. Conservative and nonpolitical in character, they were mainly concerned with issues of self-protection like the maintenance of the closed shop and of restrictions upon apprenticeship. Despite this, they were inevitably caught up in the repeal struggle, giving their enthusiastic loyalty to O'Connell until his deep-seated hostility to organized labor became too strident to be endured. The years of the famine and of post-1848 hopelessness seem to have affected them also, to the point of near-extinction.

Their regrowth in the 1850's and 1860's was slow and cautious. In 1863 the Dublin unions had recovered sufficiently to form a United Trades Association; in 1894 the Irish Trades Union Congress was established. It was proud of its craft respectability and aversion to strike action; it advised the unskilled workers to form a congress of their own. A national organization, it was thus horizontally divided; it was also vertically divided, especially between north and south, on the issues of nationality and religion. This division was reflected in the Congress's inability to make up its own mind not merely on its attitude to the nationalist movements but upon its relations with the relatively more prosperous British unions.

Into this unpromising situation came, in 1896, James Connolly, armed with the English-based logic of the Marxist Social Democratic Federation. He found a potential proletarian movement which was bedeviled by its internal class divisions, engulfed in a largely conservative agricultural society, divided by denomination but condemned by bourgeois religious orthodoxy, and distracted by the primacy of the nationalist issue. His career was accordingly dogged by frustration and poverty. He was successful in helping to inspire the foundation of a native Irish Labour Party in 1912, in which British- and Irish-based trade unions, Protestant Unionist and Catholic nationalist workers, theoretically made common cause. But he was unable to infuse it with either his own revolutionary Marxism or his conviction that this was inextricably linked with proletarian involvement in the conflict with England, which he saw in the context of the class struggle and global imperialism. He was, however, successful in building, with James Larkin, a substantial industrial base in the Irish Transport Workers' Union, a typical Irish offshoot of the militant "new unionism" of the late nineteenth and early twentieth centuries. In 1913 this Union fought the most searing industrial struggle in Irish history. It was ultimately unsuccessful, but it left two enduring influences. One was yet another tradition of implacable resentment; the other was a formal military body, the Irish Citizen Army, set up by Connolly and Larkin to protect the striking workers from police brutality. The Army stayed in existence after the strike. It was never a mass movement; one estimate places its maximum armament at 118 rifles. But it symbolized the involvement of at least a section of the Dublin proletariat in the physical struggle, and in Connolly it possessed a leader impatiently bent on revolution.

XI

By the end of 1913, the preconditions for revolution were present to an unprecedented degree. The Parliamentary Party still held unquestioned political dominance, but ready to compete with it were a constitutional alternative, Sinn Féin; two small, badly armed, but enthusiastic military movements, the Irish Volunteers and the Irish Citizen Army; and a secret cadre of revolutionaries, the Irish Republican Brotherhood. All that was lacking was a catalyst to unite them. The First World War provided it.

In September 1914 the Supreme Council of the IRB resolved to capitalize on England's difficulties by staging a rebellion before the end of the war. The young men who took that decision abandoned in doing so a resolution of 1873 in which the Brotherhood agreed to postpone the next appeal to arms until they had a mandate from the Irish people. This recourse to revolutionary conviction and contempt for what they saw by now as a depraved public opinion was to be characteristic of all the IRB leaders, most especially Pearse, who in May 1915 was appointed to a three-man Military Committee to draw up a plan for a rising. As Director of Organization of the Volunteers he was able at the same time to mobilize support in that body behind MacNeill's back. Pearse, a romantic poet and playwright of considerable stature, seems to have been convinced of the necessity for regenerative blood sacrifice rather than disposed to see any prospect of military success. So far as these prospects existed, they depended upon the combination of a massive Volunteer mobilization with the provision of German arms.

Neither prospect materialized. The German arms ship, after much elaborate and incompetent plotting, sailed from Lübeck on April 9, 1916. On April 21 she was cornered by British patrols and blown up by her captain. The rising was planned for Easter Sunday, April 23, 1916; when MacNeill discovered the duplicity of the IRB, he publicly countermanded it. Pearse and his allies postponed the uprising for twenty-four hours and attempted to rally their supporters. The result of the confusion was that only a fraction of the Volunteers mobilized on Easter Monday, and the prospect of success, if any had ever existed, was gone. After a week of savage fighting, almost entirely confined to the center of Dublin City, the rebellion was crushed.

Militarily the enterprise was a shambles. Only a handful of bewildered Dubliners gathered to hear Pearse read the Proclamation of the Irish Republic from the steps of the General Post Office on Easter Monday morning, and the proletariat, so far from grasping Connolly's Marxist purpose, jeered the republican prisoners as they were herded through the Dublin streets on their way to internment in England.

Two and a half years later public feeling had so totally reversed itself that the Parliamentary Party had been destroyed electorally and had surrendered to Sinn Féin the grip it had exerted upon the southern vote for over thirty years.

What caused this staggering reversal in Irish public opinion? The most direct cause was essentially emotional—a wave of revulsion at the severity of the executions that followed the surrender of the rebels. Fifteen of the leaders, including Pearse, Clarke, and the badly wounded James Connolly, were shot in batches over a period of ten days. This savagery, coupled with a growing appreciation of the heroism of the vastly outnumbered rebels and the sincerity of their motives, transformed them from irresponsible bandits, who had for some incomprehensible reason destroyed the center of their capital city, into nationalist martyrs. Pearse himself had predicted, indeed probably planned, this outcome of his sacrifice: "When we are wiped out, people will blame us for everything," he is reported as saying during the week's fighting. "After a few years they will see the meaning of what we tried to do." It took in fact less than a year.

But there were also less romantic reasons for the change in public sympathy. By 1917 the credibility of the Parliamentary Party as a force capable of wresting an effective measure of Home Rule from the Coalition Government in the teeth of Ulster's opposition was waning rapidly. Redmond's enthusiastic commitment of his people to the British cause in September 1914 had scarcely been in touch with popular opinion even then; two years later it was even more unrepresentative. Of the party leaders only John Dillon lived permanently in Dublin; he was the only one to respond to Irish opinion and vigorously oppose the executions: "You are washing out our whole life-work in a sea of blood," he told the House of Commons.[13] The English members were furious, but Dillon was right. The last serious hope of survival for the constitutional movement disappeared in June–July 1916 when Redmond, having first allowed Lloyd George to insert a hazily "temporary" provision for the partition of Ireland into the Home Rule Bill, was compelled to see the government publicly reassure the Ulster Unionists of its permanence. Third, and by no means least, was the growing shadow of the introduction of military conscription into Ireland as the trenches drained England's reserves of manpower. Redmond's enthusiasm for the war had been tolerable when it bore only on the imperial loyalties of Anglo-Irish volunteers and the narrow options of the proletarian unemployed. Conscription was quite another matter.

The result was that the prisoners, who were released in inverse order of seniority between December 1916 and June 1917, came home to a hero's welcome. They showed their lack of repentance by at once resuming organization, now in a much more favorable context. In particular,

---

[13] F. S. L. Lyons, "Dillon, Redmond and the Irish Home Rulers," in F. X. Martin, ed., *Leaders and Men of the Easter Rising: Dublin 1916* (London, 1967), p. 35.

a group of younger IRB members led by Michael Collins rebuilt its network with remarkable rapidity. When the Volunteers were reestablished, Collins was appointed to Pearse's old post as Director of Organization. He thus possessed a dual power, both covert and open, similar to that of Pearse in 1916; Collins's, indeed, was probably greater, since he later added the roles of Director of Intelligence in the Volunteers and Minister for Finance in the Republican Government of 1919–21. He used this dual power with consummate skill, but in the process fanned a resentment in some of his colleagues for which he and the republican movement were later to pay dearly.

The revival of Sinn Féin paralleled that of the Volunteers. Now rapidly discarding the monarchical theories of Griffith, it contested two by-elections early in 1917 on an abstentionist platform and won both of them. In June 1917 Eamon de Valera, the senior surviving 1916 officer, was released. He was elected MP for Clare in July, president of Sinn Féin in October, and president of the Volunteers in November. This triple victory not merely gave the nationalist movement a new leader; it also symbolized, first, its electoral power, second, its abandonment of Griffith's ideas in favor of the outright separatism of the 1916 Proclamation, and third, the formal association of its political and military arms. At the general election of December 1918 the Parliamentary Party was virtually wiped out, and Sinn Féin won seventy-three seats. These members, or rather those who were at liberty, met in Dublin in January 1919, proclaimed the first Dáil Eireann, and set up a "government."

XII

The next three years were the last phase of the revolutionary struggle. It was conducted not with the nineteenth-century costumed dignity of Pearse, but with the calculated, stealthy ruthlessness of men like Collins, whose military improvisations virtually invented nationalist guerrilla tactics. From the first shots at Soloheadbeg in Tipperary in January 1919, when Dan Breen, Seán Treacy, and a band of badly armed Volunteer soldiers killed two policemen for a load of gelignite, to the truce of July 1921, the country was caught up in a war of ever-increasing viciousness. British reprisals, understandable in themselves, alienated the electorate still further. The Dáil was never wholly happy about the war, which it did not officially endorse until March 1921, and the "cabinet" was never wholly in control of it. De Valera was in America, and Collins's military involvement was through the IRB rather than the cabinet. But if Sinn Féin did not control the war, it reaped the electoral rewards. In the May 1921 general election, the first in which northeast Ulster was partitioned as a political unit from the rest of Ireland, Sinn Féin won 128 seats out of 132 without opposition. In the face of military stalemate, popular hostility, and growingly critical international opinion, no device of Lloyd George's Government could now deny the revolutionaries their representative status. On June 22, 1921, King George V, opening the first session of the Northern Ireland Parliament in Belfast, delivered what was, in the circumstances, a remarkable appeal for peace. This provided the appropriate regal cue for the inevitable negotiations, and on July 9 a truce was agreed on. Five months later, on Tuesday, December 6, 1921, a treaty—forever after known in Ireland as "the Treaty"—was signed in London between the representatives of the two cabinets. In theory, the struggle had come to a successful conclusion. In practice, the signatories bequeathed to their successors a burden of unfinished business that was to determine the politics of the independent Irish State for decades to come.

The Irish delegation allowed itself to be outmaneuvered both in its own cabinet and at the conference table. The document that it signed fell far short of the thirty-two-county republic proclaimed by Pearse in 1916; it scarcely improved upon the Home Rule Bill of July 1916 sufficiently to justify the blood that had been shed since. Perhaps no such republic could have been negotiated in 1921; if so, De Valera, who returned from America in December 1920, was astute to assure his own republican purity by remaining in Dublin. In his place, he sent a negotiating team led by Griffith and Collins; Collins at least seems to have had a clear appreciation that he was placing his neck on the block. He was a sworn republican, but also a realist, who as the main architect of the military struggle knew that his army was near breaking point. Griffith, who had never been a republican, had no such problem of conscience. Under the blandishments and duress of Lloyd George they signed a treaty that excluded northeastern Ireland and gave to the Catholic nationalist south and west not a republic, but a dominion, oathbound to the British monarchy and circumscribed by military guarantees to Britain. Collins tried to repeat Pearse's trick, to hold the ranks steady through the IRB. He failed and eight months later was himself the most tragic casualty of the civil war.

Two questions about the last five years of the Irish struggle are relevant to what followed. First, why did the national alliance of 1918 disintegrate? Second, what unfinished business did the treaty leave to the Free State? In essence these two questions are one, with one answer.

The major achievement of British nineteenth-century statesmanship was largely to hive off the issues of religion and economics from that of nationality. To the bulk of the Irish Catholic Hierarchy the evangelization of England took precedence, by 1900, over the gaining of Irish independence. In turn the achievement of land reformers, from Gladstone to Wyndham, was to replace the revolutionary threat of the insecure nineteenth-century tenantry by the socially conservative influence of a nation of owner-occupiers. The revolutionary incentive of economic deprivation was consequently largely confined to the small farmers of the infertile western seaboard and the industrial proletariat. The former were distracted by the issue of nationality and indoctrinated with the virtues of juridical ownership; the later were impoverished and disorganized, and the two greatest centers of industrial population, Dublin and Belfast, were cut off from each other by sectarian religious bigotry. The ranks of western farmers and Dublin workers alike were sapped by emigration, and they themselves were cowed by the antirevolutionary strictures of an authoritarian Church. Only one bishop could be found to offer even a qualified defense of the men of 1916.

The alliance of 1917–21 was accordingly ramshackle, and collapsed once the immediate pressures of war gave way to the discussion of motivation. A hard core of officers felt they had sworn their loyalty to a republic and could not serve a Parliament that had accepted dominion status; their unity was thrown into confusion by the pragmatic support given to the treaty by Collins and the IRB leadership. The bulk of the educated bourgeoisie were symbolized by Griffith; never far away from Redmond, they had deserted him only when he proved a broken reed. The guerrilla war they had found inconvenient and distasteful; they rejoiced that it was over, prayed for order, and wondered how anyone like De Valera could be so meticulous as to countenance its resumption over words like "oath" and "republic." At the other end of the social scale was the politically inactive majority, which now included, in addition to the small farmers, urban workers living in some of the worst slums in Europe. Since 1918 they had loyally given their votes to Sinn Féin and their instinctive sympathy to the Irish Republican Army. Now they were faced first by a military, and then by a protracted political, struggle, in which one group of their former leaders summoned them to the defense of "the Treaty" and another to the defense of "the Republic."

After five years of bloody warfare it was at last native, bourgeois Irish governments who told an embittered and divided people that its social and political needs must await the resolution of its constitutional status. To give Yeats the last word:

> Parnell came down the road, he said to a cheering man:
> "Ireland shall get her freedom and you still break stone."

ONE

Political Culture and Cleavages

The political system of a country reflects, and is to a great extent the product of, the "political culture" of the society. When we refer to the "political culture" of a people we mean the general pattern of people's attitudes and beliefs about, and their knowledge of, politics and political phenomena—including matters such as political organization, the government, politicians and public servants, what the state should and should not do, and the extent and effectiveness of their own participation in politics. The concept "suggests that the traditions of a society, the spirit of its public institutions, the passions and the collective reasoning of its citizenry, and the style and operating codes of its leaders are not just random products of historical experience but fit together as a part of a meaningful whole and constitute an intelligible web of relations." It suggests, too, that "in any particular community there is a limited and distinct political culture which gives meaning, predictability, and form to the political process."[1]

All this is not to say that everyone in a community has exactly the same set of beliefs, values, and prejudices or the same knowledge about political phenomena. There exist in most communities groups whose members have a political outlook distinct from the majority and significantly different attitudes on various political matters. Their patterns of beliefs, etc., are termed "subcultures." However, it is obvious that these differences cannot be extreme or extend to every facet of politics, for in such a situation there would not be a single community at all, and the very basis of a single political system would be absent. But different combinations of cultural attitudes lead to important divisions or

[1] L. W. Pye and S. Verba, *Political Culture and Political Development* (Princeton, 1965), p. 7.

cleavages in a community, which tend in turn to be reflected in the procedures and structures of the political system.

The purpose of this chapter is to identify the main features of the
political culture of the Irish people and the major cleavages in Irish
society. Such a study should help explain many of the political institutions in Ireland and much of the political behavior of the Irish people.

II

The identification of the basic political attitudes of a community must
inevitably be a matter of impressionistic historical generalization, for
contemporary beliefs and attitudes reflect the conditions and events of
the past and are in a continuous state of change. Nowhere is this more
true than in Ireland in the late 1960's, for there is much evidence to
suggest that, currently, there is a period of very rapid social and cultural change.

The British influence. Geography and history combine to make the
British influence the most important in determining the pattern of
much of Irish political thought and practice. This is a simple matter of
the geographical propinquity of a large national group and a small one,
and the historical facts of political dominion, social and economic domination, and cultural blanketing. Ireland, like Scotland and Wales, became an English province, her politics and her economic and cultural
life dominated by, and oriented on, England. The substitution of the
English language for Irish was especially important in this respect.
During the seventeenth and eighteenth centuries the number of people
speaking Irish declined very rapidly. By 1851, less than 30 per cent of
the population could speak it and by 1871 less than 20 per cent (see
Table A.9, p. 328). Though significant (but diminishing) numbers in
the west continued to speak Irish, in Dublin and the east, which dominated social and economic life, only 5 per cent or less could speak it from
the middle of the nineteenth century.

Inevitably, in these circumstances, Irish people acquired much of the
culture, including much of the political culture, of the British and,
more particularly, the English. The process of absorption of English
ways and values was most complete in Dublin, the bigger towns, and
the east of the country generally. In addition, Ireland enjoyed standards
of public services, including education, health, and welfare services,
comparable with those of Great Britain in general. As in the case of the
white communities of the British Commonwealth, many of the currently held political traditions and values were inculcated and absorbed
during a most critical and formative period: the period of the advent

of mass democracy. As the franchise was extended in Britain, so, too, in Ireland; and Irish people acquired democratic habits and values. Political ideas were almost wholly expressed in British categories, for, from O'Connell to Parnell and beyond, the political experience of most Irish leaders was gained in British political life, and they practiced the parliamentary ways of Westminster.

However, Ireland, geographically and in other ways more peripheral than Wales or Scotland, was never integrated to the extent they were, because of the survival in greater measure of a preindustrial rural society and the centrifugal pull of national feeling and consequent nationalism. Yet Irish nationalism itself was "a revolution within and against a democracy and could not help using many of that system's institutions and procedures."[2]

There is no better way to illustrate the acceptance of democratic values and British forms than in the history of the independence movement and the formation of the new state. Though, with Sinn Féin, Irish nationalism turned away from parliamentary methods, the parliamentary tradition and the belief in the legitimacy of a democratically elected assembly can be seen to have been strongly ingrained in both the leaders and the majority of the population. The revolutionary Dáil of 1919, legitimized by election, continued in being as a parliamentary assembly through revolution and war. If it did not in fact control the situation, nevertheless it claimed the right to do so, and those who sustained it recognized its importance in the eyes of a thoroughly democratic people. The general acceptance of the most important norms of democracy is well shown by the widespread acceptance of the duly elected government in 1922 despite its rejection by De Valera and his supporters, by the rapid acceptance of this group when they abandoned force (which was getting them nowhere) for constitutional and parliamentary methods, and, finally, by their transformation into a majority government at the election of 1932. Moreover, the constitutional forms adopted were those of British parliamentary democracy. Inevitably, then, the Irish Free State was democratic, its governmental system the Westminster model. Because of this, and because the community had comparable educational standards, almost identical public services, and a full-fledged Civil Service on British lines, the country not only was wholly equipped for statehood but could embark on it with no break at all in continuity.

2 J. G. A. Pocock, "The Case of Ireland Truly Stated: Revolutionary Politics in the Context of Increasing Stabilisation" (unpublished paper, Department of History, Washington University, St. Louis, Mo., 1966).

Political independence did not automatically bring economic independence or cultural autonomy. The Irish economy was not a balanced and viable whole, and the boundaries of the new state were, and are, very permeable. Banking, insurance, industry, and trade were largely British-oriented and only slowly became centered in Dublin. Britain was and still is Ireland's chief customer and her main supplier. Even today about 70 per cent of all Irish exports are sent there (see Tables A.14 and A.15, p. 330). Likewise, people go to and come from Britain in large numbers. Since 1881 net emigration, most of it to the United Kingdom, has never been lower than 6 per 1,000 per annum of the population and at times has been nearer 16 (see Table A.2, p. 326). Today, there may be almost three-quarters of a million persons living in Great Britain who were born in the Irish Republic, and between these and seasonal or occasional migrants there is much movement in both directions. In addition, British newspapers and magazines circulate freely, British radio transmissions can be received throughout the country, British television is available to people in the north and east of the country (one-third of Irish television sets can receive it), and most of the books read in the country are published in the United Kingdom.

Britain not only influences the Irish, it also insulates them. In the words of a French writer, Jean Blanchard: "L'Irlande est une île derrière une île."[3] Very little of European thought or experience has ever been directly tapped or assimilated by the Irish. The knowledge of European languages other than English is poor, even by British standards, and very poor by the standards of many Western European countries. Because of the irredentist obsession of political leaders with the problem of the six Ulster counties, and consequent neutrality in and after the Second World War, Ireland was cut off to an extraordinary degree from the mainstream of Western European life, at least until the late 1950's.

It is not possible to illustrate the similarities in political attitudes of British and Irish people in any systematic way because there are next to no surveys covering the whole country. In respect of more concrete political phenomena, however, the British influence is strikingly clear and all-pervasive. It runs throughout Irish political organization and public administration. Time and time again throughout this book the starting point for the discussion of an institution or procedure will be the British legacy or model. The main lines and patterns of many public services were laid down under the aegis of Westminster in the forma-

---

[3] J. Blanchard, *Le droit ecclésiastique contemporain d'Irlande* (Paris, 1958), p. 11.

tive period of the modern state in the late nineteenth and early twentieth centuries, before independence. The cultural hegemony of Great Britain and, conversely, ignorance of the experience of other countries have ensured a continuing similarity, though with differences attributable to factors such as conservative Catholic influences and a gross national product per head of population little more than half the British. Thus, for example, "even the most cursory study of the development of, say, local government or education immediately reveals a continuity barely touched by the coming of the new state."[4] Only recently have the horizons of policy makers, politicians and civil servants alike, extended to other European countries.

Nationalism. Since the British influence has been so great, it may well be asked: why did not Ireland settle down as a British province? The answer lies in the fact that Ireland was more peripheral than Scotland and Wales, and, notwithstanding cultural blanketing, less assimilable. In time, nationalist feeling evolved and asserted itself, and the Irish people became, and have remained, a people with strong nationalist emotions. The state owes its existence to the successful outcome of a typical nationalist movement for independence.

When a national movement succeeds, people are very self-conscious about their statehood—however passive many of them may have been before. If the state is small and weak, anxiety about its continued existence and integrity is inevitably reflected in a heightened self-consciousness. Many of those who were young when Ireland became independent are alive today, and their firsthand memories, until recently at least, were continually being revived by political leaders who, having won power by evoking nationalist feeling, naturally continued to exploit it. After independence, there were still nationalist issues unresolved. Nationalism remained high in the consciousness of Irish people because the break with Great Britain was not complete. The new state had commonwealth status, and to some people this was not sufficient. Furthermore, the country was partitioned, and Irish nationalism continued in the form of a typical irredentist movement, doomed to sterile frustration because the majority of the unredeemed simply do not see themselves as such.

Since independence, nationalism has shown itself principally in three ways. First, constitutional issues and "the border problem" have obsessed political leaders to the exclusion of other public issues. Until very recently, those who led the successful independence struggle and

[4] D. A. Thornley, "Ireland: The End of an Era," *Studies*, LIII (1964), 7.

survived, or their kinsmen, virtually monopolized leadership positions in politics, and their failure, as they saw it, to finish the job clearly weighed on them. Also, of course, the appeal to old and familiar national issues paid them dividends in terms of support. Hence there was great political stability which in time became sterility. A largely rural population, slow to change, was exposed to unvarying appeals, and the new Ireland became a thoroughly conservative society, which until the middle 1950's failed to tackle many of its social and economic problems, let alone solve them. Hence, also, there was a tendency to ignore other international issues, a tendency increased by the insulating effect of the nearness of Britain and Ireland's small size with, in consequence, small influence. Foreign policy, except in relation to Great Britain, usually evoked little or no interest and played no part in parliamentary or electoral politics. Only in the late 1950's, when Ireland had at last been admitted to the United Nations and began to send soldiers to Cyprus and the Congo, and when the challenge of the European Community was slowly apprehended, did interest in the issues of world politics begin to grow.

Second, Irish nationalism was anti-British, making cooperation with the dominant neighbor emotionally unpalatable and politically unrewarding. But, of course, the facts of life and the exigencies imposed by propinquity could not be ignored. Considerable conformity and cooperation with the United Kingdom was, and is, obviously necessary and desirable for welfare and prosperity. Many of the advantages now accruing to citizens of the states of the European Community have always been enjoyed by Irish people in Great Britain. It is obviously to their considerable benefit that they should be able to enter the professions and the labor market and generally to enjoy the benefits of being treated like British citizens. Because of this, because of the continuing penetration of British ideas and standards, and because of emigration which has led to most Irish families having relatives "across the water," a curious, ambivalent attitude to Britain has developed. On the one hand, there is willingness (besides often a necessity) to go there and live there, a personal friendliness for British people as individuals, and a propensity to accept British standards and values; on the other hand, there is an almost ritualistic antipathy to "the British," who, the politicians have always maintained, could if they would restore the northern counties, and particularly to manifestations of British military power or symbols of British monarchy—uniforms, warships, the Union Jack, members of the Royal Family, even statues, monuments, and buildings. Once again, it is only recently that this situation has begun to change as the realities of the Ulster situation have begun to sink in and irredentism fades away.

Third, nationalism in the form of the national movement for independence was associated in typical fashion with a cultural nationalism centered mainly on the Irish language. The identification of the language with the struggle for independence has had considerable social and political consequences. The problems of reviving the Irish language, its place in education, its use in the community and for official purposes, and the treatment of those dwindling communities whose mother tongue it still is have always been exacerbated by this identification of Irish with the movement for political independence, making rational appraisal impossible and rational solutions politically inexpedient. The results for the language have sometimes been counterproductive, leading to frustration and alienation.

The Irish national movement was led mainly by people of the lower middle class; it was republican and it was against the gentry, these being an elite who were identified with Great Britain. The new state, therefore, tended to be egalitarian, an attitude symbolized by the constitutional prohibitions on instituting titles or honors. With the rapid disappearance of the Ascendancy, the former ruling class, and a marked thinning of the ranks of middle-class Protestants after independence, the community became socially more homogeneous. Considerable social mobility, especially from rural small-farm backgrounds to urban middle-class status, has aided this process.

That is not to say that Ireland is classless. Rural and urban groupings, small farmer and big farmer, middle class and working class are all apparent. Of course, also, there emerged a new elite, in politics at least. Its members came from the independence movement leaders and those active in the struggles. In Dublin, a middle-class, bourgeois elite filled the gap left by the disappearance of the old Dublin society. In business, law, and commerce in Dublin, domination by Protestants declined, as did their numbers, and they were replaced (see Table A.11, p. 329). Although the number of Protestants with large farms did not decline, the social and political leadership of the landed "West Briton" country gentry was quickly terminated. These had been the leaders of the most significant subculture in the country. Today, it exists mainly as a division based on religious, educational, and, in some respects, social separation—a cleavage in Irish society certainly, but politically of little importance. Of far greater importance was the cleavage that issued from the split in the nationalist movement itself, the split over "The Treaty," which led to civil war. These cleavages and their political manifestations are considered later in this chapter.

The dying peasant society. Ireland is a fringe country: geographically on the fringes of Europe, socially and economically on the fringes of the "British Isles," and, for long, politically a fringe province of the United Kingdom. The development of an industrial society in Great Britain tended to have its effects on the fringes—the highlands and islands of Scotland, West Wales, Cornwall, and Ireland—late in time; nor was their impact great, and the farther west, the smaller it was. Political changes have made little difference in this pattern. There exists in Ireland the remains of a "peasant society," which, though it has been progressively overwhelmed by modernizing influences that were strongly British in character, continues to influence Irish political life.

A "peasant society" proper, according to Teoder Shanin, consists of "small producers on land who, with the help of simple equipment and the labour of their families, produce mainly for their own consumption and/or the fulfilment of their duties to the holders of political and economic power. . . . The family farm is the basic unit of peasant ownership, production, consumption and social life."[5] As Shanin goes on to point out, the ties of family and the land, and the wide variety of tasks to be performed, which causes the peasant to operate at a relatively low level of specialization, lead to many of the distinguishing characteristics of peasant life and thought. "The peasantry is a pre-industrial social entity which carries into contemporary society specific, different and older elements of social inter-relation, economics, policy and culture."[6] The impact of a money economy, of towns, and of modernization generally is, however, inexorable, and makes inroads into this culture. Gradually, the peasant becomes an agricultural producer. "This pattern of development of the peasantry into a cohesive, increasingly narrowing and professionalized occupational group of farmers is seen clearly in most parts of North-Western Europe. Although increasingly tied to the industrializing society, farming still maintains some of its peculiar elements."[7]

We need not inquire to what extent this Irish peasant culture retains Gaelic or other social characteristics of a yet earlier society, or how and when that society changed. What is important here is the extent of the existence of such a culture today and its effect upon political behavior.

5 T. Shanin, "The Peasantry as a Political Factor," *Sociological Review*, XIV (1966), 7.
6 *Ibid.*, p. 10.
7 *Ibid.*, p. 17.

Ireland is an agricultural country of small, scattered family farms, as is seen from Tables A.3–8 (pp. 326–27). Just before the First World War, 70 per cent of the population lived in rural areas, and even today over half do. Many western counties have few if any large centers of population. In County Leitrim today there are no towns at all with over 1,500 people. The small towns are closely connected with the countryside they serve, and their inhabitants, especially the shopkeepers, are part of the rural community. In general, also, Ireland has a very low population density—indeed the lowest in Western Europe per square mile of agricultural land. Farming is of course the largest single occupation. In 1936 half the labor force were engaged in primary production, the vast majority of them in farming, and even today one-third are so engaged. In the Ulster counties, the proportion is well over one-half and in Connacht over two-thirds. The small family farm predominates: over 70 per cent of farms are of less than 50 acres. Hence a very large number of Irish workers are self-employed.

The tables in Appendix A show also that rapid changes have been taking place toward a more normal Western pattern, but these are comparatively recent and their impact on culture (which often lags) may not yet be fully felt. The movement of population from country to town brings a constant flow of mostly poorer country folk who retain some of their old modes of thought, which they will pass on to their children.

Just as the development of British industrial society had its least impact on the western fringes of the British Isles, so too in Ireland itself change and modern ways spread from east to west. Dr. Erhard Rumpf,[8] seeking to explain Irish nationalism and radicalism as socioeconomic phenomena, refers to a general east-west gradient in Ireland (*das allgemeine Ost-West-Gefälle*), which, he points out, corresponds to the degree of anglicization, and which can be observed in the distribution of non-Catholics in the population, in the size of farms, in the number of inhabitants per square mile of cultivated land, and in types of farming. Thus we have a picture of a modern culture permeating the older peasant culture inexorably but to differing degrees—more in the towns than in the rural areas, more in the east than in the west. The important point is that countrymen, more numerous than townsmen, are at the base of Irish political life, and their characteristics and attitudes reflect this older, preindustrial, peasant society.

The impact of the values of the countryman on Irish politics is considerable. Country people are strongly locally oriented and they set

[8] *Nationalismus und Sozialismus in Irland* (Meisenheim am Glan, 1959).

great store by face-to-face contact. Mass on Sunday, fair day, the cooperative creamery—all have significance far wider than their primary purposes for a people who are dispersed on their own small family farms. These characteristics lead to great emphasis on the personal and local in politics, a fact that is reflected in the selection of candidates for elections, in electoral behavior, and in the role of elected representatives and their relationships with their constituents.

Again, there is a strong, almost static, conservatism in most country areas. This is due to the dominance of small owner-farmers, a group produced by the land redistribution policy instituted in the late nineteenth century by the British government and continued after independence. Within the space of sixty years this policy created the family farm and a rural community of small owners (as opposed to tenants), as the tabulation on page 23 indicates. Only in the poorest areas on the periphery have discontent and misery spawned peasant radicalism. Elsewhere, their little farms secure, smallholders and their families are conservative, unimaginative, shrewd in the short run, and individualistic. They do not easily change their methods and patterns of work and life. Material incentives will not always move them to accept innovations, and, except in dairying, they have not taken to combining in cooperatives.

In these circumstances, productivity is low and the rural population declines as emigration drains off the young, this drain being very severe from the poorest areas (see Tables A.1 and A.2, pp. 325–26). Though emigration has undoubtedly been a safety valve, obviating the development of a more radical type of rural politics and perhaps deep social cleavages, it has left a sad legacy in the areas most affected. Here a torpor is evident that is death to initiative, and this, combined with the conservatism of the mass of the rural population, creates a climate unfavorable to active social and economic development. Ireland's output per head of population is in these circumstances inevitably low (see Table A.12, p. 329). What growth there is is mainly in the small industrial sector, but as yet this is proceeding at a rate insufficient to permit the country as a whole to catch up with the richer European countries.

The presence of so many self-employed in farming and the slow growth of an industrial economy have delayed the development of the familiar Western cleavage between the middle class and the working class as a dominant feature of the society. These facts, together with the disappearance of the landlord from the countryside and the flow of country people into Dublin, have combined to produce a comparative homogeneity in the community. There are no deep class divisions. The social scale is fairly short and some of the poor (though perhaps few of the very poor) are able to climb it. However, there are signs of the development of a class division based on access to education as well as of a rural-urban split as rapid industrialization and economic policies favorable to industrial expansion begin to have their effects.

Irish Catholicism. Ninety-five people out of a hundred in the Republic of Ireland are Roman Catholics (see Table A.10), and the attachment of most people to their church is strong. To a large extent Catholicism is identified with nationalism in the public mind, and this connection is sedulously fostered by the Church today. Yet, whereas the attitude of the Irish Hierarchy until the 1920's was sometimes hostile to nationalist movements, on the other hand there has also always been an important tradition of Protestant nationalism.

Most people are very conscious of religious differences, and a person's religion is almost always immediately known on first acquaintance. Education is organized to a great extent on religious lines and so are some forms of social intercourse. Intermarriage is uncommon and disapproved of by all denominations. However, there is little or no discrimination in employment or in economic associations, and, generally, the situation in Ireland does not at all resemble thoroughly segmented societies like Belgium and Holland. In politics, religious divisions are comparatively unimportant largely because of the small size of the non-Catholic element. To a great extent and over much of the country, the question of a Protestant standing for election just does not arise. Though it exhibits many of the signs of being a distinct subculture, the Protestant community is politically absorbed.

Irish Catholicism is an austere and puritanical variety that is somewhat cold and authoritarian. The Church is a folk church geared to its own idea of the needs and the limitations of a peasant people.

The traditions of the Irish Church bear the marks of a settled rural based culture which changed remarkably little over centuries. The measured pace of rural life gave a tone to the Church in its liturgies and in its style of government. There did not appear to be any good reason why the old ways should not persist until recently.[9]

In the nineteenth century, the parish priests were community leaders, the more so since many local priests identified themselves (sometimes despite the Hierarchy) with the agrarian and nationalist aims of the country people, and because the Church, not being a great landowner, was not a source of envy to landless men. To a considerable extent they have retained this leadership.

[9] Rev. Patrick J. Brophy, Professor of Dogmatic Theology at Carlow Theological Seminary, quoted in *Sunday Independent*, October 29, 1967.

The shock of first revolution and then civil war, the formal if temporary censure of half the country's political leaders, was somehow absorbed by the enormous resilience of the folk church. When the dust had settled, the parish priests were scarcely less the leaders of their communities than they had been in pre-Fenian times. Indeed, the vacuum left by the old aristocracy drew them, if anything, still closer to the centre of community decision-making. Their social and cultural eminence automatically brought them to the chairmanship of cultural, athletic and economic community organizations. The British government had historically recognized their status by tacitly incorporating them in the local management of its national education system. The twentieth century still found them playing a significant part in social and political life.[10]

This is a dominance that, in the words of Charles McCarthy, "in some of its aspects is somewhat grotesque, since almost nothing is undertaken, from drama groups to tidy town competitions, without its being under the chairmanship or presidency of the parish priest, or one of his curates. . . . The view had grown up quite strongly that no activity locally was proper or right unless it had the approval of the local clergy."[11] Nor is this phenomenon confined to the countryside or the agricultural community. Many new factories and shops of any size are blessed when they are completed; so, too, each year is the Aer Lingus fleet of aircraft at Dublin airport.

The political effects of the dominant position of the Catholic Church are immense. The Irish State was from the beginning self-consciously Catholic. Bunreacht na hEireann (Constitution of Ireland), which replaced the negotiated Irish Free State Constitution of 1922, was a self-conscious attempt to combine the liberal-democratic tradition of Great Britain with Catholic social teaching. The impact of Catholic teaching has always been evident in the content of public social policy on marriage and divorce, contraception, censorship, the pattern of health and social security services, and, above all, education. At the primary education level most schools are managed by the parish priest, and most secondary education is private and denominational.

The political weight of the Hierarchy is hard to measure, but it can be very great. The bishops have mostly been very conservative, perhaps because of their remoteness from the mainstream of Catholic thought and because they tend to be authoritarian, discouraging the more radical views of those below them. Thus the Church has often been thought of as an important force inhibiting social change. Certainly the Hierarchy has not been zealous in welcoming or implementing many of the reforms initiated by Pope John XXIII and the Vatican Council.

10 D. A. Thornley, "Ireland: The End of an Era," *Studies*, LIII (1964), 6–7.
11 C. McCarthy, *The Distasteful Challenge* (Dublin, 1968), p. 110.

Authoritarianism. Authority in Ireland—whether in the Church, school, university, or family—has until recently gone unquestioned. Undoubtedly, this authoritarianism stemmed from the attitude of the Church toward a society that is predominantly rural and partly peasant. The Church in turn passed it on to the teachers.

> In all this the national teacher is a key figure. These young men and women were drawn from the most academically able in the country, but, certainly in the case of the men, from a remarkably limited social group. It appears to me that they came primarily from small farmers and small shopkeepers in the south and west, and in many cases had themselves left home as early as thirteen or fourteen years of age, attending first the preparatory colleges (which now fortunately have been disestablished) and also the diocesan colleges, all residential in character. From there they went to a residential training college which was conducted on remarkably authoritarian lines. No doubt the Church authorities were anxious to secure this rigorous training knowing that ninety per cent of Catholic children would receive their education from national teachers.[12]

A characteristic product of this attitude is the "ban," such as the Gaelic Athletic Association's ban on its members taking part in or attending "foreign games," or the ban of the Catholic Archbishop of Dublin on the attendance of Catholics at Trinity College. Even in the independence movement itself, such an attitude was not completely absent. De Valera's assertion that a majority had no right to be wrong epitomized it. However, both in the movement and in the community generally, liberal and democratic values have predominated. Once the State was firmly established, democracy has never been seriously threatened. The hard core of intransigent republicans has always contained one or two of authoritarian leanings; in the tense period in 1932 and 1933 when De Valera came to power, there was a threat of the development of rival paramilitary organizations; in the 1930's there were a few signs of activity by individuals with fascist learnings—these manifestations are noteworthy only to illustrate how firmly democratic, rather than authoritarian, ideas have dominated politics.

More obvious than authoritarianism in politics, however, are other characteristics that are undoubtedly connected with the influence of the Church but also with the national and agrarian struggles of the past, and perhaps with the survival of a rural society. These are *loyalty* and a marked *anti-intellectualism* in Irish life.

Loyalty. Loyalty is a great virtue in, and an important feature of, Irish political life. It is a loyalty to institutions and especially persons

12 *Ibid.*, p. 109.

rather than ideas. It reinforces powerfully the natural tendency of people generally to follow their parents in their political affiliations and to support their chosen party consistently. It can be seen in most marked form in the Fianna Fáil representatives and active party workers, where an attitude of unquestioning support has led to an almost complete separation of roles between a few top leaders charged with policy making and their parliamentary and other followers who have had little or no positive part in policy formation and have expected none. In recent years it is the party leaders themselves, in both Fianna Fáil and the other parties, who have attempted to induce discussion of policy among their followers, often to be met only with apathy. It is loyalty and not the danger that deputies will lose their seats that explains the virtually complete party solidarity that is a feature of voting in the Oireachtas (Parliament).

Anti-intellectualism. The same combination of historical and social factors that produced authoritarian attitudes and a stress on the virtue of loyalty has also produced a marked anti-intellectualism in Irish society. The Church, cut off to a large extent and for a long time from European Catholic life and thought, maintained its traditional ways and attitudes to a considerable degree, as Jean Blanchard repeatedly notes in his *Le droit ecclésiastique contemporain d'Irlande*. It has never been given to speculation on the great issues that have engaged Continental Catholics. First, it lacked an intellectual center until the creation in 1795 of Maynooth College; second, that institution was, until recently, as Blanchard describes it, "very conservative." In the same tradition, McCarthy says: "Our education system conveyed the idea that the truth was known, and therefore pursuing it was offensive because it implied that there might be another solution."[13]

The disappearance of the former elite, who in any case were themselves provincials, and their replacement by leaders who achieved their positions more by doing than by thinking tended also to militate against innovation and a climate favorable to intellectual liveliness. Most of the developments in the public sector before independence had been inspired by British initiative. After the emergence of the new state, a rural, nationalist, and Catholic community neither felt the need for, nor got, intellectual stimulation from its leaders, who, until the 1950's, seemed more concerned with the remaining constitutional issues than with new ones. After 1922, few inquiries of any depth were made into social and economic problems until recently, and even those were remark-

[13] *Ibid.*, p. 110.

able for their pedestrian quality. New social services and new legislation have all too often been a copy *mutatis mutandis* of the existing British pattern. Public servants (politician or professional) and the universities have not provided new ideas, nor have there been many attempts to observe and adapt the experience of other countries.

Irish writers and artists have always been at least as much part of the British scene as of the Irish. All too many have been driven to Britain (or farther afield) by economic necessity or by the uncongenial and unsympathetic intellectual climate, reflected in such phenomena as the ubiquitous signs of tastelessness, censorship, and the cold suspicion of the Church typified in the following passage from the Archbishop's *Lenten Regulations for Dublin Diocese*: "They who give themselves the title of intellectuals have grave need of being constantly warned that a common danger exists that no one may disregard, and that artistic or literary merit does not excuse indulgence in sensuality."[14] In politics particularly, intellectuals have tended to be distrusted or ignored: "Division on personalities rather than on principles and policies has been a distinct mark of our people for a long, long time and, perhaps, is a national characteristic that is unlikely to disappear.... Irish traditions usually penalise the inquiring mind in all fields. One of the dirtiest words in Irish politics is 'intellectual.' "[15]

III

At no time in recent years has there been more evidence than now that Irish society is changing rapidly. If the tables in Appendix A show that Ireland is still, by Western European standards, a remarkably rural community, they also indicate the speed with which this pattern is changing. The urban population is growing; the number occupied in agriculture is falling and so, too, is the number of self-employed. Ireland is becoming industrialized. Growing prosperity and the impact of television are hastening the spread of urban ways and urban values into the countryside.

The passage of time in any case was bound to lead to a generational change, as the old leaders were replaced and old issues died away. But two events have powerfully contributed to this process—the challenge of the European Community, which brought Ireland face to face with unpleasant economic realities, and the great reforms in the Catholic Church instituted by Pope John XXIII and the Vatican Council. The

[14] Quoted in *Irish Times*, Feb. 6, 1967.
[15] From a lecture by Proinsias Mac Aonghusa entitled "Political Life in Ireland, 1922–67," reported in *Irish Times*, Jan. 20, 1967.

impact of the discussions and reforms in the Church, embracing the liturgy, marriage, contraception, relations between the clergy and the people, attitudes to other religions, and increasing acceptance of a positive and developmental role for the state, was the greater because of the growing questioning by urban middle-class people of the existing rules of the Church and their relationship with the clergy, which they felt were more suited to a peasant population than to a modern industrial society.

The modernization of Ireland is currently proceeding at a rapid rate. The traditional is coming under challenge, and established institutions are being forced to adapt under pressure. In politics, changing party programs and attitudes mark the disappearance of the old issues and the transition to producer-consumer politics. "Development" and "planning" are all-important words now. The Labour Party is at last making gains in Dublin, the natural stronghold of such a party in an industrialized society. Perhaps, also, agrarian problems are looming up again as the small farmers recognize the threat industrialization poses to their existence, and sense how unworkable many of their small holdings are. The familiar phenomenon of rural-urban tension—the rural commodity strike with tractors blocking the roads—has already made its appearance.

IV

This attempt to isolate some of the major ingredients of Irish political culture has brought to light a number of important cleavages in the society. A political system attempts to deal with such divisions so that they do not result in dangerous dissatisfaction or, worse, in alienation. Where conflicting groups are not represented or their interests taken account of, the system is failing to perform its function.

Nationalist cleavages. Historically, the most basic cleavage was that which produced the new nation-state and, having done so, gradually became of less and less political importance. It was in fact not one cleavage but a number of reinforcing cleavages: Catholic-Protestant, Irish-Ascendancy, Nationalist-Unionist. Because they reinforced one another and could not be resolved, they led in classic fashion to strife.

When the new independent state evolved, the essential prop of the minority was wholly removed, the old class structure finally broke down, and the Ascendancy disappeared. The minority group that remained was both small in numbers and weak in influence. Being hardly big enough to form a political party of their own (though some of those who were labeled "Independents" in the 1920's and 1930's were Unionists), the members mostly abstained from politics or joined the Treaty Party (later Cumann na nGaedheal and still later Fine Gael) as the least objectionable of those offered. To a great extent they have become assimilated politically if not socially. Thus, Unionism, like the Ascendancy, has disappeared, and only Protestantism remains, a cleavage that is religious and to some extent cultural and social, but one that has little political significance. Only in some areas of Dublin and in parts of the border counties are the Protestants numerically strong enough to be taken into political account.

These cleavages were resolved only by rebellion and the creation of an independent nation-state. Ironically, this process itself produced a cleavage that has been of greater importance than any other in modern Irish life. The division of the independence movement and, subsequently, of the country into Treaty versus anti-Treaty factions polarized Irish politics, with tremendous consequences. There is much evidence, as Rumpf has pointed out, to suggest that this division reflected regional and socioeconomic divisions as well as political and personal differences. Certainly, it exacerbated, if it did not cause, great conflict in Irish society. It has been reflected in social life, in nationalist associations and ceremonials, and in politics. In politics it was the major polarizing agent and formed the basis of party division: Fianna Fáil and Fine Gael, the two biggest parties, derive from it. Even though its causes have been removed, the polarization of politics remains to this day, for the parties have developed their own life and momentum. Yet it might be argued that by polarizing politics, they have prevented the rise of strong left or agrarian movements. Thus, it could be said that the Treaty split has inhibited or at least softened class divisions.

Although the major groups involved in the split of Sinn Féin eventually learned to live together, the extremists could not be assimilated. De Valera, for all his republican principles, was essentially practical, and entered constitutional politics when his position required it. Others were not so practical. A continuing tradition of extreme republican movements has produced people who do not recognize the government or the state and who have resorted to force and to outrage. Such people are now very few and have become increasingly estranged from the community, but they epitomize a small element of republican radicalism to be found mainly in parts of the southwest and the border counties and among members of certain social groups, usually urban workers or very small farmers.

The cleavages of an industrial society. The typical cleavages of Western industrialized societies—employer versus worker, capitalist versus socialist, middle class versus working class—have not been important in Ireland simply because the conditions that produce them have existed in only a few areas. In the nineteenth century, industrial development was limited and very localized. The area where it developed furthest, the northeast, remained part of the United Kingdom. In the new state, the Sinn Féin policy of self-reliance led to the development of protected industries, which, having grown to a size that enabled them to serve the minute home market, stagnated. Consequently, Ireland did not develop a large urban, industrial working class with proletarian attitudes. Only a small minority, though now a steadily growing minority, see society as divided along class lines. Because of the split of Sinn Féin and the emergence of the Treaty issue as the dominant issue of Irish politics, the Labour Party did not become even the party of the urban worker, let alone of the poorer people in the country generally. Only recently has industrialization become comparatively rapid, but it is far from certain that the familiar left-wing versus right-wing politics of an industrial society will become established in Ireland.

Town versus country. As industrialization proceeds in a country with a considerable peasant population, it is to be expected that a gap will open up between the rural and the industrial communities. Hitherto, Ireland has never had farmers' parties of any size or for any length of time, largely owing, perhaps, to the polarization of politics on the Treaty issue. Increasingly, however, in recent years, there have been expressions of urban-rural hostility in the Dáil, in discussions of the revision of parliamentary constituencies, when the issue of the overrepresentation of the west is raised and when fears are voiced about the power of the big cities. The emergence of a large, militant National Farmers' Association, which contrasts the earnings of city workers with those of small farmers and has in recent years defied the government and the courts, suggests that there are in Ireland today the makings of an urban-rural split.

As yet, however, one cleavage above all—the split over the Treaty—has had a dominating influence on politics. Throwing up two major parties deeply divided, it helped establish the basic pattern of Irish government and politics. Other cleavages have had to express themselves inside these parties to a great extent or outside the parties altogether, principally by interest group activity.

TWO

The Constitution

The constitution of a country is a basic document of government. When a people accept democratic values, as the Irish do, they are necessarily a law-respecting people who willingly consent to government control. The constitution is an instrument through which the government itself can be controlled. It would seem, therefore, to be an appropriate starting point for the study of the government and politics of a country.

If so, it is, however, only a starting point. A constitution contains no more than a selection of the rules governing the more formal aspects of the political process, together with an enunciation of the basic rights and duties of the citizens and declarations on matters thought to be important. It is thus only a part, though a key part, of the institutional framework of government, and an even smaller part of the total political system, which includes political processes, habits, and practices that are not expressed in formal political organizations at all.

At best, a constitution will enunciate only a general pattern of political and legal organization and relationships. The day-to-day operations of government will make necessary the creation of a body of law dealing with matters too detailed to include in the constitution, as well as the development of a series of working conventions to implement it. A constitution will reflect the basic values of the community at the time of its formulation, but values inevitably change, and standards and practices in the community become different from those prevailing when the constitution was written. Unless it is constantly being amended, the constitution will increasingly tend to contain sections that are outmoded or inappropriate.

The Constitution of Ireland gives a comparatively accurate picture of the formal organization of the Irish government as it exists today, and of the limits within which the government operates. Even so, however, such important matters as the functions of the cabinet and its relationship with the Oireachtas (Parliament) are inadequately dealt with. The values and standards of the community are generally well reflected in the document. Indeed, as we shall see, the principles of democracy on the one hand and of Catholic social teaching on the other are both clearly visible in a curious, but not unsuccessful, juxtaposition. But it would be foolish to expect to find mirrored in the Constitution the whole complex political culture of the people. It is itself only an artifact of the political culture, reflecting some aspects of that culture.

II

The Constitution in force in Ireland is Bunreacht na hEireann (Constitution of Ireland), enacted in 1937. It is thus unlike the constitutions of many countries, which are occasioned by the coming into being of an entirely new state following independence or separation, or by revolution or radical change. It represents rather an important stage in the *evolution* of the state. To understand both the occasion for it and its contents, it is necessary to see it as the successor of two previous constitutions—the Constitution of Dáil Eireann (1919) and the Constitution of the Irish Free State (1922).

The Constitution of Dáil Eireann was the constitution of a revolutionary assembly that was itself a part of an independence movement. It was not intended to provide the basic law for a full-fledged sovereign state. On the contrary, the Constitution of the Irish Free State was so intended. Occasioned by the victory of the independence movement, it marked the emergence of the state as a sovereign state internationally recognized. It was, however, the product of a negotiated treaty with the United Kingdom, and embodied arrangements agreed to by those in the independence movement who thought they were the best to be obtained in the circumstances. Some, as we know, did not think this, and when they could, they moved to change these arrangements. Thus all three constitutions were the products of the same general movement, and each succeeding version reflected another stage reached in the evolution of an Irish state with constitutional symbols and an international status broadly acceptable to the great majority. Strangely enough, the final stage—the formal declaration that the state is a republic—did not require a constitutional change at all, but was effected by ordinary legislation.

The Sinn Féin candidates who were elected at the general election of December 1918 and who constituted themselves Dáil Eireann in Janu-

ary 1919 were members of an independence movement actively engaged
in struggle. The formation and operations of a "government" and the
meetings of Dáil Eireann itself were part of the campaign. In these circumstances, their constitution was not seriously intended to meet the
needs of an effectively operating independent state, being part of what
was essentially a publicity exercise. It was short, its five sections covering the appointment of a chairman, the competence of the Dáil, the appointment of a Prime Minister and a government and their powers,
the provision of funds, and the audit of expenditure. In addition, the
Dáil passed a "Declaration of Independence" and a "Democratic Programme" of rights and duties, documents that should be read together
with the Constitution.

These enactments of Dáil Eireann reflected the democratic and republican nature of the independence movement and, at the same time,
showed how much of the British and how little of any other foreign tradition the members of the movement had absorbed. The Dáil was conceived as having overall authority over the movement and, as circumstances allowed, over the country. The Prime Minister and other
ministers were to be members of the Dáil, chosen by it, answerable to it,
and dismissable by it. The general pattern of government, insofar as it
operated, followed broadly the British. The "Democratic Programme,"
covering the ownership of property and such matters as the right to education, social welfare services, and equality, and stressing international
cooperation, reflected current British socialist thinking and was the
work of some of the leaders of the more left-wing sections of the movement. It was probably not really acceptable to the majority, or at least
many of their leaders, but those "who at this inspired moment approved
with acclamation everything that was put to them, afterwards hardly
knew what had actually been in the documents."[1]

The Constitution of the Irish Free State, together with the Treaty,
marked the success of the independence movement. It was a constitution
for an effective sovereign state brought into existence by a national
movement, but a state that had perforce to remain in a special relationship with the United Kingdom. The result of having to negotiate a
treaty with the British government was that the Irish leaders had to
accept both the then current British ideas of the proper arrangements
for emergent colonies, i.e. Commonwealth status, and also a number of
safeguards for defense and for the protection of the Protestant minority

[1] E. Rumpf, *Nationalismus und Sozialismus in Irland* (Meisenheim am Glan, 1959),
p. 43. My translation.

left in the new state. Consequently, the Irish Free State Constitution reflected two different political theories. One was of popular sovereignty, couched in dogmatic assertions about the rights of the people, and the other was of British constitutional monarchy, with roots in predemocratic monarchical theory and reflected in British Commonwealth symbols—the Crown, a governor-general, an oath of loyalty, etc.—and the constitutional fictions connected with "His Majesty's Government."

The provisions for political organization and procedures expanded the sketchy arrangements of the 1919 Constitution considerably, following quite closely the existing British patterns. However, though the British cabinet system and the Westminster model generally were the basis of the machinery of government, attempts were made to correct what the leaders of the time thought were imperfections in British government by including constitutional devices intended to increase popular and parliamentary control and to inhibit the development of a strong cabinet backed by a majority party from establishing hegemony over the Oireachtas. Such were the provisions for referendum, the initiative, and "Extern Ministers," i.e. ministers elected directly by the Dáil, who did not need to be members of the Dáil and who were not members of the cabinet. Significantly, all such "un-British" devices were removed or inoperative within five years.

With the coming to power of Eamon de Valera, a radical revision of the whole position in respect of the Commonwealth was certain, for this was after all what he had stood for and fought for. In fact, Commonwealth status did not suit the circumstances of Ireland, coming as it did too late and as the result of violence, and linked as it was with the running sore of partition. If the substance of independence had been sufficient for the moment for many in 1922—and was in any case the best that could be got—the majority accepted the need for revision, and many who had helped elect De Valera had done so to enable him to carry it out. Such a revision involved, first, the removal from the Irish Free State Constitution of all signs and symbols of Commonwealth status and, then, the construction of an entirely new constitution "unquestionably indigenous in character."[2] Such a constitution would stress the republican and popular nature of the state, superseding the Commonwealth concept entirely.

III

Bunreacht na hEireann provides for a state that is in essentials a republic. The basis of all governmental authority, including the authority to

2 N. Mansergh, *Survey of British Commonwealth Affairs: Problems of External Policy, 1931–39* (London, 1952), p. 289.

enact the constitution itself and to change it, is the people. "We, the people of Eire . . . do hereby adopt, enact, and give to ourselves this Constitution." It is important to notice, too, that the people here referred to are in principle the people of the whole island, as Article 2 makes clear: "The national territory consists of the whole island of Ireland, its islands and the territorial seas." However, in Article 3 the de facto situation is recognized, and "pending the re-integration of the national territory" the laws of the state are declared to have effect in only twenty-six counties.

In place of the symbols of British Commonwealth status, provision is made for an elected President, the symbol of republican status. Yet nowhere in the constitution is Ireland declared to be a republic. Article 4 says only that "The name of the State is *Eire*, or, in the English language, *Ireland*," and Article 5 that "Ireland is a sovereign, independent, democratic state." Surprising as this may seem, it was a deliberate omission, reflecting the evolutionary development of Ireland's constitutional status in general and De Valera's policy of "external association" and his hopes of acquiring the six Ulster counties in particular. To have formally declared the state a republic in 1937 would have involved a complete break with the Commonwealth, which at that time, it was thought, was linked by a common allegiance to the British Crown and could not include a republic. Such a break would be seen as deliberately removing all possibility of eventually wooing Northern Ireland into an all-Ireland state. De Valera made no bones about his motives: "If the Northern problem were not there . . . in all probability there would be a flat, downright proclamation of a republic in this [Constitution]."[3] He provided instead in obscure language (in Article 29.4.2°) for the continuation of arrangements devised at the abdication of King Edward VIII in 1936. At that time opportunity had been taken to remove mention of the Crown from the Irish Free State Constitution and to reinstate it in an ordinary statute, the Executive Authority (External Relations) Act, as an organ or instrument that might be used by the Irish state for some purposes in the conduct of external affairs. These arrangements, De Valera hoped, would constitute "a bridge over which the Northern Unionists might one day walk."[4]

It was a forlorn hope, but the arrangements made in 1937 had the advantage, as De Valera pointed out, of allowing for further evolution of Ireland's status without the need to change one word of the

[3] *Dáil Debates*, vol. 68, col. 430 (June 14, 1937).
[4] C. O'Leary, *The Irish Republic and Its Experiment with Proportional Representation* (South Bend, Indiana, 1961), p. 30.

Constitution. Thus, when in 1948 John Costello's coalition government decided that the time had come to declare Ireland a republic, the deed was done by ordinary legislation in the Republic of Ireland Act, which declares that "The description of the State shall be the Republic of Ireland" and which cancels the arrangement for the use of the British monarch provided for in the Executive Authority (External Relations) Act. On Easter Day, 1949, Ireland became formally and unequivocally a republic. Yet, even then, the realities of Ireland's position in relation to the United Kingdom had still to be recognized. It was neither convenient nor, indeed, practicable for the United Kingdom to regard Ireland as a foreign state. Under the Ireland Act, 1949, the Republic of Ireland, as the state was in future to be known in the United Kingdom, was not to be a foreign country or her citizens aliens. Instead, they were to have a special status and all the privileges of Commonwealth citizens. Today, they are even more privileged, for the restrictions applied to the entry of Commonwealth citizens to the United Kingdom under the Commonwealth Immigrants Act do not apply to Irish people. In this way, as in many others, the unique association of the two countries is constantly demonstrated.

The dissatisfaction of De Valera and Fianna Fáil with the Irish Free State Constitution did not extend to the system by which the country was governed. On the contrary, the trend toward a system of the British type, and operating in a similar manner, was confirmed after 1932. To a large extent Bunreacht na hEireann continued what already existed formally or in practice. The very words and phrases used were in some places identical with those used in the 1922 Constitution, or at least very similar. The most important changes that were made were those intended to increase the status and power of the Prime Minister (now called Taoiseach), though even this was to some extent only to make formal what was in fact the practice, at least since the accession of De Valera. Otherwise changes were comparatively minor, though the occasion was taken to make yet another attempt to solve the difficult problem of the composition and powers of the Senate.

However, because there are large differences in scale and complexity between Irish and British government, and because, as we have seen, the political culture of Ireland contains elements other than those derived from Britain, the conduct of government and politics is by no means exactly similar in the two countries. To a great extent, what this study of Irish government is concerned with is precisely the working of British-type institutions in a cultural setting that, though it owes much to Britain, is very different.

IV

If the enactment of Bunreacht na hEireann represented a stage in the progress of Ireland to constitutional independence from the United Kingdom, it also marked the overt recognition of Roman Catholic principles in the country's political life and institutions. Mixed with the liberal and democratic elements derived from the British tradition are principles and precepts drawn from Catholic social theory and, in particular, the papal encyclicals. This mixture is mostly to be seen in Articles 40–44, the articles dealing with the rights of the citizens, and in Article 45, which is entitled "Directive Principles of Social Policy." Elsewhere, the Constitution, though it is clearly Christian in tone, is not specially Catholic, except in Articles 18 and 19, which, taking up a political idea then much in vogue among Catholics, make provision for vocational representation in the Senate, and Article 15.2.3°, which permits the Oireachtas to establish or recognize "functional or vocational councils representing branches of the social and economic life of the people."

Article 40, entitled "Personal Rights," enunciates many of the personal and civil rights that are the product of the liberal tradition. It declares citizens to be equal before the law and to have the right of habeas corpus. Citizens' homes are not to be forcibly entered "save in accordance with law." It also guarantees the right of free expression "including criticisms of government policy," of peaceful assembly, and to form associations and unions—all "subject to public order and morality." It expressly forbids political, religious, or class discrimination. Elsewhere in the Constitution, notably in Articles 15.5 and 34–39 (the articles that deal with the courts), other liberal rights connected with legal processes are laid down.

If Article 40 is a product of liberalism, Articles 41, 42, and 43, which deal with the family, education, and property, are obviously Catholic in content and tone. Article 41 declares that "The State recognizes the Family as the natural primary and fundamental unit group of Society, and as a moral institution possessing inalienable and imprescriptible rights, antecedent and superior to all positive law." The integrity of the family is, therefore, carefully protected by constitutional safeguards. The state guarantees to guard the institution of marriage, and the enactment of laws granting a dissolution of marriage is forbidden. Further, a person who has been divorced in another country and whose marriage is "a subsisting valid marriage" in Irish law is forbidden to marry within the Republic.

In Article 42 the family is recognized as "the primary and natural educator of the child." Parents have the right and the duty to provide education for their children, but they may, if they wish, provide it in their own homes and the state steps in only in default. The enunciation in Article 43 of the right to possess property and its qualifications are unmistakably Catholic. "The State acknowledges that man, in virtue of his rational being, has the natural right, antecedent to positive law, to the private ownership of external goods." The state, therefore, will pass no law attempting to abolish the right of private ownership or the right to bequeath and inherit it. However, the exercise of property rights is to be regulated by "the principles of social justice," and the state may "delimit by law the exercise of the said rights" for "the common good."

In Article 44, the article that deals with religion, a brave attempt is made to reconcile the principles of the two bodies of thought, liberal and Catholic, which are the bases of Irish life. History and the desire not to arouse the fears of Protestants (on either side of the border) demanded that Catholic principles concerning the duty of the state to recognize and favor the one true faith, as these were understood in the 1930's, should not be strictly applied. The state acknowledges the duty to respect and honor religion and "recognizes the special position of the Holy Catholic Apostolic and Roman Church as the guardian of the Faith professed by the great majority of the citizens." It also recognizes the other religious denominations that existed in the community at the time of the enactment, and it guarantees "freedom of conscience and the free profession and practice of religion." It guarantees not to endow any religion, not to impose any disabilities on religious grounds, not to discriminate in providing aid for schools, and not to take over church property compulsorily except for "necessary works of public utility and on payment of compensation."

As in Articles 42 and 43, so too in Article 45, "Directive Principles of Social Policy," the precepts of Catholic theory dominate. Because the provisions of this article "shall not be cognisable by any court," being intended for the guidance of the Oireachtas, they have the air of pious platitudes, and have in fact been largely ignored. The state is bidden to seek "a social order in which justice and charity shall inform all the institutions of the national life," and so to organize affairs that all men and women "may through their occupations find the means of making reasonable provision for their domestic needs." It should have special care for the weaker in the community. Concerning property, the Catholic position is once again stated. The public must be protected against "unjust exploitation," and "the state shall favour and, where necessary, supplement private initiative in industry and commerce."

Finally, it should be noticed that in this article, as in the treatment of the position of mothers in Article 41, the influence of yet another cultural tradition, the rural peasant tradition, can clearly be seen. The requirement that the state shall attempt to secure "that there may be established on the land in economic security as many families as ... practicable" evokes the ideal of De Valera and others of a rural, Catholic (and Irish-speaking) society of smallholders living simply and in frugal security. The figures for population movement and emigration show how far this ideal is from realization, and perhaps even from reality.

v

Bunreacht na hEireann can be seen as a product of the political culture of the country. It mirrors some aspects of that culture quite faithfully. However, since Ireland is a democratic and, therefore, a law-respecting society, the Constitution is not merely a product of the culture, but is itself an important guide to political action. This will be seen in the chapters that follow. Even so, some of the political activities of the community are not mentioned in it, and it is often precisely activities of this type that govern the whole system. To perform the functions of translating community values into political demands and of reflecting the differences in the community that have to be resolved, political institutions are needed that seldom if ever are even mentioned in constitutions. Bunreacht na hEireann makes no mention of political parties, for example, yet it is in parties and other institutions that express and process the claims of persons and groups in the community that the political process begins. It is, therefore, to these that we must now turn our attention.

THREE

Political Parties

As earlier chapters make clear, the major political divisions in Ireland have arisen over questions of national independence—Commonwealth status, the extent of the state, and constitutional forms. The mass parties that developed in Great Britain from the late nineteenth century, reflecting as they did the social and political divisions of a metropolitan society, never had much relevance for the majority in Ireland, and it was not to be expected that they would feature in an independent Ireland. In these circumstances, there was little continuity in the party situation between the days before and after independence. Moreover, as so often happens in the evolution of a nation to statehood, the early parties of nationalist struggle were superseded or could not take the strains of momentous change and broke up. Hence the picture by the late 1920's, when stability had been achieved by the new state, bore little resemblance to the situation before independence. The Irish Parliamentary Party—the party of the middle-class, moderate nationalists—disappeared, overwhelmed by the tide of events, and the split of Sinn Féin and the resulting civil war opened up a cleavage that changed that movement entirely. Only the Labour Party, founded in 1912, still existed when a settled party system emerged in the middle 1920's. But the Labour Party, too, was changed as so much else by the events of 1916 and immediately thereafter. By and large, then, it is necessary only to consider the party system in Ireland after the inception of the state.

II

The split of Sinn Féin polarized Irish politics. From the 1920's to the 1950's Irish public opinion could be considered essentially twin-peaked; reflecting it, the party system tended to produce two groups. (However, there have never been fewer than three parties contesting elections and sometimes as many as seven.)[1] The two major parties produced by the split helped to perpetuate it. One, the Cumann na nGaedheal Party, was formed by the supporters of the Treaty in 1923; it was succeeded, in 1933, by Fine Gael. The opponents of the Treaty (or rather those of them who preferred to practice parliamentary politics with the chance of eventually winning power) formed Fianna Fáil in 1926.

These parties and the leaders who personified them were the poles around which the majority of the community gathered in groups large enough to allow, first the one, then the other, to form governments composed exclusively of their own supporters. Until 1948 at least, there was little crossing the great divide between them, though by this time the issues that had split Sinn Féin were either resolved or increasingly irrelevant. Yet the parties continued—their names evoking distinctive images in the public mind, their leaders and aspirant leaders irreconcilable, their traditions (including family traditions) hardened, and their interests vested. Although since then, and particularly from the late 1950's, these parties have changed in respect of what they actually stand for, they have the same air of permanence as those great pillars of the "stable" democracies—the Conservative and Labour parties in Great Britain and the Democratic and Republican parties in the United States.

Other parties and politicians tended inevitably to be committed one way or another on the Treaty issue. Hence they were oriented to one or the other of the major parties. Some parties presented variations on the constitutional theme. Such were the National League and Clann Eireann in the 1920's and the Centre Party in the 1930's. Others, ostensibly based on some other community interest, such as farming, were inevitably irreconcilable opponents of one major party and hence, willy-nilly, camp followers of the other. In fact, the preeminence of this issue inhibited the development of parties based on other community interests or cleavages, and at times of stress, as in the middle 1930's, those that had existed disappeared as the ranks closed and tightened. Nevertheless, because of the particular proportional representation election system that was adopted and the strength of local and personal factors in Irish politics, small parties were always likely to appear and until recently Independents were always to be found in the Dáil in numbers ranging from half a dozen to a score. Only two groups did not fit into this pattern: radical republicans because they cared too much about the issue, and the Labour Party because it said it cared very little.

From the very beginning of the state there have always been intransi-

---

[1] For details of party representation in the Dáil and the number and party affiliation of candidates at elections, see Appendix B.

gent republicans of more or less radical disposition who have not accepted the regime. From the middle 1920's onward, after the major part of the anti-Treaty party entered constitutional politics, the diehards grouped and regrouped in various radical and fissiparous organizations. Some were on the verge of constitutional politics; others, centered on the Irish Republican Army, were committed to force. Some were concerned with a republic; others, the heirs and successors of Connolly or radicals of the left, with a socialistic republic. It is in this area alone that the coverage or "reach" of the constitutional or "system" parties has not always embraced the whole political spectrum. The temporary success in 1948 of Clann na Poblachta, led by the radical republican and former member of the IRA, Seán MacBride, was due to tapping these streams and combining them with the more radical elements of the left of both Fianna Fáil and the Labour Party. However, these were notoriously unstable elements and could not be held together. Yet even as late as 1957, when IRA activity was greater than it had been for a number of years and border raids coincided with a great effort by Sinn Féin at the general election of that year to contest seats (which they would not take), it was amply demonstrated that significant republican and radical sentiment still existed in some areas.

The Labour Party, never as a whole committed to the extreme socialism of Connolly and Larkin or the extreme nationalism of Connolly and the Irish Citizen Army, and mindful of the fact that it was an all-Ireland party, was in some difficulty after 1916. It abstained from contesting the 1918 election in order to give Sinn Féin the field, and when that movement split, it affected neutrality in the civil war that ensued. Arguing that the Treaty issue was not the most important one for the Irish people, it was willing to cooperate in constitutional politics as the major opposition party until 1927; opposing the middle-class Cumann na nGaedheal on socioeconomic grounds, it became an independent ally of Fianna Fáil when De Valera led his party into the Dáil in that year. During the next twenty years, Labour was to become progressively more disenchanted with De Valera, until eventually in 1948 it tried coalition with its former bourgeois opponent. Cautious in a cagey, trade union way, and specially on its guard against "anti-Christian communist" infiltration, it failed to appeal in any wholesale way either to republican radicals, of whom there were many, or to class-conscious leftists, who have been very few in Ireland. The Party did not from the beginning quite fit into the dominant pattern of Irish politics or appeal to a mass of Irish opinion—and so far it never has.

Given two nationwide parties, each with considerable support and split upon an issue that deeply divided the community, a markedly bipolar party system was inevitable. It has persisted mainly for two reasons: first, a long-continued belief in the overriding importance of constitutional issues, a belief assiduously fostered by the party leaders themselves, and second, the great strength in the Dáil of Cumann na nGaedheal in the first ten years and of Fianna Fáil from the early 1930's, and the ability of both parties to get dependable parliamentary allies, on their own (very different) terms. The major parties have always been extremely competitive: Fianna Fáil because it could always hope to win a majority in the Dáil and Fine Gael, which had been the majority party in power, because it could not reconcile itself to any other status. Only in 1948 for a decade did Fine Gael turn to coalition politics and cooperation, and though this enabled it to resume power on a shared basis, it clearly did not enjoy the experience (nor did its major partner, the Labour Party) and returned to its former stance.

The pattern of parties outlined above has been a most important factor influencing the working of the whole governmental system. Because of the long continuation of a deep division in the community, and the consequent emergence of two major parties with strictly competitive strategies, the Irish government as a whole has developed the typical features of a bipolar system, namely,

1. A "Government" and an "Opposition"—two groups in the Oireachtas, one whose members support the government consistently, the other whose members oppose it consistently.

2. Elections at which the major question directly before the electors is: who is to form the next government?

3. The possibility of an alternation of party leaders in an "ins and outs" sequence.

But, from 1932 onward, Fianna Fáil has been in power continuously for all but six years (1948–51 and 1954–57). Thus, Ireland might best be said to have what Giovanni Sartori calls a "predominant party system," which he characterizes as a type of party pluralism in which no alternation of office occurs over time, even though alternation is not ruled out and the political system provides for the opportunities of open and effective dissent. A predominant party can at any moment cease to be predominant.[2]

This situation could be changed by parties entering into coalition. As we have seen, however, with the exception of Fine Gael and Labour in the 1950's, they prefer strict competition. If the major aim of a party is to win power or a share of power, Fianna Fáil can be said to act as it does

---

[2] G. Sartori, "The Typology of Party Systems," in E. Allardt and S. Rokkan, eds., *Mass Politics* (New York: Free Press, 1970), p. 327.

TABLE 3.1
The Party System, 1923–60

Type of party	Bases of party appeal			
	Nationalist/ constitutional	Radical	Class	Agrarian
IN THE SYSTEM "Majority parties"[a]	Fianna Fáil (1926–) Cumann na nGaedheal (1923–33) Fine Gael (1933–)			
Stable minority parties			Labour (1912–)	
Ephemeral minority parties	←————Sinn Féin[b]————→ National League (1926–27) Clann Eireann (1926–27) Centre Party (1932–33)		National Labour (1944–51)	Farmers' Party (1922–32) Clann na Talmhan (1943–61)
	←———Clann na Poblachta———→ (1947–65)			
		National Progressive Democratic Party (1957–63)		
Independents	Former Unionists			Independent Farmers
	←————————————Other Independents————————————→			
OUTSIDE THE SYSTEM	←————(Small "parties" and groups, e.g., Sinn Féin,[b] Saor Eire, often highly fissiparous and ephemeral)————→			

[a] The term "majority parties" is here used in much the same sense as Maurice Duverger used the term "partis à vocation majoritaire" in his book *Les partis politiques* (Paris, 1951). He describes them as parties that have a parliamentary majority or which think and act as though they are likely to be able to command a majority.

[b] Sinn Féin candidates contested seats in the Dáil in the 1920's and again in the 1950's, though they did not wish to occupy them, since they did not recognize the Dáil. The party also contests seats at local elections.

TABLE 3.2
The Party System, 1969

Type of party	Bases of party appeal			
	Catchall	Class	Social or national radical	Agrarian
IN THE SYSTEM "Majority parties"[a]	Fianna Fáil Fine Gael ↓			
Stable minority parties	?	Labour		
. . . .	. . . .	. . . .	. . . .	. . . .
Independents			←————Independents (fewer than at any previous time)————→	
OUTSIDE THE SYSTEM			Sinn Féin[b]	

[a] The term "majority parties" is here used in much the same sense as Maurice Duverger used the term "partis à vocation majoritaire" in his book *Les partis politiques* (Paris, 1951). He describes them as parties that have a parliamentary majority or which think and act as though they are likely to be able to command a majority.

[b] Sinn Féin candidates contested seats in the Dáil in the 1920's and again in the 1950's, though they did not wish to occupy them, since they did not recognize the Dáil. The party also contests seats at local elections.

with reason, and Fine Gael and Labour less and less realistically as time goes on. The parties, however, do not see it thus. Many in all three main parties have preferred to advocate a change in the electoral system from proportional representation to the "first past the post" system, believing that this would produce a simple two-party system (by destroying Fine Gael or Labour) and an alternation of parties in power as small changes in electoral support cause large numbers of seats to change hands. Twice in a decade, however (in 1959 and 1968), proposals for constitutional changes to this effect have been rejected by the electorate at referenda.

The same circumstances that have produced bipolar politics also account to a great extent for the failure of other parties except Labour to establish themselves on a permanent basis, despite an election system that does not make it difficult for parties to do so. In fact, only two of the minor parties that have come and gone contested elections for more than a decade.

After 1948, constitutional issues gradually ceased to be the major ones and new men came to the fore, more concerned with urgent social and economic issues, as Ireland fell further behind Western Europe. The two main parties tended to become catchall parties, pragmatic in temper and given to the incremental approach often exhibited by the large established parties of relatively satisfied societies. Such parties are described by Otto Kirchheimer as follows:

> If the party cannot hope to catch all categories of voters, it may have a reasonable expectation of catching more voters in all those categories whose interests do not adamantly conflict. . . . Even more important is the heavy concentration on issues which are scarcely liable to meet resistance in the community. National societal goals transcending group interests offer the best sales prospect for a party intent on establishing or enlarging an appeal previously limited to specific sections of the population.[3]

Sometimes, the Labour Party also has seemed to be moving in the same direction. Though it regards itself as a working-class party and has always advocated more welfare and more positive state action to develop community potential, it has not always presented a clear alternative and, in a conservative and Catholic Ireland, has never seriously advocated extensive nationalization. Indeed, on the request of the Catholic bishops in 1939, it removed that section of its constitutional aims referring to the establishment of a workers' republic. Thus, having failed, perhaps inevitably, to establish itself as a class party with a distinctive "left" program as an alternative to the two major bourgeois parties, it was once again, in the 1960's as in the 1920's, trailing third, complaining feebly (at a time when planning and state-inspired development were advocated by everyone) that the clothes they could never quite bring themselves to put on had been stolen from the wardrobe. Only in the late 1960's did it show signs of adopting a distinctive socialist policy. The thinness of its support—it has never attracted more than 16 per cent of the electorate and once as little as 6 per cent—together with parliamentary logistics and the competitive attitudes of party leaders, has prevented it from playing a critical role in the formation and maintenance of governments except, as earlier remarked, for a decade from 1948.

In the late 1960's, therefore, Ireland has, as it always has had, three main parties competing for support from a public whose opinions have become remarkably "single-peaked." This important change in the pattern of public opinion may well have considerable effects, as yet only barely recognized by the parties themselves, on the new electors' choice of party, on the intensity with which people support a party, and on the propensity to change from one party to another or to reject all of them. (The development of the party system is illustrated in Tables 3.1 and 3.2.)

[3] In J. LaPalombara and M. Weiner, eds., *Political Parties and Political Development* (Princeton, 1966), p. 186.

III

Little is yet known about the social composition of party support in Ireland. In Chapter 1, the continued existence of elements of a peasant culture was noted—a culture which, though it has been steadily eroded and is now disappearing faster than ever before, has influenced Irish political life very considerably. Mention was made of Rumpf's concept of an "east-west gradient": the farther west one goes, the more important the remaining elements of peasant culture become, and the lower down the rural social scale one goes, the more its presence is felt. The mass support for the independence movement was largely in this social group, and in Rumpf's opinion socioeconomic and cultural differences explain also, in part at least, the division of opinion over the Treaty.[4] It must be recognized of course that within the independence movement at all levels, factors such as friendship, loyalty, and personality played a part in men's decisions to go one way or the other. At all levels, also, decisions were influenced by temperament. Yet, as Rumpf suggests, in general it was the poorer and more radical element, particularly in the west, that provided the mass support for De Valera and Fianna Fáil from the beginning (see Maps 3.1–3.4).

De Valera's instinct was right. His much quoted statement "When I want to know what the Irish people are thinking, I look into my own heart" is not entirely fanciful. His vision and the Fianna Fáil program of the 1920's and early 1930's evoked an instinctive response from many of the small, and especially smallest, farmers, to some extent from the landless laborers and the land-hungry, from the former poor countryman who had become an urban worker, and from some of the middle class who had hauled themselves up from a rural small-farmer background. His—and theirs—was a vision of "a frugal Gaelic Ireland gnawed at as little as possible by the worm of civilization and especially the British, in which there were to be no rich and no poor, but many small farmers and small industries scattered over the country."[5] Such a policy had the edge on the conservative and Commonwealth policies of Cumann na nGaedheal on the one hand and the mild republicanism and welfare-statism of Labour on the other.

Later, both Fianna Fáil's moderate behavior in opposition and its responsible conduct of affairs in its first period in office brought the party

[4] See E. Rumpf, *Nationalismus und Sozialismus in Irland* (Meisenheim am Glan, 1959), pp. 48–92.
[5] *Ibid.*, pp. 126–27. My translation.

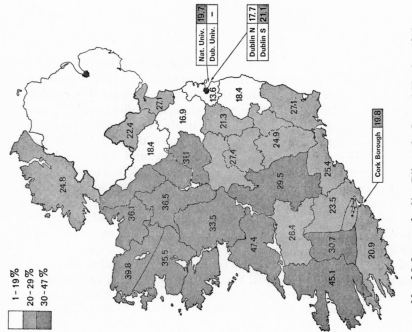

Map 3.2. Support for Sinn Féin at the General Election, 1923
(percentage of first-preference vote)

Broken lines represent county boundaries where these differ
considerably from constituency boundaries

Nat. Univ. 19.7
Dub. Univ. —

Dublin N 17.7
Dublin S 21.1

Cork Borough 19.8

1 – 19%
20 – 29%
30 – 47%

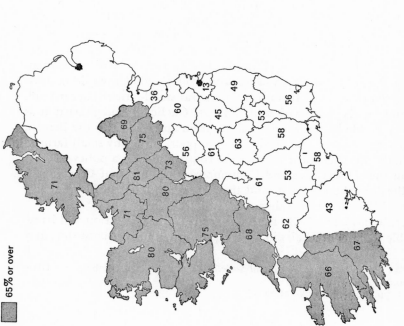

Map 3.1. Areas in which over 65 per cent of occupied persons
were engaged in agriculture in 1926

Source: *Census of Population, 1926*, vol. II, Table 3a

65% or over

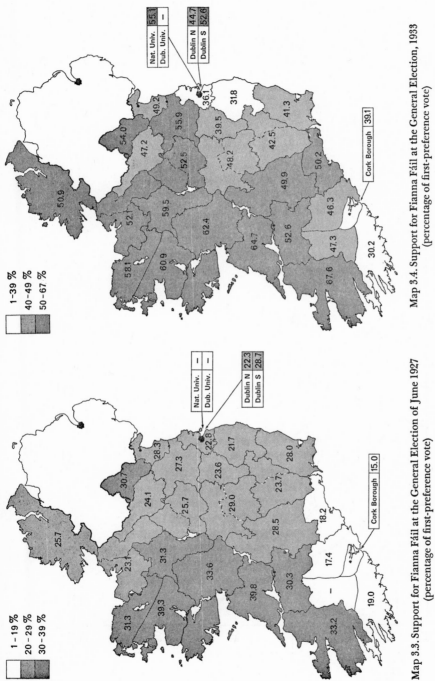

Map 3.3. Support for Fianna Fáil at the General Election of June 1927
(percentage of first-preference vote)

Broken lines represent county boundaries where these differ
considerably from constituency boundaries

Map 3.4. Support for Fianna Fáil at the General Election, 1933
(percentage of first-preference vote)

Broken lines represent county boundaries where these differ
considerably from constituency boundaries

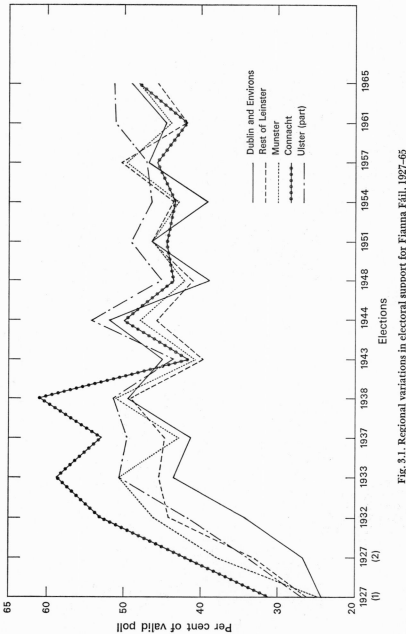

Fig. 3.1. Regional variations in electoral support for Fianna Fáil, 1927–65

votes from other sections of the electorate, as people realized that De Valera was by no means a revolutionary but, rather, a pious, bourgeois conservative. From the early 1930's Fianna Fáil added to its radical and republican base the support of a growing Catholic commercial and industrial middle class mainly composed of operators of small family businesses, who prospered in a modest way under the party's protection policies. As Fig. 3.1 shows, strong support for Fianna Fáil became nationwide in the early 1930's and has since fluctuated in national swings except in the west, where growing realization that the party was losing its radicalism and becoming as much a businessman's party as a poor man's party lost it votes permanently from the early 1940's.

The longer Fianna Fáil stayed in power, the more strongly established became the image of De Valera—not as the excommunicated rebel of 1922 but as a conservative and a devout Catholic—and the more the business community tended to support and to contribute cash to the party whose goodwill they thought might be of help to them in the conduct of their affairs. By 1965 David Thornley could write:

Mr Lemass' twenty-seven years at the helm of industry [first as Minister for Industry and Commerce and then as De Valera's successor as Taoiseach] have won Fianna Fáil a great reserve of loyalty; the political generation which knew not the polemics of the 1930's is unconscious of historical irony as it votes for Fianna Fáil and sound business administration.[6]

By this time it had become a catchall party, still able to draw upon a great reserve of instinctive loyalty, primarily from small farmers, but able also to attract votes from all other classes. Long years in office had helped establish it in the minds of many as the normal government party and the only party capable of ensuring the "stability" of single-party government.

While Fianna Fáil was originally the party of the poorer countrymen and republicans, Cumann na nGaedheal and its successor, Fine Gael, was at first the party of the Treaty and Commonwealth status, of the business world (particularly the larger and older established businesses), and of the medium and big farmers. In other words, it was primarily a party with a middle-class character. But just as Fianna Fáil became a national party and, subsequently, a catchall party, so too Fine Gael changed, though not so markedly. In the 1920's it looked and behaved like a conservative party, and attracted to itself those who desired peace and stable government, those who thought that the Treaty, the Irish Free State, and the close Commonwealth connection were the best guarantees of these,

6 "The Fianna Fáil Party," *Irish Times*, Apr. 1, 1965.

and those who could not abide De Valera. Members of the former Irish Parliamentary Party and former Unionists supported it *faute de mieux*, and, in fact, most of them were integrated into the new and independent Ireland in this way, finding in this party much that satisfied them, or at least that was better than they had expected. Also, it was probably the party of the clergy, except perhaps for some of the more radical young curates of the 1920's and 1930's from rural backgrounds and fresh from Maynooth. In the 1930's, when the party went through a number of metamorphoses to emerge as Fine Gael, it had on its right wing intellectuals who advocated the implementation of the vocationally organized society suggested in Pope Pius XI's encyclical *Quadragesimo Anno* (1931) and a few who, misunderstanding fascism, thought that in some way fascism and Catholicism might go together.

The party was strongest in Dublin and Cork (the major cities) and weakest in Leinster and Munster, where other parties, Labour at all times and in the 1920's the Farmers' Party, took some of the anti–Fianna Fáil vote. Later, in the 1940's, the same phenomenon could be observed in the west, where, for ten years or more, another and different farmers' party (Clann na Talmhan) took votes from it. As Fianna Fáil established itself in the late 1920's and the 1930's and showed that it could govern responsibly and was aiming at a Catholic, conservative republic, support for Fine Gael flagged, particularly in Dublin. Although the party continued to behave like a party that might resume office again after the next election, its image as both conservative and pro-Commonwealth was hardly calculated to attract majority support, and it went into decline. Its share of Dáil seats fell from 35 per cent in 1937 to 21 per cent in 1948, at which time it made two important changes in policy. First, it entered a coalition government and, second, as the major partner of this coalition, the so-called Inter-Party Government, it sponsored the Republic of Ireland Act, 1948, which formally declared Ireland a republic. Thus it finally laid its pro-British and Commonwealth ghost.

More recently, it has attempted with some success to appear as the national catchall alternative to Fianna Fáil. Nevertheless, "since 1932 it has never re-established its position as a 'majority-bent' party. Its national support is wide and loyal, but just that much thinner on the ground than Fianna Fáil's."[7] What is important for the political system as a whole is that it still behaves to a great extent as though it might win a majority, though after so long a Fianna Fáil hegemony, it usually has a somewhat tired air of resignation.

[7] D. Thornley, "The Fine Gael Party," *Irish Times*, Mar. 31, 1965.

The most important feature of the Labour Party is that it has never been an urban proletariat party but rather a *rural* working-class party. Its main electoral strength has always lain in the east and south, where there is a larger number of farm laborers than anywhere else in Ireland. (See Maps 3.5–3.8.) Its original core here may have been members of rural workers' organizations. Once established, this Labour support remained stable, centered more perhaps on the individual representative than on programs, let alone clear-cut ideology. Although it was founded by trade union leaders and intended to be the same sort of alliance of socialism and trade unionism as had been established in Britain, its failure to take a strong stand on the republican issue in the period from 1918, and the disunity in the Labour movement that led to the split in the giant Transport and General Workers' Union in the 1920's, made it difficult for it to establish itself in Dublin. Thus we have the astonishing fact that from 1923 until the Second World War it could muster less than 10 per cent of the poll in the biggest city in the country. Only recently has it begun to make an impact in Dublin, where, one would think, its main potential support should lie.

We can perhaps, however, find a wider explanation for the failure of Labour to be more than a poor third. David Thornley sums it up thus: "More than any other party Labour has suffered from partition, with the consequent loss of the industrial complex of Belfast, from emigration, from the division of the trade union movement . . . and from the competing claims of republicanism."[8]

The dominance of national and constitutional issues, as we have seen, inhibited the development of parties based on other community interests or divisions. Perhaps most surprising has been the failure of farmers' parties to emerge as permanent features of the system. However, it should be noted that agriculture varies considerably in Ireland, from small subsistence farming and sheep farming to dairying and the production of cattle for beef. Consequently, agrarian parties, when they have appeared, have tended to be regional. The Farmers' Party of the 1920's was predominantly a party of farmers of some substance based on a Farmers' Association with headquarters in Dublin. Though it won fifteen seats and 12.1 per cent of the valid poll in 1923, it was absorbed within the decade, mostly into Cumann na nGaedheal, which it supported in the Dáil and with which the majority of its prominent members quite obviously belonged. Likewise, in the 1940's, Clann na Talmhan (the Party of the Land) emerged, a loose-knit organization with its

8 "The Labour Party," *Irish Times*, Mar. 30, 1965.

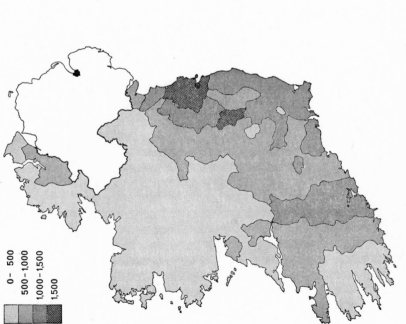

Map 3.5. Number of Farm Laborers per 1,000 Farmers, 1936
Source: After T. W. Freeman, *Ireland*, 1st ed. (London, 1950), p. 196

0– 500
500–1,000
1,000–1,500
1,500

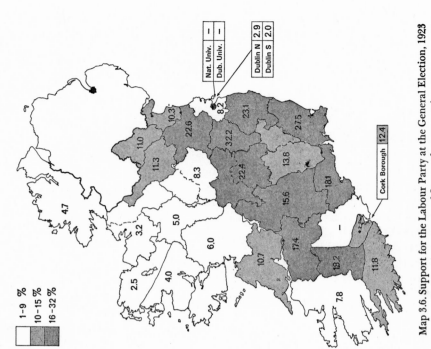

| Nat. Univ. | — |
| Dub. Univ. | — |

| Dublin N | 2.9 |
| Dublin S | 2.0 |

Cork Borough 12.4

1–9 %
10–15 %
16–32 %

Map 3.6. Support for the Labour Party at the General Election, 1923
(percentage of first-preference vote)

Broken lines represent county boundaries where these differ
considerably from constituency boundaries

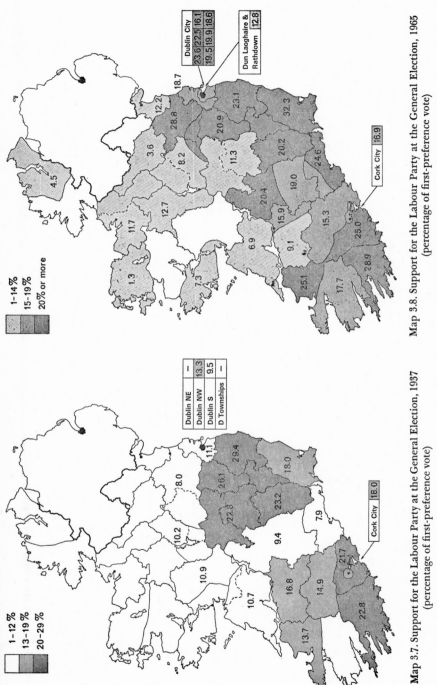

1-12 %
13-19 %
20-29 %

Dublin NE	—
Dublin NW	13.3
Dublin S	9.5
D Townships	—

10.2

8.0

11.1

29.4

26.1

22.3

18.0

23.2

7.9

9.4

10.9

10.7

16.8

14.9

13.7

22.8

2.7

Cork City 18.0

Map 3.7. Support for the Labour Party at the General Election, 1937
(percentage of first-preference vote)

Broken lines represent county boundaries where these differ
considerably from constituency boundaries

1-14 %
15-19 %
20% or more

4.5

1.3

7.3

11.7

12.7

12.2

3.6

8.2

18.7

28.8

20.9

23.1

11.3

| Dublin City | 23.6 | 22.5 | 16.1 |
| | 19.5 | 19.9 | 18.6 |

| Dun Laoghaire & Rathdown | 12.8 |

32.3

20.2

6.9

15.9

20.4

19.0

24.6

9.1

15.3

25.0

25.1

28.9

17.7

Cork City 16.9

Map 3.8. Support for the Labour Party at the General Election, 1965
(percentage of first-preference vote)

Broken lines represent county boundaries where these differ
considerably from constituency boundaries

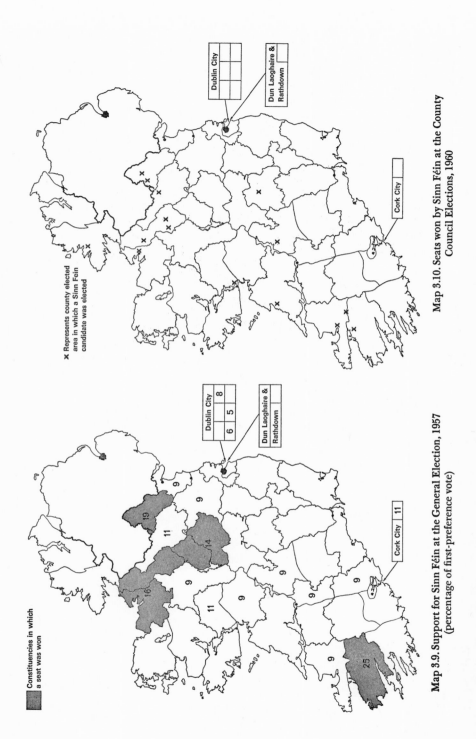

Dublin City	8
6	5

Dun Laoghaire & Rathdown	

Cork City	11

Constituencies in which a seat was won

Map 3.9. Support for Sinn Féin at the General Election, 1957
(percentage of first-preference vote)

Dublin City	

Dun Laoghaire & Rathdown	

Cork City	

x Represents county elected area in which a Sinn Féin candidate was elected

Map 3.10. Seats won by Sinn Féin at the County Council Elections, 1960

electoral strength among conservative small farmers of the west (Mayo, Galway, Roscommon), who had previously supported the major parties. Its deputies were fairly independent and locally oriented, being largely on their own when it came to fighting elections.

With the single transferable vote system of proportional representation it is perhaps easier than in most electoral systems for individual parliamentary representatives and small groups to break away from their parent body and to survive, at least for a while. Likewise, it has been possible for individuals who could touch some chord in their locality or espouse some popular cause or causes to win electoral support and even a seat. From the first days of the state until the general election of 1965 there were always twenty to thirty candidates of this sort at each election. It is not possible to generalize about them except to say that in most cases their support was personal and that in some cases they evoked remarkably stable personal loyalty. Only very occasionally can one see a distinct social or group interest basis for an individual politician of this sort. Perhaps the most obvious was the Protestant vote in the border counties. The Protestant farming vote in Donegal for an Independent, William Sheldon, was for many years a stable phenomenon, predictable to within quite narrow limits.

Finally, it should be noticed that the radical republicanism that has provided recruits to the IRA and has given rise from time to time to unconstitutional movements and extreme parties and groups has (as it has always had) its social bases in the poorer small farmer element. Its geographical home has been in the west, especially Kerry, and also, as one might expect, near the border in the Ulster counties. In Dublin, too, it attracts a small minority of radical working-class support. Map 3.9 shows where Sinn Féin got its support at the 1957 general election, when the party made a spectacular effort following a period of intense IRA activity on the border, and Map 3.10 confirms the picture.

IV

Political parties perform three main functions—we may almost call them services—in the political process. First, they mobilize the electorate. Their primary aim is to win votes. To do so involves them not only in communicating opinions and demands to political leaders and party policies to the public, but also in processing demands by combining them into coherent courses of action or policies. Thus, they perform the important tasks of "interest articulation," i.e. "the process by which individuals and groups make demands upon the political decision makers," and "interest aggregation," i.e. "converting demands into general policy alternatives."[9] Second, the parties recruit political leaders at all levels and select candidates for political posts to be filled by election. Since the spoils system does not operate to any extent in Ireland, they do not have many public offices to give. Third, they take on responsibility for central and local government, and for operating the parliamentary and representative processes of discussion, scrutiny, and criticism of government policy and administration.

The organization and procedures used to carry out these functions differ according to the size, degree of development, and culture of a country, and the nature of its political system. Irish parties, compared with those in many advanced countries (particularly large countries), are rather poorly organized and exhibit a haphazard, even amateur, approach to organization and membership building. The local orientation of politicians and politics is here very evident. The party central offices have little control over the local branches. What is more, they have little contact with them and are poorly informed about them. Thus, for example, the parties do not know exactly how many members they have or the incomes and expenditures of their local branches. In these circumstances and because no detailed studies have yet been made, it is possible to speak only in a formal way and in rather general terms about party organization and activity.

In considering party organization, a distinction may be made between the three major parties and the smaller parties that have existed from time to time and the Independents. Minor parties with pretensions have usually tried to model themselves on the major parties, with a similar pattern of organization, but a lack of resources, human and material, has been against them. Inevitably they have tended to become essentially electoral alliances of deputies who closely resemble the formally Independent members in that each has some sort of organization in his own area, often consisting mainly of personal contacts. To speak of party organization, therefore, is to speak of the three major parties.

The main institutions of the parties are the local clubs or branches (called *cumainn* in the case of Fianna Fáil), each linked to some sort of electoral constituency organization; an annual delegate meeting or convention (called Ard Fheis in the case of both Fine Gael and Fianna Fáil); a national council or executive with a smaller inner executive or standing committee; a "parliamentary party," i.e. the members of the party who have seats in the Oireachtas; and a Central Office. None of

[9] G. A. Almond and G. B. Powell, *Comparative Politics: A Developmental Approach* (Boston, 1966), pp. 73, 98.

them have permanently effective ancillary organizations, youth movements, or the like, though for a short, tense period in the 1930's the IRA on the one side and the Army Comrades Association (the Blueshirts) on the other acted as paramilitary but uncontrollable supporters of Fianna Fáil and Fine Gael, respectively.

"The old Parliamentary Party having had a committee in each parish it was natural that Sinn Féin should do likewise in its struggle with the party and that the two daughter parties, Fianna Fáil and Cumann na nGaedheal, carried on the practice."[10] The local branch or cumann tends therefore to be based on the ecclesiastical divisions, which were, however, themselves the natural community divisions. In fact, the boundaries of parishes and local government electoral areas were often identical, and as Moss pointed out, "The chapel door is one of the most suitable places for speeches and the collection of funds." Today, branches are based on the church area or polling station area in the countryside and on the local government unit (urban area or ward) in the towns and cities. Both Fianna Fáil and Fine Gael have branches almost throughout the country. In 1967 Fianna Fáil had a total of 2,015, varying from about 30 to nearly 70 in each county constituency and with a score or more in each city constituency. Fine Gael had nominally about 1,500, but only 600 of these were affiliated. In both parties many branches were almost inactive, and some were moribund. In a few cases, prominent local leaders are said to have created cumainn (composed of a few of their own supporters) where they were not needed, solely in order to increase their own influence.

The Labour Party constitution provides for setting up branches in "districts," which are defined by the central Administrative Council. In practice it has tended to have them only where there have been parliamentary representatives or aspirants, i.e. mainly in the east and south. In 1967, the party claimed to have about 500.

The major functions of the branches are to nominate candidates and to fight elections, national and local. For most branches these are the only functions. The concomitant functions of political education and recruitment of members, which one might think were continuing activities on which a successful election campaign is based, are sadly neglected by many branches. Even fund raising only assumes major importance when the annual collection is made, and immediately preceding an election campaign. The remaining function of local branches, that of acting as a channel of information and opinion to the center, tends to be con-

10 W. Moss, *Political Parties in the Irish Free State* (New York, 1933), p. 99.

fined to contact with the local public representatives, who are themselves likely to be personally in close touch with their constituents, or at least the most important ones, and who may well not welcome the intervention of the local party officers.

In fact, the level of activity of local branches varies considerably, depending almost wholly on the ardor and enthusiasm of the officers or, quite often, the local representative. Although party rules require a certain minimum number of members in a branch, in practice all that is needed is officers and the payment of the minimum registration fee (which is very low) to the national treasurer. An active Fianna Fáil party worker has stated: "Minimum cumann membership is ten, but in my experience membership of a cumann can be anything from 5 to 150."[11] Writing in 1933, Moss said of the branches that "between periods of election activity they become dormant, but the names of the principal members are known and they can be approached when election activity recommences."[12] This seems to be as true of many of them today as it was then. Although some city branches in particular are very active, almost everywhere it is an uphill fight by a few enthusiasts in the face of considerable apathy.

In these circumstances, it is not to be wondered at that individual party membership is low. Party rules require that a person seeking to become a member must declare his acceptance of the party's aims and regulations, must be elected by a branch, and having been elected must pay and maintain a subscription in order to hold a membership card. In the case of the Labour Party, following the British practice, trade unions, professional associations, cooperative societies, and similar organizations may affiliate as corporate members. In 1968, seventeen unions representing 45 per cent of trade union members were so affiliated.

In practice, it may often not be clear between elections who is or is not a member. As elections approach, however, matters like registration of branches and payment of membership dues are regularized because elections mean attendance by cumann representatives at constituency conventions for the nomination of candidates or, in the case of some local elections, nomination by the cumann itself. It is these matters that particularly interest the active members of the parties. Indeed, because of this interest, branch officers and other active members may well not be anxious for too large a local membership, preferring rather to have nominations in their own hands. It is, as they know quite well, not how many

[11] In a letter to the author.
[12] Moss, p. 99.

members they have, but their ability to get votes on election day that really matters. Also, formal membership in a party is not important in securing what few favors are open to political influence in Ireland. Thus, contributions in the case of those who have something to contribute and votes in the case of those who have not are all that is expected or given in most cases.

It is the right and duty of branches to send delegates to the party's annual convention or Ard Fheis. According to the rule books, the annual convention is the supreme authority in the party. In practice, despite some lip service to the proposition, it is nothing of the sort in the case of Fianna Fáil and Fine Gael and, until recently at least, hardly so in the case of Labour. Its very size—the Fianna Fáil Ard Fheis in 1967 was composed of 1,700 delegates—makes it too unwieldy for the effective consideration of policy. It is, rather, an occasion for a demonstration of party loyalty and for the rank-and-file workers to meet their national leaders. Very occasionally, the delegates may get a leadership policy reversed, but for the most part the resolutions that are passed are no more than guides to party opinion. The real decision makers are the leaders of the Oireachtas representatives of the party (the "parliamentary party"), together with other members of the National Executive Committee not in the Oireachtas. It is with these people and, above all, with the leaders of the party that the initiative in proposing policy and party strategy rests.

The National Executive of Fianna Fáil and the Administrative Council of the Labour Party are elected annually by the respective conferences to conduct the affairs of their parties. The National Council of Fine Gael appointed directly by the constituency organizations has the same role. In each case it consists of the national officers, together with a majority who are not members of the Oireachtas and a minority who are. Although this body—or rather, in each case, an inner executive or standing committee drawn from this body—is the organ that runs the party's affairs, it is doubtful whether the policies the party will publicly adopt are decided here. For when it comes to policy and to parliamentary tactics and strategy, the members of the parliamentary party and, in particular, its leaders (who in the case of the party in power are, of course, the government) are expected to take the initiative, and they are given a free hand to do so. Prominent, though not always predominant, among them will be the leader of the parliamentary party, who is chosen by them and who is the party leader. In the case of the party in power, he will of course be Taoiseach (Prime Minister), an office that almost inevitably puts its holder in a position above his colleagues. In practice, then, neither the rank-and-file parliamentary representatives nor the active workers in the constituencies have much to do with initiating or formulating policy. They have other tasks—the former to attend to the affairs of their constituents, the latter to get out the vote when the occasion demands.

Finally, there are the central offices. Here, perhaps as much as anywhere else in Irish politics, can be seen the effects of small scale, of amateur approach, and of local orientation. The central offices are tiny, their functions narrowly circumscribed, and their resources patently inadequate for their tasks. As yet, they have no developed research units or information services. Even the most professional of the parties—Fianna Fáil—employs only half a dozen permanent staff, whose total salaries in 1966 amounted to a little over £5,000. It has a total Central Office bill of not much more than £10,000 per annum.

v

The paucity of branch activity and the meager services given by the center to the branches and to representatives are reflected in low levels of party income and expenditure. Irish parties as such do not receive any public funds, as do the parties in some European countries, e.g. Norway, Sweden, Germany, where party political activity, including publicity and newspaper publication, is recognized as being an expense essential to democracy. The only public monies that go to parties in Ireland are the allowances paid to the leaders of the main opposition parties in the Oireachtas to help support their parliamentary activities, and a small proportion of members' salaries which the parties levy for expenses. Party finances are, therefore, the private affairs of the parties, and they are indeed very private, not to say obscure in some respects. However, the broad pattern is clear enough. In the case of all three major parties, the most important regular source of income is an annual collection made by the branches, part of which must be handed over to headquarters for Central Office expenses, the remainder being retained by the branch for use mainly to fight elections. Individual party members pay small subscriptions, which go toward financing branch activities. In the case of Labour, affiliated unions pay small annual subscriptions based on the number of their members. Until 1967, this source provided only £1,600 per annum, but this was more than doubled by the affiliation of the large Irish Transport and General Workers' Union to the party in that year.

The total amounts of regular income raised in this way are very small. In the late 1960's, Fianna Fáil had a published income of only £20,000 per annum, mostly from the national collection. The Labour Party had about £8,000, and Fine Gael, which does not publish any accounts at all, was probably in between.

Of course, at election time, parties and individual party candidates for public office spend much more than sums of the order indicated above, since special collections and appeals, both public and private, are made. It is widely believed that there is a good deal of soliciting of individuals and firms and much private giving to both parties and individuals, though the returns of election expenses, which the law required candidates to make until 1963, did not show large sums being spent. However, most of these returns may well have been incomplete. Fianna Fáil used to set up an election expenses committee when general elections became imminent, and from this has developed a more permanent organization, Taca (support). In 1967, this consisted of 200 invited members, mostly business people, each of whom subscribed £100 per annum, thus providing the party with an election fighting fund of £20,000. In the same year, unions affiliated with the Labour Party had about £120,000 in their "political funds," of which the Irish Transport and General Workers' Union had over £90,000. It would be wrong, however, to regard these funds as being at the disposal of the Labour Party. Up to the present, they have been used in a discriminating way, e.g. to help subsidize union candidates individually. Such candidates may have got as much as £500–600 each.

Incomplete as this picture is, its main feature is the modesty of the sums involved. It is obvious that many candidates must rely to a considerable extent on their own resources and ability to attract financial support, a fact that has important consequences for their position.

VI

Although party politics is a major arena of democracy, surprisingly few people play an active part in it. As Table 3.3 shows, for the vast majority voting at elections is the limit of their active participation. About 70–75 per cent of those eligible vote at general elections. At local elections the percentage is lower; in 1967 it was 68 per cent. Many, perhaps most, voters regard themselves as party adherents, though they are not party members and are not much if at all involved in party politics.

It is very difficult to estimate the number of people who play an active part. Exact figures are not available, but party membership certainly does not total more than 60,000 and is probably lower. In any case, even party membership may be more an indication of intensity of feeling than a proof of activity. In general, cumainn or branches each have five officers, and it might be argued that, unless the branch is wholly dormant (as some are), these at least are liable to be engaged in party work. They will certainly not total more than 12,000. At election time, however, there will be a flurry of activity at branch level, with many times this

TABLE 3.3

Participation in Party Politics

	Fianna Fáil	Fine Gael	Labour	Others	Total
Voters:					
General election, 1965	597,414	427,081	192,740	35,887	1,253,122
County and county borough elections, 1967	458,645	379,167	168,567	145,428	1,151,807
Estimated party members, 1967	40,000	12–15,000	5,000	Negligible	57–60,000
Estimated local branch officials active, 1967	7,000	3,000	2,000	Negligible	12,000
Local government:					
Candidates, 1967	1,022	897	525	698	3,142
Representatives, 1967	589	479	183	287	1,538
Dáil and Seanad:					
Candidates, 1965	111	102	43	24	395[a]
Representatives, 1965	103	60	28	13	204

Source: Compiled from official publications, newspapers, information supplied by the parties, and private inquiries.

[a] Including 115 for Seanad.

number being active for a few days or a week or two. When it comes to candidates and elected members, we are on surer ground. Central and local government levels together number about 3,500. All in all, then, perhaps only about 15–16,000 people (a little under one per cent of the electorate) may be said to be active in party politics, with another 40–45,000 (2.5 per cent of the electorate) committed enough to be members.

Who are the active ones? It is impossible to say much about the lower rank and file. There will not be many laborers or very small farmers; there will be better-off farmers, shopkeepers, publicans, and small businessmen, together with teachers, clerical workers, local officials, and a few professional people. Table 3.4 shows that at local government level farmers are represented roughly in proportion to their numbers in the community, though probably it is the better-off rather than the poorer farmers who engage in politics. On the contrary, shopkeepers and small businessmen are vastly overrepresented, having almost one-third of all county and county borough seats though constituting only one-thirtieth of the population. The nonagricultural working class and particularly the manual workers are greatly underrepresented. This is particularly evident at the national level, for there it becomes obvious that politics is for the few, with the active and influential posts held almost exclusively by people in certain occupations and of higher social class. At the national level, the farmers are less well represented and, in particular, provide

TABLE 3.4

Socioeconomic Status of Candidates and Elected Councilors,
Dáil Deputies, and Ministers

Socioeconomic group[a]	Popu- lation, 1961	County and county borough elections, 1967		Dáil deputies, 1965	Minis- ters, 1922–65
		Candidates	Elected		
Farming and fishing (mainly farm- ers and farmers' relatives)	34.5%	31.9%	32.3%	24.2%	7.7%
Professional	5.3	8.7	10.9	25.0	58.5
Trade union officials		1.8	1.8	6.9	4.6
Employers and managers (mainly small shopkeepers and publi- cans, owners of family busi- nesses, and contractors)	3.2	26.8	31.0	34.0	20.0
Nonmanual	23.6	12.9	12.5	2.1	4.6
Skilled manual	13.0	6.2	2.8	3.5	4.6
Semiskilled and unskilled manual	15.2	4.7	2.1	—	—
Unclassified	5.2	7.0	6.6	4.3	—
TOTAL	100.0%	100.0%	100.0%	100.0%	100.0%
	$n=$2.8m	$n=$1,723	$n=$795	$n=$144	$n=$65

Source: Compiled from *Census of Population*; data made available by Tuairim Survey, 1966, and by Department of Local Government; Flynn's *Oireachtas Companion*; newspapers; private inquiries.
[a] Groupings adapted from *Census of Population*, 1961, vol. 3.

few candidates for ministerial office. Those of them elected to the Dáil are mostly comparatively prosperous. The shopkeepers and small businessmen, on the contrary, maintain their one-third of the representation and have filled one-fifth of all cabinet posts since the inception of the state. In national politics, however, the most striking features are, first, the presence of professional people in considerable numbers—at cabinet level they dominate—and the absence of working-class people.

To what extent do the parties represent different classes? Table 3.5 shows the socioeconomic status of councilors and deputies according to party. It will be seen that Fianna Fáil and Fine Gael do not differ greatly from each other. The farmers and shopkeepers dominate at both local and central government levels. Indeed, at national level, these two groups, together with professional people, comprise the vast majority of their representatives. Labour, however, presents a rather different picture. While shopkeepers are prominent, though to a lesser extent than in the other parties, only in the Labour Party are trade union officials to be found in any numbers, and only there do manual workers appear to any extent, mainly at local government level.

This pattern of political participation is by no means unusual. Studies of the socioeconomic status of ministers and representatives in many

TABLE 3.5

Socioeconomic Status of Representatives at Local and National Level

Socioeconomic group	County and county borough councilors elected, 1967				Deputies elected, 1965[a]		
	Fianna Fáil	Fine Gael	Labour	Other	Fianna Fáil	Fine Gael	Labour
Farming and fishing (mainly farmers and farmers' relatives)	31.6%	40.9%	4.8%	34.2%	27.8%	23.4%	9.1%
Professional	11.4	12.5	3.6	10.1	23.6	36.2	9.1
Trade union officials	0.3	—	15.1	—	—	—	45.5
Employers and managers (mainly small shopkeepers and publicans, owners of family businesses, and contractors)	33.7	30.5	22.9	30.4	37.5	36.2	22.8
Nonmanual	14.2	9.3	14.5	15.1	2.8	—	4.5
Skilled manual	3.0	2.5	4.8	1.3	4.2	2.1	4.5
Semiskilled and unskilled manual	—	0.4	15.7	2.6	—	—	—
Unclassified	5.8	3.9	18.0	6.3	4.2	2.1	4.5

Source: Compiled from data made available by Department of Local Government and by the Tuairim Survey, 1966, and from newspapers.
[a] There were only three "Others" elected in 1965.

countries suggest that, as in Ireland, equality of opportunity to engage in party politics does not exist. However, as Hans Daalder has pointed out, we should be careful not to confuse inequality of influence with oligarchy or to fall into "the determinist fallacy which sees too direct a link between the social origins of politicians and class bias in their politics." As he says:

Politics is an autonomous process that certainly is affected by class factors but is not causally dependent on them. Theoretically a political elite (and above all competing elites) composed almost exclusively of a large number of upper class persons can still be fully responsive to pressures from below.[13]

In any case, parties are far from being the only channels of community opinion. All sorts of associations and organizations in the community engage in political activities, some of them continuously and with great effect. Many, indeed most of them, choose not to associate themselves too closely with any political party, their main political business being with ministers and civil servants, as the following chapter shows.

[13] In LaPalombara and Weiner, pp. 70–71.

FOUR

Interest Groups

We have seen how Irish political parties to a large extent originated in important divisions in the community. We have seen, too, that the aim of these parties is to win votes in order to obtain governmental office and power, or at least to have a voice in determining policy. In pursuing this aim, they are involved in expressing and also in molding, crystallizing, and coalescing public opinion. Thus not only do they reflect divisions in the community but they articulate and aggregate the claims of a wide variety of sectional interests and causes. In fact, the tendency in recent years has been for the biggest of them to become catchall in character. Parties are not the only channel between the community and the formal institutions of government. Along the boundary between the political system and the rest of society are a very large number and wide variety of organizations which have among their functions that of pressing the claims of their members upon those who can make, or can influence the making of, the policies, laws, and decisions of all sorts that issue from the state. They too articulate and aggregate claims as do parties.

However, a very incomplete picture of Irish government would emerge if we were to examine only those organizations that, like trade unions or farmers' associations, exist specifically to protect and further the aims and interests of their members. Interests are articulated and aggregated not only through political parties and interest organizations specifically created for the purpose, but, when necessary, by the spokesmen and leaders of important institutions in society, such as the Church, or ethnic or other basic community groups. The owners or managers of individual firms negotiate directly with the state; so too do universities and colleges. Indeed, in the modern welfare state, which attempts to plan the economy and regulate the social environment generally, almost any organization or group in the community, however remote from politics it may seem to be, might find occasion to press its case upon the government. If we concentrate upon specialized organizations for promoting interests, this is because Ireland, like all "developed" or "modern" countries, is characterized by a multiplicity of such bodies, reflecting the high degree of functional specialization that is a feature of such societies.

There is no intention to confine the term "interest group" exclusively to organizations set up *explicitly* to represent and speak for the interests of a particular group. The term covers any social group when it is attempting to influence the decision of public authorities, i.e., when it is taking part in the political process. Thus, the Irish National Teachers' Organization and the National Farmers' Association, which are vocational protection organizations, are interest groups when they are part of the political system. So, too, was the hierarchy of the Catholic Church when, for example, on various dates between 1947 and 1951 it addressed letters conveying its views to Irish governments about proposed schemes for extensions of maternity and infant care services. So also would be a deputation from a university to the Minister for Education to urge increased state assistance, or Messrs. Arthur Guinness Son & Co. Ltd., if they approached the Minister for Industry and Commerce to discuss the impact of the Common Market upon their brewing business.

Interest groups may be broadly distinguished from parties as follows:

Pressure groups do not themselves seek to win control of government by presenting a slate of candidates to the electorate. Parties differ from pressure groups particularly in the degree of their inclusiveness.... Furthermore, pressure groups can have extensive nonpolitical activities.[1]

It must be admitted, however, that the distinction is not entirely clear-cut. Although "the colonization of groups by parties and the reverse phenomenon of domination of parties by groups,"[2] which is such a feature of France and Italy, is not present to any great extent in Ireland today, some trade unions are affiliated to the Labour Party, and the Farmers' Party of the 1920's was the political arm of a farmers' association. Also, an organization at the extreme of republican politics like Sinn Féin is hard to categorize, and if, as seems most appropriate, it is regarded as a political party, there has often been considerable interpenetration between it and its consort, the IRA. In general, however, the distinction is clear enough in Ireland. Here, contrary to the situation in some European countries, most pressure groups and parties are auton-

---

1 R. Rose, *Politics in England* (London, 1965), p. 130.
2 F. G. Castles, "Towards a Theoretical Analysis of Pressure Politics," *Political Studies*, XIV (1966), 347.

omous in respect of one another, and it is unusual to be able to identify a group with any particular party.

II

It is not possible to classify Irish interest groups other than very roughly, but it will be useful to survey them in a general way and to note their most important features.

Absence of "segmented pluralism." Since the Irish community is relatively homogeneous, the phenomenon of "segmented pluralism," i.e. "the organization of complexes of competing social movements, interest groups, educational and cultural activities, and political parties based on religious affiliation (or antipathy) and ideology, religious and secular,"[3] is to a great extent absent. Ireland, unlike Holland or Switzerland, for example, does not have separate Catholic and Protestant trade unions or employers' associations. In only one or two areas of social activity does this occur: in education there are a Catholic Headmasters' Association and other associations of Catholic teachers and an Irish Schoolmasters' Association, which is Protestant; in youth movements there are the Catholic Boy Scouts of Ireland on the one hand, and the Boy Scouts of Ireland and the Boys Brigade on the other. In general, though, separate communities do not exist, each with its own complex of associations, including political associations, interrelated and interdependent.

Absence of powerful and active corporate institutions. Just as Ireland is characteristically modern in the existence of a large number of specialized interest groups, so too it is thoroughly civilian, for the army is not a factor in politics. Nor does the civil service figure as a corporate entity in society. Indeed, the only great corporate body in the community is the Catholic Church, and even the Church is not a very active or positive force in politics. In fact, there are no politically active, powerful organizations in society that really rival the parties, though the National Farmers' Association has attempted, so far unsuccessfully, to do so.

"Demand" groups. Not only are powerful corporate bodies largely absent from the scene, but also there are few groups making major demands involving very great changes. The deep division engendered by the split over the Treaty was reflected in the party system and was eventually resolved within the system. Only the tiny, shrinking republican groups that do not recognize the present regime and the small handful of Com-

---

[3] V. R. Lorwin, "Segmented Pluralism," in S. Rokkan *et al., The Politics of the Smaller European Democracies,* forthcoming.

munists and other extreme Marxists fall into this category. Even these are better thought of as political movements than as interest groups, and, in any case, they are not of much consequence. There exist comparatively few "demand" groups—groups that anyone may join, devoted to a cause such as "Ban the Bomb"—as compared with the host of "defense" or "protection" groups such as unions and trade associations. Apart from the extreme republicans, who perhaps do not belong in this category, the most important are the groups devoted to the revival of the Irish language, of which there are perhaps a score. Since this aim is, officially, government policy, though lip service only is paid to it, these groups have a special status and some receive public monies. Among the more important are Connradh na Gaeilge (the Gaelic League), the oldest, founded in 1893 as part of the nationalist revival, and Gael Linn, an organization that exploits modern mass media to promote the language. Coordinating the activities of eighteen of the language associations is the most important of them, Comhdháil Náisiúnta na Gaeilge (National Convention of the Irish Language).

The largest demand group is certainly the Pioneer Total Abstinence Association, which in 1966 claimed 400,000 members. However, many of these were enrolled *en masse* at school under the influence of clerical teachers, and some may well have fallen away. Nevertheless, the Pioneer pin, worn in the lapel or on the breast, is the most common dress decoration to be seen in Ireland, exceeding by far its nearest rival, the Fáinne, a plain circle of metal denoting a speaker of Irish and awarded by Comhdháil Náisiúnta na Gaeilge. Organizations devoted to such causes as anti-apartheid, banning the bomb, or stopping the war in Vietnam have been few, and have been confined mainly to Dublin city and to students and left-wing intellectuals. However, in 1966, for the first time a permanent police guard was placed upon the United States Embassy in Dublin, a terminal point, as almost universally, for the marches favored by such groups. (The British Embassy has always had such a guard—but for different reasons!) Among the more successful of the demand groups in recent years was one devoted to ending the export of horses for slaughter, but, in general, associations concerned with abolishing blood sports or cruelty to animals have little success.

The Catholic Church. The Catholic Church is in a unique position as an interest group. It is the only great corporate institution in the community that rivals, indeed, towers over, those of the political system. "Strictly speaking, the Church has no special legal status other than the rather vague status accorded by Article 44 of the Constitution: 'The State recognizes the special position of the Holy Catholic Apostolic and Roman Church as the guardian of the Faith professed by the great majority of the citizens.' "[4] It is legally, therefore, not an established Church; it does not need to be: "Practically all important functions—opening of the Dáil, of law terms, even of factories—are preceded by Mass. At official functions, the Cardinal takes precedence over the Prime Minister, and the Archbishop over his deputy."[5]

The Irish are a devout people and the priests are, at least in the countryside, community leaders. Virtually all school education is denominational. In the middle 1960's, 55 per cent of all secondary teachers were clerics. The following tabulation shows this control of schools in Ireland in 1964 (in percentages of total):[6]

	Primary schools	Secondary schools
Protestant control	10%	8%
Catholic control:		
Lay	1	10
Religious	89	82

The result of all this is obvious. In the words of Jean Blanchard, writing in 1958:

The Bishops of Ireland appear to have more power, in practice, than those of any other country in the world. As the natural outcome of a long historical tradition which has created exceptionally strong bonds between the nation and its clergy, their authority is great over the Faithful . . . a member of the congregation listens more readily to his Bishop than he does, for instance, to his deputy (*député*). The social importance of the head of the diocese is unrivalled. Besides, the state fixes no limit to the Bishops' powers.[7]

Members of the clergy cannot, then, but have great influence in political matters, local and national, if and when they choose to use it. But to what extent do they use it?

The clergy plays no overt part, and probably no part at all, in party politics today. This contrasts markedly with the past:

During the last century, and at the beginning of the present century, a parish priest was often seen presiding over a political meeting, because it was the time of the struggle for religious and national liberty. Today priests remain aloof from merely political controversies.[8]

---

[4] T. P. Coogan, *Ireland since the Rising* (London, 1966), p. 211.

[5] *Ibid.*, p. 213.

[6] Compiled from *Investment in Education* (Stationery Office, Dublin, 1966), Appendixes 1 and 9; and Coogan, p. 216.

[7] J. Blanchard, *The Church in Contemporary Ireland* (Dublin, 1963), pp. 18–19. (Translated from *Le droit ecclésiastique contemporain d'Irlande*, Paris, 1958.)

[8] *Ibid.*, p. 82.

Priests do not stand for political office, though no law, of either Church or State, prohibits them from doing so. Indeed, they do not *compete* for many offices of any sort, for in respect of appropriate social activities they like, and sometimes expect, to be *invited*. As local notables, they are particularly active in rural community projects, rural social organizations, and sporting associations, and to the extent that such bodies act as pressure groups, the clergy plays its part like other members. A decree of the Synod of Maynooth (the Council of the Irish hierarchy) forbids the use of the pulpit for political purposes, by which is meant party political controversy, for, of course, many matters that the Church considers within its sphere may also be "political," i.e. a matter for the attention of public authorities, notably policy in regard to education, marriage, and health services. That is not to say that individual priests and bishops do not take part in political activities. It may even be a provocative one. Father Patrick Brady, a vice-president of the National Farmers' Association when it was engaged in engineering a commodity strike involving picketing, is reported to have told a meeting of farmers in Athlone: "We want no shirkers when the commodity strike begins. We want a total standstill and if you find your neighbour sneaking away with any produce, just ram it down his throat."[9]

In national politics, however, the bishops individually or collectively exert whatever influence the Church has. They do so in two contrasting ways—either in public pronouncements in such vehicles as pastoral letters or from the pulpit, or by the most discreet of communications, perhaps not even direct, to ministers or senior civil servants. The first are well publicized; the second almost never, and this gives rise to constant rumors of clerical "pressure" or "interference." Inevitably, such rumors ascribe to the hierarchy or to individual bishops a role that they in fact do not play. Such rumor has in the past involved the Department of Education particularly.

Some individual bishops have been prone to comment publicly and even to engage in controversy, but they have been a minority. Regarded as "the archtype of the commentating Irish Bishop"[10] is Dr. Cornelius Lucey, the Bishop of Cork, who has often used the occasion of a country parish confirmation service to deplore publicly the decay of rural life and to criticize Irish governments for their failure to arrest it. "West Cork wants no hand-outs from the dispensers of patronage in Merrion Square

9 Quoted in *Irish Times*, Mar. 6, 1967.
10 Coogan, p. 239.

or elsewhere. It wants Justice, elementary Social Justice."[11] His colleague of Galway, Dr. Michael Browne, is also "a noted controversialist," as Coogan puts it. "His principal controversies have been with local authorities in Galway over the building of another school; with Lemass over vocational organization; with the Minister for Education over the new plans; and, of course, with proponents of the Mother and Child scheme."[12]

Individual bishops have also occasionally given a lead in proposing social reform. Dr. Browne was chairman of the Commission on Vocational Organization, which, following the Encyclical *Quadragesimo Anno,* propounded a scheme for a vocationally organized Irish society in 1943. A former Bishop of Clonfert, Dr. John Dignan, put forward a social insurance scheme in 1944. On the whole, however, the bishops have not been notable in the past for taking positive positions on social questions, at least in public, contenting themselves rather with pronouncing, when occasion arose, an authoritative Catholic position on proposals for changes in social policy. Yet this area of social policy is where their main political interests lie and their main influence is felt. Such influence is, as indicated above, exerted discreetly but with authority and with the expectation that their views will be accorded respect. And, of course, they are. Some political leaders have occasionally gone out of their way to underline in general terms their respect for clerical pronouncements. For example:

When we are given advice or warning by the authoritative people in the Catholic Church, on matters strictly confined to faith and morals, so long as I am here ... [we] will give to their directions, given within that scope—and I have no doubt that they do not desire in the slightest to go one fraction of an inch outside the sphere of faith and morals—our complete obedience and allegiance.[13]

I am an Irishman second; I am a Catholic first.... If the Hierarchy gives me any direction with regard to Catholic social teaching or Catholic moral teaching, I accept without qualification in all respects the teaching of the Hierarchy and the Church to which I belong.[14]

---

[11] From a sermon delivered in May 1961 in the parish of Rath and the Islands in West Cork and quoted by Coogan, p. 240. Merrion Square is where a number of government departments are located.

[12] Coogan, p. 237. The Mother and Child scheme was a proposed extension of the health services, over which there was public controversy and a ministerial resignation in 1951. Mr. Lemass is a former minister and Taoiseach from 1959 to 1966.

[13] John A. Costello, when Taoiseach; *Dáil Debates,* vol. 125, col. 783 (Apr. 12, 1951).

[14] Brendan Corish, later leader of the Labour Party; *Dáil Debates,* vol. 138, col. 840 (April 29, 1953).

As we have already mentioned, under clerical pressure the **Labour Party**, in 1939, removed the phrase "Workers' Republic" from its constitution.

This does not mean that governments have always given way to clerical pressure. Here, of course, the record of Fianna Fáil is particularly important, since this party has been in power for all but six years since 1932. It is important to recall that the first generation of Fianna Fáil leaders, who dominated the scene until the late 1950's, included men who had been excommunicated during the civil war and some who inherited the anticlerical tradition of Sinn Féin. After they came to power, they accorded respect but not subservience to the bishops, with occasional, privately expressed, signs of impatience.

It is certainly not easy to demonstrate that specific clerical pressure has had much effect upon policy. Having examined the Church's influence on foreign policy and, in particular, on the issue of neutrality in the Spanish Civil War in the late 1930's and the admission of Communist China to the UN in the late 1950's, Dr. Patrick Keatinge concluded, "the theory that the Church enjoys a direct hold on Irish foreign policy cannot be maintained."[15] In respect of social policy and particularly over a number of educational issues in recent years, Fianna Fáil has seemed to take a firm stand when controversy, or at least public controversy, has blown up. But we are here in a shadowy realm of rumor and conjecture because of the discreet, even secretive, nature of the intercourse. Moreover, it is wrong to characterize every view expressed by a cleric as the attitude of "the Church," though all too often this is done. Individual bishops may well express views not shared by their colleagues. This brings us to the nub of the difficulty of assessing the Church's influence. When is it "the Church" that is speaking? To the misunderstanding that is the inevitable result of the leaders of the Church being too discreet is added the confusion that arises from identifying the statements of clerics with the views of "the Church." In a country where the clergy has expected to have all its statements treated as authoritative, the Church has only itself to blame if it is sometimes misunderstood.

Agricultural organizations. By Western European standards the proportion of the labor force employed in agriculture and fishing (31 per cent in 1966) is high, and one might expect rural mass organizations to dominate the political scene and to speak with irresistible force. In fact, this has not been the case, partly for historical reasons. The overriding importance of national issues and the identification of the priests with these, at least at the local level, may perhaps have inhibited the growth

[15] "The Formulation of Foreign Policy in Ireland, 1921–61" (unpublished Ph.D. thesis in the Library of Trinity College, Dublin), p. 407.

of agrarian organizations with sociopolitical aims. Though there was a series of agrarian movements in the nineteenth century, culminating in the Land League in the 1880's, the land reforms of the late nineteenth century and first years of the twentieth century satisfied the aspirations of many of the rural population. Nor did cooperation develop to any extent, except in those areas where milk was produced on farms big enough to justify a collection service. From the time of independence onward for another quarter of a century or more, interest continued to center upon national and constitutional issues, and these threw up divisions that found expression in the political parties. Thus, no agrarian parties established themselves as a major or permanent feature on the political scene.

Not only has there been no development of rural mass organizations but, because of the diversity of agriculture and personal rivalries, no single protection association has been able to establish itself as the spokesman of all agricultural interests. In recent years one body, the National Farmers' Association, with a membership of perhaps 60 per cent of all farmers, has attempted unsuccessfully to assume this role and to institute the kind of annual farm price review, involving negotiations between itself and the Department of Agriculture, that takes place in Great Britain, where the Ministry and the National Farmers' Union have developed highly institutionalized procedures of this kind. Most agricultural interests are represented by sectional protection associations. In 1965 a list of client organizations compiled by the Department of Agriculture and Fisheries numbered 98 bodies, exclusive of other state organizations. These were organizations with which the Department did, or might do, business from time to time. As the following tabulation shows, most of them were narrowly based.[16]

	Number of organizations
Rural life	4
General agricultural interests	12
Cattle and other livestock	42
Milk and milk products	16
Cereals and foodstuffs	14
Poultry	3
Horticulture and beekeeping	7

Most of the major national organizations, however, are to be found in the "general agricultural interests" category, or in the "rural life" group, which contains organizations devoted to social aims or commu-

[16] Compiled from information made available by the Department of Agriculture and Fisheries.

nity development. The seven most important associations in terms of size
are the Irish Agricultural Organization Society, with 400 affiliated societies (1965); the Irish Country Women's Association, with 18,000 members (1965); the Irish Creamery Milk Suppliers' Association, with 44,000
members (1965); the Irish Sugar Beet Growers' Association, with 25,000
members (1965); Macra na Feirme (Young Men of the Farms), with
14,000 members (1965); the Muintir na Tíre (People of the Land), with
400 affiliated guilds (1965); and the National Farmers' Association, with
122,000 members (1966). Small size does not necessarily mean small influence. For example, the Irish Fresh Meat Exporters' Association and
the Irish Livestock Exporters' and Traders' Association each have fewer
than 50 members, but, involved as they are in a key economic activity,
they are very influential.

Industrial and commercial organizations. The main feature of Irish
trade and industry, as Table 4.1 shows, is the small number of large
firms and the prevalence of family-owned businesses. The small family
firm has often been slow to see the need for protection services, or at any
rate for trade associations to engage in activities on any scale. Thus,
though there are about 200 trade protection and employer associations
extending to almost every trade, they are mostly small, with little if any
full-time staff, and they engage in a very restricted range of activities.

Today, the average membership of the associations is from ten to twenty companies; their average subscription income is estimated at £250. Around a dozen
of them have professional staffs of one or two persons; the remainder have no
staff or retain part-time help, generally from chartered accountants.[17]

Of those associations registered as Friendly Societies in 1965, only seven
had an income of £5,000 per annum or more and only eight had a salary
bill of over £2,000. However, more widely representative bodies do exist,
such as the Federated Union of Employers, the Federation of Irish Industries, the Federation of Builders, Contractors and Allied Employers
of Ireland, the Association of Chambers of Commerce of Ireland, and the
Federation of Trade Associations. In recent years some of these have
begun to do more than offer negotiating and "intercessional" services
and have developed activities, such as intelligence services, sufficient to
enable them to play their part in economic planning and on advisory
bodies that the state has brought into existence. Even so, in 1966 the
Federated Union of Employers, which is perhaps the most important
employers' organization in the country, with a membership of about
1,600 manufacturing, trading, and service firms, had only a dozen execu-

[17] *Business Representation in Irish National Affairs* (Harbridge House Europe,
Dublin, 1967), p. 48.

TABLE 4.1

Estimated Number of Establishments and
Persons Engaged in Basic Industries

Sector	Number of establish- ments	Average number of persons employed	Comments
Manufacturing,[a] building, service-type[b] industries	5,000	65	80% employ 20 or less
Distributive trades:[c]			
Retail	41,000	2–3	75% employ 3 or less
Wholesale	2,400	12	75% employ 15 or less
Personal services:			
Hotels, etc.[d]	4,500	4–5	
Other	10,000	4	
Banking, insurance	400	35	
TOTAL	63,300		

Source: Adapted from *Business Representation in Irish National Affairs*, prepared by Harbridge House Europe (Dublin, 1967), p. 32.
   [a] Including mining and quarrying and turf.
   [b] Electricity, gas, water, transport, communications, storage.
   [c] Of the 43,400 establishments, only 200 employ 50 or more.
   [d] Hotels, guest houses, catering, hairdressing, cinemas.

tive and professional staff. Consequently, although the immediate needs and demands of industry are adequately conveyed to governmental agencies, it may well be that, by not giving its representative bodies sufficient resources, Irish industry has in the past not equipped itself to make its maximum impact on the state or to play its full role in planning and developmental activities. (In Table 4.2 the most important employers' organizations are listed.)

Labor. Like industry, labor is not very well organized. In 1966, the 97 Irish trade unions, some of which operate both in the Republic and in Northern Ireland, had a total membership of 472,000, of which about 364,000 were in the Republic. This represents 56 per cent of wage and salary earners, a comparatively high figure by international standards. In the same year, 77 of these unions, representing 94 per cent of union membership, were affiliated to the Irish Congress of Trade Unions, which was, therefore, able to speak for organized labor in a way that no employers' organization could for business. But the proportion of the total working population unionized is low because of the large number of small farmers, and, consequently, the Congress by no means represents the working man. The six largest unions are the Irish Transport and General Workers' Union, with 146,000 members (1967); the Amalgamated Transport and General Workers' Union, with 50,000 members (1966); the Workers' Union of Ireland, with 50,000 members (1966); the

TABLE 4.2
Principal Employers' Organizations

Name	Annual subscription income (1965 budget)	Approximate number of members	Functions and coverage of industry or sector
Federated Union of Employers	£56,000	1,600 (1966)	Labor and social affairs, collective bargaining. Variety of industries and services excluding those below. Member companies employ 125,000.
Federation of Irish Industries	£41,200	600 (1966)	General economic and commercial matters. Includes larger manufacturing and industrial units.
Association of Chambers of Commerce of Ireland	£650	35 (1966)	General and local business community interests. All Chambers of Commerce.
Dublin Chamber of Commerce		850 (1966)	As above but confined to Dublin region.
Federation of Trade Associations	£180	13	Central body for distributive trade associations.
Retail Grocery, Dairy and Allied Trades Association	£8,800	4,100 (1965)	Labor (with FUE) and commercial matters. Includes most of the largest of the 11,000 grocery outlets.
Irish Drug Association	£5,700	1,200 (1965)	Labor (with FUE) and commercial matters. Includes larger retail establishments. There are about 1,350 retail chemist establishments.
Irish Motor Traders' Association	£9,000	900 (1965)	Labor and commercial matters. Represents some motor assembly companies and larger garages and filling stations. There are about 1,200 garages and filling stations.
Licensed Grocers and Vintners Association	£7,200	1,400 (1965)	Labor and commercial matters. Membership: Dublin 600, remainder in rest of country.
Federation of Builders, Contractors & Allied Employers	£17,000	650 (1967)	Labor relations and general commercial matters. Members employ about 70% of total labor force in construction industry.
Irish Printing Federation	£4,900	55 (1963)	Labor and commercial matters. Membership mostly in Dublin region, and employs over 90% of labor in the industry in Dublin.
Irish Shipowners' Association	£2,400	5 (1965)	Labor negotiations (crews of ships) and commercial matters.
Irish Hotels Federation	£2,300	400 (1965)	Commercial matters. Over 700 hotels and 400 guest houses in the country.

Source: *Business Representation in Irish National Affairs* (Harbridge House Europe, Dublin, 1967); *Administrative Yearbook and Diary, 1967* (Institute of Public Administration); *Register of Friendly Societies* (Stationery Office, Dublin; annual); and information made available by officers of associations.

Amalgamated Engineering Union, with 27,000 members (1966); the Amalgamated Society of Woodworkers, with 17,500 members (1966); and the Irish Union of Distributive Workers and Clerks, with 14,000 members (1966). Together, these six represent over half of the membership of trade unions in Ireland, but, as Table 4.3 shows, there are a large number of very small unions. Many of these are small craft and white-collar unions. Multiplicity and small size, of course, make negotiations, whether industrial or political, more difficult.

TABLE 4.3

*Membership of Trade Unions in the
Republic of Ireland, 1966*

Members per union	Number of unions	Total number of members
1,000 or less	51	14,600
1,001–4,000	28	56,100
4,001–7,000	11	60,000
7,001–15,000	3	32,100
15,001 and over	4	201,000
TOTAL	97	363,800

Source: *Trade Union Information*, February–March 1967 (published by Irish Congress of Trade Unions).

Despite its limitations, the Irish Congress of Trade Unions is in practice treated by the state as though it speaks for labor. Hence, labor more than business or agriculture is a corporate body in society and an "estate," a fact recognized by the large number of advisory and other public bodies on which the Congress has representation. Yet labor too is comparatively poorly equipped for its role. In 1967, the Irish Congress of Trade Unions had an annual income of about £24,000 from affiliation fees and a professional staff of eight. Moreover, there is in Ireland

a practice of preserving the autonomy and identity of individual unions whenever they band together for common purposes. . . . While recognized by Government as the national spokesman on all matters relating to labour's interests, the ICTU is not itself a trade union, may not independently engage in collective bargaining, has no authority over the internal affairs of affiliated unions, and may not bind its affiliates in decisions or commitments without their concurrence.[18]

In this respect, however, they are no worse off than the representative employers' associations, and, in practice, they may be a little better off. In general, though, both sides of industry exhibit similar characteristics: many small units with considerable individual autonomy and weak rep-

18 *Business Representation in Irish National Affairs*, p. 26.

resentative bodies hampered by lack of resources from operating effectively.

Professional associations. Similar in many of their functions to trade unions are professional associations. Like business and labor, they are also represented by a large number of small bodies, which to a great extent is a result of the fact that the number of people in any given profession in a country of less than three million is necessarily low. Professions tend to be close-knit, and though there may be only small numbers of persons engaged in particular callings, very often the professional associations will include a considerable proportion of them. In 1966, the Irish Medical Association had about 1,800 members, or 60 per cent of all doctors, whereas almost all the 12,000 lay national (i.e. primary) schoolteachers were members of the Irish National Teachers' Organization. In some cases, membership in an association is a requirement of being recognized as belonging to a profession, but where this is so there is often more than one professional body. This is the case, for example, with accountants.

Consumer representation. Producers of goods and services are far better organized for protection and advancement than are nonindustrial or household consumers. Apart from the users of some particular goods or services, e.g. car owners, there are few specific consumer organizations. The only general consumers' organization equivalent to the Consumers' Association in the United Kingdom is the Irish Housewives' Association, but in 1967 this body was essentially an urban organization and had only 500 members. Though rural community organizations such as the Irish Countrywomen's Association partially fill the gap, it is probably the particular rural social structure of the country that primarily explains the weakness of consumer representation.

It can be argued of course that the more general institutions of representation, the public representatives at the national and local levels, speak for consumers, since all people consume. There is some force in this, but at the point where many political decisions are made, policies formulated, and business decided, the spokesmen of the producers are present while the public representatives—members of the Oireachtas and the local councilors—often are not. Thus the developing practices of interest consultation have important implications for democracy.

III

The activities of those who seek to influence public authorities tend to be governed by a simple and obvious principle: apply pressure where the impact is greatest. The choice of points of contact and methods of operation is governed by cultural factors, by resources, and by the political context.

As Richard Rose has pointed out: "The relationship between pressure group demands and cultural norms is of fundamental importance in analysing pressure groups."[19] In Ireland, as in the Western world generally, the legitimacy of this type of activity is fully accepted and its great development is recognized as adding another dimension to representation and, hence, democracy. Established interests expect, indeed demand, to be consulted, and recriminations will follow if they are not.

Conversely, acceptance and institutionalization of this process has led to a fairly clear agreement on what constitutes illegitimate activity. Bribery, undue entertainment, secret bargains—clandestine operations generally—are neither accepted nor, apparently, much practiced. The reputation for such behavior in politics, including party politics, which the Irish have in the United States, arose from the activities of an underprivileged minority group operating in a cultural context in which such things were accepted. At home, it seems, the Irish are more austere in their public morality. Similarly, because it is predisposed to act discreetly and sometimes deviously, the Catholic Church is seen in a sinister light as having an influence that it does not in fact possess. Threats to authority are likely to be counterproductive in a society that accords legitimacy to the elected government, and that has increasingly reacted against threats to the government and refusals to recognize it. Not only have nationalist organizations like the IRA become less and less tolerated, but reaction to the activities of the National Farmers' Association in its campaign against the government in 1966 and 1967 showed clearly that the public, and particularly the urban public, expects governments to govern and has a clear picture of what tactics are legitimate and what are not. Verbal truculence, demonstrations, threats, and withholding of rates (local taxes) are accepted; blocking the roads leading to Dublin, cutting off supplies of farm produce, and intimidation are not.

The activities of groups are inevitably influenced by whether or not their aims are widely accepted and command respect and support. In a community comparatively newly independent, in which self-conscious nationalism has remained at a high level, organizations that identify their objects with "the nation" expect, and have sometimes been accorded, special recognition, whether they are sporting organizations like the Gaelic Athletic Association, or the Irish language organizations, which, under the guidance of Comhdháil Náisiúnta na Gaeilge, dispose of

19 Rose, p. 130.

public monies. On the other hand, the Society for the Prevention of Cruelty to Animals cannot presume that it operates in a climate of opinion anything like as favorable as does its British counterpart. The Society for the Abolition of Horses for Slaughter found that it was not humanitarian considerations that finally brought it success so much as the suspicion that the Irish cattle export trade might suffer if foreigners buying "Irish beef" could not be sure it was not in fact Irish horse.

The resources, human and material, that a group has at its disposal are an important factor in governing its strategy. Money to mount campaigns and provide the necessary intelligence and representational services, and members who are potential voters on election day, are the principal weapons. However, in neither case are they as effectively deployed for the benefit of interest groups as might be expected. Even the strongest economic interests, the trade associations and the unions, have devoted quite meager sums to their intelligence and representational services. The institution with the biggest membership of all, the Catholic Church, to which 95 per cent of the people belong, does not try to mobilize its members for political ends. Organizations that do, such as trade unions, have experienced an important phenomenon of Irish politics— that at elections citizens tend to remain loyal to the party they have supported in the past even when they hold views on individual issues that are not those of the party. What Jean Blondel says of Great Britain may well be true of Ireland: "Individual issues are . . . not a predominant factor in voting behaviour. . . . Voting behaviour is usually more solid than opinions."[20]

Certainly this seems to have been borne out by the experience of the National Farmers' Association at crucial by-elections in December 1966, when, at the height of the Association's campaign against the government and with considerable public sympathy for the farmers, the government party won in circumstances in which quite small shifts in the voters' allegiance could have led to defeat. If, as seems to be the case, people are strongly oriented to political parties, associations cannot threaten the wholesale withdrawal of political support. At most, their disapproval is likely to make only a marginal difference. Yet, in practice, this will often be sufficient, and governments do tend to proceed upon the principle of modern democratic government as enunciated by Robert Dahl, that "the making of governmental decisions is not a majestic march of great majorities united upon certain matters of basic policy. It is the steady appeasement of relatively small groups."[21]

[20] *Voters, Parties and Leaders* (London, 1965), p. 80.
[21] *Preface to Democratic Theory* (Chicago, 1956), p. 146.

This strength of the voters' party allegiances is, of course, an important part of the political context, the third constraint within which interest groups operate. The political context has the greatest positive influence upon interest group tactics. Here the most important fact is that the government has considerable initiative in proposing policy and legislation amounting to a virtual monopoly, and because of the stable and assured support of loyal party members in the Oireachtas it controls the activities of that body and can govern its output. The government's hegemony is not unconditional and there is a good deal of give and take, but it remains true that one must look chiefly to the government and its professional advisers in the departments for the initiation and formulation of policy, legislation, and administrative action. Hence it is on the ministers and senior civil servants that the interest groups tend to concentrate their efforts.

The fact that many interest groups tend to center their efforts on ministers and departments by no means implies that "lobbying," i.e. the attempt to influence individual parliamentary representatives and the Oireachtas as a whole, does not occur. Interest groups circularize members, contact personally those who they think may be sympathetic, and occasionally try to impress them by processions or demonstrations, though the law prevents or restricts meetings in the vicinity of Leinster House, where the Oireachtas meets, during sessions. However, this activity, though apparently directed at the legislature, may in fact be intended as much to influence the TD's (members of Parliament) and senators in their role as party members, in order to have an impact on decisions at party meetings where the policies to be adopted in the Oireachtas chambers are approved. Attempts to promote legislation directly by means of a "private member's bill," i.e. a bill introduced by a member other than a minister, are only very occasionally made and are never successful, being at most a publicity device.

Some parliamentary representatives have close connections with interest groups. Part of the election and parliamentary expenses of some union members are met from union funds. Other deputies can be identified to some degree with occupational interest groups. Few, however, can be connected with groups except those associated with their livelihood (though almost without exception they are all members of a church). What evidence there is, and it is very meager, indicates that the members of the Oireachtas tend not to associate themselves with voluntary associations devoted to social, cultural, or religious objects, preferring perhaps to devote their energies to public bodies such as county and town councils and hospital and harbor boards, which offer opportunities for more

TABLE 4.4

*Deputies and Senators Elected in 1965: Membership of Occupational,
Sporting, Cultural, and Religious Associations*

Members of Oireachtas	TD's	Senators
Number replying to question	73	44
Number declaring themselves members of:		
Trade union	21	9
Trade association	13	4
Agricultural or rural organization	17	17
Professional association	13	11
Sporting organization[a]	44[b]	31[b]
Cultural or religious association (other than church)	30	29

Source: As declared by respondents in survey of TD's elected in 1965, made by Tuairim. See J.
Whyte, *Dáil Deputies: Their Work, Its Difficulties, Possible Remedies* (Dublin, 1966); and survey
of senators made by author.
   [a] The TD's were asked whether they were *interested* in sports. Senators were asked whether they
were *members* of any sporting organizations.
   [b] The Gaelic Athletic Association was mentioned by 21 TD's and 13 senators.

publicly recognized activity. Surveys of the TD's and senators elected in
1965 show that many recorded membership in an association appropriate
to their occupation, but few mentioned belonging to other associations
though they were specifically invited to do so (see Table 4.4).

Because of its composition, Seanad Eireann (the Senate) itself as a
body might appear to be a chamber of interest-group representatives.
Legally and formally it has such a basis, for the Constitution provides
that 43 of the 60 members be chosen from panels of candidates "having
knowledge and practical experience" of certain "interests and services,"
namely the national language and culture, agriculture, labor, industry
and commerce, and public administration and the social services. Furthermore, a proportion of the candidates for seats are nominated by appropriate voluntary associations. In practice, however, it is well known
that because the electoral college is itself composed of elected representatives chosen on a party basis, party political considerations and not vocational ones predominate. Hence the senators so chosen are not markedly more representative of vocations or interests in the community
than members of legislative bodies elected in more orthodox fashion.[22]

Because public representatives, for all their identification with specific
interests in the community, are primarily party men insulated to some
extent by the party from group pressures, and because the mainsprings
of policy and administrative decision are ministers and civil servants, it

   22 For details of the composition of the Seanad, see pp. 204–5 below.

is on these latter that the interest groups concentrate their main efforts. This is not possible for some groups, especially "demand" groups proposing sweeping reforms or major policy changes, those that defy the state itself, or those that for one reason or another are not on speaking terms with ministers. These must stay out on the streets, try to interest newspapermen and broadcasters, advertise in the newspapers, or lobby parliamentary representatives, though this is not likely to help them much. For those that seek marginal adjustments, which is what most "protection" groups seek, it is possible and infinitely more profitable to be inside—in the minister's room, in the official's office, in the department's conference room. Hence, party and parliamentary activities tend often to be subordinate and to be engaged in with caution for fear of upsetting friendly relationships.

The range of contacts between interest groups and ministers and their advisers is wide and their number enormous. In total, they comprise an important part of the ordinary day-to-day business of all ministers and many senior civil servants. They include formal deputations to make representations to the minister or his officials or to exchange information on reactions to recent events, periodic reviews to fix rates or prices or to consider the progress of an industry, and routine contacts about specific cases or detailed points of administration between the professional servants of the interest groups and appropriate-level civil servants. In addition, there is a considerable and growing exchange of information and, as far as the more widely representative bodies are concerned, an increasing amount of more positive involvement in national economic planning. It is only possible to illustrate this mass of contacts by way of example, citing some of the matters taken up between the state and some of the major organizations. An official of the major employers' organization, the Federated Union of Employers, has categorized the main types of activity as follows:[23]

1. *Representations*
    (a) to put the employers' point of view before the Government (on wage increases, changes in social security arrangements, taxation, etc.) before any irrevocable decisions affecting employer interests are taken.
    (b) state departments may specifically ask for our views on proposals which they are considering. Here it is the state which wants to find out the likely employer reaction before introducing any measure.
    (c) the initiative may be taken by the F.U.E. in trying to get the Government to introduce certain measures, for example, legislation to deal with unofficial strikes or contain wage claims.

[23] In a letter to the author.

(d) the F.U.E. may seek representation on some committee which the Government is sponsoring . . .

2. *Information*

With regard to information, there is a very considerable amount of cooperation on this between the organization, government departments, and state agencies. Statistical information, particularly on such matters as wages, salaries, and conditions of employment, will be exchanged between the F.U.E., government departments . . . and state-sponsored enterprises.

The Ninth Annual Report (for 1965–66) of the National Council of the Federation of Trade Associations, a body that represents over a dozen of the largest associations in the distributive trades, records a number of its major interventions as follows:

The National Council wrote to the Minister for Industry and Commerce to express concern at the absence of any provision in the new prices bill which would ensure that an appeal . . . would be heard by an impartial body. . . . The Council also expressed the view to the Minister that it was unrealistic for the Government to endeavour to control prices and charges unless it was prepared to control the elements, including labour costs, which went to make up prices and charges . . .

The matter [of the extent to which importers and wholesalers could recoup an import levy by charging higher prices] was raised by the Federation with the Minister who released a statement . . .

The Federation's representatives on the National Industrial Economic Council have raised this vital matter [growth of foreign investment in the distributive trades] in the Committee . . .

The Federation joined with many other organizations in protesting strongly to the Minister for Finance against the penal provisions in the Finance Bill, 1965 . . .

The National Council protested strongly to the Minister for Finance against the intrusion in private enterprise by the state organization, the Agricultural Credit Corporation, by providing hire purchase facilities for motor cars for certain state officials, veterinary officers, etc. . . .

The Federation was invited by the Minister for Transport and Power to furnish its observations on the report of the Committee of Investigation into the possibility of accelerating the movement of cargo through sea and air ports.

On the other side of the industrial fence, the Irish Congress of Trade Unions was in communication with government departments on the following matters in the years 1965–67:[24]

Department of Industry and Commerce: price control; position of motor assembly industry; registration of insurance agents; employment at Dundalk Engineering Works.

[24] Information supplied by Irish Congress of Trade Unions.

Department of Social Welfare: wet-time insurance benefits; income ceiling under Social Welfare Acts; trade dispute disqualification for Unemployment Benefit.

Department of Local Government: fair wages clause in local authority contracts.

Department of Transport and Power: nomination of workers' representatives to certain harbor boards; employment conditions of certain workers at Shannon Airport.

Department of Defence: army apprenticeship scheme.

Department of Labour: industrial relations legislation proposals; trade union legislation proposals; industrial training; recognition of trade unions in insurance industry; nomination of workers' members to Labour Court; applications for permits to employ aliens; Holidays (Employees) Act amendment proposal; applications for exclusion regulations under Conditions of Employment Act, 1936; Electricity (Special Provisions) Act; *stagiare* (trainee) agreements; ILO—ratification of conventions and reports on conventions.

Department of Education: school transport services.

Negotiations between departments and interest groups on matters such as those listed above are a regular part of the ordinary business of government. The list of organizations doing business with the Department of Agriculture (p. 105) indicates a formidable-size army of "clients" with whom one department alone has to conduct business. Other departments are in a similar position. In 1967, for example, 100 organizations (of employers and workers) held negotiating licenses (i.e. were officially recognized for purposes of wage negotiations) and were thus at some time likely to make contact with the Department of Labour; yet these do not comprise by any means the total of that Department's "clients."

Intercourse goes further, however, for the practice of appointing advisory and consultative bodies on which interests have representation has been developed consistently over many years. Increasingly, the government finds it useful and even necessary to set up committees to advise ministers on aspects of policy or administration. By so doing it hopes not only to get information and advice, both representative and technical, but also to satisfy political demands that the views of experts and interested parties should be heard, and to attempt to get consensus or, failing that, at least mutual understanding. Advisory bodies attached to central departments number between 70 and 80. They are particularly to be found connected with departments dealing with industry, labor, agriculture, justice, and some of the social services. There are in addition always *ad hoc* committees or commissions sitting to investigate particular problems. Nor is such organized consultation confined to the central government: in local government also, advisory committees are increasingly used.[25]

Membership on advisory bodies is eagerly sought after by most interest groups, for it betokens official recognition of the standing of a body. Some of the associations that are broadly representative, such as the Irish Congress of Trade Unions and the Federated Union of Employers, have places on a wide range of official committees, including some of the most important. At the end of 1966 the FUE had representatives on eleven advisory bodies and the ICTU on sixteen. Both were represented on seven bodies, namely, the National Industrial Economic Council, An Cheard Chomháirle (Apprenticeship Board), the Factories Advisory Committee, the Office Premises Advisory Committee, the Irish National Productivity Council, the Manpower Advisory Council, and the Prices Advisory Committee. In addition, each nominated delegates to the Labour Court and to the International Labour Conference.

Among the most important advisory bodies are those concerned with economic planning and development, and in particular the National Industrial Economic Council. This body, the Taoiseach said at its inaugural meeting, "is charged with the task of preparing reports from time to time on the principles which should be applied for the development of the national economy." It comments on state economic and social policy, on the progress of the national programs for economic expansion, and on proposals emanating from any department that might have some bearing on economic growth. Although it is an *advisory* body, its reports are important influences on policy makers and, therefore, on policy. Thus, at the very center of the planning process, the spokesmen of the major interests involved work closely with key civil servants. In addition, the National Industrial Economic Council is not only an advisory body vis-à-vis the government but also, conversely, a device for educating and exhorting industry, commerce, and labor; therefore it has an important role in creating a climate of opinion favorable to planned change and in "selling" government economic policy.[26]

IV

The enormous scale of this activity, which is a feature of government and administration today, is a comparatively recent phenomenon. The interest group representatives who gave evidence to the Commission on

[25] See D. E. Leon, *Advisory Bodies in Irish Government* (Dublin, 1963).
[26] See further below, p. 227.

Vocational Organization in the early 1940's were full of complaints about lack of consultation. The commission's conclusions were unequivocal:

We find that in the exercise of supervision and control over private enterprise by government departments there is relatively little consultation with vocational organizations. Such consultation as does take place is not continuous or obligatory, but is casual and haphazard. Even where bodies have been statutorily established they have been limited in function, defective in composition, and shortlived in operation.[27]

Today many interest organizations are regularly consulted and some do almost daily business with public servants; the most representative of them have more positive governmental functions in the crucial field of economic planning. Yet it is important not to create an impression of uniformly cozy relationships. In recent years, two major interest organizations—the National Farmers' Association and the Irish Medical Association—have had for long periods the worst possible relationships with the ministers and departments most closely concerned with them, bad relations that have resulted in the ministers' refusal to meet representatives and in the associations' boycott of the ministers.

Moreover, for all the volume of consultation and the number of advisory bodies, some of those who come in contact with civil servants get the impression that not all of them like genuine consultation, regarding the process as a way of getting information and compliance or as a public relations device, and that they do not see policy making as a genuinely cooperative activity. Undeniably, however, consultation is practiced to a much greater extent than it was in the past, and, inevitably, the process of planning the economy increasingly demands genuine partnership.

From a democratic point of view, the importance of widespread and systematic exchange of information, consultation, and dialogue between the government and specific interests, particularly representative associations, is clear. S. E. Finer summarizes it admirably in his *Anonymous Empire*. The process, he says,

embodies two basic democratic procedures: the right to participate in policymaking and the right to demand redress of grievances. They are best appreciated by considering . . . government without them. Suppose parties and civil servants simply refused to have any contact with the Lobby [interest groups]? Suppose the party simply claimed that it was "the will of the people" with a mandate for doing all it had proposed? Its rule would be a rigid and ignorant tyranny. And if civil servants likewise claimed to be merely the servants of the

---

27 *Report of the Commission on Vocational Organization* (Stationery Office, Dublin, 1944), para. 474.

government in power, with no mandate to cooperate with the Lobby, its rule, in its turn, would be a rigid and stupid bureaucracy. In the age of bigness and technology, the Lobby tempers the system.[28]

On the other hand, as Finer points out, although this process adds a further dimension to democracy, it is "a very 'lumpy' kind of self-government." Close relationships between government and interest groups are handy and are becoming more and more essential, but "to put the matter crudely, a close relationship tends to become a *closed* one." Moreover, many of the processes and persons traditionally and commonly associated in the public mind with democratic government and the representation of public opinion—elections, the mandate, the Oireachtas itself—in truth play a comparatively small part in shaping policy. Much of the activity of policy making and administration is carried on far from electoral politics and Parliament. Because this is so, much interest group activity, including that which is most effective, is concentrated where Parliament and the public do not and cannot see it. The increase in the volume and importance of such activity thus contributes to a growing isolation of electoral and parliamentary politics from public-policy decision making. "By the same process as it brings the 'interested' publics into consultation, it shuts the general public out of it."[29]

[28] Finer, *Anonymous Empire* (2d ed., London, 1966), p. 113.
[29] *Ibid.*, p. 114.

FIVE

Political Communication and the Mass Media

Parties and interest groups stand on the border between what might be termed "the political system" and its environment, society as a whole. They reflect interests and divisions in the community and express the aspirations and demands of their members to the government and administration. They make claims on one another and the community, and they defend their own positions and privileges against the claims of others. However, they are not to be seen solely as making demands; they also produce and mobilize the "supports" that give politicians legitimacy and power. In respect of both, they might be regarded as performing a function that is essentially one of communication. Indeed, it is possible to view government as a whole as a communications process involving a network of channels of information and institutions for transmitting ideas, demands, and orders. Certainly a communications network is "the nerves of government."

To adopt such an approach broadens immeasurably one's perspective of politics, for it is obvious when one inquires systematically "who communicates with whom and in what manner?" that the communications passing through the channels we have examined are only a portion of those with political significance. Even if such an inquiry were limited to what have been called the "inputs" of the political system, i.e. the processes by which political values, attitudes, and demands are formed and expressed to political decision makers and by which leaders aggregate interests and mobilize support, it can readily be seen that people's political opinions and actions are to a great extent governed by information, advice, and precepts coming from many sources and in many ways, some of them very far from the conventionally political.

Some of this communication is "horizontal"—ministers conferring together or with community leaders, men talking in a bar, children learning to sing "Kevin Barry" or "Derry's Walls" at school. Those who, because of their elite status in the community, can communicate horizontally in a direct manner with members of a government or other political leaders or senior public servants are likely to be comparatively well informed and influential. For most people, political information, ideas, and values are communicated either horizontally at a low level via family, school, religious group, or work place, or vertically from the top or source downward, largely by more formal media. Conversely, much information about public attitudes and demands passes vertically upward to political leaders. Obviously in a modern society television, radio, newspapers, and to a lesser extent other printed material are powerful means of wholesale vertical communication—thus the term "mass media."

It is on the extent and quality of vertical communication that the nature and efficiency of government largely depend. Where people have no access and are not exposed to the mass media because of poverty and consequent lack of social and economic development, as in primitive countries, it is hardly possible to have any national politics at all. As Richard Rose has pointed out, the great majority of people must rely on mass media as their main source of information about the actions of those in national politics.[1] What the mass media report is thus a major factor governing the quantity and quality of the political information circulating. So important are the mass media that their ownership, control, standards, and extent to which people are exposed to them are commonly and rightly regarded as matters of crucial public importance.

In general, political communications in advanced countries like Ireland consist, in the words of Lucian Pye, of "a fusion of high technology and special, professionalized processes of communication with informal, society-based and non-specialized processes of person-to-person communication."[2] We are here concerned with the "special, professionalized processes of communication," the mass media. Yet it is essential to an understanding of how political attitudes are formed and behavior shaped, and especially those attitudes that result in men and women voting this way or that (itself one of the most significant of vertical political communications), to realize that special political institutions like the parties and pressure groups or the major mass channels like TV, radio, and the press are by no means the only suppliers of political information and ideas. In fact, research findings have tended to show that,

[1] R. Rose, ed., *Studies in British Politics* (London, 1966), p. 170.
[2] L. Pye, *Communications and Political Development* (Princeton, 1963), p. 26.

in the short run at least, they may make surprisingly little impact upon many individuals. Face-to-face contacts and informal communications may be of much greater importance. In any case, there can be no doubting the preeminence of the basic social groups—the family, religious groups, school, etc.—in the political socialization of the individual and in holding him fast. Some social scientists investigating the impact of mass media claim that "Opinions and attitudes which are important to an individual's image of himself, or to his picture of society, cannot easily be changed by a fusillade of communications, however persuasive. . . . Such opinions are often anchored in and shielded by a person's primary group affiliations—'ensconced in protective group cocoons.' "[3] Whatever is said about the mass media must not obscure this most important political fact.

II

To assess the impact and political importance of the mass media, it would be necessary to investigate, first, what is available and under what conditions it is produced; second, who uses what is published; and, third, what effect it has upon the consumers' attitudes and actions. Unfortunately, little systematic information is available for Ireland on the first two points, and virtually none at all exists on the last point. Because of this, it simply is not possible to evaluate the effect of the mass media on Irish political behavior. Yet it does matter what people read, see, and hear. First we shall examine the press, which in Ireland is under private ownership and management, and then radio and television, both of which are operated by a single public authority with a legal monopoly, though a monopoly that for technical reasons is far from complete in practice.

III

A free, private enterprise press was established in Ireland parallel with its establishment in Great Britain. Mass readership daily papers, produced in Dublin, reflecting a number of shades of opinion, were well established with strong traditions of independence before the First World War. Other newspapers and journals, including those advocating the independence of Ireland, were produced and circulated, although, as the national struggle grew sharper, some extreme publications were banned from time to time. Thus, despite the fact that the press before independence had many of the essential characteristics of a free press,

[3] J. G. Blumler and J. Madge, *Citizenship and Television* (a PEP Report, London, 1967).

the limits allowed to it in respect of seditious matter sometimes resulted in the harassing of extreme nationalist publications. Also, naturally, war conditions from 1914 on subjected the entire British and Irish press to security censorship. However, comment sharply critical of government policy appeared regularly in both Irish and British newspapers, the latter circulating freely in Ireland. Thus, independent Ireland emerged with an established free press, home-produced and privately owned and operated. It embraced the full range of newspaper and journal production—national dailies, evening and Sunday newspapers, local papers, weekly and monthly journals, and magazines. British newspapers, journals, and magazines continued to circulate in small but significant numbers, and still do. Furthermore, many of the books read in Ireland are produced in the United Kingdom, and British radio and television are easily available.

At the present time there are four daily newspapers. The *Irish Independent* and the *Irish Press* might best be described as mass dailies, the *Irish Times* has some of the pretensions and characteristics of what in Great Britain is often called a "quality" paper, and the *Cork Examiner* is a regional paper, for over 90 per cent of its readers are in the province of Munster. These with their associated evening and Sunday papers make up the most important "families" of newspapers in the country. The following tabulation shows circulation figures of national newspapers for the six-month period ending June 30, 1968:[4]

Morning		Evening	
Irish Independent	172,176	*Evening Press*	149,117
Irish Press	102,073	*Evening Herald*	145,090
Cork Examiner	57,329	*Cork Evening Echo*	33,208
Irish Times	52,313		

Sunday	
Sunday Press	422,114
Sunday Independent	330,112

In 1968 there were 50 local newspapers, mostly weeklies. The circulations of 30 of them were published as follows for the same period:

Below 5,000	1	25,000–29,999	2
5,000–9,999	9	30,000–34,999	1
10,000–14,999	11	35,000–39,999	0
15,000–19,999	4	Over 40,000	1
20,000–24,999	1		

---

[4] Figures taken from *Newspaper Press Directory, 1968* (Association of Advertisers in Ireland Ltd., Dublin).

British newspapers also circulate in large numbers in Ireland. Those with the biggest circulations in 1968 were as follows:

Daily		Sunday	
Daily Express	21,040	*People*	176,046
Daily Mirror	14,000	*Sunday Express*	111,000
Daily Mail	7,121	*News of the World*	102,100
		Sunday Mirror	65,269
		Sunday Times	43,806

All these newspapers are in private hands and are run as businesses. One of them, though, the *Irish Press,* has been until recently at least closely associated with a party. It was founded by De Valera in 1931 as a weapon for his political crusade, with funds raised in the United States and from the people of Ireland, the bulk of the latter collected in small amounts. His son, Major Vivion de Valera, is controlling director of the company and Editor in Chief, in which role he influences editorial policy and decisions.

The *Irish Independent* is controlled, as it was at the beginning of the century, by the family of its famous owner before the First World War, William Martin Murphy, who clashed with Connolly and Larkin in the great showdown strike in 1913. Traditionally, it and its Sunday and evening siblings have given independent support to the Pro-Treaty–Cumann na nGaedheal–Fine Gael cause, but above all the daily has been a bourgeois, Catholic paper which, until the early 1960's at least, carried "more country news than the other nationals and at least until recently devoted a large proportion of its space to the doings of the dignitaries of the Catholic Church."[5] In some respects the *Cork Examiner* is similar. It is family-owned and -run, it is conservative, and it has given independent support to Fine Gael.

The *Irish Times,* formerly the unofficial organ of the Protestant and unionist minority, is today an outspoken, liberal, middle-class newspaper. Politically independent, it has increasingly tended in recent years to support Fianna Fáil, though in a discriminating fashion. Although it is owned and run by Protestant business and professional men, one of whom is its editor, it is far from being a Protestant newspaper reinforcing the attitudes of a distinctive "subculture," which it obviously was in former days. Through the years, it has moved, even more than the others, a long way from being the paper of a distinct group in the community. For, in the past, all the major newspapers clearly had their roots in, and served, particular publics.

In addition to the national newspapers and the regional *Cork Ex-*

---

[5] T. Gray, *The Irish Answer: An Anatomy of Ireland* (London, 1966), p. 248.

aminer, there are a large number of local newspapers, mainly weeklies, most of which are independent single units owned by individuals or small companies. They are not combined in large chains, nor do they carry much, if any, syndicated matter. Although their number is slowly decreasing—today there are 50 in the Republic; ten years ago there were 60—many of them flourish in a modest way by concentrating on local news, including "parish pump" politics, and local advertisements, and by using their presses for miscellaneous commercial printing as well as the production of a newspaper. They are of considerable importance in their local communities, but many of them studiously refrain from taking sides in the party struggles.

The Irish press is a free press. That does not mean that editors can print anything they choose under all circumstances. What it does mean, however, is that editors have a very wide freedom to print news, comment, and opinion that are unpalatable to the government without danger of penalties, legal or otherwise. Of course, there are legal limitations, but these do not usually operate to restrict the publication of political news or comment on matters of current political moment. The Censorship of Publications Act forbids the publication of matter that is "indecent or obscene" or that "advocates the unnatural prevention of conception," both prohibitions arising obviously from a zealous regard for Catholic morality. The libel laws, which are still the comparatively severe British code, and the laws concerning contempt of court are perhaps the most important editorial inhibitors, but only very infrequently do these operate to prevent publication of matter of political significance. "Parliamentary privilege" has never been invoked to inhibit political comment.

In fact, except during the Second World War, when censorship prevented publication of anything that might damage Ireland's neutrality, the only legal restrictions of any consequence are those contained in the Offences Against the State Act, 1939. Under sections 2 and 10 of this Act, newspapers are forbidden to refer to organizations declared illegal under the Act, in other words the Irish Republican Army. Although, strictly, this might be held to be political censorship, the mass media have not in fact been inhibited from reporting or commenting on the activities of the IRA. When the state has been inclined to enforce the law strictly, they have simply substituted the term "an illegal organization," for in any case the neighboring British and Northern Ireland press, radio, and TV are certain to feature such activities. In fact, the IRA and similar organizations have occasionally in the past delivered their communiqués and other statements in person to press and radio for dissemination. Such a ridiculous state of affairs serves only to confirm the freedom to publish that Irish papers enjoy and to underline the impossibility of censorship in a society that is so open to its neighbors.

What restrictions or irresistible pressures, if any, there are on editors in political matters do not arise from the law, but from inside—from the owners and boards of the papers. In practice they are probably very few. Official sanctions such as withdrawal of the right to attend press conferences or of other facilities cannot in the nature of things be effective because there are very few such privileges in any case. However, the canceling by the Department of Agriculture and Fisheries of its advertising in the *Farmers' Journal* in 1967 when the Department and the National Farmers' Association were at loggerheads might be considered a form of pressure: if so, it was very inept and counterproductive. Of course, editors (and other newsmen) are inevitably subject to unofficial representations and appeals from ministers and other political leaders as well as from officials to keep out, soft-pedal, or give prominence to items. However, many such requests might be, and probably are, resented and resisted. Of course, also, ministers and politicians generally have contacts with the press, but these exist for mutual convenience and cannot be counted as political interference. All in all, legal and other outside restrictions on editors publishing political material are very few, and newspapers are well placed to resist outside pressure and influence if they wish. Whether they are well placed to acquire information from a government and administration that are, in the British tradition, inclined to cagey secrecy is another matter.

In such circumstances of considerable freedom from outside pressures, what Irish newspapers choose to print presumably depends upon the commercial judgment and social attitudes of those who control them. Tables 5.1 and 5.2 summarize results obtained from a content analysis of

TABLE 5.1

Content of Irish Newspapers

Paper	Editorial	Advertising	Content of editorial matter					
			News	Features	Leaders	Letters	Pictures	Misc.
			DAILIES					
Cork Examiner	61%	39%	78%	4½%	2%	—ᵃ	12½%	3%
Irish Independent	61	39	69	12½	1	—	12	5½
Irish Press	78	22	67	12½	1	1½%	13½	4½
Irish Times	70	30	70	10	1½	2½	12½	3
			SUNDAYS					
Sunday Independent	63	37	52	13	1	3	18	13
Sunday Press	63	37	50	17	—	3	19	10

Source: Irish—content analysis carried out in November–December 1967. British—Raymond Williams, *Communications* (rev. ed., London, 1966, chap. 3), analysis carried out in July 1965.

ᵃ Dashes indicate less than ½ per cent.

TABLE 5.2

Analysis of the News Content of Irish Newspapers
(With some British comparisons)

Paper	Political, social, and economic news			Financial and commercial	Sport	Rest[a]
	International	Domestic	Total			
		DAILIES				
Cork Examiner	17½%	28½%	46%	12%	30½%	11½%
Irish Independent	11½	23½	35	17½	37	10½
Irish Press	12	26½	38½	11	42½	8
Irish Times	22½	19	41½	18½	25	15
London Times	13	23½	36½	28	15½	20
Daily Express	4	14½	18½	7	52½	22
Daily Mirror	2	22	24	1	49	26
		SUNDAYS				
Sunday Independent	5	21	26	3	41	30
Sunday Press	9	35	44	—	39	17
Sunday Times	13	10	23	25	21	31
News of the World	2	10	12	2	38	48[b]

Source: Same as Table 5.1.
  [a] Includes law, police, accidents, personalities, arts, and miscellaneous.
  [b] Includes no less than 32 per cent classified as law, police, and accidents.

the main Irish newspapers made in November 1967 and those of some English newspapers. Although the Irish dailies originally catered to different publics, they no longer do so to anything like the same extent, and this is borne out by the comparative uniformity in the proportion of space they give to various types of material (news, features, etc.) compared with the wide range of practices to be found in the United Kingdom. This is to be expected because of the small population and, consequently, the need to appeal to all classes in order to survive. Analysis of the content of their news items shows, however, that the proportion of political, social, and economic news that they print is high compared with the popular British dailies such as the *Daily Express* and the *Daily Mirror* and is nearer to that of the quality papers. The amount of foreign news is particularly high, but this is largely because British news comes under this heading. Moreover, Irish papers, and particularly the *Irish Times*, publish more financial and commercial news than the British popular press. Conversely, the proportion given to sports news is lower. Overall, then, the Irish dailies are comparatively serious newspapers when it comes to political, social, and economic affairs, though they do not come up to the level of the great European papers, as Table 5.3 shows.

TABLE 5.3

*Percentage of Whole Newspaper Given to Political,
Social, and Economic News*

Irish		British		Other European	
Irish Independent	15%	*Daily Telegraph*	12%	*La Stampa*	27%
Irish Press	20	*London Times*	19	*Die Welt*	33
Irish Times	20	*Guardian*	23	*Le Monde*	72
Cork Examiner	22				

Source: Same as Table 5.1.

On the contrary, the Irish Sunday papers, like the British, carry less news, and far less foreign news and financial and commercial news, than the dailies, whereas the proportion given to sports is as high as any in Great Britain. When we see how important the role of the Irish Sundays is, these facts will be seen to be of great significance.[6]

Of course, quantitative analysis does not convey at all accurately the differences between newspapers. Here it may be fair to say only that many people consider the *Irish Times* to be the nearest approach to a British quality newspaper: it certainly carries a high proportion of political, social, and economic news and of business and financial news, it gives the most extensive coverage to literature, music, and art, and it has in recent years published surveys in depth of a number of political and social questions. Nevertheless, there clearly is not as great a contrast between the Irish dailies as between the *Times, Guardian,* and *Daily Telegraph* on the one hand and the *Daily Express* and *Daily Mirror* on the other. The *Sunday Independent* and *Sunday Press,* however, are generally more like the popular British Sundays, both in their allocation of space and in their quality. Yet, overall, the Irish press is comparatively very homogeneous. Those Irish people who read newspapers get much the same facts and comment regardless of their religion, community, etc., and in this respect they contrast markedly with French people, for example, or with other European peoples, who, depending on whether they are Catholic, Communist, Protestant, or whatever, live in separate worlds of political information.

Though next to nothing is known about the effects of newspaper reading upon the Irish public, it is obvious that if a person does not see a newspaper, he cannot be influenced by it. It is particularly important, therefore, to find out which sections of the community do, and which do not, read papers.

[6] See pp. 130–31 below.

TABLE 5.4

Consumption of Newsprint in Certain European Countries, 1965

Country	GNP per capita (U.S. dollars)	Newsprint consumption per capita (kg)
Sweden	$2,500	32.2
Switzerland	2,330	20.4
Denmark	2,100	26.0 (1964)
France	1,920	11.1
Federal Republic of Germany	1,900	12.4
Norway	1,880	16.7
United Kingdom	1,810	25.3
Belgium	1,780	14.0
Netherlands	1,550	18.7
Austria	1,270	9.8
Italy	1,152	6.6
Ireland	977	17.0

Source: GNP—*OECD Observer.* Newsprint—*Statistical Yearbook, 1966* (United Nations, New York, 1967).

By Western European standards, Ireland's per capita consumption of newsprint is neither very high nor very low. Table 5.4 shows clearly, though, that *in relation to her wealth* Ireland, like the United Kingdom and the Netherlands, is a big consumer of newspapers. However, a survey of newspaper readership shows considerable variations within the country. These regional, community, and class differences may well be of great importance from the point of view of the influences that bear upon people's political behavior.

A readership survey carried out in 1968[7] showed, as Table 5.5 indicates, that more than 40 per cent of the population age 15 and over did not see an Irish morning newspaper. However, some of these, mainly in Dublin, might have seen an evening paper. More important, though, over 80 per cent of all Irish adults saw a Sunday newspaper. It is apparent, therefore, that for some people, particularly country people, the Sunday newspapers were the major source of printed political information, whereas for the vast majority they were one source.

Tables 5.5 and 5.6 show clearly, however, that there were considerable differences in the newspaper-reading habits of people according to region, type of community, and socioeconomic status. Table 5.5 indicates that the percentage of daily paper readers was lower in Connacht and the Ulster counties (Cavan, Donegal, and Monaghan) than elsewhere,

[7] *National Readership Survey in Ireland, 1968,* carried out by the British Market Research Bureau and Social Surveys (Gallup Poll) Ltd.

TABLE 5.5

Regional and Community Variations in Population Reading Irish Newspapers in May–June 1968

Readers age 15 and over	All	Region				Community	
		Dublin[a]	Rest of Leinster	Munster	Connacht and Ulster (part)[b]	Urban	Rural
Morning paper (yesterday)	59%	58%	63%	71%	39%	63%	54%
Evening paper (yesterday)	45	82	39	36	18	68	21
Sunday paper (last)	81	79	86	81	77	80	82
Provincial paper (last 7 days)	59	12	88	71	72	39	80

Source: *National Readership Survey in Ireland, 1968.*
[a] Dublin = Dublin City, Dun Laoghaire, County Dublin.
[b] Ulster (part) = Cavan, Donegal, Monaghan.

TABLE 5.6

Differences in Newspaper Reading Habits According to Socioeconomic Status, 1968

Readers age 15 and over	All	Social grade[a]					
		AB	C1	C2	DE	F1	F2
Morning paper (yesterday)	59%	86%	80%	65%	50%	61%	36%
Evening paper (yesterday)	45	58	60	65	55	17	13
Sunday paper (last)	81	83	83	86	76	85	76
Provincial paper (last 7 days)	59	36	52	52	49	86	72

Source: *National Readership Survey in Ireland, 1968.*
[a] AB = upper middle and middle class (managerial, administrative, professional).
   C1 = lower middle class (supervisory or clerical, junior managerial, etc.).
   C2 = skilled manual workers.
   DE = semiskilled and unskilled and those at lowest level of subsistence.
   F1 = those owning or working 30 acres of land or more.
   F2 = those owning or working under 30 acres.

and lower in rural than in urban communities. From Table 5.6 it is evident that fewer farmers than other people read a daily paper. Similar differences occur when it comes to exposure to television. However, both tables show that rural people are big readers of the Sunday papers (82 per cent) and the provincial papers (80 per cent). The Sundays, as we have seen, carry only a small amount of political, financial, and commercial news. The majority of the provincial papers, being weeklies, also carry little national news, and though some have a comment column or Dublin letter containing political items, many avoid partisan interpretation. They do contain local political news, especially reports of debates and proceedings of meetings of local authorities and other public bodies, and

TABLE 5.7

Readership of the Principal Morning Daily and Sunday Newspapers by Region and Community

		Region				Community	
Readers age 15 and over	All	Dub-lin[a]	Rest of Leinster	Mun-ster	Connacht and Ulster (part)[b]	Urban	Rural
Irish Independent	35%	40%	46%	29%	27%	39%	32%
Irish Press	23	19	26	25	21	23	23
Cork Examiner	10	1	0	33	0	12	9
Irish Times	8	17	4	6	3	13	3
Sunday Independent	58	62	65	53	51	61	54
Sunday Press	60	52	62	62	66	56	64

Source: *National Readership Survey in Ireland, 1968.*
   [a] Dublin = Dublin City, Dun Laoghaire, County Dublin.
   [b] Ulster (part) = Cavan, Donegal, Monaghan.

TABLE 5.8

Readership of the Principal Morning Daily and Sunday Newspapers by Socioeconomic Status

		Social grade[a]					
Readers age 15 and over	All	AB	C1	C2	DE	F1	F2
Irish Independent	35%	55%	51%	41%	30%	37%	15%
Irish Press	23	18	26	28	23	22	18
Cork Examiner	10	9	14	11	9	10	9
Irish Times	8	38	21	7	4	4	2
Sunday Independent	58	71	70	63	53	60	42
Sunday Press	60	56	62	63	56	63	62

Source: *National Readership Survey in Ireland, 1968.*
   [a] AB= upper middle and middle class (managerial, administrative, professional).
   C1 = lower middle class (supervisory or clerical, junior managerial, etc.).
   C2 = skilled manual workers.
   DE = semiskilled and unskilled and those at lowest level of subsistence.
   F1 = those owning or working 30 acres of land or more.
   F2 = those owning or working under 30 acres.

political news of local interest, for example, the parliamentary questions and other parliamentary interventions of the local TD's and senators. Such contents may well reinforce the already strong local orientations of many country people, the more so if such people do not read much national political material.

The lower readership of the national dailies in rural Ireland and particularly in the west and northwest is partly due to distribution difficulties, but it is also partly economic. As Table 5.6 indicates, readership is related to socioeconomic status. The least well off, both urban and rural, are the least likely to see a daily newspaper, and the contrast between the smaller farmers and the rest of the community is striking.

The same readership survey also provides data on who reads the various papers. Tables 5.7 and 5.8 show that of the morning papers the *Irish Independent* and the *Irish Press* were truly national, having substantial numbers of readers in all regions, in town and country, and in all social groups. The *Cork Examiner* was read only in Munster, and the *Irish Times* had a small readership, much larger in Dublin than elsewhere, much larger in urban communities than in rural, and including far more middle-class readers than any others. The Sunday papers had national coverage, and, everywhere, some people took both of them—for their contests, so it is said. In addition, English Sunday newspapers (in an Irish edition) circulate in considerable numbers in and around Dublin and Cork (see p. 125).

The readership of the *Irish Times* is thought by many to be of particular significance politically. Certainly, the majority of its readers are urban, middle-class people living in and around Dublin, as the following tabulation shows:[8]

Region		Community		Socioeconomic status	
Dublin	59%	Urban	84%	AB	29%
Rest of Leinster	11	Rural	16	C1	30
Munster	23	TOTAL	100%	C2	15
Connacht and				DE	15
Ulster (part)	7			F1	8
TOTAL	100%			F2	3
				TOTAL	100%

Also, 56 per cent of *Irish Times* readers were educated to age seventeen or over, as compared with 20 per cent for newspaper readers generally; and 34 per cent of *Times* readers have university or professional qualifications, compared with 16 per cent of readers generally. Among such people are to be found those with considerable political influence. Conversely, the paper does not reach the rural community or manual workers. But all this does not mean that the *Irish Times* is the most important middle-class paper, let alone the paper of the politically influential. Indeed, more than half of the middle class (social grades A, B, and C1) and 37 per cent of the farmers with over 30 acres read the *Irish Independent* (see Table 5.8). On the other hand, though figures are not available, it is believed that more of the "upper middle" class (social grade A), principally in and around Dublin, read the *Irish Times* than

[8] *National Readership Survey in Ireland, 1968.*

any other newspaper. In this group there are many with more than average political influence, direct or indirect. Nevertheless, assuming that the middle class as a whole includes the vast majority of the politically influential, the situation in Ireland is not the same as in Great Britain, where to a great extent the middle class reads one sort of newspaper, the working class another. In Ireland, in any case, there is not a marked contrast in content between "quality" and "popular" dailies, as there is in Britain.

IV

Broadcasting in Ireland has from the beginning been a state monopoly. In comparison with the United Kingdom, however, public control was for years more direct, since broadcasting until 1961 was under direct ministerial control. Radio Eireann (1925–61) was a branch of the Department of Posts and Telegraphs; its staff was civil servants; and its activities were subject to parliamentary scrutiny like all other public services operated directly by the central administration.

The effect of this was not to subject broadcasting to party political pressures, but rather the reverse, to insulate it entirely from politics. Radio Eireann staff members were expected as civil servants to take no overt part in politics, and the station took a strictly neutral position simply by broadcasting virtually no political material at all. In return, the mantle of civil service anonymity was cast over it, protecting it from party and parliamentary criticism. Civil service attitudes predominated, leading to an unadventurous program policy. News had to be broadcast, of course, and inevitably some of it was bound to be "political." The governing attitude, however, was that there was a certain something identifiable day by day as "news," and that this could and should be given out in "bulletins," about which there could be no argument.

Given this climate, there was no political broadcasting at all on Irish radio until 1954, when "party political broadcasts" (time allocated to parties in an agreed ratio) were introduced at election time. It was a rule also that, apart from these, no parliamentary representatives should take part in any programs of current affairs, or indeed usually in any programs of whatever description. Even after the party political broadcasts at election time began, the political campaigns were still not reported. Current affairs programs were introduced in 1953 and their scope was gradually extended, but the greatest care was taken to avoid topics and material that were at all likely to evoke even a whiff of party controversy and, if possible, any controversy at all. Radio Eireann was truly a political eunuch: in the words of Eamonn Andrews, the first chairman of its successor, Radio Telefís Eireann, "one of the worst but best-meaning radio services in the world."[9]

The introduction of a television service in Ireland in 1961 and the increasingly liberal policy of the rival British broadcasting organizations inevitably altered this situation considerably. Nevertheless, the effects of the civil service tradition of reticence are still to be seen in the marked sensitivity of unacclimatized politicians to political broadcasting, and especially to even the mildest criticism in this medium; in the feeling, still only slowly being overcome, of many in the community that broadcasting ought never to offend anyone and should, therefore, keep away from controversy altogether; and in the consequent cautious progress toward independence and the freedom to broadcast displayed by Radio Telefís Eireann, radio's successor.

The Broadcasting Authority Act, 1960, created Radio Telefís Eireann in the form of a "state-sponsored body," i.e. a statutory authority with stated functions and powers whose governing body is appointed by its sponsor minister, the Minister for Posts and Telegraphs.[10] It is charged with providing a television and broadcasting system, and in carrying out this function it is required "to secure that, when it broadcasts any information, news or feature which relates to matters of public controversy or is the subject of current public debate, the information, news or feature is presented objectively and impartially and without any expression of the Authority's own views."

Though charged with maintaining objectivity and given a legal *persona* and autonomy, Radio Telefís Eireann is obviously subject to government control to some extent. To begin with, the members of the Authority are appointed by the Minister. Although some of them are known supporters of Fianna Fáil, it might be more accurate to see them, or most of them, as deliberately chosen spokesmen of various interests in the community—the Irish language, the universities, farming, the west, etc. Obviously, also, the Authority has the ordinary obligations of state-sponsored bodies, e.g. to present its report and accounts to the Minister and to furnish him with information as required. In addition, its broadcasting hours are governed by the Minister, who also "may direct the Authority in writing to refrain from broadcasting any particular matter or matter of any particular class." He may, too, "direct the Authority in writing to allocate broadcasting time for any announcements by or on behalf of any Minister of State in connection with the

9 Quoted in *Irish Times*, Nov. 1, 1967.
10 For a description and discussion of state-sponsored bodies, see Chapter 10.

functions of that Minister." Finally, the Minister has an overall responsibility for the service. In practice, because broadcasting was historically
a part of the civil service, because of the susceptibilities and suspicions
of politicians, and because the government itself has sometimes tended
to regard the Authority, in the words of a former Taoiseach, as "an instrument of public policy,"[11] it has so far not established a fully independent position in relation to the government.

There are other pressures too. Like its predecessor, Radio Telefís
Eireann earns revenue by commercial broadcasting. These earnings, together with those from statutory broadcasting license fees, are its main
sources of revenue. In 1966–67, 41 per cent of its income of a little over
£4 million per annum came from license fees, 57 per cent from advertisers, and 2 per cent from miscellaneous sources. In the same year, sponsored programs on radio occupied 20 per cent of broadcasting time. On
television, there are no sponsored programs, and advertising is concentrated in "spots" between or during items. Whether programs are actually sponsored or not, the interests of advertisers might be a consideration
in deciding program policy, though there is no evidence that they are
at all important.

On the face of it, it is not advertisers but community interest groups
that exert pressure upon Radio Telefís Eireann, the more so because
the Authority has been trying, successfully, to break out of the old limitations on what can be broadcast, as it has had to do to compete with
programs broadcast by British stations. Many British radio programs
can be received; British TV can be seen in the north and east of the
country, and one-fifth of all homes (and well over one-third of homes
with television) are able to turn to it if they choose. Consequently, RTE
has sometimes been involved in controversy and has evoked criticism
not only from politicians but particularly from language organizations
and the Catholic Church. Indeed, as the Reverend Patrick Brophy, Professor of Dogmatic Theology at Carlow Theological Seminary, pointed
out in 1967:

At present it appears that the only widely publicized comments that our Bishops have to make about Irish television are sharply critical ones, and there is a
real risk here that the Church in its governing body will seem or appear to be
hostile to the kind of society in which television plays an actively formative part.
. . . It was regrettable that most of the official statements of Irish Bishops about
television, radio and press, particularly since the Vatican Council, had been
sharply critical.[12]

---

11 *Dáil Debates*, vol. 224, col. 1046 (Oct. 12, 1966).
12 Address reported in *Sunday Independent*, Oct. 29, 1967.

Between the bishops (especially those who, it seems, watch "The Late Late Show" on a Saturday night), language pressure groups, and sensitive and demanding politicians, the Authority has had to tread warily.

In spite of these pressures, Radio Telefís Eireann's policy has been to seek steadily increasing freedom to air any and every topic, including religious issues, birth control, and drugs, all of which were unthinkable as subjects of broadcasting programs ten years ago, and it has resolutely developed its current affairs and political broadcasts. Now, radio and television cover election campaigns and have regular political programs. Some are in the form of confrontations between ministers and other parliamentary representatives chosen by the parties. Most are interviews and discussions in magazine-type programs devised and controlled by the Authority, with a general understanding between it and the parties about political balance and the use of parliamentary representatives. Such arrangements are negotiated between the Authority and the party whips. In addition, news magazine programs have to a great extent shaken themselves free of any restraints imposed by fear of adverse comment from outside. Only the actual news broadcasts still have a slight aura of the old radio news bulletins of Radio Eireann.

While RTE has achieved considerable operational freedom, incidents in 1966 and 1967 suggested that some ministers at least did not see the Authority in principle as part of an independent "fourth estate." In October 1966, following a successful but subsequently much publicized demand by the Minister for Agriculture and Fisheries that a news item should be altered, the Minister concerned contended in the Dáil that "when I give that advice with all the authority of my office as Minister for Agriculture and Fisheries, that advice should be respected by the national television network."[13] The Taoiseach (then Lemass) went further and defined the role of the Authority in general terms as he saw it:

Radio Telefís Eireann was set up by legislation as an instrument of public policy and as such is responsible to the Government. The Government have overall responsibility for its conduct and especially the obligation to ensure that its programmes do not offend against the public interest. . . . To this extent the Government reject the view that Radio Telefís Eireann should be, either generally or in regard to its current affairs and news programmes, completely independent of Government supervision.[14]

In April 1967, Lemass's successor as Taoiseach, Jack Lynch, intervened to prevent a news team from going to North Vietnam to make a film.

13 *Dáil Debates*, vol. 224, col. 1085 (Oct. 12, 1966).
14 *Dáil Debates*, vol. 224, cols. 1045–46 (Oct. 12, 1966).

He chose to do so by making "representations" to the Authority on the telephone rather than by attempting to invoke the section of the Act that gives the Minister for Posts and Telegraphs the power to direct the Authority in writing to refrain from broadcasting any item. The Authority in turn chose to accept this rather than to insist on the letter of the law.

It is evident from these events and others like them that, although Radio Telefís Eireann has achieved substantial operational independence, it has not chosen to make an issue of principle of its status and role.[15] Perhaps the one is in part the result of the other. It is obvious from the ministerial statements and actions quoted, and others, that some ministers regard the Authority as being in the same position as any other state-sponsored body, such as the Electricity Supply Board or the Irish Sugar Company. It is this fact, rather than the fact that ministers undoubtedly and inevitably make representations in private to those who control or make programs, which gives rise to doubts about the position of the Authority. Despite its considerable freedom in day-to-day practice, Radio Telefís Eireann has not as yet achieved the independent position of the British Broadcasting Corporation.

It may well be hard for it do so, for the urge to control is not confined to ministers and the majority party. In the words of the *Irish Times* (February 21, 1968): "anyone who has to deal with the business of communication suspects that were Labour and Fine Gael in Government as a coalition today we would have something of the same degree of meddling." There is, in this area, as David Thornley has pointed out, "an essential contradiction" between party politics and the proper role of a mass communications medium, particularly if it is in a monopoly position.

Politics is a game in which only one contender can win at any particular time. The politician therefore logically views the communication medium as the cockpit of contention; he is consequently only totally satisfied with it when he is able to use it to gain an advantage over his adversaries. A "good" station is a subservient one; a "good" programme is one from which he emerges victorious.[16]

The importance of RTE achieving its freedom can be judged when one considers the extent to which people are exposed to radio or TV programs with a political content. Analysis of the content of broadcast programs shows that the proportion that might have political content, i.e. mainly news, public affairs, and talks programs, is broadly similar to

---

[15] See Senator G. FitzGerald's catalogue of incidents, *Seanad Debates*, vol. 64, cols. 1333–48 (May 8, 1968), and vol. 65, cols. 81–98 (May 29, 1968).

[16] D. Thornley, "Television and Politics," *Administration*, XV 1967), 217–18.

TABLE 5.9

Content of Irish and British Radio Programs, 1966–67
(Year ended March 31, 1967)

Type of program	RTE Hours	RTE % of total	BBC Home service Hours	BBC Home service % of total	BBC Light program Hours	BBC Light program % of total
News { in Irish	196 } 877	{ 4 } 15 } 19%	890	14%	577	7%
News { in English	681 }					
Talks and features	482	10	1,632	26	335	5

Source: *Radio Telefís Eireann Annual Report, 1967*; and *Annual Report and Accounts of the British Broadcasting Corporation, 1966–67*, Appendix 11A.

TABLE 5.10

Content of Irish and British Television Programs, 1966–67

Type of program	RTE Hours in year	RTE % of total	BBC1 Hours in year	BBC1 % of total	ITA Hours in year	ITA % of total
News	215	10%	160	4%	242	7%
Talks, public affairs, documentaries	225	10.4	472	12	377	11

Source: *Radio Telefís Eireann Annual Report, 1967* (figures for 52 weeks ended March 31, 1967); *Annual Report and Accounts of the British Broadcasting Corporation, 1966–67*; and *Independent Television Authority Annual Report and Accounts, 1965–66*, p. 13 (52-week total calculated from weekly average).

that of the British Broadcasting Corporation and British Independent Television. Tables 5.9 and 5.10 give details. Since the freedom of the Authority to include whatever material it likes in such programs is considerable, and since Irish broadcasting is influenced by the British pattern and approach, it may be supposed that the Irish citizen has offered to him fare of a kind quite similar to that of his cross-channel neighbor.

To what exent is the fare consumed? Today, nearly all homes have a radio. A TAM[17] survey made in March 1967 showed that 96 per cent of all households had a radio, though there were some small class and regional differences. The importance of radio lies of course in the news, and particularly news broadcasts that fall outside television-viewing hours. In 1966 each of the two morning newscasts was listened to by almost 30 per cent of the adult population (age 15 and over); the 1:30

[17] TAM = Television Audience Measurement. Much of the information in this section is derived from material made available by Irish TAM Ltd. and by the Television Audience Research Service of Radio Telefís Eireann.

TABLE 5.11

Reliability of News Broadcast by Radio Telefís Eireann

Statement	Agree strongly	Agree	No opinion	Disagree	Disagree strongly
You can always depend on the news from RTE	18%	54%	15%	10%	3%
For reliable news, it is better to read the newspapers than listen to radio and television	6	9	8	50	27

Source: Data from survey entitled "A News Enquiry" (unpublished), made available by the Audience Research Service of Radio Telefís Eireann.

P.M. newscast by nearly one-half; the 6:30 newscast by 20 per cent; the 10:15 newscast by 10 per cent. Only 3 to 4 per cent listen to the news in Irish. In addition, a survey made early in 1967 showed that 32 per cent of those interviewed also listened sometimes to news from stations outside the Republic of Ireland, and 14 per cent more did so two or three times a week. Except for the news, however, only 4 to 6 per cent of the population listen to Irish radio programs during television broadcasting hours.

Television is by far the more important of the electronic mass media. This is because of the numbers who watch it and because of the fact that, according to many students of communications, it is the most potent and most likely to be trusted of the mass media, a belief apparently substantiated by the findings of RTE's Audience Research Service (see Table 5.11). Although only the very poorest homes, particularly in the country, are without radio, the pattern of television ownership is *as yet* very different, as Table 5.12 shows. It must be remembered that the number of households owning television is still growing in Ireland and had not by 1967 reached saturation point. Whereas about 80 per cent of urban homes had sets (except in Connacht and Ulster, where over two-thirds had one), set ownership in rural communities was far lower, falling to 25 per cent in the west and northwest. Furthermore, in urban areas, 79 per cent of white-collar workers (professional, salaried, or nonmanual wage earners) owned television sets and 77 per cent of manual workers did; in rural areas, on the contrary, 80 per cent of white-collar workers but only 34 per cent of farmers with 30 acres or more and 34 per cent of all others owned sets. The similarity of this pattern to the newspaper readership pattern revealed in Tables 5.5 and 5.6 is striking.

Radio and TV are complementary in use. Most people do not listen to radio when television is available; in any case, apart from the news, what is broadcast during the time that television is not available is almost

TABLE 5.12

Television Ownership in 1967 by Province and Community

Region	Percentage of households		
	All	Urban[a]	Rural[b]
Dublin City and County	77%	78%	69%
Rest of Leinster	55	78	45
Munster	54	78	39
Connacht and Ulster (part)	31	67	25

Source: Data made available by Irish TAM, Ltd.

[a] Urban: towns of 1,500 or over.

[b] Rural: country districts or towns of less than 1,500 population.

wholly nonpolitical material. Both for this reason and because of television's reputedly greater impact, it is television-viewing habits that most concern the student of politics. Many TV-owning households in Ireland, like those elsewhere, are avid watchers—or at least they tend to have their sets turned on for long periods. Audiences for regular programs that in 1967 were most likely to have an important political content are set out in Table 5.13. This shows that in early 1967 each TV newscast was seen by a quarter to more than a third of the entire adult community each day, that 30 per cent watched a weekly current affairs program, and

TABLE 5.13

Audiences for Television Programs Most Likely
to Have a Political Content
(Weekly averages for 13 weeks ended March 26, 1967)

Program	Day and time	Adult viewers[a]	Percentage of adults in television homes	Percentage of adults in community
News & Newsbeat	Monday–Friday 6:15–6:45 P.M.	485,000	42%	25.7%
News	Sunday 9:00–9:15 P.M.	701,000	60	37.1
News	Monday–Saturday 9:45–10:00 P.M.	654,000	56	34.6
Seven Days (current affairs)	Monday 8:45–9:30 P.M.	559,000	48	29.6
Division (political affairs)	Friday (3 times each month) 10:45–11:15 P.M.	304,000	27	16.1
The Politicians (discussion between party leaders)	Friday (once a month) 10:45–11:15 P.M.	235,000	20	12.4

Source: Compiled from information supplied by Audience Research Service of Radio Telefís Eireann and Irish TAM, Ltd.

[a] Adult = age 15 and over.

TABLE 5.14

Television Audiences for Party Political Broadcasts at Election Time

Election	Adult viewers	Percentage of adults in television homes	Percentage of adults in private households
General election, 1965 (14 party political broadcasts):			
Maximum viewing	525,000	54%	29%
Minimum viewing	401,000	41	22
Presidential election, 1966 (4 party political broadcasts):			
Maximum viewing	455,000	42	25
Minimum viewing	444,000	41	24

Source: Data made available by Irish TAM, Ltd.

that audiences for explicitly political programs late at night were from 12 to 16 per cent. At election times, the high point of community interest in politics, party political broadcasts attract far higher audiences than this (see Table 5.14), even averaging above the normal number of viewers for the times they were screened, and this in circumstances under which one-third of TV homes can switch to an alternative British program.

These figures are averages for the whole country, but set ownership is far from evenly spread. Thus, while considerable numbers of people in the east and in the towns are exposed continuously to programs with a political content, the great majority in the west and in the countryside generally are not.

v

The effect of the mass media upon political attitudes and behavior is a subject that has come to be widely recognized as among the most important and perplexing in modern politics. In the case of Ireland, very little indeed can be said because of the lack of data. We may suspect that the mass media actually communicate less to politicians about the feelings and desires of the public and less to the public about the whys and wherefores of ministerial action than either politicians or newsmen like to believe. Perhaps, as Rudolf Klein has argued,

Newspapers and politicians have an almost incestuous relationship: they tend to have closer ties with each other than the newspapers have with their readers and politicians have with their voters. The result is that they both tend to overestimate their influence on the country at large—when, in fact, their main influence is often on each other.[18]

18 *The Observer*, Apr. 7, 1968.

It should not be imagined that a free press and an independent radio and TV service are cast-iron guarantees of close contact and mutual understanding between the government and the governed. In some of the larger democracies, the problem of the remoteness of the government from the citizens has recently come to be seen as most urgent and basic for the future of democracy, despite the existence of mass media on a scale greater than ever before. The closer contacts between Irish ministers and rank-and-file deputies and party workers, which small scale makes possible, no doubt help them keep in touch in a way that perhaps is more difficult for the ministers of much larger countries. Even in Ireland, however, the failure of some ministers and some important sectional interests to see each other's point of view and the bewilderment and increasing frustration of a public that cannot understand what the real issues are seem to point, at the very least, to serious failures to communicate.

Some important contrasts in exposure, if not in communication, that *might* have political significance have emerged from this survey. These are the differences in exposure to the mass media between the people of the west and those of the east, between rural and urban people, and between farmers and those in nonagricultural occupations. Whatever impact the mass media have, e.g. in inculcating in the consumer the basic values of the community, in reinforcing the values and attitudes the individual has acquired in his community groups, or in introducing new ideas and values, has not been experienced by considerable numbers in the west, in the countryside, and in farming, for they have not had access to them. This deprivation probably has effects, though they are unmeasurable, far wider than its political effect, embracing social attitudes in general. The contrast presented in the figures thus raises an obvious question: is this high degree of nonexposure of rural, and particularly rural western, people to the national mass media a factor in the persistence of elements of a different and older political culture, to which attention was drawn earlier (see p. 51)? Relative poverty (unrelieved by adequate social policies) is a partial explanation of these exposure differences, for such differences are repeated in figures for the ownership of many consumer goods (e.g. refrigerators, vacuum cleaners, cameras). It follows that, with growing prosperity, the position may alter and these differences may disappear, as they have tended to do in many countries.

While it is impossible for lack of information to generalize about the impact of the mass media, let alone to measure the contrasts which we may suspect arise from differing degrees of exposure, there is a small amount of information about Dubliners. A survey of the political attitudes of Dubliners, carried out in 1966 by students of the Institute of

TABLE 5.15

Political Interest and Knowledge

Category	Dublin	U.S.	U.K.	Germany	Italy	Mexico
Proportion of people following accounts of political affairs:						
Regularly	30%	27%	23%	34%	11%	15%
From time to time	41	53	45	38	26	40
Never	29	19	32	25	62	44
Other and don't know	—	1	1	3	1	1
Proportion able to name some party leaders (7 asked for from major parties):						
Four or more	64	65	42	69	36	5
None	5	16	20	12	40	53

Source: Dublin—Munger Survey (not yet published). U.S., etc.—G. Almond and S. Verba, *The Civic Culture* (Princeton, 1963), pp. 89, 96.

Note: In the Almond and Verba survey, the samples in the cases of the U.S., the U.K., Germany, and Italy included both urban and rural people. Only in the case of Mexico was the survey confined to townspeople.

Public Administration under the direction of Professor Frank Munger of Syracuse University, provided material that may be compared with that in Almond and Verba, *The Civic Culture,* a study based on surveys made in five democratic countries with differing levels of development and different historical experiences. Although it does not prove anything about the effects of reading newspapers or watching television, it does suggest that the Dubliner, who is the most exposed of all Irishmen to "modernizing" influences of all sorts, approximates quite closely in the extent of his political interest and knowledge to the citizens of the most industrialized and modern of the five democratic countries surveyed by Almond and Verba (see Table 5.15).

Political communication, however, is a two-way process. The purpose of this chapter has been to show that Irish people have very different degrees of access, according to region, community, and class, to the mass media, which may be among the most potent of the influences that help form and affect people's political attitudes and behavior. In a democracy the feedback includes those most important of all political signals, election results. What we know of political inputs does not as yet permit us to explain the resultant output, people's political behavior, and particularly their votes. Between this chapter and the next, therefore, there is a formidable gap, the measure of our lack of understanding of political behavior.

SIX

Elections

In earlier chapters we examined the various organizations in the community that express the political desires of their members and compete with one another for their many political ends. Prominent among these are the political parties. In *Political Oppositions in Western Democracies*,[1] Robert Dahl identifies a number of "sites" where party encounters take place and categorizes states according to the relative importance of these sites. In this respect Ireland resembles the United Kingdom, for in Ireland the parliamentary elections are where political parties fight their most important battles and where victory or defeat is usually decisive.

Formally, the Constitution assigns to the Dáil the function of choosing a Taoiseach and approving a government. In practice, general elections to the Dáil usually determine which party or group of parties shall form the government, while the Dáil merely ratifies a decision already made. That a party or coalition of parties should win a majority of seats at a general election and form a government is in practice also the condition of achieving an almost exclusive power to change state policies, for that is the power of the government. It is "a condition that is ordinarily both necessary and sufficient."[2] Government in this style is quite distinctive, and we shall identify its characteristics in later chapters. Here we are concerned with the decisive battle site, the election. This is not to say that other sites are unimportant or that "elections make a democracy." However, elections usually do make governments with a monopoly of initiative in policy decisions and with great power to get their decisions accepted in the Oireachtas.

The major issue of general elections tends to be who is to form the

---

[1] Robert A. Dahl, ed., *Political Oppositions in Western Democracies* (New Haven and London, 1966).
[2] *Ibid.*, p. 339.

next government, and this affects electoral strategy and behavior. A natural consequence of the fact that elections are for governments—that the electorate will be presented by the contending parties with clear alternatives—has not always occurred. At general elections up to 1937, and again in 1951, 1954, and 1957, there was a clear choice between two viable alternatives, in the first period between the Pro-Treaty party (Cumann na nGaedheal) and the Anti-Treaty party (Fianna Fáil) and, in the second, between Fianna Fáil and a coalition of the rest. In 1948 a coalition was mooted and effected after the results were known. At the elections from 1938 to 1944, however, and again at the 1961 and 1965 elections, no workable alternative was presented because of the unwillingness of parties to cooperate or form an alliance, and the only question was: will Fianna Fáil obtain a working majority or not?

II

If general elections are for governments, it is often argued, election systems should be judged by their propensity to produce effective governments. For many, however, the most important criteria of an election system are elector satisfaction, substantial equality between one voter and another, and the reflection of as many opinions as possible. For those who hold this view, the Irish election system is of great importance, for it offers a case study in the working of a system that in theory is directed toward these very ends. In addition, general elections are elections to Dáil Eireann and one might reasonably ask: does the system help or hinder the production of an assembly that is competent for its job?

The system used in general elections to the Dáil and which is also used in elections for the Seanad and for local authorities, is proportional representation by means of the single transferable vote in multi-member constituencies. This is the system that has been so strongly advocated in English-speaking countries for eighty years or more by the Proportional Representation Society (now the Electoral Reform Society) that it is almost always known in the United Kingdom and Ireland simply as "Proportional Representation" or "PR," as though there were no other proportional systems.

At first it might seem strange that a state whose political institutions and procedures derive from British practice should have adopted any proportional representation system, let alone a system that, for all its theoretical attraction, has been very little used. In 1968 Ireland and Malta were the only countries whose national representative assemblies were elected according to this system. That Ireland adopted PR was due to the fact that at the Treaty both the leaders of the independence movement and the British Government were in favor of it. Owing to the activities of the Proportional Representation Society, the single transferable vote system was being much canvassed in the United Kingdom in the early part of the century. On the Irish side, it was espoused by Arthur Griffith, who was a founder member of the Proportional Representation Society of Ireland, and adopted as an aim by the Sinn Féin movement to provide proper minority representation. On the British side, it was adopted for Ireland in the Home Rule Bill of 1914 and in subsequent legislation for Ireland as a device to ensure full representation for minority, i.e. Protestant and unionist, opinion. The single transferable vote was first used in December 1918 in the two-member Dublin University constituency. The first real PR election in Ireland took place in January 1919 in Sligo, where the Corporation was elected as provided in the Sligo Corporation Act of the previous year. In the negotiations leading up to the Treaty in December 1921, the leader of the Irish plenipotentiaries, Arthur Griffith, promised the adoption of PR in elections to the Dáil as one of the safeguards for the Southern Unionists, and the Irish Free State Constitution made provision for it.

Under this system, the elector casts a single transferable vote, that is, a vote given in such a way as to indicate the voter's preference for candidates in order. If the voter so indicates, this vote can be transferred from a choice to a next choice when it is not required to give the prior choice the necessary quota of votes to secure election or when, owing to the poor support given for the prior choice, that choice is eliminated from the contest. The voter does this by placing numbers against the names of the candidates on the ballot paper in the order of his choice. He need not vote for all the candidates, but he must number his preferences continuously, 1, 2, 3, etc. To ascertain who has been elected, votes are initially sorted according to first preferences and any candidate who obtains the "quota" or more is elected. The quota used in Irish elections is the "Droop quota," so called because it was propounded by H. R. Droop in 1869. It is the smallest number of votes that suffices to elect enough candidates to fill all the seats being contested while being just big enough to prevent any more being elected. It is expressed in the following formula:

$$\text{Quota} = \frac{\text{No. of valid votes}}{\text{No. of seats} + 1} + 1 \, .$$

If, as is usually the case, the first count does not result in the necessary number of candidates getting a quota, a process of transferring votes takes place in subsequent counts until all the seats are filled. First, the "excess votes" of any candidate—i.e., votes not needed by him—are distributed proportionally to the second or next available choices of his supporters. When no surpluses remain to be distributed and there are seats still to be filled, the candidate with the fewest votes is eliminated and his votes are redistributed according to the next available preferences indicated. This process continues until all the places are filled. A fuller description of the system and of the procedures of an Irish election is given in Appendix E.

When a country has an election system that is said to be a proportional representation system, much attention is naturally paid to equality of representation. One of the key factors in the proportionality of the single transferable vote system is the number of seats in each constituency. The bigger the constituency and the greater the number of members it returns, the more closely will the results approximate to proportionality. The Constitution provides only that "no law shall be enacted whereby the number of members to be returned for any constituency shall be less than three." In other respects, however, it makes specific provision for equal representation, for it requires that "the total number of members of Dáil Eireann shall not be fixed at less than one member for each 30,000 of the population, or at more than one member for each 20,000 of the population," and that the ratio between the number of members for each constituency and its population "shall, so far as it is practicable, be the same throughout the country." The Constitution further requires that the constituencies shall be revised according to these principles at least once in every twelve years.

In practice, convenience has led governments to stretch constitutional provisions to the utmost, and on one occasion too far. Until recently, as Table 6.1 shows, there was a marked tendency for governments to break up the bigger constituencies and to increase the number of three-member constituencies at successive constituency revisions. This was done deliberately and was frankly justified in the Dáil on the ground that "it is made easier for a party which may be called upon to shoulder the responsibility of government to get sufficient seats to enable them to undertake that task with adequate parliamentary support."[3]

Convenience of another sort, this time the convenience of deputies and their constituents (together with a strong rural bias among the deputies), led successive governments on the occasion of constituency revisions to sacrifice mathematical accuracy in order to favor rural areas—especially the western seaboard areas, which have been steadily losing population—

[3] *Dáil Debates*, vol. 108, col. 924 (Oct. 23, 1947). See also vol. 51, col. 1283 (Mar. 23, 1934).

TABLE 6.1

Constituencies and Members

Electoral Act	Number of constituencies	Number of members per constituency							Total number of members	Average number of persons per member
		9	8	7	6	5	4	3		
1923	30	1	3	5	–	9	4	8	153	21,358
1935	34	–	–	3	–	8	8	15	138	21,536
1947	40	–	–	–	–	9	9	22	147	20,103
1959a	39	–	–	–	–	9	9	21	144	20,127
1961	38	–	–	–	–	9	12	17	144	20,127
1969	42	–	–	–	–	2	14	26	144	20,028

Source: *Report of the Committee on the Constitution*, December 1967. Figures for 1959 and 1969 added.

a Some sections of this Act were held to be repugnant to the Constitution, and it never operated. The scheme it envisaged was replaced by that laid out in the 1961 Act.

as against Dublin, whose population has been increasing rapidly. With each revision this became more marked, while, in addition, the average ratio of members to population was kept to the lowest constitutional limit. Consequently, many constituencies were below the constitutional limit and with the passage of time became more so.

The least favored constituencies have always been in and around Dublin, the most favored in the west. Indeed, by the 1959 Electoral Act the western counties of Donegal, Galway, Mayo, and Kerry, with a 1951 population of 532,736, returned 30 deputies (one deputy to 17,758), whereas the city of Dublin, with a population of 568,838, returned only 25 deputies (one deputy to 22,753). However, this time the government had gone too far. In 1961, some sections of that Act were declared unconstitutional by the High Court (*O'Donovan* v. *Attorney General*, 1961, I.R.114) on the grounds that the ratio of population to seats in each constituency was not as near as possible to the national average, as the Constitution requires, thus causing substantial inequalities, and that the government when revising the constituencies had not paid due regard to changes in the distribution of population as required by the Constitution. The subsequent act, the Electoral (Amendment) Act of 1961, went a long way toward eliminating the inequalities sanctioned by the 1959 Act. However, the constant movement of population from the countryside, and especially the west, to Dublin and its environs means that inequalities continually develop and grow. The 1966 census revealed that Dublin County had over 29,000 people for each member and two other Dublin constituencies over 27,000, while declining areas like Mayo, Roscommon, Sligo, and Leitrim had fewer than 17,000 for each member. Nevertheless, an attempt by the government in 1968 to alter the Constitution to allow a greater "tolerance," and to permit considerations such as community boundaries and the convenience of TD's in servicing their constituents to be taken into account when fixing constituency boundaries, was rejected by the people in a referendum. The subsequent Electoral (Amendment) Act, 1969, once again eliminated inequalities, though only at the expense of ignoring county boundaries to a far greater extent than ever before. However, it is clear that unless the Constitution is amended, frequent readjustments must continue to be made.

Clearly, substantial mathematical equality is a desirable thing in the eyes of many, besides remaining in any case the constitutional requirement. Equally clearly, there is much strength in the arguments used in the O'Donovan case and subsequently by the government: that since deputies are required to keep in continuous touch with their constituents to help them secure their rights in housing, health, and other social services and in connection with agricultural subsidies and grants, it is necessary to have a higher ratio of members to population on the western seaboard in order to achieve substantial (as opposed to numerical) equality.

III

The tendency for politicians willy-nilly to be concerned with local matters and the personal affairs of their constituents, together with the comparative weakness of party organizations, has important effects on election practices, as regards both the nomination of candidates and the waging of campaigns.

The two biggest parties have always operated on a national scale, usually with candidates in every constituency and in numbers sufficient to provide a majority.[4] The Labour Party is altogether smaller and has tended to be a regional party, with its strength mainly in rural areas of the east and south. Other parties have tended to be either regional— as, for example, Clann na Talmhan, which was based on small western farmer support—or nationalist and radical in their inspiration and able to rally the support of a minority wherever a leader or a small group of active people emerged. The persistence of Independent candidates is due to the opportunities the election system offers, particularly in the larger constituencies, in a social situation where personal and local elements have considerable weight in politics. The system allows electors to combine in groups that do not coincide with established party divisions and to back candidates who are not necessarily party choices. In these cir-

---

4 For details of candidates and elected members, see Table B.4, p. 333.

cumstances, the unionist minority, although it did not form a party, returned candidates in the first years of the state's existence. In these circumstances also, party rebels have been elected and might be again; "Independent Farmers" have been given local support, often connected with some agricultural organization; personalities have had safe seats, and one of them, Alderman "Alfy" Byrne, a former Lord Mayor of Dublin, actually founded a family dynasty. Even oddities have in the past slipped into a fifth seat. Probably the most famous of these, and certainly the strangest, was Thomas Burke, a member for County Clare from 1933 to 1951, who was locally famous as a "bone-setter" and whose appeal for votes was made frankly on the grounds of medical services rendered.

Because parties have small and comparatively undeveloped central offices and lack funds, candidates depend greatly on their own efforts and on those of their local supporters. Formal party organization at the local level is often vestigial between elections, many branches having but a shadowy existence. Some TD's build more active organizations, but significantly these are often as much their own as those of the party. At election times, all these organizations spring to life, the level of their activity depending on the enthusiasm and energy of the candidate or key branch officials. To a great extent they are on their own, and they know it. Consequently, the control the central party organization exercises over the activities of the local organizations is comparatively small. This can be seen both in the selection of candidates and in the conduct of campaigns.

In selecting candidates, the initiative rests to a large extent with the local constituency organizations, though the national executives of the parties decide how many candidates shall be put forward in each constituency, an important matter if the party's strength is to be exploited to the full. Candidates are selected at constituency conventions at which representatives of each branch in the constituency put forward names and ballot on them. These meetings, which might comprise up to 400 delegates, are presided over by chairmen (often party leaders) selected by the national executives. Nominations have to be ratified by the national executives, which have the right to add names. However, this is usually so fiercely resented in the constituency that they are slow to do it. It is, therefore, the job of these chairmen to guide the deliberations and decisions of the conventions in such a way that local differences are composed, a suitable team of candidates is selected, and the wishes of the national executive are followed.

In selecting candidates, the two major parties in particular have an eye to covering the constituency effectively, and of course local branches are anxious to get a local candidate if they can. Consequently, the tendency is to choose candidates from different parts of the constituency, often according to its natural divisions. Although a party's candidates are formally a team, in the rural constituencies particularly each candidate tends to have his own territory and his own following and does not invade the territory of a teammate.

To some extent, the Labour Party resembles the two biggest parties, but control over where candidates should stand has in the past seemed to rest more with local branches. Until the late 1960's, when the party increased its scale of activities considerably, there was in most cases only one candidate in a constituency and the party did not contest all constituencies. In the smaller parties, the decision to put up a candidate rests entirely with a local branch and usually depends upon funds. The choice of candidates in these parties, as of Independent candidates, is therefore a local, even personal, matter.

Consequently, although the law does not require it, candidates are predominantly local men in the sense that they live and belong in their constituencies. In the 1957 election, for example, only 30 of the 288 candidates had their residences outside the constituencies they were contesting, and of these 30, thirteen were ministers, former ministers, or national heroes. Many, and perhaps most, candidates live in or are identified with a particular part of the constituency where they have a following and which they regard as their area. Only a man with a "national record" or a minister, or a relative of such, can expect to be adopted in a constituency in which he does not live or with which he has no close ties. As a result, most candidates for rural constituencies are countrymen, and there are very few urban carpetbaggers. Dublin middle-class professional people, particularly lawyers, with political ambitions are therefore considerably hampered, for they must usually find seats in Dublin itself. This requirement of local residence has a marked effect on the composition and competence of the Dáil.

Because local government is dominated by party politics and because local government service is an important route to parliamentary office, many candidates are members of local authorities. Since this is a stable and conservative society, great account is taken of seniority and record of service. Many candidates are, therefore, councilors of some seniority, for they must often earn their nomination by long and assiduous devotion to their constituents' interests in local government matters. It is possible, however, for a person with the right name and connections to achieve the same results by inheritance, or for a famous footballer, who is a hero in his county, to have candidature and office thrust upon him. Only from the middle 1960's, when a general desire for a change from the old ways and a concern with social and economic issues were evident, were there signs that youth of itself was other than a positive disadvantage.

IV

The campaigns waged by these locally selected and usually local candidates have also tended to be to a considerable extent self-contained and self-sufficient, with the central organization of the big parties playing only a supporting role. The three major parties provide their candidates with a small amount of financial help, some national publicity, and some advice in the form of election handbooks and "Notes for Speakers."

Financial help varies, but in general all constituency party organizations are expected to finance their own campaigns. Fianna Fáil guarantees its candidates' deposits and usually loses very few. The expenses of some candidates, Labour and other, are met from trade union funds. Fine Gael candidates seem to be virtually on their own.

Until 1965, the campaign at the national level was waged with two main weapons, party leaders and posters. The speaking tours of the party leaders are an established feature of Irish elections. By tradition, the leaders are expected to visit certain regional centers, and offense would be caused if they did not. The ceremony of these visits is time-honored; while De Valera was active, they were old-fashioned and impressive, with torchlight processions and bands. By tradition, also, the leaders address mass meetings in Dublin on the eve of the poll. In 1965 television was available for the first time, and the parties paid greater attention to party political broadcasts than they ever did with radio. The parties have radio and TV time allotted by agreement. Their use of radio has always been very poor; by British standards their use of television in 1965 was also amateur and they had not yet learned how to exploit the medium.

The main parties have usually issued party programs, sometimes in very general terms. When social and economic matters loomed large in the 1965 election, all the parties produced programs and plans, but since to most people they must have looked very alike, it is doubtful whether they swung many votes or made much impact. Typically in the past, campaigns have been waged on the issues and events connected with the civil war. Early elections, up to and including 1933, were often conducted in an atmosphere of tension. In 1932 and 1933, indeed, many believed that a coup d'état was possible and the end of democratic processes quite likely. Long after the constitutional issues involved were settled or dead, they still dominated electioneering in a ritual that took the form of charge and countercharge with the civil war, the Oath, and the Commonwealth being dragged out of Irish history and exacerbated by personal animosity. These were the coinage of Irish elections until the late 1950's. Even in 1957, De Valera felt impelled to defend himself on the radio against a newspaper charge about actions 30 years before.

Only in recent years have social and economic issues—growth rates, planning, and the social services—come to be the major national talking points, and even here the parties are not easily pinpointed on a left-right spectrum, socialist to conservative. Prosperity might help the government, recession do it harm. To a few, one party might seem to be more concerned with improving social services than another, but for most there have been few national issues on which to fasten. The only persistent theme of recent years has in fact been an institutional one, the desirability of one-party governments as against coalitions. At every election since 1948, when a coalition government was formed, Fianna Fáil has tried to establish this as an issue, arguing that coalition government is necessarily weak and indecisive.

National issues and activities designed to influence electors at large are, however, a backdrop against which a candidate seeks the support of his locality. His best asset by far is his record of service in his own district. Here, naturally, the sitting deputy has a great advantage, for he can offer—and in many cases has already given—service as a contact man and advocate at central government level as well as at the County Council offices. Although a good record of service is an asset to anyone and is the foundation of the position of many deputies of the small parties and Independents, the candidates of the main parties use it chiefly not against political opponents of other parties, but against their fellow candidates of the same party. Under the single transferable vote system in multi-member constituencies, candidates of the same party are in competition with one another for a relatively fixed number of votes. A candidate cannot fight his fellow candidate on policy; he tries to seem a more assiduous and more successful servant of his constituents. Politicians know this well and act accordingly. A former leader of the Labour Party put it thus: "the service which a candidate gives to his constituents prior to the election determines in large measure the vote which he secures in an election."[5]

For this reason, a candidate's election address, a copy of which is delivered free by post to each elector, always includes a short autobiography laying out meticulously the public positions he has held and the voluntary organizations of which he is a member. In the past some have

[5] Deputy William Norton, quoted in D. E. Butler, ed., *Elections Abroad* (London, 1959), chap. 3 by B. Chubb, p. 202.

listed the benefits the candidate alleges he has obtained for his district.

Concentration on the personal and local is more evident in the rural areas than in the big cities, and this can be seen particularly in canvassing activities. All candidates and all party officials believe that canvassing is the most effective method of electioneering, but whereas in the city it does not matter much who the canvassers are, in the villages and in the countryside the candidate himself must personally approach all supporters of consequence in his area and as many others as he can besides. In turn, his prominent supporters seek the votes of their neighbors. Thus links in a chain of personal approach are forged, a matter of necessity in dealing with a rural population, which values face-to-face contacts, which regards personal influence as an important factor in the conduct of any business of importance, and which likes to feel that a potentially influential man has asked a favor and is obligated.

Although election meetings have declined in number and importance in the urban areas, the pattern in the countryside is uniform and comparatively unchanging, being dictated by the pattern of social intercourse. Throughout the country the meeting at the church gate after Mass is the most important—and perhaps the only—opportunity of reaching everyone. Regardless of the political affiliations of the speaker, most people stay and listen attentively. Even in the towns and cities, these are the best opportunities of getting a worthwhile audience. In the rural areas the local market is also an important opportunity to reach sizable audiences.

For most people exposure to election propaganda has probably been low, at least until recently. This is a matter of conjecture, for no studies of any sort have been made. In the cities and big towns it has comprised a few election addresses, a few posters and advertisements, possibly a canvasser or two, the daily or evening paper if one is taken and read, and on polling day loudspeaker vans. In the country it can rarely have been more than a couple of election addresses; very few posters; possibly a visit from the candidate, more likely from a locally prominent supporter; after-Mass meetings; and, for some, market day meetings. As the newspaper readership figures in Table 5.5 show (p. 131), many country people (in Connacht and Ulster more than 60 per cent of the population) do not see a daily newspaper and are likely to see only a Sunday paper and the local weekly. Party political broadcasts on the radio probably reach very few, for most people do not listen to Radio Eireann in the evenings. On the other hand, television broadcasts in 1965 were seen by a far larger number of voters, although at that time television was installed in rather less than half the homes in the country (see p. 142). But, of course, exposure to television varied considerably between the east and the west and between the city and the countryside.

v

The effect of all this electioneering on the voters is to a great extent unknown, for there have been no pre-election polls or surveys. Only the published election results are available, and it is impossible to learn much about local community voting behavior from this source. However, the published results do give for constituencies the number of valid and invalid votes, the number of votes each candidate received at each stage, and the number of transfers and nontransferable votes. From these data it is possible to make a few observations.

The percentage of electors who vote (the turnout) has varied from 62 per cent in 1922 and 61 per cent in 1923, when unsettled conditions obtained, to 81 per cent at the 1933 election, where there was great excitement and tension. Since the 1930's, when polls were generally high (76 to 81 per cent), the turnout has been between 70 and 75 per cent. Regional differences are well marked and have been consistent over the years. The lowest polls occur in Dublin and its surrounding urban area (and to a lesser extent in Cork city), and in the western seaboard counties of Donegal and Mayo and parts of Galway and Kerry. The low polls in and around Dublin are partly due no doubt to the fact that the population is more mobile, but it is noticeable that these areas are also more volatile in their voting habits (above the average rise in 1965; above the average fall in 1957). This suggests that living in or near the city has an effect on people's propensity to vote. The low turnout in the west is probably due largely to two factors. First, some people who are registered are not in fact in residence. These include seasonal workers in Great Britain and people who have in fact emigrated, but whose names are kept on the register. Second, difficulties of communication and consequent lower political interest contribute to lower turnout. However, it is noticeable that southwest Cork, with quite similar geographical features to other western counties, often has a high turnout, while neighboring south Kerry, with a long tradition of support for radical agrarian policies and a tendency to support extreme candidates, has a low turnout. The highest polls occur in two of the Ulster border counties, Cavan and Monaghan, where, significantly, people have good reason to be politically self-conscious, and in the southwest, in Tipperary and some parts of County Cork, which, perhaps again significantly, were among the main centers of nationalism and military activity in the independence struggle between 1919 and 1921.

What little can be learned from the published results about the habits of those who do vote suggests a number of hypotheses, though—in the absence of survey data—these must be very tentative. First, it is apparent that Irish electors are strongly oriented to their parties. Throughout the history of the state never fewer than six and usually seven or eight out of ten of all electors have supported one or the other of the two major parties and another one has supported the Labour Party. Moreover, analyses of the results of the elections of 1957, 1961, and 1965 show that almost all electors who gave their first preferences to major party candidates elected at the first count gave their second preferences to other candidates of the same party. For Fianna Fáil it was 88.0 per cent in 1957, 83.3 per cent in 1961, and 88.2 per cent in 1965; and for Fine Gael it was 82.0 per cent in 1957, 80.6 per cent in 1961, and 85.5 per cent in 1965. In other words, they seem to have exhibited loyalty to the party as such. Electors who support smaller parties do not have such an opportunity, but there is some evidence that these voters too are influenced by their party's advice. For example, when the Sinn Féin Party appealed to its supporters in 1957 not to give lower preferences to candidates of other parties, the number of votes that became nontransferable as Sinn Féin candidates were eliminated was very much higher than normal.

Besides clear evidence of support for political parties as such, there is some evidence of general movements to and from the major parties. Because of the presence of candidates of smaller parties and Independents, it is not possible to talk in terms of anything so uniform as "swing." Moreover, too many other local and personal factors may be operating for the change in a party's share of the poll in a constituency ever to be fully explained by a national or even regional phenomenon of this sort. Nevertheless, in most elections since the Second World War the rise and fall of support for the major parties was broadly on a national scale, i.e. when a party gained, it gained almost everywhere, and vice versa. (See, for example, Fig. 3.1, p. 80.)

Although party loyalty seems strong, it does not follow that a party is able to dictate its supporters' choice between candidates. On the contrary, there is abundant evidence that voters use the freedom of the election system to take other factors into account. Most electors, all those who are Fianna Fáil or Fine Gael and some Labour supporters, have a choice between two or more candidates of their party, and the party does not try to influence the order of their choice. These candidates, it must be repeated, are as much in competition with their fellow party candidates as with candidates of other parties, and they try to build up and hold a body of support which is their own and which they foster carefully. Some rural deputies seem to know to a surprisingly accurate degree exactly who their supporters are.

People tend to give their first preference to the senior and best known of the party team or to the candidate from their own district, whom they are likely to know. They also take into account the candidate's reputation for serving his constituents. The politicians know this, and the election figures sometimes bear striking testimony to it. Members might and do lose seats because they cease to pay attention to their constituents or because a fellow candidate shows himself to be more assiduous (see Table 6.2). Even senior party members and former ministers have lost popularity and their seats in this way.

Personal and local factors, too, explain the success in the past of farmer candidates (whether in a farmer's party or not) and of Independents generally. These rely particularly on their reputation for serving their constituents. In Dublin there have often been one or more such members, whose position has been entirely based on "citizen's advice" type of service and on success in obtaining public housing and other benefits. For this reason, also, some deputies who have broken with their parties have nevertheless retained their seats. However, the number of Independents and quasi-Independents (the members of the smallest parties) has been falling and is now at its lowest ever. In 1965, they were all but wiped out, and it may be becoming increasingly difficult for an Independent to win a seat, or to hold a seat once won, hard work notwithstanding.

The importance of personal factors can perhaps be seen as clearly as anywhere in the appeal of sports and in the vote-drawing power of personal sympathy for a bereavement. Increasingly, prominence in Gaelic games has replaced "a national record" as a vote catcher, a fact that the parties have exploited. The Dáil is more and more studded with former Gaelic stars. Perhaps, however, the more striking example of the influence of personal factors on electors is the "sympathy vote" that serves to

TABLE 6.2

Changes in Candidates' Popularity at General Elections

Candidates	1954 and 1957	1961 and 1965
Number of pairs or trios who stood in consecutive elections	51	49
Number of cases where order of popularity changed	15	13
Number of cases where loss of popularity was followed by loss of seat[a]	6	8

[a] It cannot be said that a member lost his seat solely because his popularity declined and his opponent's increased. Other factors might have played a part, e.g., intervention of other candidates of the same party or a new candidate from his own district.

put a son or a widow into a dead man's seat, which can be retained at subsequent elections if he or she works hard. The last five by-elections before the 1965 general election saw the return of three widows and one son. Of these four relatives, three held their seats at the general election and one did not stand. This strengthens an already strong dynastic element in Irish politics. At the 1965 election, 41 of the elected members (28 per cent) were connected with former or already sitting deputies. One of the most striking cases of the sympathy vote was the election of E. O hAnnluain (Sinn Féin) in Monaghan in 1957. He almost certainly owed his election to the fact that his brother had been killed taking part in an IRA raid shortly before.

VI

How do Irish elections measure up to the criteria that were identified at the beginning of this chapter? First, elector satisfaction, equality, and accurate representation. It is often said (in English-speaking countries at least) that it takes too long to count the votes and declare the results under this system and that it is too complicated for the ordinary person. In fact, all the counts are usually completed within 48 hours. However, in 1965, when it was possible for the first time to demand a full recount (i.e. of all counts completed and not the last completed count only), two disputed elections took five days to resolve, owing largely to the fact that candidates and their agents scrutinized each ballot paper closely. As for complexity, the electors at least do not seem to have found it difficult to do what is required of them. An average of under one per cent of invalid votes compares well with the lowest European results.[6]

TABLE 6.3

Percentage of Voters Whose First-Preference Choices
Were Elected at General Elections

Area	1957	1961	1965
Whole country	70%	70%	73%
Highest constituency percentage	86	87	86
Lowest constituency percentage	51	51	56

The percentage of electors who see their first choices elected and—provided the choice put before them is adequate—can be presumed to be satisfied is high. As Table 6.3 shows, in the 1957, 1961, and 1965 elections it was 70 per cent or over. On the other hand, in these same three elec-

6 See Table B.3, p. 332, for details.

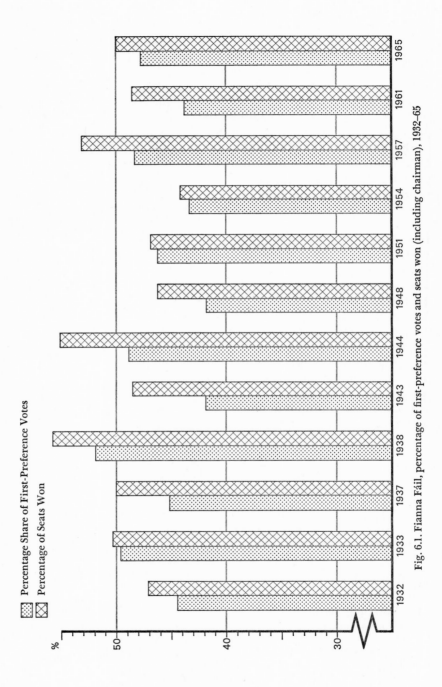

Fig. 6.1. Fianna Fáil, percentage of first-preference votes and seats won (including chairman), 1932–65

Percentage Share of First-Preference Votes

Percentage of Seats Won

tions the percentages of votes that did not help elect anyone were as follows: 23.7 per cent in 1957, 22.4 per cent in 1961, and 21.6 per cent in 1965. However, these were not all "wasted" votes, since 4 per cent in 1957, 5 per cent in 1961, and 3 per cent in 1965 of the total valid poll became nontransferable, which represents a deliberate choice by voters to abstain if their first choices were not used.

Undoubtedly, however, the most important criterion for many is that of proportionality: are the seats won by each party proportional to the votes cast for that party? As the system has worked so far in Irish conditions, Fianna Fáil and (until 1965) Fine Gael have consistently won a few more seats than their first-preference votes entitled them to, and Labour usually fewer. (Table 6.4 gives details.) In the case of small parties, those that put up a large number of candidates fare badly, whereas those with a small number of locally popular candidates have usually done well.

The reason the big parties do better than their share of first-preference votes warrants is because, having put up more than one candidate in each constituency and having obtained a good share of the total poll, they usually have candidates still available in the later stages of the count. These candidates attract lower-preference support. As Figure 6.1 shows, this "bonus" has long been of critical importance to Fianna Fáil, for the party has had to rely on it to get an absolute majority or to get near enough to be able to form a government. Because it is a vital point and probably an unpredictable one, Irish elections tend inexorably to resolve themselves into a single question: will Fianna Fáil get a majority?

In Ireland the production of effective governments, the second criterion of a good election system, means a Dáil in which one group of party leaders has a stable majority. Following the British tradition, party leaders have looked for certain majorities as a condition of assuming responsibility and have never had to govern for any length of time in conditions in which their measures might be defeated while they themselves remained. Usually, too, but not always, they have thought in terms of strict competition and single-party governments, though, as much European experience shows, this is not necessary to effective government. A result of this sort is not of course produced by election systems alone. Political habits and political divisions in the country must also be conducive to it. What an election system might do is to facilitate single-party rule, perhaps at the price of equality, or to thwart it by making it easier for small groups. Table 6.5 shows the frequency with which single-party governments have been produced. It reveals that single-party governments with majorities have alternated with single-party governments

TABLE 6.4

Index of Proportionality for Major Parties, Elections 1923–65

Year	Fianna Fáil	Fine Gael	Labour
1923	104	105	79
1927 (1)	111	110	115
1927 (2)	107	105	96
1932	108	106	61
1933	101	104	92
1937	110	102	93
1938	107	99	66
1943	115	100	79
1944	111	106	68
1948	110	107	110
1951	101	105	94
1954	102	107	100
1957	110	102	85
1961	112	103	90
1965	105	97	96

Source: C. O'Leary, *The Irish Republic and Its Experiment with Proportional Representation* (South Bend, Indiana, 1961), pp. 50–52, brought up to date.

Note: The value for each party at each election is arrived at by taking seats won as a percentage of the seats that would have been won had full proportionality operated. Full proportionality equals 100.

dependent on allies (usually dependable allies and camp-followers), or on two occasions with coalitions. The average duration of governments (three years) is by no means short by European standards, as the following tabulation of governments since the Second World War indicates:[7]

Australia	7.0	Norway	3.3	Denmark	2.1
Canada	5.2	Ireland	3.0	Belgium	1.2
Sweden	5.0	Austria	2.3	Finland	1.0
New Zealand	4.4	Luxembourg	2.3	Italy	0.9
United Kingdom	3.3	Iceland	2.3	France	0.7
Germany	3.3	Netherlands	2.2		

However, although governments composed of the members of a single party have been formed on fourteen out of sixteen occasions, only in seven cases had they absolute majorities of their own supporters, and two of these arose from the fact that the members of the major opposition party did not take their seats. Furthermore, though the failure of a party to get an absolute majority has by no means meant that it could not govern with comparative ease, owing to the support of dependable allies, on four occasions it has led to a second election following closely

[7] J. Blondel, "Party Systems and Patterns of Government in Western Democracies," *Canadian Journal of Political Science*, I (1968), 191.

TABLE 6.5

Nature of Governments, 1922–65

Election	Government	Single-party government with majority of own supporters	Single-party government w/o majority of own supporters	Coalition	Duration
1922	Pro-Treaty[a]	×[b]			11 mos.
1923	Cumann na nGaedheal	×[b]			3 yrs., 8 mos.
1927(1)	Cumann na nGaedheal		×		2 mos.
1927(2)	Cumann na nGaedheal		×[c]		4 yrs., 3 mos.
1932	Fianna Fáil		×		10 mos.
1933	Fianna Fáil	×			4 yrs., 4 mos.
1937	Fianna Fáil		×		10 mos.
1938	Fianna Fáil	×			5 yrs.
1943	Fianna Fáil		×		11 mos.
1944	Fianna Fáil	×			3 yrs., 7 mos.
1948	Inter-Party[d]			×	3 yrs., 2 mos.
1951	Fianna Fáil		×		2 yrs., 10 mos.
1954	Inter-Party[e]			×	2 yrs., 8 mos.
1957	Fianna Fáil[f]	×			4 yrs., 5 mos.
1961	Fianna Fáil		×		3 yrs., 5 mos.
1965	Fianna Fáil	×[g]			3 yrs., 5 mos.

[a] From spring 1923 called Cumann na nGaedheal.

[b] Government majority was due to the fact that the biggest opposition party (Fianna Fáil) did not take their seats.

[c] Although the government (i.e., cabinet) consisted of members of a single party, Cumann na nGaedheal, that party had a formal agreement with the Farmers' Party, and one Farmers' Party member held a post of Parliamentary Secretary.

[d] A coalition of all parties except Fianna Fáil.

[e] A coalition of Fine Gael, the Labour Party, and Clann na Talmhan.

[f] In 1959 Eamon de Valera was elected President and was succeeded as Taoiseach by Seán F. Lemass without an election.

[g] Fianna Fáil won exactly half the seats.

on the first. Thus, it is apparent that though the single transferable vote system has favored the big parties, and particularly the biggest, it has not given a bonus big enough to produce absolute majorities regularly in the political circumstances that have obtained so far.

The governing factor and the cause of the remarkable stability of this apparently unstable position is, to repeat, the critical size of Fianna Fáil support, which has permitted it always to hope for a majority. This made the party from the beginning strongly competitive and unwilling to contemplate coalition or cooperation in any form. Accordingly, Irish government assumed to a large extent the classic alternating "ins and outs" pattern that is a feature of two-party systems. Because Fianna Fáil's opponents would not enter coalitions, except for the decade 1948–57, the Irish party system is now in fact a predominant party system—though only barely so.

Faced with the thwarting situation that Figure 6.1 reveals, it is not surprising that Fianna Fáil at least should contemplate changing the election system. To do so necessitates amending the Constitution, the procedure for which, under Article 46, involves the passing of a constitutional amendment act by the Oireachtas and its approval by the electorate at a referendum. Attempts by Fianna Fáil in 1959 and 1968 to abolish the single transferable vote in multi-member constituencies and to substitute in its place the single nontransferable vote in single-member constituencies were both rejected by the electorate at referenda.[8]

Finally, it is obviously necessary to pay attention to the fact that general elections produce not only governments but Dála (assemblies). Indeed, constitutional theory suggests that it is for this purpose alone that elections are held, though, as we have seen, practice is rather different. Hence, the third criterion: does the election system help to produce Dála composed of members effective for the role they play, or—given the political system in general—the role they might play? When we come to consider the Dáil, there are good grounds for arguing that the election system may be an important factor in producing an assembly that is less than effective even for the somewhat modest role it is called upon to play. By giving extensive opportunities for local views and values to carry weight, it produces an assembly composed of deputies too obsessed with local matters and their local positions and not well enough equipped in professional knowledge and experience to be an adequate check upon the government. (See pp. 213–16 below.)

VII

Elections do not, of course, take place in a social and political vacuum. The results they produce are factors as much of the culture of the community, its political habits and conventions, and the political situation as of the system itself. A particular election system might aid certain results and satisfy certain criteria, perhaps at the expense of others. If, as is the case in Ireland, elections are the sites of the really decisive political battles, it might well be argued that the major criterion ought to be the production of effective governments and that "what elections should do is to face the elector with a choice, which he is to make in a particular set

[8] For details of the referenda results, see Tables B.7 and B.8, p. 336.

of circumstances between alternatives which are real and present."[9] To arrange for him to do so, however, may involve sacrificing proportionality, and the opponents of Proportional Representation are prepared to do just this. The single transferable vote system, as Irish experience shows, allows all sorts of considerations to have due weight, and in its operation seems to favor the view that the elector should have great freedom to put local candidates in the order of his choice for whatever reasons move him. In so doing, the danger is that the electors may deprive themselves of the opportunity of choosing the government.

[9] W. J. M. Mackenzie, *Free Elections* (London, 1958), p. 53.

SEVEN

The Government

Governments are usually produced as a direct result of general elections, which are to a great extent contests between political leaders for the right to assume office. The government (sometimes called the Cabinet) consists, then, of those parliamentary leaders of the party or combination of parties that has won a majority in the Dáil. These leaders meet as a committee to decide the major issues of public policy and the measures they intend to present to the Oireachtas for approval, to coordinate the work of the departments they control, and generally to manage the affairs of the state. They meet under the chairmanship of the Taoiseach, who chooses them (at least formally); he is also their party leader, or, in the case of a coalition, a leader agreeable to all the partners. Both in the Dáil and in the Seanad they introduce the legislative measures and policies they have decided on and pilot them through the various parliamentary stages; they explain and defend their policies and actions and those of their departments; and they provide the main source of information on public affairs. While they command the confidence of a majority in the Dáil, they hold a virtual monopoly of initiative in proposing legislation and policy for approval, and they govern the timetable and legislative output of the Oireachtas. Since they do ordinarily command such confidence, it will be apparent that the Oireachtas as such has a comparatively minor role in formulating policy and legislation; and, since members have fallen into the habit of trusting and not embarrassing their leaders, its performance as a public watchdog over the activities of the government is a modest one. As Dr. K. C. Wheare says, this is a system where "the Government makes the laws with the advice and consent of the representative assembly."[1]

In order to understand this monopoly that governments enjoy, it is

1 K. C. Wheare, *Legislatures* (London, 1963), p. 163.

necessary to know not only the formal rules governing their appointment, functions, and tenure but, more important, who the members are, what their actual role is in the system, and what are the effective conditions under which they fulfill it. To do so involves exploring the "singular approximation," as Walter Bagehot called it, of the government and the Oireachtas and elucidating the relations of party leaders with their supporters.

Rules governing the government are, of course, to be found in the constitutions of all countries. In countries with a constitutional tradition, these basic rules provide a framework within which the organs of government actually operate. This is the case in Ireland. But the Irish Constitution gives a picture that from an operational point of view is inadequate and, in some important respects, misleading. It gives a woefully poor description of the functions of the government: it suggests a division of governmental powers that does not—and could not—exist, and it gives the impression that the Dáil has powers that it does not possess. Nevertheless, these constitutional provisions, together with a number of constitutional conventions or practices, are important in governing the government and it is essential to look at them first.

II

Article 13 of the Constitution provides that the President of Ireland, the formal head of the state, shall appoint the Taoiseach on the nomination of the Dáil and that he shall appoint the other members of the government "on the nomination of the Taoiseach with the previous approval" of the Dáil. Up to the limit of the life of the Oireachtas, which is five years, the Taoiseach holds office either until he chooses to resign, in which case the other members of the government are deemed also to have resigned, or until he "has ceased to retain the support of a majority in Dáil Eireann." In this case, he must resign unless on his advice the President chooses to dissolve the Dáil and thus to precipitate a general election. Except in the circumstance outlined above, the Taoiseach may also secure a dissolution of the Dáil—and thus a general election—on request to the President, a request with which he must comply.

Concerning the appointment of the Taoiseach and the government, the function of the Dáil has in practice usually been purely formal. Once, however, in 1948, a parliamentary coalition of all parties other than Fianna Fáil with the support of a number of Independents was formed by the leaders of the newly elected representatives after the election results were known and before the Dáil met. This resulted in the "Inter-Party" government. If the relative strengths of the parties were favorable and they were so inclined, such a procedure could recur. Thus it is by no means inevitable that the role of the Dáil should be a formal one.

Fourteen of the sixteen governments that have emerged from general elections since June 1922 have been composed of members of a single party, and governments so composed have succeeded one another in the manner typical of bipolar politics. However, the alternation of parties in power has not been regular or rapid, owing to the dominance of Fianna Fáil after 1932 and the unwillingness of other parties to enter a coalition except in the decade 1948–57. Although seven of these fourteen single-party governments have had to rely on the support of other parties and Independents in the Dáil, such support has usually been unconditional and dependable. There is not much evidence that reliance on other groups and individuals has thwarted any government, and certainly the problems involved in conducting the nation's business in these circumstances seem to have been little, if at all, greater than those that large parties encounter with their own supporters from time to time. Thus, the characteristic style of Irish government has been that of single-party governments operating with assured, though sometimes small, majorities. To a great extent the practices of this type of government are regarded as the norm.

The nomination of the members of the government is made by the Taoiseach. The new Dáil, having nominated the leader of the majority party or group after a short and usually ritualistic debate, adjourns for a few hours while the leader calls upon the President and is formally appointed. He then returns to the Dáil and puts forward the names of the members of his government. These are approved *en bloc* by the Dáil, though in the early days of the state there was some attempt to have them discussed and approved individually. They are then appointed by the President and assigned their departments by the Taoiseach. It should be noted that appointment to the government and appointment as head of a department are quite distinct. The Taoiseach has the right to assign departments to the members of his government. He informs the Dáil, but the Dáil is not required specifically to approve the allocation.

If, as has usually been the case, the government consists of members of a single party, the incoming Prime Minister as party leader will probably have had considerable freedom of choice, though powerful colleagues and the expectations of the party have no doubt imposed some constraints on some prime ministers. W. T. Cosgrave in the early days of the state led a loose party and was surrounded by strong personalities, and he may have had less freedom to dispose than De Valera, who from the beginning possessed considerable charisma and dominated his col-

leagues. The case of the coalition governments in 1948 and 1954 was obviously different again. In the first, in 1948, the leader himself, John A.
Costello, was not at the time the leader of his party, Fine Gael. He had
little to say in the initial choice of his ministers except perhaps in the
case of some of his party colleagues. The number of posts for each party
group was proportionate to their voting strength in the Dáil, and it was
necessary, under the agreement between the parties, to allocate certain
posts to certain parties. In the case of the Labour Party, the elected members held an election for the posts allocated to it.

By 1954, Costello's personal position was stronger, for he was seen by
the public as the alternative to De Valera. It was necessary once again,
however, to agree on a share-out of offices and each party filled its own
posts, the Labour Party again by election. Costello's position in his own
party probably gave him considerable freedom to choose his party colleagues and to allocate posts, and he may have had some negative influence on the choice of other parties. The extent to which, during these
years, cabinet posts were regarded as being at the disposal of the party to
which they were allocated is illustrated by the fact that when the Labour
Minister for Local Government died in 1949, his party met to elect his
successor and the Taoiseach nominated their choice immediately. Even
temporary transfers were kept within the party, for when the Minister
for External Affairs, who was the leader of Clann na Poblachta, was out
of the country for a short while, his department was entrusted to his
party colleague, despite the fact that he was the most junior member of
the government.

The Constitution (Article 8) requires that the government shall consist of no fewer than seven and no more than fifteen members. The Taoiseach, the Tánaiste (Deputy Prime Minister), and the Minister for
Finance must be members of the Dáil. The other members must be members of the Dáil or the Seanad, but not more than two may be members
of the Seanad. Every member of the government has the right to attend
and speak in each house. In practice, in the whole history of the state
there have been only two Senator ministers. Senator Connolly combined
a ministerial post and the party leadership of the Seanad from 1932 to
1936, but the use of a minister in this way has never been repeated. The
only other Senator minister, Seán Moylan, was a senior Fianna Fáil minister who was defeated at the 1957 general election, and he was nominated to the Seanad by the Taoiseach so that he would be able to continue in office.

Although there is a legal distinction between membership of the government and the post of head of department, they are in fact virtually

synonymous. There is, it is true, provision in the Ministers and Secretaries (Amendment) Act, 1939, for the appointment of members of the government without departmental responsibilities. Such a person "shall be known as a Minister without Portfolio," but the government may "assign to any particular minister without portfolio a specific style or title." One such equivocal "Minister without Portfolio" was appointed, a Minister for the Coordination of Defensive Measures, who held office from 1939 to 1945.

Usually each member of the government heads one department, but not infrequently a minister is put in charge of more than one. This is a matter of convenience. De Valera himself was both Taoiseach and Minister for External Affairs from 1932 to 1948, and for a period at the beginning of the Second World War he was also Minister for Education. The number of departments has increased somewhat since the beginning of the state. In 1924 there were eleven; in 1968 there were sixteen, but in two cases ministers controlled two departments and the Cabinet numbered only fourteen.[2]

Since all ministers are members of the government and the government is composed exclusively of ministers, the structure is simple. In fact, there are few other politician officeholders of any sort in the administration. The government may appoint parliamentary secretaries, i.e. underministers, up to a maximum of seven, who must be members of the Oireachtas. In 1968 there were five. In addition, there is a law officer, the Attorney General, with a small department, who, though he is not (and under the Constitution cannot be) a member of the government, is the government's adviser in matters of law and represents the state in important legal proceedings. He is not required to be a member of the Oireachtas and in practice he is not; he may engage in private practice in addition to his state duties and he has in fact done so in recent years.

This simple pattern, which has been in operation since the beginning of the state, has sufficed in spite of the great increase in the range and amount of state activity. Governments have apparently not felt the need to develop an extensive system of permanent Cabinet committees to relieve the government itself or to process or coordinate business. This comparative lack of a committee structure is no doubt due to the small size of the country and the opportunity that smallness gives for direct and personal negotiation between ministers themselves and between ministers and officials.

[2] For details of the development of the central administration, see Figure 9.1, pp. 224–25 below.

III

A state that emerges as a result of a war of independence is naturally governed in its first years by the surviving leaders in that struggle, men who have come to the top by routes that are not necessarily the ordinary paths to democratic office. An examination of the personnel of Irish governments shows that the independence struggle and the subsequent civil war cast long shadows.

Naturally, the first government of the independent state, the Provisional Government, was composed entirely of leading figures, military and civilian, of the independence movement, and six out of seven of them had held ministerial office in the Dáil governments of 1919–22. That it did not include all the leaders was due, of course, to the split over the Treaty. In 1932, when Fianna Fáil took office, most of its ministers were leading veterans of the same struggle. Because many of the leaders were young at the time of independence, because Ireland is a conservative society with a respect for seniority, and because one party had ten consecutive years of office and its successor sixteen, the original groups on both sides remained exceptionally stable, with few changes of personnel. Hence, the pattern was one of low turnover of ministers, long service, and aging cabinets. Even after 1948, when a new variation, the so-called "Inter-Party" government, emerged, this pattern still persisted. Although the assumption of power by the Inter-Party government meant new ministers, many of them were senior in their parties and had given long service in the Dáil. Because Fianna Fáil held power for so long and so often and because De Valera felt great loyalty to his old comrades, his ministers tended to continue in office until eventually old age overtook them.

Table 7.1 shows the number of ministers entering each of the three groups into which Irish governments from 1922 to 1965 may be classified, i.e. Cumann na nGaedheal, 1922–32; Fianna Fáil, 1932–48, 1951–54, and 1957–65; Inter-Party, 1948–51 and 1954–57. During the 27 years that Fianna Fáil was in office between 1932 and 1965, only 30 people manned an administration that grew in size from ten departments to fifteen. De Valera's last government in 1957 contained four out of the nine whom he first chose to work with him 25 years before. After his retirement, these four remained in office until April 1965, and even in 1968, one, Frank Aiken, was still there. While they were in office, Cumann na nGaedheal exhibited the same conservative tendencies. Only seventeen persons in all manned the government in the first ten years of the state's existence. The Inter-Party governments had a larger turnover as the more fissipar-

TABLE 7.1
Recruitment of Ministers, January 1922–April 1965

Group	Head	Ministers
Provisional Government and Cumann na nGaedheal, 1922–32:		
Original government	Collins	7
New entries:		
Jan. 1922–Aug. 1922	Collins	1
Aug. 1922–Sept. 1923	Cosgrave	4
Sept. 1923–June 1927	Cosgrave	4
June 1927–Oct. 1927	Cosgrave	—
Oct. 1927–March 1932	Cosgrave	1
TOTAL		17
Fianna Fáil, 1932–48, 1951–54, 1957–65:		
Original government	De Valera	10
New entries:		
March 1932–Feb. 1933	De Valera	—
Feb. 1933–July 1937	De Valera	2
July 1937–June 1938	De Valera	—
June 1938–July 1943	De Valera	1
July 1943–May 1944	De Valera	1
May 1944–Feb. 1948	De Valera	1
June 1951–June 1954	De Valera	2
March 1957–June 1959	De Valera	5
June 1959–Oct. 1961	Lemass	3
Oct. 1961–April 1965	Lemass	2
April 1965–	Lemass	3
TOTAL		30
Inter-Party, 1948–51, 1954–57:		
Original government	Costello	13[a]
New entries:		
Feb. 1948–June 1951	Costello	1
June 1954–March 1957	Costello	6
TOTAL		20

[a] Two members of this government had been members of Cumann na nGaedheal governments before 1932. They are included here again.

ous elements left the coalition, but despite this, the overall picture is one of comparatively small turnover (except of course when a party went out of office) and of many ministers with long service. From the inception of the Provisional Government in 1922 to the eve of the 1965 election, no fewer than fifteen ministers, almost one-quarter of those who had held office, had served for ten years or more, and five, all Fianna Fáil, for twenty years or more.

With comparatively unchanging personnel the average age of gov-

TABLE 7.2

Ages of Ministers on First Entry to Government,
January 1922–April 1965

Age	All[a]	1922–31[a]	1932–47	1948–56	1957–65	Government of April 21, 1965
Under 30	–	–	–	–	–	–
30–39	25	11	3	5	6	3
40–49	21	4	7	7	3	5
50–59	16	1	5	7	3	2
60–69	2	–	–	1	1	4

Source: Flynn's *Oireachtas Companion*, other published sources, and private inquiries.
[a] The date of birth of one minister cannot be ascertained.

ernments tended to get higher during the long periods of stability that have marked Irish governmental history. The average age of the government of January 1922 was 33 years; Cosgrave's government of 1927 averaged 41 years. De Valera's first government in 1932 also averaged 41 years, while his 1951 government had an average age of 57 years. However, by 1957, when De Valera chose his last Cabinet, the process of renewal had at last begun and the average age was 55 years. Lemass's government of April 1965 averaged 49 years. Table 7.2, which shows the ages of ministers on first assuming office, confirms the impression to be gained by looking at the average ages of individual governments. It is clear from all this that Irish governments were for many years recruited on the basis of service in the independence movement and for a very long time remained dominated by those so chosen. The conservatism, and at times almost stagnation, of Irish social and economic development and of politics generally from the 1920's to the 1950's is perhaps partly attributable to this fact.

Inevitably, though slowly, other considerations have come to be taken into account. Particularly in the case of Fianna Fáil, because of the party's long periods in office, it is possible to see a number of routes to office emerging. All except four of the twenty appointments to the government made after the first Fianna Fáil team was chosen in 1932 had had five or more years of experience in the Oireachtas, but there is a sharp distinction between those with service as Parliamentary Secretary and those without. De Valera's first appointments to fill places falling vacant were mostly senior party colleagues, some with "a national record" and most with long parliamentary and junior minister service. Later, he appointed direct to cabinet rank, and out of the six Fianna Fáil ministers who were appointed without Parliamentary Secretary experience after

1932, four were appointed in his last government in 1957. Lemass's appointments from 1959 were of men with junior minister experience, and, increasingly, of quite young professional men, as he, like De Valera in 1957, faced the problem of finding able successors to the first generation. Among this new generation of ministers who have come to office since the mid-1950's, there have been a number of sons and relations of old party leaders. One, the son of a retiring minister who had been an old comrade of De Valera, was appointed by him to office without any parliamentary experience at all.

So far as the Inter-Party governments were concerned, the constituent parties had to be represented whatever the seniority or records of their leaders. Nevertheless, all but two members of the 1948 government had had considerable parliamentary experience, half of them going back to the 1920's, and, in general, Cabinet rank in the two Inter-Party governments was achieved by party seniority and service. Only in the case of the two Clann na Poblachta ministers can it be said that office came their way by a political accident. One of them had had under four months' experience in the Dáil, the other none at all.

The roads to ministerial office were originally, then, service in the independence movement and consequent seniority in the party; later, junior office; and, more recently, promise of ability and family connection, these two being by no means mutually exclusive. Since the same is true of opposition leaders as well, political leadership in Ireland today is to a considerable extent in the hands of the sons and other relatives of former party leaders. However, because of the paucity of ministerial and leader talent in the Oireachtas as a whole, any able professional man may well have a good chance of quick preferment.

Because the country is, comparatively speaking, homogeneous, the Taoiseach does not have to worry, like the Prime Ministers of some countries, about giving representation to particular sections or regions. For many years there has been one Protestant in the present government, but he does not hold office because of his religion and there is certainly no obligation to replace one Protestant by another. Only in the case of the Department of the Gaeltacht is a special qualification necessary. This department deals with the particular problems of those areas where the people speak Irish as their first language, and it is appropriate that the minister charged with their welfare should be either a "native speaker" or at least very proficient in the language, which most TD's are not.

Although there do not appear to be any absolute socioeconomic criteria of eligibility for office and the first leaders on both sides were "politicians by accident," some occupational groups have always been strongly

TABLE 7.3

Socioeconomic Status of the 65 Ministers Who Held Office Between 1922 and 1965

Socioeconomic group[a]	Per cent
Farming and fishing (mainly farmers)	7.7%
Professional	58.5
Trade union officials	4.6
Employers and managers (mainly small shopkeepers and publicans, owners of family businesses, and contractors)	20.0
Nonmanual	4.6
Skilled manual	4.6
Semiskilled and unskilled manual	—

Source: Flynn's *Oireachtas Companion*, other published sources, and private inquiries.
[a] Groupings adapted from *Census of Population*, III (1961).

represented, others strikingly absent. As Table 7.3 indicates, the dominance of the professional men (there has only been one woman minister and that was before independence) is overwhelming. Fifty-eight per cent of all ministers since 1922 have been members of a profession. Rarely has there been a government without a majority of professional men. Professional status does not necessarily mean a middle-class background, especially in Ireland and especially if schoolteachers are included, but it does tend to mean an essentially middle-class life.

In the first governments, before and immediately after independence, journalists and teachers were specially strongly represented, and this reflected their predominance in the leadership of the independence movement generally. But, as Table 7.4 indicates, members of these two professions did not continue to be attracted to politics and, overall, the most conspicuous group has been the lawyers. Thirty-two per cent of all ministers since 1922 have been in the law. In Ireland, as in so many countries, the law and politics are a fruitful combination. On the contrary, though Ireland is an agricultural country and one-quarter of the TD's are farmers, very few farmers have held office. Again, though 20 per cent of all ministers have been in business, few have been industrialists or big businessmen. Likewise, trade union officials have been in government only when the Labour Party participated in the Inter-Party governments. Finally, working-class people hardly appear at all in office. The fact is that at this level politics is a middle-class occupation involving the better-educated or trained man; yet, at the same time "the organization man" from the bigger businesses tends to eschew politics, while farmers and shopkeepers, though they get into the Dáil in fair numbers, do not often rise to leadership positions. Thus, the field is left for the professional man.

TABLE 7.4
Professional Men in Government, 1922–65

Profession	Ministers, 1922–65	Profession	Professional men in certain governments, 1922–65				
			Aug. 1922	March 1932	Feb. 1948	March 1957	April 1965
Accountants	1	Accountants	–	–	–	–	1
Barristers	13	Barristers	1	1	3	1	2
Solicitors	8	Solicitors	1	1	–	–	2
Engineers	3	Engineers	–	1	–	2	2
Journalists	3	Journalists	2	1	–	–	–
Medical doctors	4	Medical doctors	–	1	2	1	1
Teachers	6	Teachers	2	2	–	1	–
TOTAL	38	TOTAL	6	7	5	5	8
Total number of ministers	65	Total number in government	10	10	13	11	14

Source: Flynn's *Oireachtas Companion*, other published sources, and private inquiries.

IV

Although the above analysis shows that many have acquired ministerial office because they have been national leaders or party leaders or their relatives, the powerful position of the members of the government arises as much or more from the role they play in office as from who they are or what they have done. They owe their domination of the political scene to the fact that, whether or not they were political leaders before, on being appointed to the Cabinet they certainly become leading figures in their party, more particularly in the Oireachtas party and therefore in the Oireachtas, while at the same time they assume the headship of a government department. In their persons they link the majority party, the management of the Oireachtas, and the control of the central administration. This combination of positions of leadership gives the members of the government their preeminence. This in turn conveys social prestige, for they are at the very center of affairs. Their position is the stronger if, as certainly has been the case with Fianna Fáil, they are well known to one another and to their followers and form a ready-made team, which is accustomed and expected to take the initiative in forming the party's objectives and program.

The position of ministers is the stronger, also, since they have a virtual monopoly of political leadership. There are few, if any, other party leaders outside the Oireachtas, though one or two trade union officials in the Labour Party might be politically important, as in Great Britain, while the national executives of the three main parties may exert some influence as corporate bodies. There are none on the majority side in the Oireachtas, for the only other officials are the Parliamentary Secretaries, the Chief Whip (who is usually a Parliamentary Secretary in any case), and the majority leader in the Seanad, none of whom have the status of ministers. Moreover, the Oireachtas does not have a strong parliamentary committee system with powerful chairmen or rapporteurs; nor does it have a developed party committee system; nor, indeed, do the members as a whole have a strong sense of the dignity of the Oireachtas or a high view of its functions and powers, as, say, members of the United States Congress have. Finally, there are no rival leaders in the departments, for the members of the government are themselves the department heads and, as such, are both constitutionally and legally responsible for departmental actions and conventionally, in the British manner, the sole source of decisions and information.

In this triple role, members of the government assume the major responsibility for governing the country, although this is by no means obvious from reading the Constitution. That document states (in Article

28) that the *executive* power of the state shall be exercised by or on behalf of the government; it makes the government responsible for the
work of the departments; it requires the government to prepare estimates of expenditure and present them to the Dáil, and (in Article 17)
it gives the government an exclusive initiative in respect of proposing
public expenditure. These constitutional provisions show how closely
British practice was followed, and they are, in fact, an attempt—as were
the similar provisions of the previous Constitution, the Irish Free State
Constitution of 1922—"to capture the essential elements of cabinet
government and squeeze them into the phraseology of constitutional
clauses."[3]

The elements of cabinet government are not so easily captured, however, particularly if the statement of them is couched in terms of the con-
ventional separation-of-powers theory. Even the classic British definition
of the functions of the Cabinet in the *Report of the Machinery of Government Committee* (the Haldane Committee) fails us in this respect.
The main functions of the Cabinet, according to this report, are
(*a*) the final determination of the policy to be submitted to Parliament;
(*b*) the supreme control of the national executive in accordance with
the policy prescribed by Parliament; and (*c*) the continuous coordination and delimitation of the activities of the several departments of state.
This is, however, to concentrate unduly on the activities of the government at Cabinet meetings, and it ignores both the parliamentary and
departmental functions, let alone the party functions of the members of
the government, which are inseparable from those stated. Furthermore,
it does not convey completely the overall responsibility of this group for
the general welfare of the community and the consequent initiative the
community expects them to take to identify public problems and to
solve them. With Muirís O Muimhneacháin, a former Secretary to the
government, we may say that it is the government's job "to govern, to see
that the peace is kept and the law enforced, to keep the varying needs of
the community as a whole and of its different sections constantly in
mind, to concert measures, so far as it can, for averting any danger that
may threaten the community and for creating conditions that will help
the people to advance in welfare and prosperity."[4]

To do this requires the exercise of continuous leadership not only in
the Oireachtas and the party, where members of the government have
formal leader positions, but among the many social organizations that

---

[3] F. A. Ogg, *English Government and Politics* (New York, 1936), p. 731.
[4] "The Functions of the Department of the Taoiseach," *Administration*, VII (1959–
60), 291.

are concerned with public policy and, in Ireland today, increasingly take a part in its formulation. In exercising this leadership, members of the government are continuously aware of the fact that they do so because they are successful party politicians. They take their decisions, both in Cabinet and individually in their departments, in the light not only of their personal views but of the wishes of their party and their public pledges, of the information, advice, and proposals of the civil service, and of the views of interested organizations in the community. They will remember that they have to get Oireachtas agreement to their policies, and that it will fall to them also to answer for their success or failure in implementing them. Often, too, they will keep in mind the *next* election, which may be as important a determinant of government policy as the previous one.

v

In exercising their considerable initiative and powers, members of the government depend for their continuance in office on maintaining an adequate level of satisfaction in their party, in the Oireachtas, and in the community. They hold their positions on certain conditions. To understand the government of the country and to be able to assess to what extent it can be called democratic, it is necessary to know what these conditions are.

There are, first, some constitutional requirements to be observed, but these do not take us very far. Once appointed, the government is "responsible to Dáil Eireann," and its leader, the Taoiseach, must retain the support of a majority in the Dáil. If he does not, he must resign unless the President grants him a dissolution and, thus, an appeal to the electorate. When the Taoiseach resigns, all the members of the government are deemed to have resigned also, as are the Parliamentary Secretaries and the Attorney General. By mentioning the Dáil specifically, the Constitution emphasizes the minor role and importance of the Seanad, whose power is limited to forcing the Dáil to reaffirm a previous decision. This responsibility is stated to be collective and the government is required to "meet and act as a collective authority." Collective responsibility is, however, an elusive concept. It suggests that ministers are a team—but how united a team? It suggests that they must answer for their performance and might be removed—but in what circumstances?

In *The Government of Great Britain*, Graeme Moodie describes collective responsibility in general terms that would be acceptable in constitutional theory in Ireland:

All members of the administration are expected publicly to support its policies and its actions, regardless of their private feelings on the matter. Should they for any reason no longer be prepared to do so, they must resign their office (although not, usually, their seats in Parliament). Constitutionally, they cannot acquiesce in a decision and then, at some later stage when for example, it becomes unpopular, claim that they were opposed to it and thus seek personally to escape the political penalties. . . . By the same token, it is impossible for the House of Commons to vote for the removal of a particular member of the Government, unless it is clear that the Government is prepared to sacrifice that individual either as a scapegoat or because no collective responsibility is involved.[5]

Now, this does not mean that all are equally involved in decisions. Ministers have their own departments and their own interests. While the Parliamentary Secretaries and the Attorney General are politically as liable as the members of the government, they do not participate in the making of most Cabinet decisions. Nor does it mean that all members are equally in favor, or even in favor at all, of a particular proposal. All it requires, as Moodie points out, is "that the arguments be conducted in private" (hence the necessary corollary of secrecy) and that members accept or acquiesce in public.

However, it is important to notice that the Irish government as such remains the chief center of decision making to an extent that perhaps no longer obtains in Great Britain. There, the size and range of state business have necessitated the development of an extensive Cabinet committee system, so that many decisions ostensibly made by the Cabinet are in fact only ratified by it. That is not to say that there are no Cabinet committees at all in Ireland. There are known to have been committees from time to time in the past, as, for example, during the Second World War for defense purposes and during the Inter-Party governments to compose differences. In recent years, also, committees *ad hoc* have been appointed to deal with matters that have provoked disagreement in the government or where a problem has demanded the close attention of a small group of ministers. It seems that one committee at least, concerned with economic affairs, though appointed *ad hoc* has tended to last the lifetime of governments and to be reappointed. This reflects the growing need for closely integrated action on the part of certain ministers and departments.

The practice of collective responsibility must depend to a great extent on the likemindedness and coherence of the group of ministers and upon its leadership. All parties are coalitions, and the practice of collec-

[5] G. Moodie, *The Government of Great Britain* (London, 1964), p. 88.

tive responsibility will vary with the composition of the party or group of parties making up the government at any given time and with the position and personality of the Taoiseach. Irish experience falls into three phases, the Cumann na nGaedheal governments, the Fianna Fáil governments, and the Inter-Party governments.

Although the experience and predilections of most of the leaders in 1922 led them without hesitation to adopt British institutions and practices, there were a few who hankered after the ideal of a Parliament consisting of independent groups, which would in fact legislate and govern through ministers individually appointed and responsible to the Dáil. Kevin O'Higgins told the Dáil in 1922:

We will have groups here, small groups of seven or eight. We will not have parties on definite lines of political cleavage.... In these circumstances you would not have a stable government if you had normal cabinet government. ... We want to have the Parliament of Saorstát Eireann [the Irish Free State] a deliberative assembly in the fullest sense of the word.... You will not have that by adhering to collective responsibility.[6]

This ideal did not materialize. The plan for a small Cabinet on normal lines, plus "extern ministers," administrative experts who were to be elected individually by the Dáil and to be directly and individually responsible, was enacted in only an emasculated form and abandoned after six years. Political divisions and the exigencies of government produced big parties and majorities. The Cumann na nGaedheal governments supported by their reliable followers in the Dáil assumed to a large extent the functions and powers of a British Cabinet. They were, it is true, broad-based governments containing "men who ranged all the way from the extreme protectionist views of Mr. Walsh, the Minister for Posts and Telegraphs, to the free trade views of Mr. Hogan, the Minister for Agriculture,"[7] for the party was a pro-Treaty party only, though tending to conservatism rather than the left. While ministers clearly had considerable freedom to conduct their own departments in their own way, the three resignations that occurred in that period were all the result of disagreements over important items of policy and show that the theory as outlined by Moodie was fully accepted by both the Cabinet and its parliamentary supporters. The divergent views of individuals—about free trade, for example—were known, but open public disagreement was avoided and there was no question of any formal "agreement to differ" as there was in Britain in 1932.

[6] *Dáil Debates*, vol. 1, cols. 1558–60 (Oct. 12, 1922).
[7] W. Moss, *Political Parties in the Irish Free State* (New York, 1933), p. 29.

With the advent of Fianna Fáil to power, De Valera's dominating position and preference for firm Cabinet government and definite leadership resulted in Cabinets with more monolithic public faces. There were no resignations over policy and no overt disagreements in his time. His successor, Seán Lemass, inherited a party long schooled in this tradition, and being so clearly an unrivaled master of the economic policy issues, which had come to dominate politics, he seemed also to dominate his government. The resignation in 1964 of Patrick Smith, Minister for Agriculture, over a disagreement not directly concerning agriculture but about the attitude to be taken to wage claims, indicates that in the Lemass era, too, the doctrine outlined above was accepted. There were, however, signs of a loosening of the conventions in Jack Lynch's first years, and the significant formula "the minister was speaking as an individual" had sometimes to be used.

With the Inter-Party governments, as might be expected, necessity sometimes demanded similar practices. The first Inter-Party government was a coalition not only of all the other parties but also of some Independents, who, for the sake of convenience, were regarded as a coherent group with the right to a ministerial post in the parceling out of offices, which was based on party strength. The basic coalition agreement was confined to a number of points: "Any points on which we have not agreed have been left in abeyance," John Costello, its leader, told the Dáil.[8] Moreover, it was a government of parties, each party having the right to nominate to certain offices and to fill them again if death or resignation removed a minister. During this government's period of office, the leader of Clann na Poblachta demanded and got the resignation of his party colleague directly, sending a copy of his letter to the Taoiseach.

Although the Inter-Party government was in the circumstances comparatively effective, its members could not always avoid explicit public disagreement. Sometimes ministerial statements, both in the Dáil and outside, revealed differences of view on policy matters. The government maintained in public, and some of its members perhaps even believed, that a minister could properly speak "as an individual" on current policy issues.

Deputies on the other side of the House have anguished themselves with talk about the public embarrassment which there is over the fact that the Minister for External Affairs does not talk the same financial language as myself. I have yet to meet anybody outside the ranks of the professional politicians who is worried about that. Nobody is worried. Have we got to the stage in this country

---

8 *Dáil Debates*, vol. 110, col. 67 (Feb. 18, 1948).

when, on a matter which may be an important point of policy when it is decided, we cannot have freedom of speech? Have we got to the stage when men, just because they join the Government circle, must all, as one Deputy said, when they go out of the council chambers speak the same language?[9]

Significantly, the period of these governments also saw the use on a regular basis of Cabinet committees, on economic affairs and the annual estimates of public expenditure, both to hammer out agreed policies before Cabinet consideration took place and to resolve differences. In the latter stages of the first Inter-Party government, disagreement and poor communications between members seem to have led in some cases to a state of uncoordinated independence. In the Dáil itself, it was necessary on a few occasions to resort to the "free vote" when the Inter-Party group was divided, and even some members of the government itself voted against the government.

These modifications of the previous practice, while significant and with potentially important implications, did not alter the style of Cabinet government in any fundamental or permanent way. The Inter-Party government's area of agreement was small, but, within it, the members operated in broadly the customary manner, and their Dáil supporters generally spoke and voted as a stable coalition until the government was brought down by its extreme elements and the defection of Independents. Any changes of practice were made of necessity and in general were recognized as deviations from the norms followed by previous governments.

The term "collective responsibility" suggests not only a publicly united government but a government that is accountable as a whole and might be removed. In constitutional theory the government *executes* the policies decided upon by the Oireachtas and must account to it for its administration of these policies. In practice, as we have observed, the government itself is the originator of policy and the manager of the Dáil. It is able to be so because it is supported consistently by a unified party or group of parties in the Dáil. Because of this, the electorate can usually in fact choose the Taoiseach, and because of this, also, the Dáil does not usually dismiss the government either, though it might. In fact, governments are rarely defeated. Since 1922, governments have been defeated on only six occasions, the last time being as long ago as 1949. Even among these six defeats, one at least was an accident, and in no case at all was it obvious that the Taoiseach had in any general way "ceased to retain the support of a majority in Dáil Eireann." On no occasion has

[9] Deputy P. McGilligan (then Minister for Finance), *Dáil Debates*, vol. 119, col. 2521 (Mar. 23, 1950).

TABLE 7.5

Reasons for Dissolution of Dáil Eireann, 1923–65

Reason	Number of occasions
Government coming to end of term of office	8
Tactical:	
Government chooses to dissolve	2
Government welcomes defeat to get new election	2
Danger of Dáil defeat	3

defeat led to a change of government. In only two cases was it followed by a dissolution, and in both these cases the defeat was welcomed by the governments concerned as an opportunity to improve their position at a general election, for they made no attempt to reverse the decision, though they could have done so. It is rather the threat of defeat that has more often led to a dissolution, for this has occurred on at least three occasions. In two cases coalitions were involved (in 1951 and 1957), while the third arose from the changed position when the Fianna Fáil deputies, who had hitherto refused to take their seats in the Dáil, decided in August 1927 to do so. It may be said, then, that the Dáil can and does force governments to submit to the electorate, though this is only likely to occur in periods of coalition government, but it does not dismiss them. As Table 7.5 shows, dissolutions have usually occurred when governments were coming toward the end of their term of office or for tactical reasons.

The all-important fact of party solidarity is thus clear enough, but what are its conditions? First, it cannot be denied that for many TD's there is some element of risk both to their seats and to their parliamentary careers in opposing their leaders, but it is less than the risk that representatives run in countries where the party label is everything, and for some it is negligible. Because of the election system and the weight attached by voters to personal and local factors, the Irish TD who rebels and is expelled from, or leaves, his party is not automatically doomed by any means. Moreover, many, particularly of the rural members, are unlikely ever to get ministerial office, and would not in any case seek it, so that their careers are not jeopardized. And though no ordinary member ever wants a dissolution, a threat by the Taoiseach to dissolve would be unlikely to deter any but a few Independents.

In general, then, the position of governments does not rely to any extent upon sanctions. Rather, it rests upon strong feelings of loyalty and a considerable willingness on the part of the ordinary TD to let his party leaders get on with what he regards as *their* business of government and opposition, assured of his support, while he attends to *his* business, notably his constituents. This almost seems to amount to unconcern about many matters of general policy except where they impinge on his own locality. Governments operate therefore with no great volume of party and parliamentary debate and comment and without the need to argue general issues, and even compromise on them, which characterizes their behavior in many other countries. Of course, there are a few TD's (and Senators) who are interested in broad issues of social, economic, and foreign policy to the extent of wishing to contribute to policy formation or debate; of course, ministers pay attention to rank-and-file representations, and, indeed, the numbers involved are small enough for communications to be swift, direct, and easy. But, as becomes clear on examination of the Oireachtas, the contribution of the parliamentary representative to general legislation and broad policy formation is a minor one indeed. Governments generally do not have constantly to revise or adjust their policies, once formulated, to meet the demands and criticisms of their supporters, let alone the views of the Oireachtas as a body. Insofar as they are sensitive to their followers and the Oireachtas, it is because they believe that they ought to be—i.e. that that is how democratic governments behave—and because they wish to create in the mind of the public an image of a party that is united and contented, led by men who are reasonable and accommodating.

More immediately important than the Oireachtas, in many instances, are the organized interest groups, some of them now directly involved in policy formation by way of advisory bodies, whose views have to be weighed and considered. Particularly in the formation of economic policy, the support or acquiescence of employers' or farmers' organizations and the trade unions is critical to the government, and the Dáil's contribution sometimes seems to be too little and too late.

Ministers are not only collectively responsible; they are also individually responsible for their own activities and those of the departments they control. Legally this is clear enough; politically it tends to be obscured by doubts about the limits of a minister's responsibility, first, in some areas of public administration such as some of the activities of public enterprises, and second, for personal wrongdoing or inefficient action on the part of his civil servants about which he could not have been expected to know. The general principles and the parliamentary methods here are familiar enough. The minister speaks for his department, both in the Oireachtas and outside, and he explains and defends government decisions on matters within the purview of his department, his own decisions and actions, and those of his officials. Because he has the right to the last say, he is held to have had that say and all decisions are regarded as his. The corollary is that civil servants do not defend state decisions or public action publicly and are not subject to direct parliamentary inquisition except in the case of the inquiries made by the Public Accounts Committee and the Seanad Select Committee on Statutory Instruments, both of which deal with rather technical matters. Yet while he is responsible for matters within his competence, it is he who in practice decides what are the limits of his responsibilities and what he will and will not answer for. That such is the case arises from a considerable failure on the part of the Oireachtas to devise and operate efficient methods of eliciting information and assessing it (see pp. 195ff).

Even more uncertain are the circumstances under which an individual minister may be forced to resign, and to what extent such a decision would be the Taoiseach's or the government's as a whole. It is certain that a minister could be forced to resign only if the government, or the Taoiseach with government support, decided to abandon him when in difficulties or to disown or sacrifice him, perhaps in order to save the government as a whole. This might be a question of deciding which would harm the government more, a forced resignation with its attendant publicity, or casting the mantle of collective responsibility over him and making the matter one of confidence. In any case, the decision is the government's—or more likely (except in a coalition) the Taoiseach's—for no government is going to be forced against its will to part with a colleague at the behest of the Dáil.

We are here, however, to some extent in the realm of conjecture, for there are very few cases on which to generalize. Only eight ministers individually resigned between 1922 and 1968. Four of them resigned or were forced to resign because of disagreement with the Cabinet over policy, and another, MacNeill, was in effect disowned in 1926. In these five cases, collective responsibility was clearly involved, the outgoing ministers in each case having taken positions that their colleagues disagreed with. The other three are rather different. Two resigned for health reasons, and another, Senator Connolly, resigned on the abolition in 1936 of the Senate, of which he was the majority leader. In addition, in 1946, a Parliamentary Secretary was forced to resign after a judicial inquiry into the affairs of a firm he was connected with.

Paradoxically, because there is even less evidence to go on, the position of a minister where an official has acted wrongly or inefficiently is clearer. Where the occurrence is an isolated one and he could not have known, there is no serious question of resignation. In the discussion on an Indemnity Bill made necessary by the failure of a junior civil servant to carry out his duties, the minister involved explained the circumstances and added:

It is quite true that, as Minister for Health, I carry full responsibility to this House for the manner in which my Department is administered but in these matters there must be some realism.... Am I to accept responsibility for the fact that an officer of my Department suffers a breakdown in health?... Is there anything I could possibly have done to ensure that this would not have occurred?[10]

This realistic approach was generally agreed to be the right one. Where more general departmental incompetence or failure is involved, it is virtually certain that the principle of collective responsibility will operate, the matter will be made one of confidence, and no question of individual resignation will arise, at least for the moment. Certainly none has. In general, it may be concluded that individual responsibility is largely thwarted by collective responsibility, and it cannot be said that a minister will be punished by loss of office for his failure or incompetence or that of his civil servants.

VI

So far we have talked of the government as a corporate body and of ministers in general terms as though they were all equal. However, the position of the Taoiseach, the leader of the government, demands special consideration, and with it that of the President of Ireland (Uachtarán na hEireann), the head of the state. In Ireland, as in most democratic countries, there is a very clear distinction between the two. In Bunreacht na hEireann the Taoiseach is defined as "the head of the Government, or Prime Minister," a phrase that evokes the concept of a British Prime Minister while at the same time pointedly denying the British constitutional myth that the government is the government of the head of the state. In fact, this definition sums up Irish constitutional development quite accurately.

The position of the Taoiseach was, one may surmise, of particular interest to De Valera when he was preparing Bunreacht na hEireann; it certainly featured largely in the comments of the opposition when the draft Constitution was being debated in 1937. In defining him as the head of the government, De Valera's intention was to do away with the constitutional fiction of "His Majesty's Government," and at the same time to make the Taoiseach and not the President the head of the government. The Taoiseach is only required to keep the President "gen-

[10] S. MacEntee (then Minister for Health), *Dáil Debates*, vol. 187, col. 67 (Mar. 7, 1961).

erally informed on matters of domestic and international policy." This he does by making a regular monthly visit, but the President does not see Cabinet papers.

The President is, then, on the whole a formal head of state who is both the symbol of the state and the center of ceremonial. He performs many acts of government in a formal way at the request of those who have the real power, the Taoiseach and the government. Yet he is conceived of as much more than this. In the words of his creator, De Valera, "he is there to guard the people's rights and mainly to guard the Constitution," and he is endowed with certain real powers to this end. These powers are of four kinds. In the exercise of the first three he is obliged to consult, though not necessarily to follow the advice of, the Council of State, a body consisting of named officeholders (such as the Chief Justice and the Chairmen of the Dáil and Seanad), former holders of offices (such as President and Taoiseach), and not more than seven others appointed by the President himself. First, he may refer any bill to the Supreme Court to be tested for repugnancy; since 1937, three bills have been so referred. Second, if a majority of the Seanad and not less than one-third of the Dáil request him to decline to sign a bill on the ground that it "contains a proposal of such national importance that the will of the people thereon ought to be ascertained," he may, if he so decides, accede to the request and precipitate a referendum on the measure. Third, he may at any time convene a meeting of either or both houses of the Oireachtas, a power obviously intended to be used in an emergency. Finally, he has it "in his absolute discretion" to refuse a dissolution to a Taoiseach who has ceased to retain the support of a majority in the Dáil or who, having been defeated, chooses to interpret the defeat as loss of confidence. In fact, on the only two occasions when this has occurred, a dissolution was granted, and except in case of emergency, it is difficult to see a President doing anything else.

Without doubt these powers of the President, which are intended to be used precisely at periods of crisis or disagreement, might involve him in considerable political controversy, the more so since he is likely to have been selected at an election fought on party lines. In fact, few occasions for their use have so far arisen. Yet, though successive Presidents have by their scrupulous avoidance of partisan words and behavior lifted the office to that of a dignified symbol of the whole community insulated from party political argument, the reaction of the opposition on the two occasions when a defeated Taoiseach sought and was granted a dissolution suggests that it would be all too easy for the President to become involved in politics.

To compare the Taoiseach with a British Prime Minister is not to say very much. It does suggest that he is the central figure, to a great extent the centerpiece and symbol of the government. His preeminence among his colleagues stems from four facts. First, he is usually the party leader; second, elections have often taken the form of gladiatorial contests between two designated party leaders, thus emphasizing the personal leadership of the victor; third, except in the case of coalition governments, he chooses his colleagues; and, fourth, by the very nature of his position he has a very special responsibility to take the lead or speak when authority is needed.

The role of the Taoiseach has been described as follows:

He is the central coordinating figure, who takes an interest in the work of all Departments, the figure to whom ministers naturally turn for advice and guidance when faced with problems involving large questions of policy or otherwise of special difficulty and whose leadership is essential to the successful working of the Government as a collective authority, collectively responsible to Dáil Eireann, but acting through members each of whom is charged with specific Departmental tasks. He may often have to inform himself in considerable detail of particular matters with which other members of the Government are primarily concerned. He may have to make public statements on such matters, as well as on general matters of broad policy, internal and external. He answers Dáil questions where the attitude of the Government towards important matters of policy is involved. He may occasionally sponsor Bills which represent important new developments of policy, even when the legislation, when enacted, will be the particular concern of the Minister in charge of some other Department of State. His Department is the sole channel of communication between Departments generally and the President's secretariat, except in minor and routine matters. Through his Parliamentary Secretary...he secures the coordination, in a comprehensive Parliamentary programme, of the proposals of the various Ministers for legislative and other measures in the Houses of the Oireachtas.[11]

Seán Lemass, himself Taoiseach from 1959 to 1966, also put the emphasis on the coordinating role:

The Taoiseach's primary task, apart from acting as spokesman for the Government on major issues of policy, is to ensure that governmental plans are fully coordinated, that the inevitable conflicts between Departments are resolved, that Cabinet decisions are facilitated and that the implications of Government policy are fully understood by all his Cabinet colleagues and influence the shaping of their departmental plans.[12]

---

[11] M. O Muimhneacháin, "The Functions of the Department of the Taoiseach," *Administration*, VII (1959–60), 293.

[12] Interview quoted in *Léargas* (Institute of Public Administration, Dublin, 1968), No. 12, p. 3.

Beyond this, as Byrum E. Carter has written of the British Prime Minister, "the Office cannot be defined; it can only be described in terms of the use to which it was put by different individuals of varying abilities, who faced different problems and dealt with different colleagues."[13] It is the more difficult because Cabinet business is confidential and state records, even those of the very beginning of its existence, are not yet available. Also, Irish political leaders have been slow to write their autobiographies or memoirs. Again, because of the continued presence of leading survivors of the civil war, and because, to Irish people with long political memories, the unhappy events of 1922 and after still seem very near, historians of contemporary Ireland do not yet have available much of the material on which political judgments at this level can be made.

Both constitutionally and in practice the role and power of the Prime Minister have increased since 1922. In the Irish Free State Constitution the "President of the Executive Council," as he was called, did not have the full position and powers of a British Prime Minister, and some of the wording and provisions of that Constitution revealed the intention to reduce his status and role. Not only the rules governing his appointment and that of his colleagues (though to some extent they were only formalities), but also the provisions for resignation and dissolution indicated the intention "to deprive the head of the Council of those powers which *par excellence* distinguish his position from that of his colleagues."[14] In fact, the President of the Executive Council did have the position of a British Prime Minister to a greater extent than the words of the Constitution might suggest. But W. T. Cosgrave, who was President of the Executive Council from 1922 to 1932, was surrounded by strong personalities, and he may not have had much choice, especially at first, of who his senior colleagues would be. Perhaps, as was suggested, "he was never more than a leader among equals."[15] In some of his public utterances at least, he seemed to go out of his way to belittle his own position and stress that of the Council as a whole. In 1937, speaking of the dismissal and resignation of ministers in his time, he said he had not had the power to compel the resignation of his ministers, and he thought this a good thing. "Ministers in my view ought to possess security and a measure of independence."[16] He was perhaps pointedly contrasting

13 B. E. Carter, *The Office of the Prime Minister* (London, 1956), p. 200.

14 N. Mansergh, *The Irish Free State, Its Government and Politics* (London, 1934), p. 174.

15 D. O'Sullivan, *The Irish Free State and Its Senate* (London, 1940), p. 6.

16 *Dáil Debates*, vol. 68, col. 348 (June 14, 1937).

himself with De Valera, who from the beginning had much greater status and power under the same constitutional rules, because he led a much more united party accustomed to his strong leadership.

From 1932, De Valera was able not only to exploit the possibilities that lay open to him under the Irish Free State Constitution, but also to embody his view of the proper position and powers of a Prime Minister in his own Constitution. The very title he chose, Taoiseach, though it is far from connoting an absolute ruler, suggests, in his own words, that he is "the essential pivot on which the whole Government was arranged." Whereas the Irish Free State Constitution gave powers and duties to the Executive Council as a whole, Bunreacht na hEireann gives them to the Taoiseach in most vital and many purely formal matters. He fixes the dates of assembly and dissolution of the Dáil; he nominates the members of the government; he assigns them to their departments and is not obliged to get the Dáil's assent to his allocation; ministers must resign when he requires them to do so, and the government comes to an end when he chooses; his signature is necessary before the Dáil can debate any motion for granting funds; he presents bills to the President for signature; he nominates eleven of the sixty members of the Seanad. In practice, too, De Valera towered above his colleagues as Cosgrave never did. Revered as "the Chief" by ministerial colleagues and party followers alike, he could and did dominate when he cared to, and in cases of difficulty he dealt individually with his ministers and not through Cabinet procedures.

With Lemass there was little if any diminution of the role or dominant position of the Taoiseach, though he had not the charisma of De Valera. As Tánaiste (literally in Irish, "heir apparent") he inherited an established position with a set pattern of behavior associated with it. Moreover, social and economic planning and development had by the late 1950's become the dominant items of politics and this was where his strength lay. Because it fell to him, almost single-handed, to attempt the task of bringing home to the community the need for radical changes if the country was to develop in line with other Western European countries, he established a dominant position not only in politics in the narrow sense but in the community as a whole.

The position of J. A. Costello as leader of the Inter-Party governments and the role he played were, of course, different. He was a compromise choice, drafted where others were unacceptable. He led a government of parties containing many diverse elements, and some of his colleagues lacked parliamentary, let alone ministerial, experience. The area of agreement between the partners in the coalition was limited, and issues outside this area were always likely to cause disagreement. He was, then, *primus inter pares*, a chairman in the Cabinet and a coordinator of government business. Yet such is the nature of the position and such the inevitable tendency, as the Taoiseach is constantly thrust forward as spokesman and symbol, for the public to see a government as being somebody's government, that he soon became in the public eye the alternative leader to De Valera. Consequently, in his second government, he appeared to have a stronger personal position. However, it could never have equaled that of the acknowledged leader of a single unified party.

Thus the variations between successive holders of the office of Prime Minister, so different in character and so differently placed, make it difficult to generalize. The office is, indeed, "what its holder chooses and is able to make of it."

VII

The characteristics of Irish government that have emerged so far are, first, a powerful government; second, strict competition between parties whose parliamentary representatives form stable groups, the one a majority "government" group, the other, a minority "opposition"; and, third, the great importance of general elections as the decisive political battleground. The rigor of this pattern is only slightly softened by tenuous Dáil majorities and the inclusion in them of Independents. The functions and role of the legislature in systems that exhibit these characteristics are usually limited, and Ireland is no exception to this general pattern.

EIGHT

The Oireachtas

The Oireachtas, like the "Mother of Parliaments" on which it is modeled, has a role in the governmental process which, if not minor, certainly compares poorly with that of the legislatures of many European countries or the Congress of the United States. In many countries, e.g. the Scandinavian countries and the Netherlands, the long-continued coexistence in the past of independent parliaments with largely independent cabinets has contributed to a tradition among parliamentarians of insistence on their rights. They have sought to preserve their powers and autonomy, to be constantly on guard to prevent governments from assuming control of parliament's internal procedures or business, and to make their contributions as genuine legislators. In some cases, this independence is symbolized by the exclusion of holders of ministerial posts from membership of parliament, and, in general, parliamentary procedures reflect it.

This is all a far cry from British constitutional development and the British tradition. Yet, strangely, the comparatively minor role of the Oireachtas has not, until recently at least, been at all widely recognized in Ireland, even by politicians and those interested in politics. In general, a widespread acceptance of the legal fictions of the constitutional lawyers has obscured the facts of the situation. Or rather, the generally accepted propositions about government do not reflect the facts, though the tactics of those engaged in politics show that they recognize them at the level of action, if not of abstraction.

Before pursuing an investigation into the actual functions and role of the Oireachtas, however, it is necessary to define exactly what is meant by the term. Strictly, following the British conception that Parliament consists of the King, the House of Lords, and the House of Commons, the Oireachtas must be defined, as it is in the Constitution, as consisting not only of two houses, Dáil Eireann and Seanad Eireann, but of the President also. In practice, however, the term is used to refer to the two houses alone. Ireland has, then, a bicameral legislature, though the Seanad, like many senates, plays a minor and subordinate role. To a great extent in this chapter, it is the Dáil with which we are concerned, and only consequentially the Seanad.

II

In his book entitled *Legislatures*, K. C. Wheare discusses the functions of parliaments under the following heads: making (and breaking) the government, making the government behave, making the laws, and making peace and war (i.e. the conduct of foreign relations and defense). Although the Oireachtas has constitutionally and formally an authoritative say in its performance of all these functions, the agreement of its majority makes it not only a comparatively passive agent, acquiescing in the government's proposals, but also a not very inquisitive or noisy watchdog.

In the choice of government, the function of the Dáil (for in this case the Seanad has no part at all to play) has already been examined (pp. 166–68). Usually the Dáil registers a result, that of the general election by which it was itself elected. However, this need not necessarily be so. Given the presence of more than two parties and Independents, it is possible in some circumstances that post-election bargains, not explained in advance to the electorate, might be struck and coalitions put together or narrow minorities turned into majorities; this did in fact happen in 1948. In the last chapter we saw, too, that the choice of the members of a government is made by the incoming Taoiseach and approved *en bloc* by the Dáil, though the freedom of choice a Taoiseach has and the extent of the influence upon him of members of the parliamentary party may vary considerably with the party and the circumstances. All in all, this hardly adds up to a picture of the Dáil as the maker of governments, and there is an obvious contrast here with those countries where, after election results are known, consultations usually *have* to take place between the parties before a government can be constructed.

It cannot be said either that the Dáil dismisses the government, if by this is meant that it is likely to pass an adverse vote that would necessitate either the government's resignation and replacement by another or a general election. Table 7.5 (p. 184) shows a quite different picture. What can happen—and has happened—is that the rising discontent of a few members who have been supporting the government, or their threatened defection, has forced it to dissolve the Dáil and hold an election. Important as this is, nevertheless here again a contrast can be drawn with countries whose parliaments might and do overthrow governments.

"Making the government behave" is recognized as a major function of parliament in all democratic countries. It was John Stuart Mill's belief, indeed, that this is its "proper office" rather than legislating, and certainly some would regard the adequate performance of this function as a test of democracy. Yet it is a notorious fact that Ireland's model, the British Parliament, failed to develop procedures adequate to make effective its scrutiny of the growing range of state activity since it fell under government domination in the late nineteenth century. The Oireachtas, having taken over the British parliamentary procedures and traditions of the early twentieth century, has neglected to develop them even to the extent, meager as it is, that has occurred in Britain. Even by British standards the Oireachtas shows up poorly in its ability to acquire and appraise information and to supervise and influence the conduct of government.

The Oireachtas is deficient on three counts. First, its procedures and techniques are archaic and ineffective; second, the staff and facilities available to members are meager; and, third, too few of the members are equipped by education or experience to make the kinds of inquiries that are necessary or to appreciate the kind of data that ought to be made available in order to judge performance. Thus, neither the methods employed nor the personnel involved, whether representative or professional, are adequate to appraise large programs of public expenditure upon an ever increasing range of economic and social objectives, including long-term capital programs and extensive subsidies. Even if they were, the style and demeanor of opposition—and it is the opposition on which the performance of this function to a great extent depends—and the conception members generally have of their functions do not favor really effective or hard-hitting criticism.

The procedures used by the Oireachtas are those evolved by the British Parliament in the nineteenth century. Parliaments are basically debating assemblies. In the Dáil, as in the House of Commons, ministers explain and defend, and members comment in public debates using a variety of procedural pegs on which to hang discussions of administrative performance. These include debates on the annual estimates and on financial legislation generally, and on motions of various kinds, including motions of censure and "no confidence" and adjournment motions. In addition, arising out of their legislative functions, members of the Oireachtas may avail themselves of the opportunities to inquire and criticize that arise in debates on proposed legislation. But whatever its usefulness as a publicity device, the quality of public debate on the performance of the administration must depend on the quality of the information on which the discussion takes place. Debate is not, and cannot be, in itself an effective method of eliciting information or probing government activity. In fact, ministers, briefed by their civil servants, are often the only well-informed participants; the opposition and ordinary members generally have no comparable resources for acquiring and appraising information. Moreover, not only are debates usually gladiatorial set-pieces conducted on party lines, but also many of the participants may well be using the opportunity to pursue a rather different object, local publicity for themselves, and will feature local matters for local consumption.

It is not possible to measure the quality of debate in any objective fashion. We can only say that in Ireland debates are often discursive and uninformed, and sometimes irrelevant to the major issues of the topic under discussion. They are, no doubt, of some value as a device to deploy the pros and cons of a proposed course of action, e.g. legislative proposals. As a device for making the government behave, they are, publicity apart, very inefficient.

Much of what has been said of debates applies also to parliamentary questions. The Dáil has a question time on the well-known Westminster model, and, as in Britain, parliamentary questions are "a simple, convenient and speedy routine . . . available to Deputies for getting information from the Government."[1] Table 8.1 shows the considerable extent to which it is used. But analysis of questions asked shows not only that party considerations arise (from October 1956 to July 1957, for example, only 390 questions out of 1,800 were asked by government deputies) but that, to a great extent, questions are concerned with local, and often very minor, matters. In recent years at least half the questions asked have clearly and explicitly concerned a local or personal matter and many more have had some bearing on a local interest of the questioner. Certainly, some questions are aimed at getting justice or redress of a genuine grievance and there is no doubt that question time is valuable in this respect. In many cases, however, what a questioner is aiming at is to demonstrate for local public consumption his interest in the problems of his constituents, and here we should note that parliamentary questions of this type are but a small proportion of a continuous flood of inquiries and representations to ministers and departments

[1] T. Troy, "Some Aspects of Parliamentary Questions," *Administration*, VII (1959), 252.

TABLE 8.1

Sittings and Business of Dáil Eireann

Year	Number of sittings of Dáil	Total hours of sitting	Number of parliamentary questions		Hours of financial business	Hours of private members' business
			Oral	Written		
1960	76	559	2,483	270	237	31½[a]
1961	75	562	2,944	187	214	32[b]
1962	77	581	5,055	357	298	29½[c]
1963	86	606	4,107	316	295	54
1964	70	510	3,429	271	245	16½

Source: For 1960–62, J. C. Smyth, *The Houses of the Oireachtas* (2d ed., 1964), p. 50; for 1963–64, *Returns Relating to Sittings and Business of the Seventeenth Dáil* (Stationery Office, Dublin, 1965).
[a] Includes 11 hours of government time.
[b] Includes 18½ hours of government time.
[c] Includes 8 hours of government time.

made by TD's, and to a lesser extent by Senators. This is part of the service that is so important in getting and holding electoral support.

Because the incidence of questions is casual and capricious, they may have some value as a deterrent, but the very fact that they are random means that this is not an adequate method for systematic appraisal of government action. They are inadequate also since, in replying, a minister may reveal only what he chooses: "it will be sufficient if he can demonstrate *some* tenable basis for his action."[2]

In many legislatures the main procedural device for making the government behave is the committee. "Outside Britain and Commonwealth countries," writes Wheare, "it is common to find that legislatures set up a series of committees to each of which is assigned a field of governmental activity . . . and they regard themselves as entitled to find out what the Government is doing in these fields."[3] Such committees have a dual role, for they also consider proposed legislation in their own area. Great Britain never developed a strong committee system of this sort, dominant governments arguing that the doctrine of ministerial responsibility demands that ministers should answer to the full house. There, committees (called "standing committees") to which bills are referred after a general debate are constituted *ad hoc* and are not specialized in any area of state business. It is only in the "select committees," and more especially in the newly established Select Committees on Agriculture and on Science and Technology, that there is anything approaching expert and systematic inquiry into government action.

[2] *Ibid.*
[3] K. C. Wheare, *Legislatures* (London, 1963), p. 136.

Because of differences of scale, the Dáil has little need for standing committees of the traditional British type, and the fact that they are not often appointed is reflected in their title, for they are called "special committees." When it comes to select committees, the field is once again barer than in Great Britain. At the time when the Irish Free State was set up, the House of Commons had, as it happened, only one select committee to examine the conduct of government business, the Public Accounts Committee. The function of this committee was (and is) to examine the audited accounts of the government departments, which it does by way of considering the report of the parliamentary auditor—the Comptroller and Auditor General—taking up points sieved out by him as a result of his audit. The Irish Free State Constitution provided for such an officer, and the Dáil instituted a Public Accounts Committee consisting of twelve members appointed annually, its chairman being a member of an opposition party.

Later, in 1948, again following the British lead, another scrutiny committee was set up, this time in the Seanad. The Seanad Select Committee on Statutory Instruments (of nine members) is modeled very closely on a similar House of Commons committee. Its function is to examine the orders made under enabling legislation by the government or other public bodies to ensure that they do not offend against a number of criteria covering the use of powers, form, language, and publicity. Both these committees proceed by way of written and verbal inquiry and they interrogate civil servants, but not usually ministers. Neither has any powers except that of reporting to the parent bodies, which might, but usually do not, debate their reports. Both are precluded from questioning policy.

These committees are without doubt effective within their very considerable limitations. They are conducive to more careful administration, but their coverage even in their own fields is far from complete and they are mainly concerned with form and trivia. They are not, and are not intended to be, a means by which the Oireachtas investigates and appraises the government's policy and handling of affairs or the effectiveness and efficiency of the central administration. Moreover, they have often been desultory in their working, and there is very little sign that most members of either house are interested in the further development of the select committee device, limited as it is. Until recently, there has not even been a serious demand for a committee to examine the state enterprises ("state-sponsored bodies," as they are called), which might have been expected after the setting up and immediate success of the Select Committee on the Nationalized Industries of Great Britain in 1957.

The truth is that no really effective committees to investigate and appraise the entire range of state activity (such as experience in other countries suggests are the appropriate instruments for the purpose) can be set up in Ireland unless the government wishes to see them initiated. For the Oireachtas, unlike Congress in the United States, for example, has no will of its own and no conception of itself as a corporate body intended to be a constitutional instrument to perform functions that involve controlling the government. Its ruling majority looks exclusively to the government itself for guidance and direction. But governments naturally do not want effective critics, and will not have them if they do not have to have them. Neither do their professional advisers in the civil service. By tradition and training they abhor public investigation and publicity, and most of them do not in any case believe that parliamentary scrutiny would improve administrative performance.

The ineffectiveness of procedures for making the government behave is increased by two factors: the paucity of facilities available to members, and their own attitude—particularly that of the opposition—to this job. As individuals, most TD's simply cannot equip themselves adequately. In the past they were poorly paid, the salary (called an "allowance") being too small for most of them to regard the office as a full-time occupation, let alone to employ secretarial or other assistance. In 1968, their salaries were raised to £2,500 per annum, and those of Senators to £1,500, both subject to income tax. In addition, they have free travel between their homes and Leinster House and free postage. Even so, very few of them have even part-time secretarial assistance, and, clearly, a more professional type of help is out of the question.

In many parliaments official provision is made for services such as these. The Oireachtas, however, is served by a staff of only eighteen "clerks," plus a small ancillary staff. Their time is mostly taken up with servicing the meetings of the two houses and the various committees. In these circumstances, no committee gets the help of more than one clerk, and that often part-time. Individual members cannot get much more than advice on procedural matters from them. There is an Oireachtas library with a staff of two, who give some assistance, but no organized research or information services are available. Members do not even have private or shared offices, only party rooms. Nor is this failure of the Oireachtas to equip itself compensated for by facilities provided by the parties. The parties are poor and, in any case, have never made a feature of research and intelligence services for their parliamentary members.

Naturally, the main task in examining and criticizing the government, particularly in debates and other proceedings of the Oireachtas itself, falls to the party or parties in opposition. The concept of "the Opposition" as an essential complement of "the Government" is recognized in Ireland, and a special allowance is paid to the leader of the opposition party or, if there is more than one opposition party, to the leaders of the two biggest opposition groups. The style and demeanor of the opposition resembles what Wheare describes as typical of the British system, a style that he contrasts with European and American legislatures. "The leading idea upon which it is organized is that it offers itself before the country as an alternative government. It criticizes upon the understanding that, given the opportunity, it could do better itself."[4] Because of party solidarity, its efforts are not likely to be successful in the sense that parliamentary votes will be swayed. Rather, the Dáil is a platform from which to conduct a continuous appeal to the electorate. Whatever might seem to be the likelihood of the opposition actually taking office, the fact is that it behaves as though there were. For example, the main opposition party has a full team of "shadow" ministers. These behave in an appropriately responsible fashion and urge their followers to do likewise. Only a few individual TD's have occasionally conducted a different kind of opposition, more outspoken, more wholesale, more truculent, but effective; and one or two independent-minded and outspoken Senators have also behaved in somewhat similar fashion.

Many of the weaknesses from which the Oireachtas suffers in respect of scrutinizing government action are equally evident when it comes to making the laws, and the same contrasts may be made with other countries. Lacking an adequate committee system and facilities or assistance for members, it is not well adapted for considering the adequacy of proposed legislation or for searching out its weaknesses. The same criticisms of debate as a method of procedure apply here also. But there is, in addition, one respect in which the Oireachtas, like all parliaments on the British model, contrasts even more markedly with parliaments elsewhere. This is in the monopoly control the government has of legislation, both in introducing proposed legislation to the Dáil and in getting it processed into law in large measure unaltered. This fact perhaps more than any other is the distinguishing characteristic of the Oireachtas and parliaments like it. They are not "legislatures" in the sense in which the United States Congress is a legislature, nor do the members consider themselves "legislators" as congressmen do. These facts are reflected in turn in the legislative procedure, the leadership, and the general conduct of business both in the Dáil and in the Seanad.

Bills are proposed mainly by the government, the legislative program

4 *Ibid.*, p. 119.

(some 50 or so bills each year) being decided in Cabinet and each bill being prepared with overall Cabinet approval by the appropriate department after such consultation as it deems necessary. It is at this stage that the effective pressures are brought to bear and the important interests considered. The minister thus introduces a bill, a government measure, which the party will be expected to support and which the government considers has already taken major interests and views into account. Almost all bills are introduced and passed in the Dáil and proceed thence to the Seanad. There is a provision in each house for "private member's bills," but in practice these are insignificant.

> The chances of a private member's bill reaching the statute book are remote, for even when the Government accepts the principle involved the member is normally requested to withdraw the bill on the assurance that the Government will introduce a measure officially drafted to meet his case.[5]

The private member's bill is in fact often a publicity device.

Between preparation and introduction in the Dáil or consideration at the second stage—i.e. a general debate on the principles of a measure —there is one procedure that might lead the government to make changes or even to have second thoughts. That is the parliamentary party meeting. The Oireachtas members of each of the three major parties meet, in the case of Fianna Fáil once a week during the session, to discuss parliamentary business. In recent years the parliamentary members of the Fianna Fáil party, which has been the party in power, have expected to have all proposed bills explained to them and to have a chance to criticize them before they are introduced. Forthcoming legislation is a regular item of business at each meeting.

It is hard to know what positive influence these meetings have on the content of legislation. It is probably very little, both because the legislative proposals they discuss are already drafted and, in effect, the decisions have been taken, and also because the members are neither organized, equipped, nor minded to make a systematic scrutiny of bills. None of the parties, it should be noted, had any regular specialist committees continuously considering particular areas of public business until recently, but in the 1961–65 Dáil Fianna Fáil set up a standing committee on agriculture, and since then it has developed a number of committees that meet from time to time with the appropriate minister. From these and from the more general meetings the government gets an indication of feeling in the party and whether a proposal that touches some prejudice or interest of the rural community is going to be badly

[5] J. C. Smyth, *The Houses of the Oireachtas* (2d ed., Dublin, 1954), p. 41.

received. In recent years two bills were much criticized at the Fianna Fáil Oireachtas party meetings and both had to be amended. Significantly, they were a succession bill (curtailing the right to bequeath property) and a land bill. Some Fianna Fáil leaders say that parliamentary party meetings have assumed great importance in recent years as the government has tackled the problems of social and economic development in a more wholesale way, with a consequent increase in the number of bills affecting the community intimately.

The parliamentary party meeting is probably, however, of less importance as a *formative* influence than the day-to-day contacts leaders have with party members and the representations of individual members in the early stages of preparation of bills. For the salient fact is that the parliamentary party's consideration of a bill takes place *after* departmental and governmental decisions have been made and the bill is drafted. This applies also to the proceedings of the Oireachtas in general. The government is committed, and the bill is sponsored and conducted during its passage through the Oireachtas by the minister. Backed by the government majority, he expects to get it through relatively unscathed, though amendments may be accepted and, even at this late stage, proposed by himself to improve the bill.

Legislative procedure follows the characteristic pattern of this type of assembly. After a formal introduction (first stage), there is a general debate followed by a vote (second stage), after which the bill is regarded as having been approved in principle and not subject to serious alteration. This is followed by a third stage, an examination of the bill section by section, at which amendments may be proposed that do not negate the bill as a whole. The bill as amended is then considered once again before being passed on to the other house, usually the Seanad.

The principles governing legislative procedure seem to be four. First, the house is considering proposals in an advanced stage of preparation. The idea that governs the legislative procedures of many parliaments, namely that a bill is only a proposal to be investigated by a committee that will interrogate its authors and hear interested parties before preparing its own revised version to present to the full house, is entirely alien to Irish parliamentary tradition. Second, the principles of a bill are debated first and in full house and, having been agreed upon, are not thereafter open to amendment. Third, it is ordinarily the job of ministers to bring in bills and to sponsor them; the Oireachtas expects this and is organized accordingly. Fourth, business is so arranged and rules so framed that the government can get its bills passed without too much delay, while at the same time the opposition has opportunities to deploy its case against them, a case made principally not to influence the government or the house, but to persuade the public that the running of the country would be better placed in their hands. The orderly passage of business is assured by the government's majority and by the activities of the party whips, who manage their respective parties, arrange the timetable, and make sure of the vote.

Foreign affairs and the conduct of defense are notoriously areas where, by the very nature of the subject and of the procedures involved, parliaments are in the hands of governments. Ireland is no exception. The Constitution requires that war shall not be declared nor shall the state participate in any war without the assent of the Dáil, but if it comes to war, this requirement is likely to be only a formality. More important, Article 29.5 requires that international agreements "shall be laid before the Dáil," i.e. published, and therefore subject to parliamentary questions, and that any agreement involving expenditure of public money shall have the approval of the Dáil. But the texts of agreements represent things already done and commitments entered into, and though Dáil Eireann does in fact have to approve, for example, the sending of soldiers to serve in UN forces, its grip on the state's foreign commitments is palpably weak. Some matters, no doubt, cannot be the subject of debate while they are in course of being negotiated, but the result is that even an agreement involving fundamental social and economic change, such as entry into the European Economic Community or agreement on a free trade area, might well in fact be presented virtually as a *fait accompli.*

The position is no different in respect to the development of foreign policies in general. Matters such as the interpretation of neutrality, relations with power blocs, or—a hardy annual of a few years back—the admission of China to the UN, indeed Ireland's UN policies as a whole, are developed without the government seeking approval for them. White papers on foreign policy are rarely published. The state's attitude and actions are explained only later at some convenient parliamentary opportunity, perhaps in the debate on the estimates for the Department of External Affairs, and even these explanations have often been cursory and inadequate.[6]

The conclusion is inevitable: the Oireachtas is neither very efficient at appraising government policy and administration—least of all foreign affairs—nor a creative force in legislation. It serves to ratify deci-

---

[6] See P. Keatinge, "The Formulation of Foreign Policy in Ireland, 1921–61" (unpublished Ph.D. thesis in the Library of Trinity College, Dublin), chap. 10.

sions made elsewhere, it legitimizes, it gives valuable publicity to public business, and it provides an important forum for the expression of opinions and the voicing of grievances.

III

In this survey of the performance of the Oireachtas, attention has mainly, and rightly, been focused on the Dáil. The relative inferiority of the second house is, of course, a common, though not universal, phenomenon of modern democratic states. In the case of Seanad Eireann, it is the sequel to a troubled past.

The first Parliament in 1919 consisted of a single house, for the independence movement neither needed nor wanted more in the circumstances. When the Treaty was being negotiated, however, promises were demanded and given that the new state should have a Senate in which the unionist minority would be strongly represented, and provision was made for this in the Irish Free State Constitution. That Senate had a checkered career. No satisfactory formula for its composition could be found, and when it exercised its right to hold up legislation that had been passed in the Dáil, it was immediately open to the charge not only of thwarting the real representatives of the people but of being un-Irish as well. It was especially anathema to De Valera and Fianna Fáil and it did not long survive their accession to office, being abolished in 1936 after acrimonious debates during which De Valera declared himself unconvinced of the value of any Senate but open to conviction. However, a general belief in the usefulness of second houses prevailed, and the 1937 Constitution made provision for a new Senate, Seanad Eireann.

Seanad Eireann is both singular in its composition and circumscribed in its powers. In considering a new Senate, De Valera was attracted by one of the proposals of a commission set up to advise on the composition of a new house, a proposal for a body selected on a vocational basis and obviously inspired by the principles enunciated in the encyclical *Quadragesimo Anno* of Pope Pius XI. However, he recognized that the country was not in fact sufficiently organized on vocational lines to allow direct choice by vocational bodies, and he was also concerned not to have a body so composed as to be likely to oppose the government of the day. The scheme he evolved, therefore, provided for a body composed of three groups. Six members are elected by the Irish graduates of the two universities, three from each. Forty-three are elected by an electoral college of nearly 900 composed of the members of the Oireachtas and the county and county borough councilors, from five panels of candidates nominated in part by bodies representing five groups of interests—education and culture, agriculture, industry and commerce, labor, and public administration and social services—and in part by members of the Oireachtas. The remaining eleven are nominated by the Taoiseach himself after all the others have been chosen, thus providing him with an opportunity to give representation to any group that he thinks needs it, to bring in persons of eminence, and—De Valera frankly admitted when proposing it—to ensure a government majority.

The scheme for the election of the forty-three was admitted to be only a step toward vocational representation. Yet in itself it was defective, for not only did the structure of the community not correspond to vocational principles, but also the composition of the panels, with labor separated from management, seemed actually to go contrary to those very principles. More serious for genuine vocational representation, the dilution of direct representation of vocational organizations in order to make the system more democratic permitted party domination, which has in fact been complete. The parties have controlled the elections to the exclusion of almost all the truly vocational elements. Since the Taoiseach's nominees tend also to be party men, the Seanad is composed largely of party politicians not very different from their colleagues in the Dáil and, in the case of many of them, with only tenuous connections with the interests they affect to represent. Almost one-third of them are usually in fact former TD's, defeated or retired, and almost all the rest are party men who have earned a reward or a consolation prize—"unlike deputies, many senators are not 'front rank' party men: rather, they are party 'back-room' boys, policy designers, influential backers and organization workers, and some of them are veterans or even 'hacks.' There are many 'hacks,' but not so many as we are sometimes told, and their numbers seem to have diminished since the generation of the Revolution started to leave politics."[7] Naturally, they tend to speak and vote on party lines; they also sit in party groups. Only the university representatives, included to compensate the universities for having lost their representation in the Dáil in 1936, tend to approximate the vocational type, representing professions such as law and medicine and the professional classes generally. Naturally, the prestige of the house suffers from the fact that it is not composed on any basis that corresponds with the social structure of the community but is merely another selection of party politicians chosen in an unnecessarily complicated manner.

[7] T. Garvin, "The Irish Senate in Theory and Practice, 1937–66" (unpublished M.A. thesis in the Library of University College, Dublin), p. 85.

The Seanad suffers also from its evident inferiority and subordination to the Dáil. The Constitution makes clear that the Dáil is regarded as representing the people. The Seanad is deliberately placed to one side of the political stage, for the Dáil nominates the Taoiseach and approves his government; the government is constitutionally responsible to the Dáil and there it must maintain a majority; the Dáil is required by the Constitution to consider the estimates of public expenditure, to ratify international agreements, and to approve any declaration of war; almost all legislation is introduced in the Dáil and there all major policy statements are made. The Seanad's meager powers to amend or delay emphasize the point that it is primarily a revising body with the power to draw public attention to a proposal by compelling the Dáil to reconsider it.

The subordinate status of the Seanad in law and in practice and its lack of prestige are emphasized and underlined by three facts. First, the house contains no ministers. The Constitution permits up to two members of the government to be Senators, but in its whole history since 1938 only one minister has been a member and this only because he was defeated at a Dáil election. The majority side of the house is led and business is controlled by a majority leader who, though he is always senior, does not have ministerial rank. Second, the Seanad's business is subordinated to that of the Dáil. Since most bills are considered by the Dáil first, the Seanad, which spends nine-tenths of its time debating bills, sometimes has little business in the early part of the sessions, only to be forced into an unseemly rush at the end, processing without proper consideration a number of bills that the government wishes to have passed before the recess. Third, sometimes in the past its consideration of items on its agenda has been delayed, interrupted, or impaired by the failure of ministers to attend as arranged.

There is a vicious circle here: lacking prestige and being government-controlled, the Seanad cannot insist on a more active role or more consideration for its dignity or convenience. Because it does not do so, it is condemned to hold an undignified position and to waste what potential it does have. It does do some useful work. Largely because it contains a larger number of professional people than the Dáil, its debates on current issues are sometimes important; bills are improved, some considerably, as a result of its work; its Select Committee on Statutory Instruments does effect a check on the administration. However, the air of leisure that pervades its debates, its light program (in recent years it has met 20 to 30 times and for an average of about 160 hours in each year), the absence of any feeling of urgency or of momentous political cut and thrust, and the comparatively poor publicity it gets all emphasize its lack of importance and contribute to its low prestige. If it were more important, its composition would undoubtedly evoke more than the halfhearted criticism that is now heard from time to time, but to government and to community alike, this does not seem to be a matter of much importance.

IV

The poor performance of both houses of the Oireachtas arises partly from the fact that they are badly equipped and organized and poorly informed. There are, however, more fundamental causes: first, a general acceptance by members of the dominant role of the government as policy maker, and second, the preoccupation of many members with their own local positions. These considerations have led them to see themselves as having another function to perform, the function of "servicing" their constituents. In so doing, members of the Oireachtas generally, and TD's in particular, constitute themselves more a factor in the *administration* of state policy—particularly in detailed administration—than *legislators* as conventionally conceived. They adopt this role both by inclination and by force of circumstances, a fact best explained by considering who and what they are and how they attain office.

In the chapter on elections, the point was made that almost all Dáil candidates are local people; so then are most TD's, as Table 8.2 illustrates. Fewer than 10 per cent live far out of their constituencies and fewer than 20 per cent were born elsewhere. Of those who do not live in or near their constituencies, the greater number are ministers (who may in fact have two homes), national heroes, or members of a family dynasty founded on a national hero; for all others, it is essential to live nearby, and this has consistently been the case since 1922. In fact,

TABLE 8.2

Birthplace and Residence of TD's

Place of birth or residence	1922	1932	1944	1965
Born in constituency	56%	60%	68%	60%[a]
Born nearby[b]	—	—	—	21[a]
Resident in constituency	72	83	84	78
Resident nearby[b]	—	—	—	14

Source: Data for 1922–44 are from J. L. McCracken, *Representative Government in Ireland* (London, 1958), p. 90; data for 1965 are from John Whyte, *Dáil Deputies*, Tuairim pamphlet No. 15 (Dublin, 1966).

[a] Percentage relates to 110 members only.

[b] I.e., in an adjacent constituency or another constituency in the same county.

TABLE 8.3

Changes in Age Distribution of TD's

Age group	Dáil				
	1919	1922	1932	1944	1965
20–29	21%	14%	1%	2%	6%
30–39	37	38	27	12	20
40–49	25	24	39	31	31
50–59	13	18	26	37	24
60–69	3	4	5	17	14
70 or over	—	2	2	1	5

Source: Data for the years 1919–44 are taken from J. L. McCracken, *Representative Government in Ireland*, pp. 31–91. The data for 1965 are from the Tuairim Survey and private inquiries.
Note: Percentages are given to the nearest 1 per cent and do not necessarily total 100.

ties are even more specific, for many and perhaps most members are identified with the particular part of the constituency in which they live or which they are reckoned specially to represent. Senators, of course, except the university representatives, do not have constituencies. Nevertheless, though one-third of the 1965 Seanad lived in Dublin, many of the rest were identified with their home areas in much the same manner as TD's, and in practice they performed the same role.

Since TD's are predominantly local men and since Ireland is overwhelmingly a Catholic country, there are few Protestant members. These have tended to represent parts of constituencies where the people of their faith could muster a quota of votes, e.g. in Donegal until recently, or in some Dublin constituencies. In the Dála of the 1920's there were a dozen or more; in 1965 there were four. The Seanad in the same year had five out of sixty, and of these, two were elected by Dublin University and three were nominated by the Taoiseach (two from border counties whose Protestants could no longer muster a quota).

The revolutionary Dáil of 1919 contained a large proportion of young men, and over half the 1922 Dáil were under forty. But once they were selected, it was comparatively easy to retain their seats, and the turnover was fairly low. Moreover, new entrants tended to be over forty. Accordingly, as Table 8.3 shows, the Dáil was a steadily aging body until the 1950's, when inevitably senior men began to be replaced more quickly. So, too, in the Seanad, where the renewal process began later. "Proportionately the Upper House retains more older members than does the Dáil, and the thinning out [of the "Old Guard"] has not affected it so noticeably until fairly recently."[8]

[8] *Ibid.*, p. 132.

TABLE 8.4

Education of TD's for Various Years, 1922–65

Year	Level attained		
	Primary	Secondary, vocational or technical	University or professional
1922	40%	34%	26%
1932	44	32	24
1944	48	29	22
1965	20	50ª	30

Source: Data for the years 1922–44 are adapted from J. L. McCracken, *Representative Government in Ireland*, p. 93. Data for 1965 are from John Whyte, *Dáil Deputies* (Tuairim pamphlet No. 15, Dublin, 1966), p. 33.

ª Of these, 47 per cent were on the secondary level and 3 per cent on the vocational or technical level.

TABLE 8.5

Education of TD's, 1965, by Party

Party	Level attained			
	Primary	Secondary	Vocational or technical	University or professional
All	28 (20%)	68 (47%)	5 (3%)	43 (30%)
Fianna Fáil	10 (14)	36 (50)	5 (7)	21 (29)
Fine Gael	9 (20)	19 (40)	– –	19 (40)
Labour	7 (32)	12 (54)	– –	3 (14)
Others	2	1	—	—

Source: Data from the Tuairim Survey.

The first Dáil was also very strong in professional men. Over 40 per cent were in a profession, especially teaching, journalism, and medicine, and others were students. In the 1920's the character of the house changed markedly. Already in 1922 the numerical predominance of people with university or professional education had disappeared (see Table 8.4). To this day the Dáil has a very low proportion of such people compared with many countries. It will be seen from Tables 8.4 and 8.5 that it was not until recently that the number of members with secondary education rose sharply. Analysis of the 1965 Dáil by party reveals that Fianna Fáil is proportionately less well provided with graduates than Fine Gael, while the Labour Party is even weaker.

Just as the number of highly educated people dropped in 1922 and after, so too did the number of professional people. Table 8.6 shows that, whereas professional people comprised 30 per cent in 1922, they had fallen to less than 20 per cent by the middle 1940's. Teachers and journalists especially fell away, the decline in the former being acceler-

TABLE 8.6

Occupations of TD's, 1922–65

Occupation[a]	1922		1932		1944		1965[b]	
Professional:								
Accountants	2		–		–		1	
Barristers	3		11		6		7	
Solicitors	3		6		6		7	
Engineers	1		1		2		1	
Journalists	6		2		2		1	
Medical doctors	9		6		4		3	
Teachers	13		13		5		8	
Veterinary surgeons	1		–		–		–	
TOTAL	38	(29.7%)	39	(25.5%)	25	(18.1%)	28	(19.4%)
Industrial and commercial:								
Auctioneers	1		1		1		3	
Company directors, managers	3		13		10		14	
Publicans	1		4		1		7	
Shopkeepers or general merchants	12		15		17		8	
Others	6		6		4		9	
TOTAL	23	(17.9%)	39	(25.5%)	33	(24.0%)	41	(28.4%)
Farmers	14	(10.9)	41	(27.0)	39	(28.3)	33	(23.0)
Trade union officials	11	(8.6)	5	(3.2)	6	(4.3)	10	(7.0)
Clerical workers	3	(2.4)	2	(1.3)	3	(2.2)	3	(2.1)
Artisans and tradesmen	5	(3.9)	4	(2.6)	5	(3.6)	5	(3.5)
Housewives} Politicians[b]}	33	(25.8)	22	(14.3)	23	(16.6)	{ 4 {18	(2.7) (12.5)
Miscellaneous	1	(0.8)	1	(0.6)	4	(2.9)	2	(1.4)
GRAND TOTAL	128	(100%)	153	(100%)	138	(100%)	144	(100%)

Source: For the years 1922–44 the tables in J. L. McCracken, *Representative Government in Ireland*, pp. 96–99, have been used and adapted. Data for 1965 are taken from the Tuairim Survey.

[a] Some members have more than one occupation. All have been classified according to their main occupation.

[b] The figures for 1965 are somewhat different from those given in Table 3.4. The differences arise because the categories used are not the same and because all ministers have been classified here as politicians, as McCracken did in his tables.

ated by the ending of direct university representation in 1936. Lawyers, on the other hand, increased: from the 1930's half the professional people have been barristers or solicitors, and especially country solicitors. Lawyers are particularly strong in Fine Gael, whose proportion of professional men generally is far higher than the other parties.

In contrast with the professions, farmers were conspicuously absent from the first Dáil, which "could make no claim to being a cross-section of the whole community."[9] However, the farmers naturally soon took

[9] J. L. McCracken, *Representative Government in Ireland* (London, 1958), p. 33.

their place in a body in which local men represent local communities, and they now number nearly one-quarter of the total. Besides those recorded as farmers, there are always others with a secondary interest in farming, for it is quite common for people to combine their principal profession or business, especially keeping a shop, with farming.

If the farmers are naturally thought of as representing rural communities, it should not be supposed that those classed in industrial and commercial occupations are necessarily city people or in big business. Far from it; directors and executives of large firms are, in fact, conspicuously absent. The industrial and commercial group are mostly owners of small family businesses, local contractors, publicans (barkeepers), and shopkeepers, and there is a strong rural and small-community element among them. Together with the farmers, they form the solid core of the Dáil and comprise more than half of its total membership.

With half the Dáil in farming or small-scale business, there are few people with higher education and professional or business experience of a kind that would enable them to bring modern knowledge and techniques of business management to bear on large-scale state activity. In this respect, the Seanad is better placed, as the following tabulation on occupations of Senators elected in 1965 shows:[10]

Professional	32%	Trade union officials	7%
Commerce, finance, and insurance (mostly shopkeepers and publicans)	22	Persons engaged in politics	5
Agriculture	27	Others	8

While the small business element (shopkeepers, publicans, etc.) and the farmers make up half the house, as they do in the Dáil, the proportion of professional people is significantly higher (32 per cent as against 19 per cent), largely because of the university representatives and the presence of other middle-class professional people who can combine their occupation with the lesser demands of the Seanad in a way not possible for TD's.

Although the Dáil is deficient in professional and big business experience, it is strong in knowledge of local community affairs. Deputies are particularly active in local government, which is one of the routes to parliamentary office and which offers the most frequent opportunities for service to their constituents. By far the most important local authorities in Ireland are the county and county borough councils. In 1965, 56

[10] T. Garvin, "The Irish Senate in Theory and Practice" (unpublished M.A. thesis in the Library of University College, Dublin).

TABLE 8.7
*Local Government Experience of TD's Elected
to the Eighteenth Dáil, 1965*

Experience	All	Fianna Fáil	Fine Gael	Labour	Other
Not at present a county or county borough councilor, but has been in the past	15	11	3	1	–
Currently a member of a county or county borough council:					
Service before being first elected to the Dáil	67	26	24	15	2
First elected to council after becoming a TD	14	8	5	1	–
TOTAL	81	34	29	16	2
Percentage	56%	47%	62%	73%	
Percentage of members who do not hold ministerial or Parliamentary Secretary office	66%	67%	62%	73%	

Source: Data collected by the Tuairim Survey, 1965.

per cent of deputies were members of such councils, and if we exclude ministers and Parliamentary Secretaries, who find it difficult and embarrassing to attend local authority meetings, the percentage was 66 (see Table 8.7). So, too, were almost half the Senators. Some of those who were county councilors served also on urban authorities (there are no rural district or parish councils), and almost all, county and county borough councilors alike, were serving on one or more of a variety of other local authorities such as county committees of agriculture, vocational education committees, harbor boards, joint authorities administering health services, and "visiting committees" which inspect local authority hospitals, mental institutions, and the "county homes" (for the aged). All these offer opportunities for influence and service that enhance a man's local reputation and help him secure a quota of first preferences. Nor is this to be thought of as a phenomenon of the countryside. Eleven of the twenty-five Dublin City representatives in 1965 were councilors, and of the fourteen who were not, five were ministers or former ministers. Four out of five of the Cork City deputies were also councilors and the other was a minister.

In addition, members of the Oireachtas are to be found in all kinds of voluntary bodies, particularly trade unions and trade associations. Yet, strangely, they are not as frequently to be found in social, cultural, or religious organizations as might be expected. However, for electoral purposes, membership of bodies such as the Gaelic Athletic Association is generally reckoned to be particularly useful.[11] McCracken in his *Representative Government in Ireland* notes that of the twelve women who sat in the Dáil between 1922 and 1948, three were widows and three sisters of prominent leaders of the independence movement, and five others were widows of former TD's. Among the men, he found eight sons of members and twelve close relatives of leaders. In 1965 there were four widows and twenty-eight sons or daughters of former members, and nine nephews or other close relatives.

These data provide a fairly clear picture of the membership of the Oireachtas. Most members of the Dáil are "local people," they live and belong in their constituencies, their work or business is local, and their very position may largely depend upon their activities in local government and local life generally. Whereas the Seanad contains a bigger proportion than the Dáil of a different element—those with middle-class and urban occupations—and Senators do not depend so directly on the goodwill of the public of their areas, the majority of them are also of much the same type, engaged in much the same activities. The majority of the members of the Oireachtas are, in fact, the most important "public persons" in their districts.

How do they see themselves? Although there are no systematic data on this, there can be little doubt of what the answer is. For most of them a public representative is, as Léo Hamon said of the French deputy, "a man at the beck and call of his electors,"[12] though they themselves would not put it quite like that, preferring to use words such as "service," and "available" instead. The public expect this; "there is a fixed notion that cannot be got out of people's heads that Deputies can get you something that you cannot get from anybody else."[13] The election system puts a premium on it: "of course you must canvass in another form from the day on which the election is over till the date of the next election."[14] For a good many the *cursus honorum* may well be via service at local government level, and the maintenance of one's position certainly requires continuing to provide it. Service of this kind is thus an integral part of the web of personal contact and influence that is the foundation of the

[11] See Table 4.4, p. 114 above.

[12] "Members of the French Parliament," *International Social Science Journal*, **XIII** (1961), 557.

[13] Senator M. Hayes, *Seanad Debates*, vol. 55, col. 1686 (Dec. 19, 1962).

[14] Deputy M. Hilliard, quoted in D. E. Butler, ed., *Elections Abroad* (London, 1959), p. 202.

position of the public person, at least in the rural areas and to some extent in urban working-class areas too.

The service that representatives give covers a wide range of minor administrative matters at both local and central government levels. Members of the Oireachtas, particularly TD's but also Senators, are expected to give advice, to help prepare applications to public authorities, and to make inquiries, representations, and appeals for any person or group in their own constituency, but particularly in their own district. Matters they deal with include housing and housing grants, entitlement to health services and other public social service benefits, health service facilities, roads, drainage and flood control, land redistribution, and compulsory purchase. Also, their help may be sought and given in matters such as children's allowances and old-age pensions, where the decisions are automatic and the procedures routine and simple and where, therefore, the representative's intervention is superfluous. In only one matter, jobs, is there little scope for representations. At the central government level there are only a few post office appointments and jobs for laborers on drainage projects and on similar types of work. At the local level, only rate collectors and some posts in the vocational education and local agricultural services are in the giving of the local representative bodies and, therefore, open to influence.

Whether the representative can help or not, he has to intervene and to be seen to be doing so. This has direct effects on minor administrative procedures. For example, to facilitate members in their duties, "most of the departments send out their replies [to the deputies' representations] with carbon copies. The deputy sends the carbon reply to the constituent."[15] For this reason also, questions and debates that are useful publicity media often have a strong local and personal flavor.

What proportion of the time of a member of the Oireachtas does all this take? Evidence given in a case in the High Court in 1961[16] and the impression to be gained by talking to members make it clear that, for many country TD's and some city TD's, it constitutes a heavy burden and may be their most time-consuming activity. Yet most of them accept it without resentment. On the contrary, there is some evidence that they value it and exploit it. There are officials who will say that some deputies deliberately create the impression among their constituents that their intervention is necessary or helpful, and thus they build up a profes-

[15] Senator M. Hayes, *Seanad Debates*, vol. 55, col. 1687 (Dec. 19, 1962).
[16] See *O'Donovan* v. *Attorney General*, 1961, I.R.114, and the evidence in this case reported in the *Irish Times*, Jan. 12–26, 1961.

sional-client relationship. Certainly, there have in the past been instances where attempts by departments to alter procedures so that representations by deputies would become unnecessary have been resented and, indeed, thwarted.

This preoccupation with minor administrative matters on one's constituents' behalf, which makes the representative a factor in administration, might be seen as the obverse of his comparative torpor in other roles. To borrow the terminology of Wahlke and his colleagues in *The Legislative System*,[17] most members of the Oireachtas do not see themselves in respect of policy and legislation as "inventors," i.e. as being there to devise legislation, or even "brokers," i.e. referees in the struggle to compose conflicting interests. These are in their view the functions of the government. Many probably do see themselves as "tribunes," their job being to discover and reflect the opinion of their constituents. Some, in fact, argue (though it may be a rationalization) that their "contact man" activities enable them the better to perform this role.

A small group of members, both TD's and Senators, do not conform to the general pattern of local representative outlined above. Besides the members of the government themselves, there are a few more active parliamentarians comprising mainly the opposition "shadow cabinet" or "front bench" and a few others who carry a great load of parliamentary work, both debating policy in a general way and scrutinizing bills in detail at the committee stage. These are the professional politicians, the politician lawyers, a few academics in the Seanad, and one or two others, almost all—except perhaps in Labour—with middle-class and urban backgrounds.

Locally oriented though so many members are, they do not carry their local interests to the point of voting contrary to the party line. They express their views at the party meeting and in speeches, but, this done, they support their party when it comes to a vote, and they are expected to do so by their constituents. Besides being locally oriented, representatives are also strongly party-oriented and are able to reconcile the two because most of their supporters have strong party allegiances also, which are not affected by the party's policies at any given time. Thus the voting records of TD's are consistent. They average a 70 per cent attendance to vote and very rarely vote against their parties. At most, a dissident will abstain unless, being on the government side, his vote is critical. Significantly, perhaps, the only recent case of a government supporter voting against the government arose over a local government mat-

[17] J. C. Wahlke *et al.*, *The Legislative System* (New York, 1962).

TABLE 8.8
Voting Record of Senators, 1957–61

Number of votes cast (maximum: 44)	Number of consistent party supporters	Number of independent voters	Number whose records are inconclusive
30 or above	33	2	–
20–29	12	1	–
10–19	7	1	–
Less than 10	5	–	4
TOTAL	57	4	4

Note: During this period six Senators died and were replaced. The Cathaoirleach (chairman) is omitted. The total number of Senators covered is, therefore, 65.

ter concerning the dissident's own county, and the member himself was senior, individualistic, particularly locally oriented, and something of a character. Only in the Seanad, where it is not politically important, are there to be found a few genuine independents. In a recent study, T. Garvin concluded that "there are probably about four or five independent Senators in a typical Senate."[18] As Table 8.8 indicates, the voting record ten years ago showed that this was also the case at that time.

v

The member of the Oireachtas, and particularly the TD, is more a factor in administration and a "consumer representative" than a legislator. However, it is important to note that the Constitution as interpreted by those brought up upon traditional constitutional theory does not recognize this. The judge in the *O'Donovan* case declared:

Most important duties are positively assigned to Deputies by the Constitution, the paramount duty being that of making laws for the country.... It will be found again, however, that the Constitution does not anywhere in the Articles relating to the functions of Deputies recognize or sanction their intervention in administrative affairs.[19]

The welfare state creates the opportunities and the need for this type of activity. What might be doubted is whether the parliamentary representative should perform it, or at least the more routine elements in it. Yet, rightly or wrongly, it may well be that, as the citizen sees it, the representative engaged in these activities is performing "an indispensable function which no other political unit or device can perform so well."[20] Nor does it follow that he would give it up, if he was no longer forced by

18 Garvin, p. 85.
19 *O'Donovan* v. *Attorney General*, 1961, I.R.114.
20 J. D. B. Miller, *Australian Government and Politics* (2d ed., London, 1959), p. 116.

the election system to do it. This kind of activity by public persons and this kind of relationship between them and their clients are deep-rooted in Irish experience. For generations, Irish people saw that to get the benefits that public authorities bestow, the help of a man with connections and influence was necessary. All that democracy has meant is that such a man has been laid on officially, as it were, and is now no longer a master but a servant.

NINE

The Central Administration and the Civil Service

The nineteenth century saw the gradual replacement of old governmental and administrative organizations in Great Britain by a completely new and integrated system and the creation of a remarkable Civil Service, "the one great political invention of the nineteenth century," as Graham Wallas called it. This process, which was complete by the end of the century, was one not only of modernization and tidying up, but of democratization as well. It was based upon the principle that there should be two systems of government, central government and local government: the one responsible to Parliament via ministers controlling departments manned by a professional "career" Civil Service; the other, a subordinate system, ultimately controlled by Parliament, but administered by locally elected councils, which, in the case of some towns, were the direct descendants of the self-governing communities of the past. Almost all public business was to be subsumed under one or other of these heads. Ireland as part of the United Kingdom was as far as possible fitted into this pattern. Since, however, it had been a separate kingdom with its own administration, it had perforce to be treated in some respects as a special case, both in administrative structure, where a measure of decentralization was both necessary and convenient, and in the extent and allocation of governmental functions, where the security needs of imperial rule and its paternalism meant that the arrangements made for Ireland were in some respects different from those of Great Britain.

Concerning administrative structure, the principle of union was not applied systematically and neither was the principle of consolidating all central activities in a number of uniform departments. Indeed, by the end of the century, when the state began to intervene on a more massive scale and when, because of the home rule movement, there was a desire to associate Irish people more closely with the administration of their state services, there was a marked increase in the variety of organizations administering public services. The result was a veritable administrative jungle.

In his book *The Irish Administration, 1801–1914*, McDowell sums up the position as follows:

It is apparent from a cursory glance at Irish administrative history in the nineteenth century that there was a strong tendency to tackle newly-appreciated problems on simple *ad hoc* lines, which often meant the creation of a new department with little regard for the general structure. Though functions were from time to time transferred between departments, no attempt was made to plan systematically the distribution of duties between all the departments, British and Irish, functioning in Ireland, nor were the arrangements for controlling and cooperating their activities adequate.[1]

After the Union, some Irish departments were merged in their British equivalents but others were not. In the course of the century, some British departments got new duties in respect of Ireland, while in other cases Irish departments or offices were set up, some administered by boards. Indeed, Ireland, it was said at the turn of the century, had as many boards as would make her coffin. The control of the Chief Secretary (a sort of Minister for Irish Affairs) over the various offices varied considerably and, in respect of at least one department, the Department of Agriculture and Technical Instruction, was very tenuous indeed, since he was intended to be but a figurehead and that department had its own Junior Minister. Tidy-minded colonial administrators with experience in India, like J. W. Ridgeway, Under-Secretary from 1887 to 1893, and Lord McDonnell, who held the same office from 1902 to 1908, fretted at the lack of overall control they were able to exercise, owing to the institution of semi-independent boards, on the one hand, and the interference of the British Treasury, on the other. It should be noted, however, that while the emerging development and welfare services were in a variety of hands, the basic essentials of law and order were very firmly and directly controlled by "the Castle,"[2] which, by and large, was the center of influence and patronage. Moreover, the scale of the administration was so modest, Dublin so small and compact, and the senior officials so homogeneous and used to meeting one another at their clubs that, as McDowell recalls, George Wyndham, Chief Secretary from 1900 to 1905, found that the government of Ireland was "conducted only by continuous conversation."

[1] R. B. McDowell, *The Irish Administration, 1801–1914* (London, 1964), p. 27.

[2] Dublin Castle was the center of the Irish Administration, where the Chief Secretary had his office, and the headquarters of the police and security forces, besides home affairs and justice generally.

Concerning the extent and allocation of the functions of the state, Ireland exhibited variations on the British theme. "Irish conditions encouraged or compelled the state to exert itself vigorously on a more extensive front than in contemporary England."[3] Departments such as the Board of Works and the Local Government Board tended to pursue active policies of relief, improvement, and development, and after 1880 the state began to operate in Ireland "on, by contemporary British standards, a large front."[4] The Land Commission, the Department of Agriculture and Technical Instruction, and the Congested Districts Board, all set up in the last twenty years of the century, were part of a massive reorganization and development of the agricultural community.

If Ireland, being "underdeveloped," qualified for more paternal treatment, the local government system at least was in most respects the same as that evolved in Great Britain itself, and was democratized by the same stages. The allocation of functions between central and local government was obviously on the British pattern. The basis of local government in Ireland, as in Great Britain, was mainly roads and the environmental health services ("public health" and the "sanitary services," as they were called), and the relief of the poor, including the provision of medical services. But, unlike Great Britain's, Ireland's police were nationalized and education largely so, and at the end of the century the development of agriculture and the resuscitation of the poorest rural areas were all central services, though administered by or with the advice of boards on which Irishmen sat, rather than by standard departments headed by civil servants answering directly to the Chief Secretary or some other minister.

Although Ireland was something of a special case in regard to both administrative structure and functions, the same could not be said of the public service, at least from the time of the Civil Service reforms of the third quarter of the century onward. The development of a Civil Service divided into distinct classes common to all departments, mostly appointed by a competitive examination set on ordinary school or university subjects and advanced by bureaucratic promotion procedures, applied to Ireland as to Great Britain. Since Irish educational standards were approximately the same as those in Great Britain, Irishmen could and did join the Civil Service in large numbers and served both in Ireland and in Great Britain. Nor were they barred from the higher posts. True, it was a standing complaint that the Treasury was niggardly in the number of "First Division" (i.e. top administrative cadre) posts that it would authorize for Irish departments, but those that did exist, to-

[3] McDowell, p. viii.
[4] *Ibid.*, p. 27.

gether with other senior posts, were likely to be occupied by Irishmen. In an analysis of the 48 most senior civil servants in 1914, McDowell points out that they were "overwhelmingly Irish," only 10 of them having come from across the Channel. On the other hand, 28 of them were Protestants and 20 were Catholics, a manifestation of the favorable social and economic position of the Protestant community and yet at the same time evidence of the fact that it was far from a monopoly.[5]

It will readily be seen from all this that political independence for Ireland did not precipitate the problems that beset many of the states of Asia and Africa as they emerged to independence. "Ireland inherited a complete apparatus of government, both central and local,"[6] with its own public service, which had a sure source of recruits from well-established secondary schools and universities. The formative period of these institutions, during the period of "the Union," meant that they were inevitably closely assimilated into the emerging British system and in essentials on the British pattern. Only in two respects were there significant differences: first, a greater propensity to turn to the state to solve social and economic problems; and, second, a messy pattern of authorities, which contrasted with the comparative uniformity of the British administrative structure of the early twentieth century.

II

In a notice dated January 19, 1922, the Provisional Government announced that the business of the new state would for the moment be carried on by nine departments, which would incorporate the various existing departments, boards, and other offices of the previous regime. "It will be obvious," the notice said, "that under the altered circumstances certain of the [existing] departments ... will be no longer required." This presaged a drastic reduction of the jungle to uniformity, which was, indeed, accomplished to a large extent by the Ministers and Secretaries Act, 1924, section 1 of which reads as follows:

There shall be established in Saorstát Eireann the several Departments of State specified and named in the eleven following sub-paragraphs, amongst which the administration and business of the public services in Saorstát Eireann shall be distributed as in the said sub-paragraphs ... and each of which said Departments and the powers, duties and functions thereof shall be assigned to and administered by the Minister hereinafter named as head thereof.

All at once, it seemed, Irish administration was forced into the neat dichotomy of a central administration subdivided into ministerial de-

---

[5] *Ibid.*, pp. 47–48.

[6] T. J. Barrington, "Public Administration, 1927–36," *Administration*, XIII (1965), 316.

TABLE 9.1

Employment in the Public Service, 1940–65

Category	1940	1947	1953	1965
Public service employment:				
Civil Service	25,387	28,832	33,299	34,361
Local authorities	57,300	49,365	55,739	47,351
State-sponsored bodies[a]	7,803	11,988	39,534	52,494
TOTAL	90,490	90,185	128,572	134,206
Total labor force	1,307,000[b]	1,298,000	1,231,000	1,108,000
Public service employment as percentage of total labor force	6.9%	6.9%	10.4%	12.1%

Source: T. P. Linehan, "Growth of the Civil Service," *Administration*, II, No. 2 (Summer, 1954); National Industrial Economic Council, Report on Full Employment, Table 2; reports and information supplied by the Department of Local Government; and information supplied by the Central Statistics Office, the Department of Finance, and individual organizations.

[a] Figures were collected for the 15 largest state-sponsored bodies, accounting for 96 per cent of the total in 1965. The number in the remainder was estimated.

[b] Estimated.

partments and a system of local authorities subordinate and answerable to the Oireachtas through the Minister for Local Government and Public Health and other ministers, but administering their services under the direction and control of locally elected representatives. This was not to last for long, however. Within five years the first of a series of boards and commissions had emerged, the prolific growth of which has been one of the features of modern Irish government. A Civil Service Commission to examine candidates and recruits to the service, insulated from direct ministerial control on the British pattern, was perhaps to be expected. The assigning in 1927 of the ownership and control of the generation and distribution of electricity to a semi-independent public corporation was also not at all strange, since it was universally agreed in the British Isles that "the Civil Service was not recruited for the purpose of running business undertakings like this."[7] However, these were but the first of many such bodies set up to carry out an ever-widening range of activities embracing not only "business undertakings" but also regulatory, social service, and developmental functions. A generic name has been given to bodies of this sort: they are known as "state-sponsored bodies." However, the limits of the term are far from precise. They form one, now the largest, of three main groups of public organizations— ministerial departments, state-sponsored bodies, and local authorities— and their staffs are one of three sections of the public service. Table 9.1 shows their enormous growth since 1940.

[7] Deputy P. McGilligan, Minister for Industry and Commerce, *Dáil Debates*, vol. 18, col. 1907 (Mar. 15, 1927).

The principles on which functions have been allocated among departments, local authorities, and these boards are hard to discern if one looks for logic or applies administrative theory. There are many apparent discrepancies and inconsistencies which can only be explained by history, contemporary reasons of convenience, an *ad hoc* approach by ministers at least as pragmatic as that of the Irish Administration in the nineteenth century, and a continuing and growing belief in the limitations of the Civil Service.

We shall deal with the central administration in this chapter and with state-sponsored bodies and local government in the chapters that follow.

III

The basic statute that governs the central administration is the Ministers and Secretaries Act, 1924. It regularized the *ad hoc* reduction and grouping of the forty-seven departments, boards, and other offices that existed before the Treaty, and created eleven departments including a Department of the President of the Executive Council (Prime Minister). Most of the new departments encompassed a collection of the previous offices within each new department itself, but some assumed control over offices that were still to remain separate. (For details, see Figure 9.1.) The circumstances of the time precluded any comprehensive survey of the functions of the state and their allocation to administrative organizations, central or local, on some overall scheme based on administrative principles. Introducing the bill, W. T. Cosgrave, President of the Executive Council, told the Dáil: "As the House well knows, there were, during the British administration, quite a multiplicity of Boards and Statutory bodies, and during the last two years it has not been possible to survey the whole field and to see how better we may construct the Government machine."[8]

With few exceptions, the existing offices as they stood were accepted and were combined into commonsense groupings. The offices of the Dáil Government (1919–22), which, except for Justice and Local Government, had had a rather shadowy existence, were wound up. However, some of their staffs joined the existing Civil Service, which was taken over in complete working order. To a large extent the offices of the previous administration fell into natural enough groupings by reason of either proximity of purpose or historic connections. In addition, two departments had to be created, for under the Union there had obviously been no call for them. These were Finance and External Affairs,

[8] *Dáil Debates*, vol. 5, cols. 917–18 (Nov. 16, 1923).

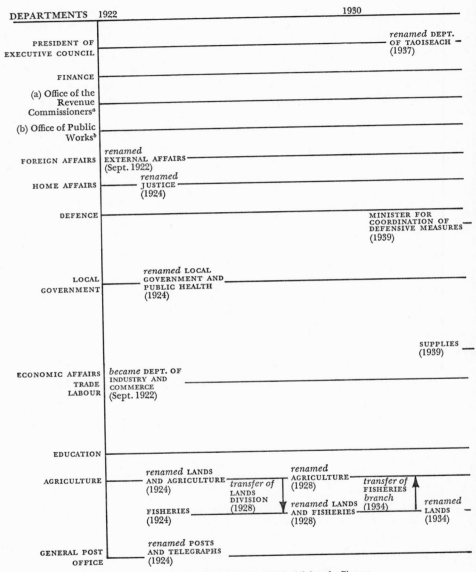

DEPARTMENTS 1922   1930

PRESIDENT OF   *renamed* DEPT.
EXECUTIVE COUNCIL   OF TAOISEACH —
                                                                   (1937)

FINANCE

(a) Office of the
Revenue
Commissioners[a]

(b) Office of Public
Works[b]

FOREIGN AFFAIRS   *renamed*
                   EXTERNAL AFFAIRS
                   (Sept. 1922)
HOME AFFAIRS   *renamed*
                   JUSTICE
                   (1924)

DEFENCE   MINISTER FOR
                                                                   COORDINATION OF —
                                                                   DEFENSIVE MEASURES
                                                                   (1939)

LOCAL   *renamed* LOCAL
GOVERNMENT   GOVERNMENT AND
                   PUBLIC HEALTH
                   (1924)

                                                                   SUPPLIES —
                                                                   (1939)

ECONOMIC AFFAIRS   *became* DEPT. OF
TRADE   INDUSTRY AND
LABOUR   COMMERCE
                   (Sept. 1922)

EDUCATION

AGRICULTURE   *renamed* LANDS   *transfer of*   *renamed*   *transfer of*
                   AND AGRICULTURE   LANDS   AGRICULTURE   FISHERIES
                   (1924)   DIVISION   (1928)   branch   *renamed*
                                       (1928)   (1934)   LANDS —
                   FISHERIES   *renamed* LANDS   (1934)
                   (1924)   AND FISHERIES
                                                        (1928)

GENERAL POST   *renamed* POSTS
OFFICE   AND TELEGRAPHS
                   (1924)

[a] The Revenue Commissioners operate under the general control of the Minister for Finance.
[b] The Parliamentary Secretary to the Minister for Finance acts as a Minister for Public Works.

Fig. 9.1. Development of the Central

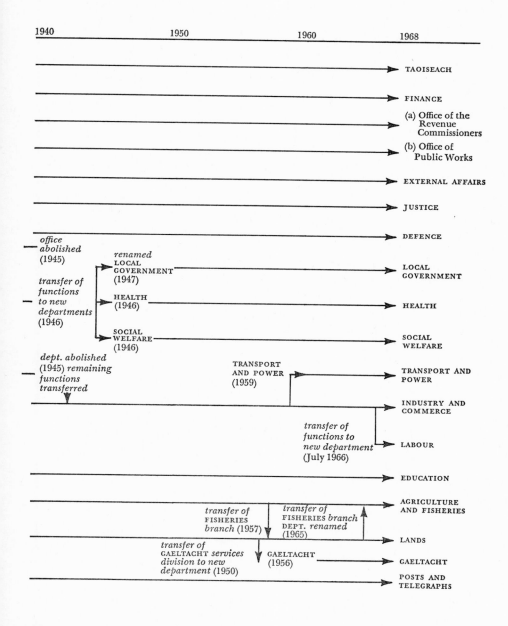

1940   1950   1960   1968

TAOISEACH

FINANCE

(a) Office of the Revenue Commissioners

(b) Office of Public Works

EXTERNAL AFFAIRS

JUSTICE

DEFENCE

office abolished (1945)

transfer of functions to new departments (1946)

renamed LOCAL GOVERNMENT (1947)

LOCAL GOVERNMENT

HEALTH (1946)

HEALTH

SOCIAL WELFARE (1946)

SOCIAL WELFARE

dept. abolished (1945) *remaining functions transferred*

TRANSPORT AND POWER (1959)

TRANSPORT AND POWER

INDUSTRY AND COMMERCE

transfer of functions to new department (July 1966)

LABOUR

EDUCATION

AGRICULTURE AND FISHERIES

transfer of FISHERIES *branch* (1957)

transfer of FISHERIES *branch* DEPT. *renamed* (1965)

LANDS

transfer of GAELTACHT *services division to new department* (1950)

GAELTACHT (1956)

GAELTACHT

POSTS AND TELEGRAPHS

Administration in Ireland, 1922–68

though the latter was essentially a continuation of the Dáil Government department, which had consisted of a minister and a number of diplomatic representatives, many of whom had been stationed in Paris, where they had sought recognition from the powers negotiating the peace treaty after the First World War.

For all the consolidation, some British anomalies remained. For example, the Office of Public Works continued in board form, but as a protégé of the Department of Finance and with the Parliamentary Secretary to the Minister for Finance acting in effect as its minister. Also, the customs and tax administrations were combined into a single unit under Revenue Commissioners, who were, as in the case of Works, under the general aegis of Finance.

The allocation of functions made in 1924 was not systematically reviewed until a committee of inquiry was appointed with wide terms of reference in 1966, over forty years later. As yet, no major changes have actually been made in the pattern then established. Over the years, a few new departments have been set up, and a few transfers of divisions from one department to another (and, in at least one case, back again) have been effected. The number of departments has been increased from eleven in 1924 to sixteen in 1968.

The biggest increase resulted from the growth of the social services, which occurred after the Second World War. The Department of Local Government and Public Health was split up and three separate departments—Local Government, Health, and Social Welfare—emerged. The great increase in the functions of the state in respect of planning, development, and control of the economy that occurred more recently led to another increase. In 1959 some divisions of the Department of Industry and Commerce were separated from the parent department and established as a new department, Transport and Power, and in 1966 others were hived off to become the Department of Labour. However, no planning department or department of economic affairs has come on the scene. Instead, the functions and responsibilities of the Department of Finance have been greatly increased, and to its role as controller of public expenditure and the Civil Service and manager of taxation and borrowing have been added, in the last ten years, the tasks of economic forecasting and programming and the responsibility for the general economic development of the community. (See Figure 9.2.) Planning as it is conceived in Ireland requires a central coordinating department, and that is what the Department of Finance preeminently is. The questions that have been raised again and again since the Second World War in Great Britain about the proper role of the Treasury and whether economic planning functions are best located there have not been much debated.

The first attempts to devise appropriate machinery for full-scale planning and state-guided development of a democratic community have tended, rather, to concentrate on the creation of new types of public body somewhat akin to ordinary advisory bodies, but including in their membership not only representatives of employers, workers, and the state-sponsored bodies but powerful Civil Service representation. The National Industrial Economic Council, established in 1963, is primarily an important sounding board and a device for educating, persuading, and cajoling not only industry, commerce, and the unions, but also government departments and the public sector generally. Significantly, it has become an increasingly important independent commentator on social and economic policy and problems and, perhaps, an important influence on policy makers. However, the Secretary of the Department of Finance has been the Council's chairman and the Council's material is prepared by a Civil Service secretariat. Such arrangements may well mean that in the long run the initiative in the Council will lie with the bureaucracy. At this important "elbow of government" the Civil Service and, more narrowly, the Department of Finance bid fair to dominate.

The assumption of new duties and the creation of new departments, as state services expanded, have naturally brought an increase in the number of civil servants, but this has not been of such an order as to alter the scale of the administration. Table 9.2 shows the number of civil servants at various dates. It will be seen that the total number did not increase at all in the first decade of the state's existence. During the next twenty years there was continuous and steady growth as the social services developed. By 1953 the service had increased in size by 55 per cent. Since 1953, a period in which the state has added greatly to its functions in the economic field, there has been no comparable increase, for in 1968 the total of all civil servants was less than 10 per cent higher than it had been fifteen years earlier.

Table 9.3, which shows the numbers and proportions of civil servants engaged in the various activities of government, reveals that in the middle 1960's, as at the beginning of the state's existence, the great proportion of civil servants were employed either in the postal services or in providing basic services such as justice, defense, and public works, and in the collection of taxes and customs. These activities include those largely handled directly by the central government. However, the number engaged in them has risen only modestly and, as a percentage of the total service, declined from over 80 per cent in 1923 to 70 per cent in

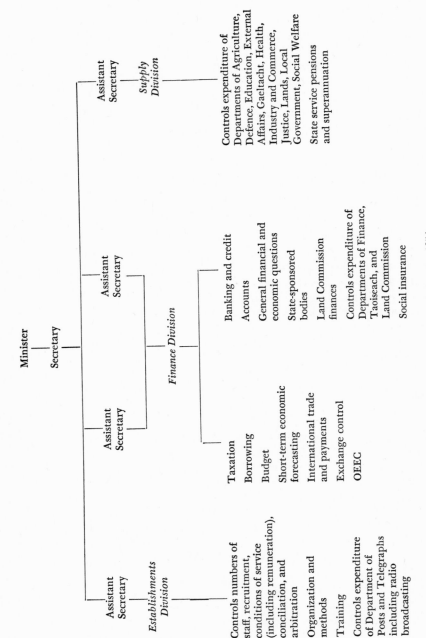

Fig. 9.2a. Department of Finance, 1954

Minister

Secretary

Assistant Secretary — Establishments Division

Assistant Secretary

Assistant Secretary — Finance Division

Assistant Secretary — Supply Division

Establishments Division:
- Controls numbers of staff, recruitment, conditions of service (including remuneration), conciliation, and arbitration
- Organization and methods
- Training
- Controls expenditure of Department of Posts and Telegraphs including radio broadcasting

Finance Division:
- Taxation
- Borrowing
- Budget
- Short-term economic forecasting
- International trade and payments
- Exchange control
- OEEC
- Banking and credit
- Accounts
- General financial and economic questions
- State-sponsored bodies
- Land Commission finances
- Controls expenditure of Departments of Finance, Taoiseach, and Land Commission
- Social insurance

Supply Division:
- Controls expenditure of Departments of Agriculture, Defence, Education, External Affairs, Gaeltacht, Health, Industry and Commerce, Justice, Lands, Local Government, Social Welfare
- State service pensions and superannuation

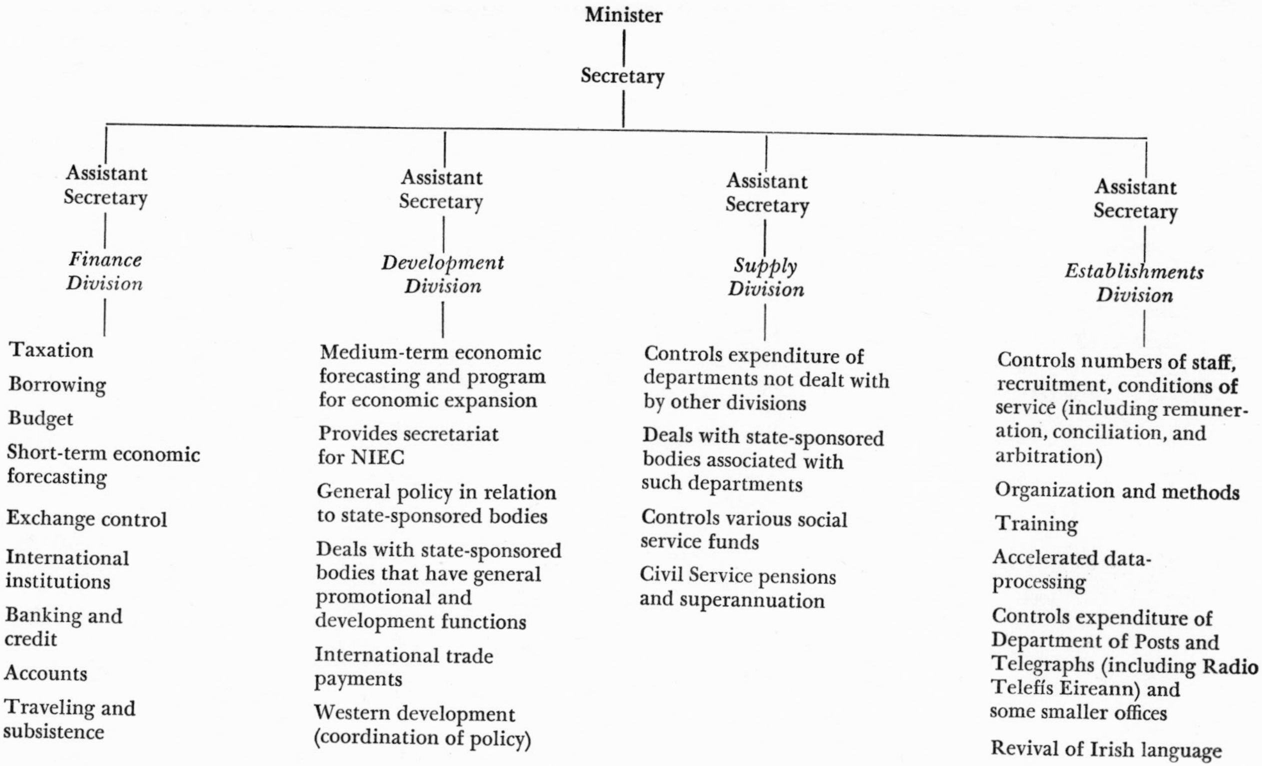

Minister

Secretary

Assistant Secretary	Assistant Secretary	Assistant Secretary	Assistant Secretary
Finance Division	*Development Division*	*Supply Division*	*Establishments Division*

Finance Division

Taxation

Borrowing

Budget

Short-term economic forecasting

Exchange control

International institutions

Banking and credit

Accounts

Traveling and subsistence

Development Division

Medium-term economic forecasting and program for economic expansion

Provides secretariat for NIEC

General policy in relation to state-sponsored bodies

Deals with state-sponsored bodies that have general promotional and development functions

International trade payments

Western development (coordination of policy)

Supply Division

Controls expenditure of departments not dealt with by other divisions

Deals with state-sponsored bodies associated with such departments

Controls various social service funds

Civil Service pensions and superannuation

Establishments Division

Controls numbers of staff, recruitment, conditions of service (including remuneration, conciliation, and arbitration)

Organization and methods

Training

Accelerated data-processing

Controls expenditure of Department of Posts and Telegraphs (including Radio Telefís Eireann) and some smaller offices

Revival of Irish language

Fig. 9.2b. Department of Finance, 1968

TABLE 9.2

Number and Percentage of Civil Servants, by Grade, 1922–65

Group	1922	1934	1940	1947	1953	1965	1968
Administrative and executive		1,740 (8.1%)	2,217 (8.7%)	2,303 (8.0%)	2,715 (8.2%)	3,054 (8.9%)	3,409 (9.4%)
Clerical, subclerical, and typing grades		4,596 (21.3)	6,562 (25.9)	7,480 (25.9)	7,826 (23.5)	7,700 (22.4)	8,278 (22.7)
Inspectorate		549 (2.6)	774 (3.0)	1,094 (3.8)	758 (2.3)[a]	1,211 (3.5)	1,304 (3.6)
Professional, scientific, and technical		1,026 (4.8)	1,111 (4.4)	1,296 (4.5)	2,076 (6.2)[a]	2,622 (7.6)	2,909 (8.0)
Supervisory, minor, and manipulative[b]		10,337 (48.0)	10,724 (42.3)	11,516 (39.9)	13,186 (39.6)	15,200 (44.2)	15,822 (43.5)
Messengers, cleaners, etc.		1,370 (6.4)	1,657 (6.5)	1,883 (6.6)	2,137 (6.4)	1,888 (5.6)	1,967 (5.4)
Industrial staff		1,904 (8.8)	2,342 (9.2)	3,260 (11.3)	4,601 (13.8)	2,686 (7.8)	2,699 (7.4)
TOTAL	21,035	21,522 (100%)	25,387 (100%)	28,832 (100%)	33,299 (100%)	34,361 (100%)	36,388 (100%)

Source: *Return of Staff in Government Departments* (Stationery Office, Dublin, 1924); T. P. Linehan, "Growth of the Civil Service," *Administration*, II, No. 2 (Summer, 1954); information supplied by the Central Statistics Office and the Department of Finance.

[a] In 1953 all persons with professional qualifications were classed in the professional, scientific, and technical group.

[b] Mainly in the Department of Posts and Telegraphs.

TABLE 9.3

*Number and Percentage of Civil Servants Engaged in the Provision
of the Various State Services, 1922–65*

Sector[a]	April 1, 1922[b]	October 1, 1923[c]	1950	1965
Basic services	3,163 (15.0%)	4,666 (21.0%)	5,705 (22.8%)	8,870 (25.8%)
Postal and telecommu-				
nications services	13,518 (64.3)	13,418 (60.2)	10,849 (43.4)	15,225 (44.3)
Economic services	3,388 (16.1)	3,180 (14.3)	4,652 (18.6)	6,158 (17.9)
Social services	904 (4.3)	891 (4.0)	3,090 (12.4)	3,278 (9.5)
Other	62 (0.3)	114 (0.5)	688 (2.8)	830 (2.5)
TOTAL	21,035 (100%)	22,269 (100%)	24,984 (100%)	34,361 (100%)

Source: Figures for 1922 and 1923 are from *Return of Staff in Government Departments* (Stationery Office, Dublin, 1924); for 1950 and 1965 from information supplied by the Central Statistics Office and the Department of Finance.

[a] Basic services: Justice, Defence, External Affairs, Taoiseach, Public Works, Revenue.
Postal and telecommunications services: Posts and Telegraphs.
Economic services: Finance, Industry and Commerce, Transport and Power, Agriculture, Fisheries, Lands.
Social services: Education, Health, Local Government, Social Welfare, Gaeltacht.
Other: Valuation and Ordnance Survey, Stationery Office, and a number of other small offices not easily classifiable.

[b] The date of the formal transfer of staff from British to Irish control.

[c] By October 1923 many of the new services necessitated by the establishment of the Irish Free State had been instituted.

1965. The development of state services and activities in the economic and social service fields has, of course, occasioned a rise, but even so, these activities involved less than 30 per cent of the whole in 1965. This reflects, as does the small increase in total numbers, the fact that the actual provision of services or performance of functions, as opposed to their oversight and control, has been provided by public authorities other than the central administration—particularly local authorities and, more particularly, as Table 9.1 shows, state-sponsored bodies.

The inevitable increase in coordination and overall control of a widening range of functions that led to the addition of new departments and of new divisions in existing departments naturally caused the number of the very top ranks (Assistant Secretaries and Secretaries and their equivalents) to double. In the early 1920's there were somewhat over 30; in 1939 about 40; in 1950 about 50; and in 1965 about 65. However, this increase was not matched in the higher Civil Service as a whole. The size of the administrative and executive group increased by less than 1 per cent (from 8.1 per cent to 8.9 per cent of the total) between 1934 and 1965, and in 1968 it was only 9.4 per cent.

Naturally it is easy enough to point to apparent discrepancies in an administration that has been developed in a most pragmatic way. Criticisms such as the following can readily be made:

Considered from the viewpoint of any given area—a town or county—who is responsible for the state of housing, considered as a whole, in that area? The answer is "no one." No one is clearly and ultimately responsible. . . .

If promotional work is not appropriate to the Civil Service, but is appropriate to state-sponsored bodies like the Industrial Development Authority or Bord Fáilte Eireann or Córas Tráchtála, why is so much promotional work still inside the Civil Service? It is probably true to say that much the greatest part of Civil Service work still is promotional work. . . .

If a state-sponsored body (Aer Rianta) should run Dublin Airport, why does the Department of Transport and Power run Shannon and Cork Airports?[9]

Review of the whole administration, now being undertaken, is a formidable job, the more so since those being reviewed, the civil servants themselves, have spent their whole working careers in the administration as it is, acquiring loyalties to this or that existing department, and they tend inevitably, as Walter Bagehot observed a century ago, to see the organization as "a grand and achieved result, not a working and changeable instrument." Although a climate of change has undoubtedly been created in recent years, the pace of change has so far seemed, to the outsider at least, to be painfully slow.

IV

The *Report of the Commission of Enquiry into the Civil Service, 1932–35* describes the impact on the Civil Service of the change to independence as follows:

The passing of the State services into the control of a native Government, however revolutionary it may have been as a step in the political development of the nation, entailed, broadly speaking, no immediate disturbance of any fundamental kind in the daily work of the average Civil Servant. Under changed masters the same main tasks of administration continued to be performed by the same staffs on the same general lines of organization and procedure.

The Civil Service was simply taken over. It was in fact already prepared for this, for under the abortive Government of Ireland Act, 1920, provision had been made for dividing the personnel of the various Irish offices between Dublin and Belfast, the capital of the new Northern Ireland. During 1921, a committee of civil servants representing the Civil Service associations (the staff side) and the state (the official side) had been at work on this. In the event, men working in the south who had worried whether they would (or would not) be transferred to Belfast under that arrangement now found that they could decide for themselves. Those few (a hundred or so) who wished to go north did so and joined the new Northern Ireland administration. Swiftly, something

9 T. J. Barrington, "Machinery of Government," *Administration*, XI (1963), 192–93. In 1968 the administration of the airports was transferred to Aer Rianta Teo.

like an iron curtain came down between the two administrations, partly perhaps because many of the Northern Ireland senior officers were not Irish or had no Dublin connections, but also, obviously, because at the political level the atmosphere was glacial. There had to be some contacts, of course, but they were mainly confined to technical matters and technical men for many years.

Under the Treaty the future tenure and conditions of employment of the officers transferred to the service of the Irish Free State were protected, and generous provision was made for compensation in the event of retirement. It is no wonder, therefore, that the Treaty was welcomed with relief by most civil servants. The number who transferred to the service of the new state was about 21,000 out of a total of 28,000 who were then working in Ireland. Of these 21,000, fewer than 1,000 decided to retire prematurely under favorable conditions in the first few years. To what was thus virtually a complete service were added 131 people who had served in the Dáil Administration service and 88 who had formerly been in the Civil Service but who had resigned or been dismissed because of nationalist sympathies or activities. In addition, 64 officers holding posts in departments in Great Britain were invited to transfer and returned to Ireland in the next year or two.

Naturally, there were unrivaled opportunities for advancement, for each of the new departments had to be provided with a full headquarters organization and top management. In fact, the process was remarkably free from nepotism and there was no great scramble for place, owing largely to the presence in the Department of Finance, which controls personnel, of austere senior officers strongly imbued with British Civil Service traditions, among them officials lent to the new Irish government by its erstwhile foes. An analysis of the careers of the 34 Secretaries and Assistant Secretaries or their equivalents in the new departments reveals that 21 of them were transferred officers, 2 from departments in London; 5 were former members of the Dáil Administration; and 5, including 2 more Dáil civil servants, were former civil servants who were reinstated. Only 3 came from elsewhere, 2 from the army to the Garda Síochána (the new police force) and one, a barrister, brought in from outside. Thus, 26 out of 34 of the top men were career civil servants, though a few of them suddenly found themselves considerably higher in the hierarchy than they could otherwise have expected to be. Among those who retired, there may well have been a few who were in effect forced to retire, but there was nothing in the nature of a purge.

We have dwelt on the transfer at some length, since it was the smoothness of the operation and the overwhelming sense of continuity that led

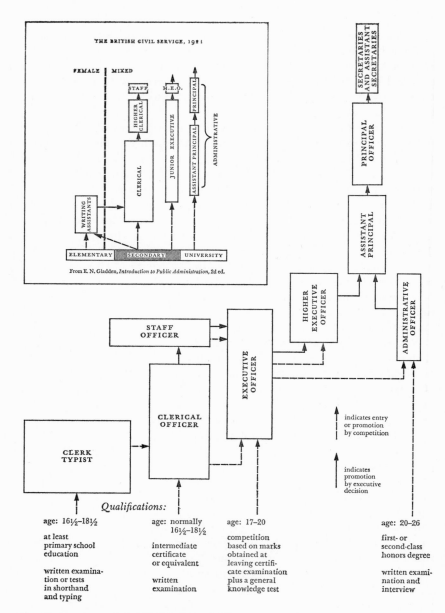

Fig. 9.3. Structure of the Civil Service, 1965; general service grades. (The areas of the figures in the diagram representing the various groups are roughly proportional to the membership of the groups, and their positioning is intended to indicate their relative status.)

to the central administration being carried over into the new regime to a great extent unaltered and in perfect working order. The departments themselves were new, but most of them were largely composed of working units transferred *en bloc* as going concerns. This was no doubt a powerful aid to the development—or rather, continuation in new circumstances—of constitutional government. As F. M. Marx has observed, the permanence of the civil servant and his commitment to government as an endless activity, his monopoly of knowledge, and his bringing of objective facts to bear, all erect barriers to despotic fiat or rash judgment.[10]

The new Irish Civil Service was a British Civil Service in miniature: in many respects it still is. This continuity during nearly fifty years of native government is strikingly illustrated by reference to the structure of the service. As in Great Britain, the major part of the service is grouped into a number of grades common to all departments. These are the "general service grades" and are clearly the same as the British "classes." A glance at Figure 9.3 is sufficient to show the strong resemblance of the Irish structure to the British. This is then a "class" system, each class performing work suited to the ability of the people in it, theoretically at least, and each being recruited either directly from school or university or, except in the case of the lowest, from the class below by competitive examination. In addition, there are "departmental grades" in departments with specialized duties, such as the Office of the Revenue Commissioners, though in general these grades are closely related to one or other of the general service grades and promotion from them by competition to a general service grade is possible. Thus there exists the possibility for almost all of promotion from grade to grade, and, in fact, there is considerable movement of this sort. For example, in the years 1950–60, 41 per cent of the appointments to the Executive Officer grade were filled by confined competition from lower grades, and from 1955 to 1964, 44 per cent of appointments to Administrative Officer were filled from the Executive Officer grade or other grades.

It will be seen from Figure 9.3 also that the higher posts, those of Assistant Principal and above, are appointed both from Administrative Officers (who might in turn, as we have indicated, have come from the Executive Officer grade) and from Higher Executive Officers, who are the best of the Executive Officers, promoted on an average after twelve years in the service. Administrative Officers and Higher Executive Officers thus form a pool from which higher officers are selected, and they

[10] In J. LaPalombara, ed., *Bureaucracy and Political Development* (Princeton, 1963), p. 64.

perform the same type of duties, being interchangeable with each other. This arrangement is one of the few major deviations from the British pattern. It is the result of the belief of the first Establishment Officers in the Department of Finance that the work in Ireland would continue to need comparatively few "First Division" people, as they had been called in the British Civil Service, a point upon which the Treasury had always stood firm against the pressure of the heads of the Irish departments and offices. It was a mistaken belief, for it ignored the new need for top management of a now entirely self-governing country, however small. It has led to a situation where the top jobs are not only open to people recruited at secondary school level but largely filled by them. In fact, because of the paucity of graduates coming forward from the universities to compete for Administrative Officer posts in the past, about 90 per cent of posts from Assistant Principal upward are at present occupied by people recruited at secondary school level. That is not to say that their education did in fact end at secondary level, for some of them obtained diplomas, degrees, and professional qualifications by evening study. However, this tendency for higher civil servants to come into the service from school and not from university is clearly very important in influencing the character of the service and has increased its needs in respect of education and training.

Although the structure that was taken over has not been much modified, it has sometimes been argued that it should have been. Whereas the majority of the Commission of Enquiry into the Civil Service, 1932–35, clearly did not think that there was much basically wrong with the service, one of the service associations that gave evidence, the Civil Service Clerical Association, condemned the structure as in many ways "unnecessarily complicated and cumbersome," and one member of the Commission in a minority report argued likewise and proposed a simpler grading system. In an article entitled, significantly, "Elaborate Contrivance," in *Administration*, the journal of the Institute of Public Administration, T. J. Barrington, a senior civil servant, made a strong attack along the same lines in 1955.

It was an ingenious thought to break up the inflow of general service work into five main streams and to try to match the inflow of recruits to each of these streams . . . but it was not devised for our conditions and it does not work. . . . The variation in the level of work passing through a Government department is not as great as the number of grades that handle it. Thus each grade tends to overlap the other . . . and indefensible lines of demarcation tend to be drawn between the grades.[11]

---

[11] T. J. Barrington, "Elaborate Contrivance," *Administration*, III (1955), 97.

The Report of a British Committee on the Civil Service in 1968 (the Fulton Committee) made the same criticism of the much larger British service.

v

Although the formal structure of the Civil Service has changed relatively little, it was not to be expected that so British an organization would remain for long unaltered in its character and mores. True, given great continuity and the acceptance by politicians and public servants alike of the British Cabinet system and the minister–civil servant relationships that go with it, and given also a high level of morality in public affairs, it was only natural that the Civil Service should remain an incorruptible, nonpartisan, and usually anonymous corps with security of tenure, considering itself the servant of the legitimate government, whoever they may be; and that it should tend to conservative austerity with regard to the functions of the state and to its role within the state. Yet, although Ireland was comparatively assimilated to Great Britain culturally and enjoyed comparable types and levels of education, the social structure was always different and became more so after the Treaty. After independence it was to be expected that Irish institutions would increasingly reflect Irish rather than British conditions.

To begin with, the British Civil Service like many European services had a distinctively upper-class tradition in its higher ranks, and its social tone in the early twentieth century was still rather superior. The administrative class was largely filled by graduates of Oxford and Cambridge, which, even after the First World War, continued to be overwhelmingly the preserves of the public schools and of the upper middle and upper classes. By reason of this background, by membership in their gentlemen's clubs, and by the socialization process they underwent in their first years in the service, members of the administrative class were well endowed to become part of the "Establishment" and as a body to form a well-defined subgroup within it. The tone of the British Service, especially its gentlemanly "generalist" tradition and relationships between the ranks, was set by this group and continued to be so until quite recently.

Notwithstanding the distance and differences between Dublin and London, these values had applied in Dublin also. And while higher civil servants in Ireland before the Treaty were by no means so uniform in origin and training, they, too, could be said to be part of a local "establishment." McDowell's analysis of the 48 top officials in 1914 shows them to have been middle- and upper-middle-class, the sons of professional men and lesser landowners, and 43 at least of them had had university—mainly Dublin (Trinity College), Oxford, or Cambridge—or professional education and training.

This situation could hardly continue in the new Ireland. Independence marked formally the end of the dominance of the Anglo-Irish "Establishment," and though the independence movement had been inspired and led largely by middle-class people, they were on the whole not people aspiring to higher social position and they led a movement that cut across the class lines of the lower strata of society. The character of the newly independent community reflected this. It was bourgeois and republican, and though the class lines that have developed are hard to trace, it is clear enough at least that there is no aristocracy and no "Establishment." This was bound, naturally, to be reflected in the Civil Service, which soon became peopled at the top levels by officers who, though middle-class, were often lower- rather than upper-middle-class and who were by no means out of the same mold as their equivalents in the British service. The higher Civil Service quickly ceased to be an upper-class preserve. One of the most obvious results of this is that senior officers tend to have an understanding of, and affinity with, the *administrés*, which comes from close association and personal knowledge. Thus, one of the necessary changes in the character of a bureaucracy suited to a modern democratic state was quickly and easily effected.

Because university graduates entered the service in only small numbers and because of the arrangement by which top jobs are open to Higher Executive Officers, the higher Civil Service became increasingly composed of people who had entered the service directly from secondary school. Perhaps 90 per cent of the posts from Assistant Principal upward are today filled by these people. Further, the tabulation below indicates that, though in the upper reaches a larger proportion of persons entered as graduates, no fewer than 39 out of 65 (60 per cent) of the posts of Secretaries of departments and Assistant Secretaries were in 1963 held by people who had entered the service from secondary school. At the very top, 8 of the 15 heads of departments in 1963 started similarly, 4 of them, including the Secretary of the Department of Finance, as Clerical Officers. The contrast with McDowell's 1914 group is very striking.[12]

Mode of entry	Number
Competition for:	
Clerical Officers	9
Executive Officers	30
Administrative Officers	18
Professional post	6
Transferred from Dáil Administration	2
TOTAL	65

[12] Source: Personal inquiries by author.

What are the results of the higher Civil Service being largely composed of people who entered from secondary school? Since secondary education was not free before 1967 and since many country people were not close enough to a school for their children to attend daily, the children of the poor, especially poor country people, tended to have a Civil Service career barred to them. With this important exception, many children of all social classes attended schools run by religious orders, which provided the bulk of Irish secondary education remarkably cheaply, and it is from these that most of the recruits have come. Some were the sons of salaried people or of farmers of some substance, albeit far from rich. At the poorer end of the scale, however, there were many whose parents could hardly afford even the small expense of sending their children to these very cheap schools. For them particularly, success at the Civil Service examinations was more prized than a university scholarship, for the latter was until very recently inadequate by itself to maintain a student, while the former offered a prospect of a good career and immediate self-sufficiency. With too few job opportunities available owing to inadequate economic development, there was a certain inevitability about a career in the Civil Service for the poor and unconnected secondary school student of above-average ability.

Thus, although the higher Civil Service is definitely not open to all classes, it is equally clearly not an upper- or even a middle-class preserve. Indeed, because of the education that has been provided cheaply by religious orders, it is within wide limits classless. Many civil servants, however, tend to reflect other characteristics of their schooling, and this is to be seen most obviously in the case of the men who have been educated at schools run by the Christian Brothers, a Catholic order founded in 1808 to provide education for poor boys and now engaged in providing secondary education for all classes. The schools of this order owe their popularity to their remarkable record of success at public examinations. Though they cater for all classes, they are still a major source of secondary education for the children of those who cannot afford high-price secondary education. Thus we come to a remarkable phenomenon of the Irish Civil Service: whereas the Christian Brothers provide about one-third of the secondary school teaching for males, something like three-quarters of the men who enter the general service grades come from their schools.

If these schools give an education of a particular type and tend to produce men with certain characteristics, it is inherently probable that the service will reflect these characteristics, though the organization itself will no doubt make its own contribution to the formation of its members. It has been said that this is in fact the case. A senior civil servant,

S. O Mathuna, himself a product of a Christian Brothers school, has suggested that the Christian Brothers' necessary concentration on preparing boys for examinations was paralleled, perhaps inevitably, by a comparative neglect of nonacademic and extracurricular activities.[13] Moreover, "though the development of character was always in the forefront of their teaching, those who passed through their schools were liable to acquire a slightly over-academic education and to lack in some degree a fully rounded personality." His view was confirmed by another distinguished Christian Brothers product, Dr. Jeremiah Dempsey: "If the education was intensive, it was also narrow. For years after I left, I was unaware of anything around me that didn't belong to the work in hand."[14] In contrast with the British tradition, O Mathuna also noted that "there is little solidarity, in the old school tie sense, between ex-pupils of the Christian Brothers." These characteristics, he argued, have had an important influence on the character of the service, which was, in his opinion, a very homogeneous group, as was to be expected when one considers the remarkable uniformity of their origins, education, experience, and point of entry.

Although no systematic study has been made to substantiate these hypotheses, many have acknowledged the insight of O Mathuna's article, and it may be suggested that there is indeed a Christian Brothers stereotype in the higher Civil Service which has dominated the service and has given it some of its most marked characteristics. Higher civil servants generally perhaps tend to be intellectually able and hard working, but rather narrowly practical in their approach and inclined to be concerned with the short-term objective. They are little prone to speculate broadly or to reflect on long-term ends or cultural values. With rather narrow secondary education in the case of so many, or at best for some others the limited opportunities offered by an evening degree course and no other professional training or outside experience, they may well have restricted horizons. They are from their schooling likely to accept "the system" with little question, though in this they do not differ from civil servants almost everywhere. Also, they tend to share with the public servants of many, perhaps most, countries the belief that the outsider probably has little to contribute.

Such a service was (and is) admirable at "running the machine" and adequate to administer comparatively modest state services. However, because of its very virtues and because of its considerable homogeneity,

---

[13] S. O Mathuna, "The Christian Brothers and the Civil Service," *Administration*, III (1955), 69–74.
[14] Quoted in M. Viney, "The Christian Brothers," *Irish Times*, Nov. 17, 1967.

which deprived it of the stimulus of varied intellectual formation and experience, it became slowly less adequate to recognize or cope with the demands arising from the great increase since the Second World War in the state's role in social and economic life, or to spearhead a drive for the expansion of the country's wealth and prosperity at a rate comparable with that of Western Europe generally. This might not have mattered so much had there been others in politics and public life or in the universities to supply the vision, and in government to supply the drive. But there were not.

It is easy enough now with hindsight to see what was happening in the years immediately after the Second World War and to contrast this with what, it is now obvious, was needed. It is possible even to look further back, as some have done, and to declare that the Irish State, faced as it was with a need to build a balanced economy and to stem emigration, required from the very beginning a breed of public servants who would play a major role not merely in the implementing of modest state services but in actively planning and developing the infrastructure of the community, in other words, a Civil Service very different from the one that was inherited. It might even have been expected that such a service would be called for if the ideals of Sinn Féin were ever to be realized.

This is, however, to ignore a number of important facts. Given the inheritance and the continuity of the public service, it was not reasonable to expect a service with different characteristics either to be quickly evolved or indeed to be called for. Sinn Féin radicalism gave way to the cautious conservatism of Cumann na nGaedheal. The truth is that contemporary opinion simply did not envisage the Civil Service (or indeed the state) as having an active role in planning or developing the community. When the Dáil in 1927 debated the organizational form and management of the new state electricity venture, there was no question of having the Civil Service man it and, as the minister remarked, "In saying that, I am passing no criticism on the Civil Service as we find it at the moment."[15] Almost a decade later the Commission of Enquiry into the Civil Service found no major fault with the service. Only a single member in a minority report criticized it as "too cautious and too rooted in different traditions," and there is no evidence that this view was at all widely held at the time. As the role of the state increased, the tendency to adopt the "state-sponsored body" form of organization, not only for the conduct of economic activities but also for a growing range

[15] *Dáil Debates*, vol. 18, col. 1927 (Mar. 15, 1927).

of social services and development services such as tourism and exports, reflected the continuing general view that the proper role of the Civil Service was restricted.

By the time the rebuilding of Western Europe got under way in the late 1940's and early 1950's and governments of necessity assumed the role of community developers, Ireland was to a greater extent than ever before or since in recent times isolated from the mainstream of European politics, social thought, and economic and social development. Ireland had been neutral in the war, was unwilling to join military alliances, and was kept out of the United Nations organization. Higher civil servants like the politically influential in the community in general tended to conservatism and to be inward-looking and, like many bureaucracies, had "a professional predilection for the status quo."[16] Moreover, unlike the situation in many European countries, continuity had not been broken by violent changes occasioned by the war and thus no sudden need or clear-cut opportunity for radical change presented itself. The developments that did occur, for example in the social services, owed little to Civil Service inspiration. For a decade or more the exciting changes that transformed Western Europe made little impact on Ireland, the more so because of the slowness of Great Britain, whose culture and values so influence and insulate Ireland, to respond to them, since Britain, like Ireland, had been able to preserve a considerable continuity.

It was not indeed until a recession in the middle 1950's brought a growing awareness of the gap that was opening up between Ireland and the rest of Europe that a change came. It came with the preparation and publication in 1958 of *Economic Development* (a study of national development problems and opportunities) and the first five-year economic development program. With dramatic suddenness the state lurched into the middle of the twentieth century, at least so far as the development of the economy was concerned. And for all the apparent conservatism of the Civil Service as a whole, *Economic Development* and the first economic program, together with the rapid developments that immediately followed the assumption by the government of full responsibility for directing the economy, were to a great extent the work of civil servants in the economic and financial departments.

Although this dramatic development was due to the inspiration of a small number of individuals and to the fruitful partnership of a few ministers and a few civil servants, and not to a change in the attitude

16 F. M. Marx, in J. LaPalombara, p. 87.

of higher civil servants generally, the volumes of *Administration* (the journal of the Institute of Public Administration), first published in 1953, testify to a growing awareness, on the part of a minority at least, of a new and more positive role for departments and of the need for thoroughgoing reforms if higher civil servants were to be—as they had to be—the architects of the community.

In contrast to the initiative symbolized by *Economic Development*, the response of the Civil Service as a whole to the rapidly emerging needs was, it seems, recognized to be hardly adequate, for the Taoiseach himself told a conference of senior officers in 1961:

I think it is true to say that in some government departments there is still a tendency to wait for new ideas to walk in through the door. It is perhaps the normal attitude of an administrative department of government to be passive rather than active, to await proposals from outside, to react mainly to criticism or to pressure of public demand, to avoid the risks of experimentation and innovation and to confine themselves to vetting and improving proposals brought to them by private interests and individuals rather than to generate new ideas themselves.[17]

He said frankly that doubts about the suitability of the Civil Service to do development and promotional work had led to the widespread use of the state-sponsored body type of organization. He urged the need for departments to think in terms of new opportunities and to provide leadership, but, he asked, "does the existing organization of civil service departments encourage this attitude in their staffs?"[18] The Permanent Secretary of the Department of Finance echoed him: "What is needed is a more lively and general appreciation by the Civil Service of the part it can and should play in promoting national development."[19]

Under the impact of all this, the higher Civil Service began a reappraisal. However, as F. M. Marx has observed, "Civil servants do not drift naturally into the camp of change," and this has turned out to be an agonizing process. Events have overtaken a machine hardly adapted to cope with the tasks now being demanded of it. However, in 1966, the Minister for Finance appointed a committee to inquire into the organization of the departments of state. Although, in making the announcement he said that "the Civil Service has shown a remarkable capacity to adapt itself to new functions," he can hardly have meant this seriously.

[17] S. F. Lemass, "The Organization Behind the Economic Programme," *Administration*, IX (1961), 5.
[18] *Ibid.* He was still saying much the same in 1968. See *Léargas*, No. 12 (1968), p. 2. See also below, pp. 257–58.
[19] T. K. Whitaker, "The Civil Service and Development," *Administration*, IX (1961), 84.

Nevertheless, the full implications of the changes in the content and techniques of modern government are now coming to be realized, though, as yet, they have not been fully accepted in all departments.

The advance of the social sciences and of accounting and statistical techniques to the point where they are essential tools for policy making and management have made it vital for public services everywhere to be peopled by a more professional race than has usually been found in the higher administrative ranks of British-style civil services. Increasing numbers of senior officers have to be capable of absorbing, appreciating, and using large amounts of systematic economic and social data in order to elucidate problems and to formulate adequate plans to place before their ministers. If, as in Ireland, the vast majority of senior officials are recruited at secondary school level, formidable education and training problems are posed, embracing the appropriate social sciences including management, not to be solved by programs measured—as most have been in the past—in days or weeks, but demanding months or years.

A more positive role for the Civil Service—the concept of Lemass of departments as "development corporations"—also poses problems of organization. It may be that planning and administration should be more separated than they often are at present, at least into separate units in each department. In fact, separate and specially staffed research and development units of one sort and another in, or connected with, departments began to be set up in the early 1960's, for example in the Departments of Finance and Local Government, in the Department of Education in 1966, following a survey on *Investment in Education* sponsored by the Organization for European Cooperation and Development, and in the Department of Agriculture in 1964. Such units may well be needed for most departments. More widely, the proper relationship of departments to state-sponsored or -financed research organizations also needs to be settled on a more systematic basis than has yet been attempted in recent years in the case of such organizations as An Foras Talúntais (the Agricultural Research Institute), the Economic and Social Research Institute, or An Foras Forbartha (the Institute of Physical Planning and Construction Research). Again, as more research organizations come into existence, there is a danger, already apparent, that exclusiveness, demarcation jealousies, and even empire building may prevent full cooperation.

Beyond these lie more fundamental problems still. An increased supply of highly trained social scientists has been pointed to as essential to the development of the community generally. The implications of this need go far beyond questions of Civil Service recruitment and education, but they clearly affect the Civil Service intimately, as the shortages of economists and physical planners experienced by the departments in the middle 1960's showed all too clearly. The full exploitation of those who are available, and the tapping both of the knowledge and experience of academic social scientists and of the experience of the private sector, whether formally by contract employment in the Civil Service proper or in some way outside it, is an immediate problem, the key to which lies partly in changes in Civil Service attitudes and procedures.

Finally, it is already obvious that the day-to-day exigencies of planning and of persuading industry, agriculture, the unions, and the state-sponsored bodies to make their individual decisions within the context of governmental plans have forced civil servants to consultation on a scale hitherto unthought of. It is now becoming apparent that the relationships between the state and other organizations in the community, and the attitude of civil servants to consultation in a community that is rapidly becoming corporate in structure, will be vital not only to economic well-being but to freedom itself. The working relationships between organized interests, public and private, in the new planned society are evolving pragmatically and to a large extent under Civil Service and ministerial guidance, undiscussed and perhaps even unnoticed by the ordinary public representative, let alone the ordinary citizen. It may well become more and more difficult for democracy to keep a toehold in the crevices between the great organizations of the public and private sectors.

TEN

State-sponsored Bodies

The considerable variety of administrative bodies that was a feature of Irish government before independence was, as the previous chapter showed, only temporarily reduced to uniformity when the new state took over. This uniformity was never in any case complete, and within a few years new public authorities in forms other than that of a ministerial department began to be set up. Since then, with the great growth in the range and volume of state activity, the number and variety of such bodies has increased considerably. They now surround the central administration like satellites, each one to a greater or lesser degree under the surveillance or control of a department. A general term has been coined to describe them, though its connotation is, as yet, far from precise. They are generally known as "state-sponsored bodies," a term that has now to a large extent superseded a similar descriptive term, "semi-state bodies," once much used.

In general, the term "state-sponsored bodies" is used to describe those public bodies endowed with powers and duties by statute or by ministerial authority whose staffs are not civil servants and to whose governing boards or councils the government or ministers in the government appoint some or all of the members. Use of the term does not, however, extend to bodies engaged in judicial activities, e.g. the Censorship of Publications Board, or bodies whose duties are essentially advisory.[1] In form, they are generally statutory corporations or companies set up under the Companies Acts, i.e. the normal private enterprise form of organization. In their operation they are free both from the full rigor of detailed Department of Finance control, which bears upon the central departments, and from detailed Oireachtas scrutiny. In every case, how-

---

[1] This definition is adapted from that suggested by Garret FitzGerald, *State-sponsored Bodies* (2d ed., Dublin, 1964), p. 5. This is the only book on the subject, and Chapter 10 relies heavily upon it.

ever, they have a sponsor minister who is ultimately responsible to the Oireachtas for them.

This type of organization in many forms is used for a wide variety of purposes including the regulation of certain economic and social activities; the provision of certain social services, especially health services; the management of public utilities and a wide range of business enterprises; the provision of financing to both the private and the public sector; and economic development work generally. There were over 70 state-sponsored bodies in 1968 (see Appendix D). In 1965 their staffs amounted to almost 40 per cent of public service employment and almost 5 per cent of the total labor force (see Table 9.1, p. 222).

It should be said at once that the state-sponsored bodies do not constitute a neat or even coherent group. There is no use in looking for logic or order here; it is even misleading to attempt to rely on such a formal criterion as legal status. A thoroughgoing pragmatism, uninfluenced by socialist doctrine or administrative theory, has indeed been the main feature of the development of the Irish administration. A general acceptance of the proposition that ministerial departments are suitable only for the direct administration of a comparatively narrow range of state activities has clearly been the starting point of a search for the most practicable form of organization, as a new problem arose or the need for a new state initiative was realized. But the search has never been a long one and never systematic. Governments and ministers have adopted strictly practical solutions, sometimes paying scant attention to the provision of adequate legal instruments or to the need for parliamentary control, and individual departments have even developed their own particular traditions in this matter. The British inheritance, itself notoriously pragmatic, is no doubt clearly to be seen, e.g. in the fact that the telephone service and forestry development, which might be thought to be candidates for the status of state-sponsored body, are both administered by departments, and that the railways are run by a public corporation. British influence is also obvious in the public corporation form of organization that the public utilities usually take. But it is in this area, perhaps as much as in any other, that Irish development has been to a great extent a native product, and a largely unplanned one at that.

Vague and embracing as the term state-sponsored body is, and doubtful as it seems to be, even in the minds of politicians and public servants, whether certain public bodies are or are not included in the category, it by no means covers all public bodies other than central departments and local authorities.[2] The great variety of public bodies is not wholly

---

[2] See FitzGerald, pp. 5–6, for examples of other categories.

subsumed in this trilogy. In particular, there are a number of authorities that lie between the ministerial department and the state-sponsored body, to which attention must be drawn. Closest to departments both in form and in relationships with each other are some organizations that are perhaps best thought of as departments, lacking only direct ministerial heads of their own. They are answered for by an appropriate minister to whose department they are appendages, though in some cases appendages considerably larger than the parent bodies. Like departments, they are staffed by civil servants, operated according to Civil Service rules and procedures, and paid for by monies voted directly by the Oireachtas. Unlike them, they are headed either by government-appointed commissioners—as, for example, the Office of the Revenue Commissioners, the Land Commission, and the Civil Service Commission—or by a public official such as the Comptroller and Auditor General, who heads the Exchequer and Audit Department and is a servant of the Oireachtas, or the Director of the Stationery Office, who is an ordinary civil servant. In the case of many of these bodies, there is some obvious historical explanation for their having "semidetached" status, and perhaps some continuing valid constitutional or operational reason also.

One step further removed from the ministerial department and nearer the state-sponsored body is the statutory body wholly (or almost wholly) staffed by civil servants but directed by a board which, though appointed by the minister, is not composed of civil servants, and which, unlike a department, is financed by a grant-in-aid (i.e. a block grant) but, like a department, accounts in detail to the Comptroller and Auditor General. The history of the development of two of these is particularly significant. Both the Industrial Development Authority and An Foras Tionscal (the Industrial Institute) grew out of developmental activities of the Department of Industry and Commerce, and it is clear that they owed their existence to the desire to give the necessary freedom from Civil Service procedures to those engaged in developmental work, while still retaining close departmental control. Apparently, this arrangement also was too constricting, because in 1968 it was announced that they were to be amalgamated and given the status of a state-sponsored body. Similar in position are bodies like the Labour Court, connected with the Department of Labour, and the Agricultural Wages Board, under the aegis of the Department of Agriculture.

The essence of the state-sponsored bodies as the term is used in Ireland lies, it might be thought, in some degree of independence, legal and operational, but we should beware of referring to them as "independent" or "autonomous" public bodies. A separate legal existence they do have, but this by no means ensures operational independence from their sponsor departments. Independence clearly does not spring from their having their own staffs rather than Civil Service staffs, nor from their not being bound to comply with Civil Service procedures. In any case, some state-sponsored bodies, although they have their own staffs, nevertheless have Civil Service directors appointed by the sponsor minister from his own department. Nor does independence follow from their being free from detailed Oireachtas scrutiny. In fact, the degree of independence varies enormously and depends in each case on one or more of three main factors: the nature of the function performed and particularly its political significance or sensitivity, the financial position of the body and especially its sources of funds, and the habits of departmental control that have become established and that may perhaps have originated largely in accidents of personality.

In this connection, state-sponsored bodies are better thought of not as one group but as two: those established to administer or regulate some area of social or economic activity or to provide a social service, and those established to engage in producing goods and services for trade, or to carry out developmental activities connected with trade and industry. Even such a broad division as this, however, is not without difficulties. For example, the operations of the Electricity Supply Board in respect of rural electrification or some of those of An Bord Iascaigh Mhara (the Sea Fisheries Board) and Arramara Teo.[3] (seaweed-processing) have elements of social service in them; and promotional bodies, though closely related to the "public enterprise" bodies engaged in trade, operate on grants-in-aid and are clearly not in the same position vis-à-vis ministers as commercial bodies with their own sources of funds, e.g. the Irish Life Assurance Company, which competes successfully on equal terms with private insurance companies. The truth is that generalization is very difficult here. Broadly, however, there does seem to be a difference between bodies giving services or regulating some social activity and those engaged in trade, development, or promotion. Such a difference depends upon the nature of the activity, and this difference may be of some importance when one comes to consider the extent and nature of ministerial and Oireachtas control that ought to be imposed upon them.

II

It will be seen from the classified list of state-sponsored bodies in Appendix D that the administrative, regulatory, and social service group, which comprises 30 bodies, can be divided into three main subgroups: (1) bod-

---

[3] Teo. = Teoranta, the Irish equivalent of Ltd, i.e. a limited company.

ies established for the government of certain professions, (2) bodies set up to control certain economic activities, and (3) bodies set up to provide or administer certain social services, mainly health services. Little need be said about the first. Almost by definition professions are self-governing, getting their powers in the past by charters from the British Crown and in more modern times by statute. The bodies in the second and third categories, however, represent deliberate decisions on the part of governments not to hand over the control of some area of activity coming under state supervision either to ministerial departments or to local authorities. In the case of many of them the reason seems to have been the desire to associate interested parties with the administration of their own business, or the users or recipients of a service with the administration of that service, which would not be possible with central or local authority control. Their existence in such numbers suggests a strong attachment to the vocational principle. In some cases, particularly in the field of agriculture, members of the governing boards are, indeed, elected by producers, distributors, or others directly concerned, e.g. the Milk Boards. In the case of one of these bodies, the Foyle Fisheries Commission, the corporate body form is a convenient vehicle for cooperating with a neighboring country (Northern Ireland) in the control of the fisheries of an estuary that marks the boundary between them.

The propensity of Irish governments to adopt *ad hoc* solutions to particular organizational problems in this area is well illustrated by some of the health service bodies that make up the majority of the social services group. They were originally set up to provide services which, as the Department of Health put it in a memorandum, "while not appropriate to be dealt with by the Department of Health were not of a local nature and were therefore unsuitable for administration by local health authorities," which are the main providers of personal health services in Ireland. In such cases, which included, for example, blood transfusion facilities and the mass X-ray service, Ministers of Health developed the practice of setting up companies under the Companies Acts, a procedure that was no doubt convenient and speedy but that, as the Department admitted, was "not entirely appropriate for the establishment of bodies such as these," financed largely by state and local authority grants.[4] In 1961, the Health Corporate Bodies Act empowered the Minister to establish by order corporate bodies to provide health services, and such health service bodies are now, if not literally statutory bodies, at least corporate bodies established pursuant to a statute.

---

[4] Explanatory Memorandum issued to members of Dáil Eireann with the Health Corporate Bodies Bill, 1961.

The other main group of state-sponsored bodies comprises, first, the public enterprise sector of trading bodies, which in 1968 contained no fewer than 31 corporations and companies engaged in transport, in radio and television, in banking and finance, and in the production of a wide range of commodities from electricity and steel to fertilizers and toffees. Second, it comprises an ever-increasing number and range of research, marketing, and development bodies that the state has found it necessary to set up in order to promote the social and economic progress of the country; in 1968, they numbered 17, with one more in the process of being created (see Appendix D for details).

As is the case in most countries, the trading bodies in Ireland include the bulk of the infrastructure industries—fuel and power (except oil), transport, central banking, radio and television—and like them, too, a miscellaneous collection of other industries and enterprises whose presence in the public sector owes more to particular circumstances than to a general policy. It is almost impossible to measure precisely the extent of state-owned trading enterprises, but their importance can be gauged from the fact that they employ almost 5 per cent of the country's labor force and their staffs comprise over one-third of all public servants. Table 10.1 provides a very rough comparison of their employment and investment with those of other European countries in 1957. It shows that, whereas the percentage of the active population engaged in public

TABLE 10.1

Employment and Investment of State-owned Trading and Industrial Enterprises in Some European Countries, 1957

Country	Percentage of active population employed	Percentage of total gross fixed investment
Austria	8%	27%
Belgium	4	10
Denmark	4	12
Finland	n.a.	9
France	7 (1956)	25
Ireland	5	23
Italy	n.a.	27
Netherlands	n.a.	13
Norway	n.a.	14
Sweden	7	15
United Kingdom	14	32

Source: Ireland—G. FitzGerald, *State-sponsored Bodies,* pp. 1–2. Other countries—*Economic Survey of Europe for 1959.*
Note: Including postal and telecommunications services in Ireland, which were in fact provided directly by a ministerial department. They are, however, included in the Irish figures in this table in order to validate the comparisons.

enterprises was quite low, the percentage of the total of gross fixed investment held by them was among the largest. The public enterprise sector in Ireland is, therefore, as FitzGerald says, "relatively highly developed ... bearing in mind the absence of heavy industrial activity which in some other European countries is partly or even largely under the control of the state."[5]

How has this come about? It owes little to socialist theory. After the eclipse of the left wing of the labor movement during the latter part of the First World War, there were few socialists in Ireland, no socialist movement worth the name, and no developing body of socialist doctrine. The very term socialism was anathema to most, the more so because, following the lead of the Catholic Church, most people identified it with communism. The Irish Free State was liberal-democratic and conservative. Its governments and those that have followed have reflected public opinion generally in showing no lack of confidence in private enterprise. Irish opinion was and still is truly reflected in Article 45.3.1° of the 1937 Constitution (one of the "Directive Principles of Social Policy"), which declares that "the state shall favour and, where necessary, supplement private initiative in industry and commerce." This attitude was echoed in 1961 by the then Taoiseach, Seán Lemass, when he stated: "Even the most conservative among us understands why we cannot rely on private enterprise alone, and state enterprise in fields of activity where private enterprise has failed or has shown itself to be disinterested, has not only been accepted but is expected. ... Nobody thinks of us as doctrinaire socialists."[6] It has, however, been precisely the considerable need to "supplement private initiative in industry and commerce," and at times to rescue it, together with the inexorable and universal tendency for public utilities to come under public management, that has led to the sizable public enterprise sector. Thus, there has been little nationalization of already existing business enterprises; only some half dozen businesses have been taken over, in every case either as a rescue operation or in response to the need to ensure an adequate public service. On the other hand, there has been considerable state initiative in starting enterprises.

It should be remembered of course that the Irish state started out with considerable economic handicaps. Although the Treaty ushered in an Irish state independent of the British state, it did not create an economically independent community. Ireland remained very much part of a

[5] FitzGerald, p. 1.
[6] S. F. Lemass, "The Organization Behind the Economic Programme," *Administration*, IX (1961), 3.

larger economic and financial unit that was London-oriented, and it was, considered as a unit by itself, in some respects relatively underdeveloped and certainly unbalanced, as was the rural western seaboard of the British Isles generally. This situation was exacerbated by the exclusion from the Irish state of the only industrial area in the island, Belfast and its environs. Because of this and because of the more attractive prospects for capital on the London market, which was still open to Irish investors, private capital was not available to the extent necessary for development, and private enterprise was distinctly unenterprising.

Conservative in outlook though it was, the first government of the Irish Free State nevertheless inherited the traditions of Sinn Féin, whose National Land Bank and surveys of the industrial resources of Ireland made in the period before the Treaty symbolized its policy of actively developing the country. Willing though it was to work with London-oriented banks and to rely on the investing public, the Cumann na nGaedheal government soon found that funds for the development of agriculture and industry were not forthcoming from these sources. A definite line of development leading to state enterprise is here discernible. In 1926, we find the government taking up shares in a recently formed private finance company, the Industrial Trust Company of Ireland, and appointing two directors, but the company failed. In 1927, the Agricultural Credit Act authorized the setting up of an ordinary limited liability company to make long-term capital available to farmers, the shares to be offered to the public in the first instance and only to be taken up by the state if necessary. The public did not respond, and though this was a mixed enterprise company, the state was overwhelmingly the dominant partner, a fact that was recognized in 1947 when it was reorganized as a wholly owned state company.

Following the failure of the Industrial Trust Company, the Fianna Fáil government in 1933 launched a venture similar to the Agricultural Credit Corporation. Introducing a bill for an Industrial Credit Company, the minister explained that "so far as possible, the functions of the Government will be confined to the initiation and launching of the project, and the control and management of it, until such time as the public show that they are ready to step in to relieve the Government of its duties and responsibilities in this regard."[7] It met the same response, and the state had once again to become the dominant shareholder, and thus the controller, of the company.

Another line of development was the exploitation by the state itself

[7] *Dáil Debates*, vol. 48, col. 1539 (July 4, 1933).

of the natural resources of the country. This, too, derived from Sinn Féin policy and was made necessary by the absence of private initiative or by its unsuitability. Obviously, in making decisions about which industries the state should take up, social policy considerations were important. Such considerations have become increasingly important, and with the growing ability to see, and to be able to calculate, the worth to the economy as a whole of setting up particular industries, state initiative has been more frequently exercised. When the completion of the River Shannon hydroelectric scheme in 1927 made necessary a decision about how the bulk generation and supply of electricity should be organized, there was no disagreement about its being placed under public control, since it was recognized that the pace of rural electrification could not be allowed to depend on private enterprise decisions. Subsequently, public bodies producing turf (peat), minerals, sugar, processed foods, grass meal, and other agricultural products have all owed their origin to the desire to exploit or develop resources that were not in fact being developed. So, too, does Arramara Teo., the seaweed-processing firm, which is a company owned jointly by the state and English business interests.

In the case of a few bodies in this trading group, special circumstances as much as any general line of development explain their existence. For example, the strikingly misnamed Dairy Disposal Company was set up in 1927 to acquire a number of creameries with a view to disposing of them to a few large cooperative creameries in an effort to reform the industry. The cooperatives, however, never developed and the company remained in business.

In transport, although the exact circumstances under which the state started companies (as in the case of the airlines and Irish Shipping Ltd.) or nationalized them (as in the case of the railways and road services) differ from case to case, their inclusion in the public sector is in line with development in many other countries. This is so, also, in the nationalization of central banking, and radio and television.

The remaining trading enterprises either owe their origin to rescue operations or have a social service origin. Examples of the first are the Irish Life Assurance Co. Ltd. and Irish Steel Holdings Ltd. Examples of the second are An Bord Iascaigh Mhara (the Irish Sea Fisheries Board), whose origins are well illustrated by the fact that it was originally registered as a "Friendly Society," i.e. an association registered under the Friendly Societies Act, the chief purpose of which is to assist necessitous members, and Gaeltarra Eireann (Irish Gaeltacht Industries), formerly a division of the Department of the Gaeltacht, which promotes cottage industries on the underdeveloped and mountainous western seaboard. That is not to say, of course, that all the others in the trading group are to be regarded as strictly business enterprises and therefore subject to business criteria, notably the need to make profits. Clearly this is not so in the case of the public utilities, especially the railways, though it has taken a long time for the fact to be appreciated. Increasingly, however, it is becoming recognized that state trading enterprises generally have social responsibilities and objectives that sometimes oblige them to lines of action they would not follow if profit making were their sole objective. The implications of this for control of major policy and even for their nature and role are considerable, though these have never yet been clearly spelled out. Nevertheless, we should not go to the other extreme and imagine, as so many do, that state trading enterprises are all primarily social services inevitably losing money. With only two exceptions—Córas Iompair Eireann and Gaeltarra Eireann, both of which have substantial social policy obligations—trading enterprises do not normally lose money or regularly need substantial subsidies.

Finally, we should notice a category of state-sponsored bodies that have come into existence recently, as the Irish state, like most other states, has assumed responsibility for the development of the economy as a whole. The organizations in this group have been created to aid and to stimulate Irish enterprise by promoting markets for Irish goods or services (including tourism), by engaging directly in marketing, or by encouraging and facilitating the setting up of industries in Ireland by foreign businessmen through the provision of grants, loans, tax concessions, and other inducements. An example of the first is Córas Tráchtála (the Irish Export Board); of the second, Bord Bainne (the Milk Marketing Board); of the third, the Shannon Free Airport Development Company Ltd., which builds and rents factories and runs a trading estate and entrepôt facilities. These bodies, while closely allied to business enterprise, are in one important respect very different from ordinary business firms and the state trading enterprises in that to a great extent they are development services and in some cases rely almost wholly on state grants for their income. Therefore, even less than in the case of the trading bodies can we think of them as being in business to make profits.

III

So far we have categorized those state-sponsored bodies engaged in trading, marketing, or economic development work by reference to their functions and have explained the reasons for state initiative in these areas. What has not been explained is why this particular form of public body should be used rather than direct departmental administration or local authority control. Most of these bodies are either statutory corporations or joint stock companies set up under the Companies Act. It may be asked then, first, what led to the practice of establishing state-sponsored bodies for these activities and, second, what has governed the choice between a statutory corporation and a company?

The views expressed by the Minister for Industry and Commerce when the Electricity Supply Board, the first of the public utilities, was being established in 1927 have already been referred to (p. 241). They reflect the general thinking of the time. It was necessary for the state to act, certainly, but it was essential also, as he said, to make any such state venture "as independent as possible of government."[8] The Minister's survey of the experience in other states led him to conclude that "where any degree of public ownership had been settled upon, there was pretty definitely in every case an equally strong decision that public ownership and administration should not mean ownership and administration by a state department in the ordinary way." There was no hint of any loss of confidence in private enterprise or its forms and procedures: "their whole aim and object was to achieve all that was advantageous arising out of state control and to add to that all that seemed to be advantageous from business management.... Something in between had to be found." These views, which were strikingly similar to those expressed later by Herbert Morrison in Great Britain and widely accepted there by all political parties,[9] gave rise to the concept of the "independent" or "autonomous" public corporation, run by a state-appointed board but "removed as far as possible from political pressure ... from incessant government and parliamentary interference." In fact, for all the references in the Minister's speech to investigations in South Africa, Sweden, and Germany, the Electricity Supply Board provided for in his bill was very similar to the Central Electricity Board that had been created very shortly before in Great Britain. There can be little doubt, in any case, but that the concept of the public corporation as it developed from then on in Ireland owed something to British example.

In the case of the other state venture of that formative year, 1927, the Agricultural Credit Corporation, the state was intended to be a mere shareholder in an ordinary company, taking up the shares the public did

---

[8] This quotation and those that follow are from *Dáil Debates*, vol. 18, cols. 1902ff (Mar. 15, 1927).

[9] See H. Morrison, *Socialisation and Transport* (London, 1933), chaps. 8 and 9. For a general account of the development of British ideas about the public corporation, see A. H. Hanson, *Parliament and Public Ownership* (London, 1961), chap. 2.

not want and having the right to appoint a minority of directors. The failure of the public to invest in this and similar ventures forced the state into the position of being the sole owner and controller of companies it felt necessary to promote. Thus, almost by accident, the state-owned company form appeared in Ireland. This development contrasts markedly with that of the United Kingdom, where there have been comparatively few state companies. On the other hand, in some other European countries the publicly owned joint stock company is "probably the most widespread type of public enterprise."[10]

Since the 1920's and 1930's there have been three main developments. First, the state-sponsored body has been used to an increasing extent and for many jobs besides trading; second, insofar as it ever really existed in practice, the "autonomous" or "independent" body has largely disappeared and state-sponsored bodies tend to be subjected to considerable government control; third, the flexibility of the company form and the comparative ease with which companies could be set up led to the increasing use of this device, sometimes for purposes far removed from those normally associated with joint stock companies. Each of these changes, which we shall now examine, reflects the growing power of governments, and each has exacerbated what is undoubtedly the major problem posed by the existence and operations of these bodies, namely the problem of effective parliamentary control.

Since the Second World War a practice has developed of setting up state-sponsored bodies for an ever-widening range of functions, including, most notably, the promotion of markets and other developmental work. It arises in particular, it seems, from the experience of governments that the suitability of the Civil Service to engage in development work is limited, and in general it reflects a lack of confidence in the ability of departments as at present organized and staffed to cope with some of the new tasks of the modern state. Speaking in 1961, the Taoiseach, Seán Lemass, was quite explicit about this:

It is fair to assume that it was the persistence of doubt about the suitability of Government Departments, as now organized, to operate as development corporations and to perform, in the manner desired, particular functions deemed to be necessary for the nation's progress—functions which required exceptional initiative and innovation—which have led to decisions of the Government from time to time to set up by statute or otherwise a number of more or less independent authorities. I am not referring to the administration of state-owned commercial-type undertakings. . . . I have in mind the administration of activities of another kind, where the purpose is to provide services to promote development generally or to help private concerns to make headway—such as aids

---

[10] *Economic Survey of Europe for 1959* (United Nations, Geneva), chap. 5, p. 34.

to industrial development, export trade, tourism and so forth. In these instances the decision might have been either way—either to administer these schemes directly through the appropriate Departments, or to set up boards and authorities outside the departmental system for the purpose. If Ministers decided to do it one way rather than the other, it was because they believed that the results would be better.[11]

There were, he conceded, other reasons also: the need to attract the services of people who were not, and would not become, civil servants; the desire to be free of detailed departmental and Oireachtas control; the hope that the public would cooperate more readily. "It may be," he speculated, "that whether by accident or by design, we have in fact devised a better system of administration ... and that activities which are still direct departmental responsibilities could, with increased efficiency, be passed out to similar extern authorities."[12] In this respect, the example of Sweden springs immediately to mind.

Since the Second World War also, the growth of the public sector and the key role played by many of the state enterprises in it, together with the advent of state planning, have made it necessary for governments to assume more and more control of the policy decisions of state-sponsored bodies. The extent of this control is often considerable, though—because, as Lemass said, it "is settled on a pragmatic rather than theoretical basis"[13]—it is hard to generalize about it. Certainly it is often hardly appreciated by the public that to speak of "independent" public bodies is now an anomaly. This is, however, largely explicable by the fact that the statutes and other legal instruments have not been amended in the case of older bodies, and in the case of more recent bodies they give no adequate picture of the respective roles of ministers and boards.

The same unsatisfactory result arises from the third development. The procedure of setting up a company was soon recognized to be simpler, quicker, and far less trouble than the more ponderous business of establishing a statutory corporation, which, of course, involves the full parliamentary process. Indeed, the practice adopted in setting up some companies has been so casual and informal that they have come into existence without any specific Oireachtas sanction at all, as for example in the case of Irish Shipping Ltd. and Irish Steel Holdings Ltd. Lemass, who before he was Taoiseach had been Minister for Industry and Commerce and the creator of many state-sponsored bodies, has claimed that

[11] Lemass, "The Organization Behind the Economic Programme," pp. 5–6.

[12] *Ibid.*, p. 8.

[13] S. F. Lemass, *The Role of the State-sponsored Bodies in the Economy* (Dublin, 1959), p. 1.

the statutory corporation "was the device which was deemed to be appropriate where the task was to provide essential services on a nationwide, non-competitive basis," whereas "for the more directly commercial type of operation, the device used was the state-financed corporation, with the characteristics of a joint stock company, registered under the Companies Acts."[14] In fact, most of the "infrastructure" industries and public utilities are in statutory corporation form, and where they are not—for example shipping or the airlines—it could be argued that these bodies are in practice in competition, as ordinary commercial concerns, with other non-Irish carriers. However, it is harder to accept some of the other reasons given by ministers to explain the choice of form, namely, that the company form is suitable for ventures that may not survive but less appropriate when the venture has established itself as a permanent feature, or that the corporation form has greater prestige and standing.[15]

What is quite clear in all this is, as Lemass once put it: "We do not work on the basis of theory. We work always on the basis of the best method of getting a particular job done."[16] Some of the inevitable results are equally clear and, from the point of view of good government, equally unsatisfactory. Whereas few doubt that most of these bodies have been successful and, in Garret FitzGerald's words, "the net contribution by these bodies in the economic and social life of the Irish community has been a remarkable one," nevertheless the failure to draw up adequate and up-to-date legal instruments reflecting the realities of growing state control, and the expediency, even casualness, evident in their inception have contributed materially to the problems of effective Oireachtas scrutiny and control.

IV

The increased use of state-sponsored bodies, which has been such an important feature since the Second World War, has been accompanied by a failure of the Oireachtas to supervise and control their activities. This was perhaps not so important when there were comparatively few of them and when many of those that did exist had, originally, commercial objectives. It was possible to contend—and, in fact, it was contended, in both Britain and Ireland—that such "business" bodies should be "removed as far as it is possible from political pressure."[17] Conse-

---

14 *Ibid.*

15 See *Dáil Debates*, vol. 176, cols. 990ff (July 9, 1959).

16 *Seanad Debates*, vol. 33, col. 1583 (Apr. 16, 1947).

17 P. M. McGilligan, Minister for Industry and Commerce, *Dáil Debates*, vol. 18, col. 1919 (Mar. 15, 1927).

quently, as the example of the Electricity Supply Board shows, "there had to be set up a business board . . .[which] should be independent of Parliament and Government as far as that could reasonably be arranged."[18] Accordingly, the minister was not endowed with powers over finance or general policy, nor was he able to direct the Board "in the national interest."

Postwar developments have changed the picture considerably, extending the number of these bodies and their use for social service or developmental activities and bringing all of them inevitably under closer government control as the state accepts responsibility for national development. Today, few even of the trading organizations can claim to be simply business enterprises and all are to some extent public services. The old concept of the autonomous body (never, in any case, applicable to bodies providing social services or engaged in regulatory functions) is patently unsatisfactory in these circumstances. But politicians, faced with a confusing array of these bodies set up with no attempt to secure uniformity of organization, powers, or finance, and in the case of many of them operating on insufficient or anomalous statutory bases, have not so far evolved any clear categories or principles of board-minister-Oireachtas relationships adequate to the needs of the situation. In any case, very few members of the Oireachtas are interested, except in parochial matters or to make party political capital.

It is necessary here to distinguish between government control and Oireachtas control. According to the "autonomous corporation" theory, neither was to extend very far in the case of trading bodies, except in emergencies. Ministers being responsible for very little, it followed that the Oireachtas could hold them accountable for very little. Today, no one doubts that ministers often have considerable powers, sometimes extending from the most general policy to matters of comparative detail; but the Oireachtas does not, and cannot, bring them to account, first, because it is often not clear either what the objectives of the bodies are or who (minister or board) is responsible for what, and, second, because the Oireachtas has neither the information nor the equipment to effect adequate control. Ministers may, therefore, wield power without responsibility.

Ministerial (or governmental) power over state-sponsored bodies is of four kinds. First, the sponsor minister (sometimes with the consent of another interested minister) or the government appoints some or all of the members of the governing boards of these bodies, and may dismiss

18 *Ibid.*, cols. 1818–19.

them. This power is a potential source of great patronage, and if a party is in power for a long time, as has been the case, it might be expected that the boards would become peopled by its supporters and those who have deserved well of it. In fact this has not happened to anything like the extent many people in Ireland firmly believe. Members of the Oireachtas, who are of course the leading and most active politicians, are in many cases barred by statute from holding such posts, and where no such legal barrier exists, the convention has been established. In fact, nominations to boards may often originate with the Civil Service rather than the minister, since departmental officials are commonly asked to suggest names and they place lists of possible candidates before their ministers. Taken as a whole, the choice of directors of state-sponsored bodies is probably more often explicable in terms of relevant experience, representation of interests, and Civil Service preference than in terms of party politics, let alone nepotism.

Second, in each case, the appropriate minister sees that the organization's operations are "kept in line . . . with the overall development plans of the Government."[19] This involves approval for new capital projects, for important policy proposals, and for such matters as major wage and salary increases. Such ministerial control may, however, extend much further, for, third, ministers have a general power of surveillance and right to intervene on behalf of the community. The extent and degree of control vary greatly from body to body and perhaps from time to time. Bodies that are dependent on the government for their finances because they operate on an annual grant-in-aid or, in the case of trading bodies, because they have to have losses made good or need new finance seem to be inevitably more vulnerable than those that are not, but it would be dangerous to draw a distinction along these lines. The Minister for Transport and Power, who is the sponsor minister for seven trading bodies, including the biggest and most important public utilities, attempted to explain the functions of his department in relation to his charges as follows:

The purpose of the Department is, first of all, to prepare legislation when it is required, to examine the demands for capital for future productive purposes and the promotion of the various companies, to examine how capital already provided is being spent and whether or not it should be remunerated at any given stage in a company's operations, to examine the general policy of each of these companies in relation to the national economy, and to see if there are any elements in their operations which are hindering other companies or other interests. In that we should also have regard to the necessity of there being rea-

---

[19] Lemass, *Role of the State-sponsored Bodies*, p. 9.

sonably good relations between employers and workers in these companies and we like to assure ourselves in every way possible that industrial relations are operating on what might be described as an optimum basis.

It is the duty of the Department also to exhort all companies at every possible opportunity to adopt dynamic cost reducing output raising techniques, to lower their costs as much as possible, to provide the very best possible service at the lowest cost, and to keep in line with modern practice.[20]

The control effected under these two heads sometimes has no statutory or other formal sanction, and the minister may well have no explicit legal power to direct a body—indeed, this usually *is* the case for the trading bodies in corporation form. The following extract from the *Dáil Debates* of 1963 illustrates the point clearly and indicates a thoroughly unsatisfactory state of affairs.

Dr. Browne and Mr. McQuillan asked the Minister for Industry and Commerce under what powers vested in him by the Oireachtas he can direct the Board of CIE [Córas Iompair Eireann, the state transport corporation] to accept his proposals, as referred to in a letter by him to CIE on 1st April 1963.

M. J. Lynch [the Minister]: ... I have no statutory power to issue directions to CIE in relation to trade disputes between the company and its employees. In view of the functions assigned to me under the Ministers and Secretaries Act, I do not need to have special powers to enable me to make a strong request to the company.

Dr. Browne: What is the position of the company in relation to a strong request? Do they have to accept it or can they reject it? What is the position?

Mr. J. Lynch: When I issued a direction to the company in the first place, the company knew well that I had not the power to direct them to do anything but knew I was making an attempt to solve the strike and they agreed to accept my direction in the matter.[21]

At the other extreme, the Minister for Health has very wide powers granted to him by statute concerning the performance of health services by corporate bodies set up under the Health (Corporate Bodies) Act, 1961.[22] He is explicitly enabled to establish such bodies, to control them virtually in all respects, and, if he wishes, to abolish them—all by ministerial order. Likewise, Taisci Stáit Teo. (set up to finance industrial enterprises) is required under its statute to perform its functions "as and when directed by the Minister," and, in any case, its board is composed wholly of civil servants. That ministers do in fact control state-sponsored bodies in some cases, whatever the legal position, is evident from the following extract from an advertisement inserted in the

---

20 *Dáil Debates*, vol. 182, cols. 999–1000 (June 10, 1960).
21 *Dáil Debates*, vol. 202, cols. 33–34 (Apr. 23, 1963).
22 For a list of these bodies, see Appendix D.

national dailies on September 3, 1966, by the Dairy Disposal Company (whose full-time chairman is a civil servant):

In accordance with the desire of the Minister for Agriculture and Fisheries who has indicated that it is his wish that suppliers affected by the strike should be treated as sympathetically as possible, the Company is now working out arrangements for payment to the milk suppliers concerned on the basis of milk deliveries in other comparable periods.

Finally, the minister has powers to govern the presentation and form of reports and accounts, and to provide for audit, and he also has the right to be given whatever information he requires. These matters are usually specifically provided for in statutes, orders, or articles of association.

The ministerial supervision and control outlined under the four heads above make it necessary for departments to have an intimate knowledge of the activities of the bodies they sponsor. Clearly ministers and chairmen must keep in touch. The Minister for Transport and Power has adopted the practice of holding a regular monthly meeting of the chairmen of the bodies whose sponsor minister he is. However, contacts are by no means confined to the boards and senior executives on the one side and the minister and his senior civil servants on the other. Garret FitzGerald, who had personal experience in one of the trading bodies, describes civil servants as "having frequent routine contact with officials of the state-sponsored bodies at various management and supervisory levels." He notes that "in some of these instances the matters dealt with may well be of such a character as to require clearance by the Minister, or at least to require that he should be informed of what is passing. But in many instances—probably the majority—the contacts are confined to the civil servant/management level." He comments that "these 'second-level' contacts, many of them of a very informal nature, are an essential part of a smooth-running administrative machine that involves the implementation of many aspects of state policy through state-sponsored bodies."[23]

Supervision and control might also be effected by the device of appointing serving civil servants to boards. The extent to which this practice was being followed in 1966 is shown in Table 10.2. It will be seen that in the administrative, regulatory, and social service group, 9 out of 29 boards contained civil servants. They were mostly to be found in the social service agencies sponsored by the Department of Health. In no cases were civil servants in a majority. Among the bodies engaged in

[23] FitzGerald, pp. 49–50.

TABLE 10.2

Civil Service Members of Boards of State-sponsored Bodies in 1966

Type of body	Number of Civil Service directors						Civil servant chairman
	None	One	Minority	Half	Majority	All	
Administrative or regulatory (10)	8	–	1	1[a]	–	–	1[a]
Social service (19)	12	–	7	–	–	–	1
Trading, i.e. production of goods and services (31)[b]	23	5	2	1	–	–	3
Marketing, research and development (17)[b]	5	7	2	–	–	3	5

Source: Compiled from information given in the *Directory of State Services*, 1966; *Dáil Debates*, vol. 221, cols. 463ff and 954ff (Feb. 24 and Mar. 3, 1966); and information supplied by departments.

[a] The Foyle Fisheries Commission. Half the board of this Commission are nominated by the Northern Ireland Government and are civil servants. The chairmanship rotates.

[b] Including subsidiaries.

trading, marketing, and development, there were civil service directors in 20 out of 48 cases. It is significant, however, that this practice was most common in the marketing, research, and development subgroup (12 out of 17). In this group, of course, are the bodies that operate on grants and the bodies whose activities are not—and could not possibly be—considered primarily commercial. According to Lemass, the Civil Service is not well adapted for development work, and other organizations have consequently had to be used; nevertheless it is necessary that such work be subordinated to departmental policy and closely integrated with departmental activities, which might well also be of a developmental character. If this is so, the presence of civil servants on boards is the handiest coordinating device. In the great majority of cases in both groups, boards contained a minority of civil servants or only one. However, it is not so easy to justify on this ground the practice of civil servants acting as chairmen of boards.

Although the placing of civil servants on boards is clearly useful, some criticisms have been made of it. C. S. Andrews, former chairman of Córas Iompair Eireann, condemned the practice, saying, "I cannot see how a civil servant functions properly if he is wearing two hats and if, having participated in the councils of a board, he returns to his Department and sits in judgement on the decisions reached."[24] Obviously, also, the practice could (but should not) be used as a means of effecting departmental control while avoiding detailed parliamentary control. Certainly, unless the circumstances are exceptional, a board composed wholly of civil servants would seem to be undesirable, for this is in

24 *Administration*, VI (1958–59), 298.

effect departmental administration without the normal parliamentary safeguards. As Table 10.2 shows, this did in fact occur in three cases: An Foras Forbartha and the National Building Agency, both sponsored by the Department of Local Government, and Taisci Stáit Teo., sponsored by the Department of Finance. It is hard to see these bodies as other than ministerial creatures removed to some degree from the normal rigors (such as they are) of Oireachtas control over the Civil Service.

It should be noted finally that civil servants are sometimes involved as secretaries or key personnel in state-sponsored bodies. Some have been appointed part-time secretaries of boards. For example, this was the case in the Socio-Medical Research Board, which was not much more than an advisory body in fact, and in other health bodies. In some cases, civil servants have been seconded as executives of state-sponsored bodies, a practice justified by Lemass "where there are reserves of ability in a department," and contrariwise, because, if such officers proved to be failures, "the difficulties of displacement would be less"![25] Both these procedures might in practice enhance coordination between department and enterprise, and perhaps make departmental control more effective.

The considerable variation in practice in the extent of governmental control over state-sponsored bodies makes it difficult to generalize except to observe that control has inevitably increased in recent years. By means of the procedures mentioned above, the government should usually be able, whatever the legal position, to exert effective control even in considerable detail. There is some evidence, however, that chairmen and boards have occasionally resisted ministers and even defied them. The Electricity Supply Board is said to have attempted to resist government pressure to use turf for the generation of electricity when cheaper fuels were available, but such differences were never publicly referred to, least of all in the Board's annual reports. On the other hand, considerable publicity attendant upon the resignation in 1966 of Lieutenant-General M. J. Costello, managing director of the Irish Sugar Company and its subsidiary, Erin Foods Ltd., confirmed that he had been at loggerheads with the Department of Finance for years over the policies of Erin Foods. This fact was widely known but never publicly stated, owing to the inadequacy of the company's reports and the failure of the Oireachtas to elicit information about its affairs. According to the American management consultants called in to report, "they found 'no evidence of a rigorous analysis or meeting of minds' between the Minister for Finance and the company's management on the real objective

[25] "The Organization Behind the Economic Programme," pp. 6–7.

of the project. . . . There had not been . . . full agreement on the resources to be made available."[26]

It is possible also that in recent years some state-sponsored bodies, perhaps the well-established and least enterprising, have been slow to respond positively to the government's development plans. A Report on Economic Planning by the National Industrial Economic Council in 1965 made clear that national planning policies were not always acted on by boards.

> The need for steps to ensure that all departments of the public service and state enterprises play their full part in implementing the programme is reinforced by the priority given to the attainment of economic growth in the Second Programme. The implication of this development and the need for a realignment of policies and administrative machinery may not be completely realized as yet in some parts of the public service and in all the state enterprises.

Earlier, in 1959, Lemass made the same point: "There develops a tendency in some boards to think of themselves rather as sovereign independent authorities than as integral parts of a larger organization and they are sometimes disposed to resent pressures to keep them in line."[27] Lemass has also argued, contrary to what is usually believed, that a minister, far from being a restraining influence, is essentially a stimulator. "The difficulty is where a board is dragging its heels, or is so excessively cautious or dilatory that it fails to keep its place in the general advance. The minister has the task of stimulating greater activity in such cases and it is not always easy to do so without friction." He added that, "as a general rule, the relations between the Minister and the board should never be too cordial."[28] The picture presented here, of the minister as a constructive critic stimulating and exhorting from outside, is a somewhat surprising one, and it may be an ideal of Lemass's, put forward when he was talking in speculative and normative terms. In everyday practice, most of the civil servants concerned, like many ministers, would probably prefer to have their state-sponsored bodies comfortably under their eye, pursuing safe policies in such a way as to generate little friction, thus minimizing the risk of causing political discontent or ministerial embarrassment.

Whereas the ability of the government to control state-sponsored bodies is potentially very great (though it may not exercise its power in all cases), the Oireachtas is far less well placed. The constitutional position is, of course, clear enough. Ministers are responsible to the Dáil not

26 Reported in *Irish Times*, Oct. 14, 1966.
27 *Role of the State-sponsored Bodies*, p. 9.
28 *Ibid.*

only for those duties laid upon them by the Constitution and the statutes, including their failure to act when they should have acted, but for all their actions as ministers and for those of their departmental officials. There is a political obligation upon them to explain and defend, and the Dáil (with the Seanad as a potentially useful auxiliary) ought to be in a position to make this responsibility a reality. However, the Oireachtas suffers from the basic handicap that the precise objectives of some state-sponsored bodies are not clearly stated and, more generally, that the statutes and legal instruments constituting and regulating them are often inadequate and sometimes anomalous, particularly in defining the relations between boards and their ministers. Ministers might (and do—as the quotation on p. 262 from the *Dáil Debates* about the CIE strike shows) wield considerable powers without specific authority and often without being held accountable.

There is another view: "There has arisen . . . in recent times, in Dáil Eireann, and perhaps even more surprisingly in Seanad Eireann, a tendency towards endeavouring to make the decisions of some statutory boards, taken within the powers given to them by law, subject to review and even to veto in the legislature."[29] According to Lemass, this might be partly due to "woolly thinking." Given the situation described above, this is no wonder. Moreover, there is a vicious spiral here. To quote Lemass again:

It is probable that when any semi-state board becomes the centre of controversy—as is not unlikely at some period of its existence—its independence is likely to be in serious jeopardy, because Ministers, realizing the folly of accepting responsibility without effective power, will be disposed to bring their operations under closer supervision, which could reduce if not eliminate their special utility as an administrative device.

But such an increase in ministerial control in turn only makes the gap between it and parliamentary control the greater, since to the extent that state-sponsored bodies approximate to government departments, the same deficiencies of the Oireachtas to which attention has already been drawn in Chapter 8 (pp. 195–200) manifest themselves, namely inadequate methods of acquiring information and inadequate expertise in assessing it. Reports and accounts vary considerably in the extent and usefulness of the information they give, in the case of some of the bodies in company form telling little or nothing; they are rarely debated; and, in any case, they are useful only as the starting points of systematic inquiry, itself a prelude to informed parliamentary debate. Dáil Eireann

---

[29] Lemass, "The Organization Behind the Economic Programme," p. 7.

has not even established a select committee on state enterprises, as the British House of Commons did in the middle 1950's, though all parties have advocated it—when they have been in opposition—including Lemass himself for Fianna Fáil.[30] In contrast to Lemass's views in opposition, it seems generally to have been his view in office and Fianna Fáil policy that ministerial control is sufficient and that select committee scrutiny is unnecessary, inhibiting to the state-sponsored bodies, and, notwithstanding British experience to the contrary, constitutionally dangerous.[31]

The problem of the control of state-sponsored bodies is not, of course, the same as that of controlling government departments. Despite the tendency of all of them, including the trading bodies, to become increasingly instruments of government policy, it does not follow that the extent of control and the methods of control appropriate to departmental administration apply also to them. There is still some validity in the argument that, as Lemass put it, "these bodies were set up with the deliberate intention of avoiding close state control."[32] What is not valid is to argue, as he did, that "additional parliamentary control is unnecessary having regard to the wide ministerial powers in relation to state-sponsored bodies."[33] It is indeed exactly the reverse. Additional parliamentary control is necessary precisely because ministers have wide powers.

These are very familiar problems to students of government, and particularly of British government. There can, however, be few developed countries in which so little attention has been paid to them and in which the legislature has so completely failed to fulfill its proper functions in relation to what has now become, because of its versatility, a most important administrative device.

[30] See *Dáil Debates*, vol. 119, cols. 367–70 (Feb. 21, 1950).
[31] In February 1967 an opposition motion for a select committee was rejected. See *Dáil Debates*, vol. 226, cols. 1317–42 and 1677–1701 (Feb. 15 and 22, 1967).
[32] *Role of the State-sponsored Bodies*, p. 11.
[33] *Ibid.*

ELEVEN

Local Government and Politics

The third of the three main groups of authorities that administer public services are the local authorities. However, local authorities are not to be regarded *simply* as administrative organs, allocated functions by the central authorities as convenience dictates, though this is to a large extent what they have become. The system of local government developed in Great Britain and Ireland in the nineteenth century was one of two systems of government (central and local) to cope with virtually all public business. It was intended to be local *self*-government; democracy carried down to the smallest community unit practicable and, by the device of committee administration of all services, to the most intimate details of their application. Whereas the great growth of the state-sponsored bodies may be seen simply as the development of decentralized administration of central government functions, since they answer to the Cabinet and the Oireachtas, local government should not be similarly viewed. To do so is to ignore both its history and its rationale.

It cannot be denied, of course, that local government is subordinate government, since local authorities, having no inherent authority of their own, derive their functions and powers from the Oireachtas. Nevertheless, local authorities are different in kind from state-sponsored bodies, for they are in themselves representative, and local government embodies the concept of local representation as an integral feature. Services are administered under the supervision of locally elected persons who have some discretion in their conduct of affairs and who can be called to account. No doubt, in the twentieth century, the exigencies of the welfare state have pressed inexorably in upon the body of local self-government, crushing it almost to death. Nevertheless, local government will not be understood unless it is remembered that originally the ratepayers (for local government has a source of funds of its own—the "rates") were intended to have considerable independence and autonomy.

Following this tradition, there is a generally accepted belief in Ireland in the value of local government as a *democratic* institution, perhaps even an essential part of democracy. This legacy of Victorian liberalism was summed up by the Royal Commission on the Government of Greater London in terms that would be generally accepted in Ireland today: "Local government is with us an instance of democracy at work, and no amount of potential administrative efficiency could make up for the loss of active participation in the work by capable, public-spirited people elected by, responsible to, and in touch with those who elect them." Nevertheless, Ireland now has a council-manager system of

TABLE 11.1

Expenditure of Local Authorities as a Percentage of Total Public Sector Budget and of Gross National Product, 1939–65

Expenditure	Year ending March 31			
	1939	1949	1959	1965
Total expenditure of local authorities[a] (£ million)	16.0	30.2	65.6	106.0
Total public sector budget (£ million)	47.7[b]	97.2	182.8	332.8
Local authorities' expenditure as percentage of total public sector budget	33.5%	31.1%	35.9%	31.9%
GNP at factor cost (£ million)	161.6	333.7	517.8	826.0
Local authorities' expenditure as percentage of GNP	9.9%	9.1%	12.7%	12.8%

Source: Compiled from *Irish Statistical Survey* and *National Income and Expenditure*, both published annually by the Stationery Office, Dublin.

[a] The term "local authorities" here includes county councils, county borough councils, urban councils, town commissioners, vocational education committees, committees of agriculture, and health bodies.

[b] This excludes a special payment of £10 million to the British Government under a Treaty agreement.

TABLE 11.2

Local Authorities; Major Categories of Expenditure, 1962–63

Category	Current		Capital		Total	
	£ thousand	Per cent	£ thousand	Per cent	£ thousand	Per cent
Education	3,785	4.5%	786	0.9%	4,571	5.4%
Health	22,556	26.9	690	0.8	23,246	27.7
Housing	5,575	6.7	11,079	13.3	16,654	20.0
Social welfare	2,008	2.4	1	—	2,009	2.4
Transport and commerce	9,595	11.4	7,382	8.8	16,977	20.2
Other	17,211	20.6	3,067	3.7	20,278	24.3
TOTAL	60,730	72.5%	23,005	27.5%	83,735	100.0%

Source: Based on figures supplied by the Central Statistics Office, Dublin.

local government, having largely abandoned the British principle of direct committee administration of services in favor of the conduct of all services under the direction of a single individual, the City or County Manager, who answers to his council but yet has a statutory position and statutory powers. Since managers are appointed and local government committees in the British tradition consist of elected councilors, there is obviously a greater willingness in Ireland to forfeit, or at least to risk, democracy in order to achieve efficiency. Perhaps, also, Irish people do not feel very strongly about local government. When, in the 1960's, local elections were postponed for up to two years to suit the convenience of the national political timetable, hardly a voice was raised in protest; when councils were suspended or abolished for nonperformance of their duties, they went out of existence with scarcely a whimper or cry of alarm. Even the suspension of the Dublin City Council in 1969 for failure to strike an adequate rate did not arouse much public hostility.

There is apparently a fundamental problem here—how are democratic procedures and local autonomy and variety to survive in the face of the evident trend of modern welfare states toward ever-rising and uniform standards of service? The importance of this problem may be measured by the size, range, and nature of the services provided by local authorities. Table 11.1 shows their total expenditure to be no less than one-third of all public spending and to consume an increasing proportion of the gross national product, amounting to about one-eighth in 1965. When we go further and examine the objects of expenditure, it is apparent that local authorities provide many of the most important basic environmental and personal services on which people's health, comfort, and even lives depend from cradle to grave. Table 11.2 gives a summary of the main categories of local expenditure in 1962–63, and Table 11.3 lists local government functions by class of authority.

II

Concerning its institutions, local government derives on the one hand from the British tradition of civic autonomy dating from medieval times and symbolized by the royal charters granted to towns by monarchs, and on the other from the habit of providing for law and order in the countryside by placing the onus on local gentry, who were expected in addition to administer on an amateur and unpaid basis such state regulations as applied in their neighborhood and such public services as were absolutely essential. From a functional point of view, its historical core lies in the relief of destitution and in the provision of basic environmental services such as roads, sanitation, water, and other "public health" services. In the nineteenth century, a new and unified

TABLE 11.3

Principal Functions of the Major Local Authorities

Functions	County councils	County borough councils	Borough and urban district councils	Town commissioners
ROADS AND PUBLIC WORKS	Main and county roads	Urban roads	Urban roads	
	Maintenance of public works	Maintenance of public works	Maintenance of public works	
PUBLIC ASSISTANCE	Public assistance (except Cork, Dublin, Limerick, and Waterford)			
HEALTH	Dispensary medical (doctor, medicines) Maternity School health Child dental Tuberculosis Hospitals Mental health Child welfare Food hygiene Control of infectious disease (except Cork, Dublin, Limerick, and Waterford)	Performed by joint health authorities of city and adjacent county (see note below)		
SANITARY SERVICES	Water supply Sewerage Collection of refuse and cleansing Public lighting Burial grounds Parks and playgrounds	Water supply Sewerage Collection of refuse and cleansing Public lighting Burial grounds Parks and playgrounds	Water supply Sewerage Collection of refuse and cleansing Public lighting Burial grounds Parks and playgrounds	Parks and playgrounds

TABLE 11.3 *(cont.)*

Functions	County councils	County borough councils	Borough and urban district councils	Town com- missioners
HOUSING	House build- ing and renting House loans and grants	House build- ing and renting	House build- ing and renting House loans and grants	Renting houses
PHYSICAL PLANNING	Preparation and imple- mentation of develop- ment plan	Preparation and imple- mentation of develop- ment plan	Administering planning Acts	
MISCEL- LANEOUS	Scholarships Fire brigades Public li- braries and museums, etc. Elections	Scholarships Fire brigades Public li- braries and museums, etc. Elections Markets	Provision of allotments Control of fairs and markets Fire brigades School meals	Provision of allotments Control of fairs and markets School meals

Notice three other important local authorities. *Health authorities:* the Cork, Dublin, Limerick, and Waterford Health Authorities perform the health and public assistance functions of the four city councils and their adjacent county councils. The Western Health Institutions Board (of two representatives of each of five Connacht counties) controls joint hospital services. *Vocational Educational Committees:* every county and county borough council and seven borough and urban district councils appoint a Vocational Educational Committee to provide education for trades and business, in science and art, and in agricultural subjects. *County Committees of Agriculture:* every county appoints a County Committee of Agriculture, whose main function is to provide assistance and instruction in agriculture and horticulture. The committees employ agricultural instructors.

system was slowly created to deal with the social problems of the Industrial Revolution when and as they were perceived in Great Britain; it was completed by the end of the century. The authorities created were democratic or were democratized. With few modifications this system was applied to Ireland, democracy and all—though conditions in Ireland were often very different. Thus, again, it is necessary to begin with British experience and British solutions in an Irish setting. However, the twenty years from independence to the Second World War brought modifications and additions of such magnitude that the resultant system is by no means merely a variation of the British pattern.

The reforms and developments of the nineteenth century centered principally on three groups of authorities—the counties, the boroughs and other town authorities, and the boards of guardians of the poor law "unions," which were newly created authorities set up to administer the relief of poverty. As the Anglo-Normans conquered Ireland from the middle of the twelfth century, they divided the territory they subdued into counties on the British pattern, their boundaries determined largely by the accidents of war and the dynastic fortunes of Irish chiefs. It was a long process, but it was completed by the early seventeenth century. Sheriffs appointed by the central government handled those functions of government that needed to be decentralized in these counties. The sheriffs called together twice in each year two dozen of the biggest landowners of the county to prepare business for, and to meet, the royal judges proceeding around the country "on circuit." This body, which was called "the Grand Jury," had both legal and administrative duties and was responsible for raising the necessary funds by levying taxes upon occupiers of land in the country.

There were somewhat similar arrangements in towns that in Anglo-Norman times were fortified and given charters, similar to those given by the Crown to English towns, granting certain powers of self-government. These powers were formally vested in corporate bodies consisting of the "freemen" of the town, men with property or in certain occupations, who elected a leader, the mayor, and a council to conduct their corporate business and attend to legal and administrative duties. By the early nineteenth century, there were nearly 70 of these boroughs, many very small and many, big and small, badly governed by their corporations, but all with considerable autonomy.

To these two types of local authority there was added a third in the early nineteenth century in an attempt to cope with the rapidly growing problem of destitution. After an inquiry, whose findings were largely ignored, the new British poor law system was extended to Ireland in 1838. This new system, which superseded the organization devised in Tudor times, was based on harsh principles, among them the requirement that public assistance should only be given inside institutions known as workhouses in almost prisonlike conditions. It was administered under strong and uniform central controls by local bodies called boards of guardians, an administrative pattern that contrasted sharply with the loosely supervised oligarchic government of the towns and counties. In England the unit was "the union" of parishes, the basic social unit of that country; in Ireland, however, "the union" was an area of ten miles radius around each of 130 market towns. In each, a workhouse was erected and its operations were supervised by a board of guardians, which was partly composed of appointed magistrates and partly of elected representatives of those citizens who were obliged to foot the bills, that is, the middle and upper classes.

It was to these three groups of authorities that the state turned from the 1830's on, to administer a growing range of new services, particularly public health and other environmental services designed to protect the community and to relieve the worst hardships of its poorer members; these authorities were reorganized and reformed when rising standards of efficiency and a growing acceptance of the principle of democracy so demanded. To a great extent reforming legislation was very similar in content to that devised for Great Britain and followed it closely in time.

Following on the reforms of government in the British towns in 1835, the Municipal Corporations (Ireland) Act, 1840, swept away 58 of the existing 68 boroughs and, in the 10 that remained, provided for new councils elected by substantial property owners and composed of a mayor, aldermen (i.e. senior councilors), and councilors. Smaller towns were able under permissive legislation of 1828 to acquire powers to provide a very limited range of services such as lighting and cleaning, and in 1854 the Towns Improvement (Ireland) Act extended this arrangement. All towns with a population of 1,500 or more could, if the inhabitants wished, take powers to provide lighting, paving, cleaning, and water supply services, which services were administered by elected "commissioners." Originally these and other local authorities were to a great extent free of central control. It was not until 1872 that a central government department, the Local Government Board, was established to supervise them. Between this date and the end of the century, central control of the rapidly burgeoning local government system increased considerably. Nevertheless, the principle that local authorities were autonomous governmental units, masters in their own houses, was still accepted, and there was a marked contrast between the control exercised by the Local Government Board and that of the poor law commissioners, who imposed rigid uniformity.

The great extension and consolidation of public health services in Great Britain effected by the Public Health Act of 1875 were paralleled in Ireland with acts of 1874 and 1878. The 1874 Act established a comprehensive system of "sanitary authorities," which in the case of urban areas were towns of over 6,000. Thus the boroughs and the bigger of the towns that were not boroughs came to form one group of urban authorities, which under the 1878 Act and subsequent legislation acquired considerable duties and powers in health and other environmental services including housing. Elsewhere, i.e. in the countryside and the smaller towns, public health and environmental services were allocated not to the county authorities, the grand juries, but to the poor law guardians, whose relative efficiency led to their being used for a growing range of duties, notably the "dispensary system," a general practitioner service that provided a doctor and dispensaries in each district over the whole country. Established in 1851, it remains to this day the basic personal health service for most Irish people.

Thus, by 1880 two types of urban authority had been created: the councils of the larger towns (including the boroughs)—the "urban district councils" as they came to be called—developing as major multipurpose authorities; and the representative bodies of the smaller towns, called "town commissioners," whose responsibilities did not extend to public health services, for the provision of which they were not separated from the appropriate union (later county authority). These emerging arrangements embodied an important principle of British local government, namely that towns are different from the countryside in many of their needs and in the governmental arrangements appropriate to them. This principle was further applied at the end of the century when county government was reformed and a third type of urban authority, the county borough council, came into being.

The county authorities, the grand juries, tended to be bypassed in favor of the relatively more efficient poor law authorities, who by the end of the century not only relieved destitution and furnished public and personal health services, but, from 1883, provided rural housing as well. With the reform of county government in Great Britain in 1888 and 1896, the government of the Irish countryside was clearly due for a change, the more so since the contrast between the oligarchic and increasingly anachronistic grand jury system and the representative and increasingly democratic urban government was becoming ever sharper. Under the Local Government (Ireland) Act, 1898, the functions of the grand juries were handed over to democratically elected county councils. As the franchise was wide, being extended to male householders or occupiers, a considerable measure of democracy came to the Irish countryside with dramatic suddenness and was immediately turned to account in the developing national struggle for independence.

Besides providing democratic government at county level, the 1898 Act arranged for the transfer of the public health functions of the poor law guardians to rural district councils, thus setting up a two-tier system in the countryside as in the towns. However, the largest boroughs (Dublin, Cork, Limerick, and Waterford) were created counties (termed county boroughs) as were the largest British towns in 1888, and were completely divorced for local government purposes from the adjoining county areas. The county borough councils thus became almost all-purpose local authorities.

By the end of the century, then, a more or less coherent pattern of authorities was established to replace the confusing mass of overlapping bodies that had been created *ad hoc* earlier in the century, while a simplified taxation system in the form of the rates, a tax on housing and other fixed property, provided an autonomous source of funds. Yet, even now, not all "local government" had been subsumed in this set of authorities. Apart from services such as police and education—which, in contrast to Great Britain, had been nationalized and were administered bureaucratically by central government departments—there still existed local public bodies such as harbor boards and port sanitary authorities, and, of course, the boards of guardians, which were now, however, fully democratized and partly assimilated to the main system, being composed of members of the appropriate urban and rural authorities. On paper at least, this system resembled very closely the British pattern, lacking only the parish councils that in Britain formed a third or bottom tier of local authorities in the rural areas and were the culmination of Victorian grass-roots democracy.

Between 1898 and independence, local government was dominated by national political issues and movements. The new franchise brought about a great change in the composition of the councils. The county councils in particular became centers of nationalism. In 1906, a French writer, L. Paul-Dubois, pointed out that the 1898 Act was "revolutionizing the antiquated local government system. . . . By providing the popular movement with a lever against the Castle and at the same time a permanent local focus, it gave Ireland a new weapon to advance its claims."[1] Thus, as J. J. Horgan put it, "the Local Government Act of 1898, although indeed its authors knew it not, was the legislative father of the Irish Free State."[2]

After the Dáil Government was established in 1919, the large majority of local councils, in the words of the First Report of the Department of Local Government, "challenged the authority of the Imperial Parliament by refusing to recognize the control of the Local Government Board and by making declarations of allegiance to Dáil Eireann."[3] Of all the Dáil Government departments, Local Government was the most successful and least shadowy. In this heady atmosphere, local government itself suffered somewhat, a decline that was hastened by the finan-

[1] L. Paul-Dubois, *L'Irlande contemporaine et la question irlandaise* (Paris, 1907), pp. 183, 186. My translation.
[2] J. J. Horgan, "Local Government Developments at Home and Abroad," *Studies*, XV (1926), 535.
[3] *First Report of the Department of Local Government and Public Health, 1922–25* (Stationery Office, Dublin, 1927), p. 11.

cial disabilities placed by the British on recalcitrant authorities, by the breakdown in the collection of rates, and by the fact that civil war followed immediately after the Treaty. The combined effect of all this on a local government system that was not in any case working well in the cities and in which committee administration, the democratic power-house of the British system, was patently inefficient and conducive to nepotism, was to force the new government to suspend some authorities for incompetence or neglect and to consider the whole question of the machinery and procedures of local government. Two decades of reform followed. The result is that, whereas the pattern of Irish local authorities today is largely a late-nineteenth-century creation, the machinery and processes of local government are products of the first generations of independent rule.

III

The first rulers of the Irish Free State approached local government with the view that as the elected representatives of the Irish people, now come into their own, they had a duty to organize an honest and efficient government and to do so quickly and with no nonsense. Local authorities, for all their displays of national fervor, were in many cases not particularly efficient. Their administration was often sloppy and tainted with nepotism and jobbery, which were anathema to many of the austere and high-minded ministers and their even more austere civil servants. Imbued with the ideals of Sinn Féin and supported by middle-class and influential business interests in Cork and Dublin, they began at once to think in terms of less democratic procedures to produce more efficient administration, and, from 1922 on, a second phase of reforms took place. It was not completed for twenty years. Between 1922 and 1942 the machinery and procedures of Irish local government were transformed from a close, and apparently unsatisfactory, imitation of those of Britain to a unique system of managerial government and central supervision that is undoubtedly more bureaucratic in its operation than what went before, but more suited to Irish conditions.

Although the general trend of local government development after independence was away from the Victorian democratic ideal of the greatest possible devolution of appropriate functions to elected representatives, democracy in one respect was quickly achieved. The restrictions on full adult franchise in the 1898 Act and plural voting by reason of ownership of property were removed by 1935, and from that date the qualifications for registration as a local elector have been only adult status (i.e. 21 or over) and residence.

The Victorian concept of local democracy, which in Great Britain resulted in a two- or three-tier system of authorities everywhere except in the largest cities, was never fully implemented in Ireland, for parish councils were never set up. Indeed, after independence, the trend toward grass-roots authorities was reversed, a process that has continued ever since. The poor law guardians were abolished in 1923 and the rural district councils in 1925; in both cases their functions were transferred to the county councils. The smaller urban authorities have come under increasing strain and have tended to lose or give up their functions and powers. Not only were there always at any one time a handful of town authorities suspended by ministerial order for nonperformance of their duties, but by 1940 a few of the smaller town councils had ceased to exist altogether. By 1960 six town commissions had disappeared, while four of the councils of urban districts (the larger town authorities) had given up their urban district status in favor of the lowlier "town" status. Increasingly, town councils have been permitted to hand over the actual performance of their duties—for example house building, paving, lighting, and cleaning—to the county councils, and have done so.

This trend reflected the increasing inadequacy of small units technically, administratively, and financially when faced with the growing range and rising level of public services. It meant that the counties, together with the city authorities and county boroughs, came more and more to dominate local government. Local government in Ireland became, and is now, primarily county council government.

The movement to bigger units has by no means come to an end. The county in its turn is coming under strain. Even in 1898 the decision to make the county the major unit was not arrived at rationally. The counties were there and, though county boundaries were in origin largely the product of accidents, they were accepted without question and without reference to the large differences among them in area, wealth, and population. Population changes, the increase in public services, and scientific and technical advances have exacerbated these differences while putting strain upon all, big and small. Even comparatively strong county authorities are not big enough units for today's hospital services, for example. These demand large catchment areas to justify the degree of specialization and the levels of expenditure of resources they require.

Faced with this problem, county authorities have increasingly joined together in "joint authorities" to provide services, particularly health services. In 1960, health services in the four county boroughs and their surrounding county areas were by statute put into the hands of separate health authorities composed of representatives of each of the councils involved. Since then, regional health authorities have been proposed for the whole country. Similarly, physical planning has been undertaken on a regional basis. The county, then, is coming to be recognized as less suitable than the region from technical and administrative points of view. But sentiment, both patriotic and sporting, has attached itself to the county units since the end of the nineteenth century. Moreover, there is widespread awareness in both official and political circles that the bigger the unit, the further removed is the elector from the government of his local area. Thus, Ireland is experiencing the classic local government problem of efficiency versus community sentiment and personal involvement.

The chief instrument of the efficiency of advanced countries of the modern world is, as Max Weber pointed out, the "bureau" or office; the key occupation, the bureaucrat. From the very beginning of the state, and particularly in its first twenty years, local government became markedly more bureaucratic—and more efficient. Bureaucratization took three forms: increasing central government control; the creation of a single local government service, centrally selected by open competition, and central control of personnel matters; and—most important in its consequences—the institution of the manager system.

Central control by ministerial departments increased steadily from the 1920's to the 1950's, by which time it was ubiquitous, unsystematic, and uneven in its incidence. Increasingly, the older conception of local government as a separate governmental system gave way to the idea of local authorities as agents of central departments. Certainly, more functions were allocated to local authorities, but their freedom to decide for themselves whether to provide services or not, or at what level to provide them, tended to diminish. Increasing financial dependence on the central government inevitably meant control, the more detailed in its incidence since grants were often allocated for given purposes and hedged about with stringent conditions ranging from prior and detailed approval of plans to payment after inspection or on proof of attaining certain standards and, of course, stringent audit. (Table 11.4 illustrates the growth of central government grants.)

Not only did central control increase in volume, but the number of departments involved in supervision grew. Today, local authorities by no means deal only with the Department of Local Government, but also with Health, Agriculture, Education, Justice, Social Welfare, Transport and Power, and Defence. Sometimes new schemes have occasioned new,

TABLE 11.4

Sources of Local Authority Revenue, 1939–65

Source	1939 £ thousand	1939 Per cent	1949 £ thousand	1949 Per cent	1959 £ thousand	1959 Per cent	1965[a] £ thousand	1965[a] Per cent
Rates	6,271	50%	10,358	41%	20,561	40%	25,863	33%
State grants	4,697	37	11,139	44	22,230	43	38,247	49
Other receipts (mainly rents and repayments for housing)	1,672	13	3,590	15	8,753	17	14,241	18
TOTAL	12,640	100%	25,087	100%	51,544	100%	78,351	100%

Source: *Returns of Local Taxation* (annual).
   Note: Receipts in year ended March 31.
   [a] Estimates.

single-purpose authorities separate from the county and urban authorities, though linked with them by representation. The most important of these are the county committees of agriculture and the vocational education committees, which operate under their own statutes and under the supervision of their own sponsor departments.

The impact of detailed, complicated, and confusing controls has inevitably frustrated councilors and officials alike, whatever their advantages in producing uniformly high standards. In face of this frustration, there have been some signs of a changing attitude in the Department of Local Government in recent years. In 1963, J. L. Garvin, then Secretary of the Department, admitted to "the ever-present tendency in supervising authorities to concentrate on controls as being easier to operate than to curtail, involving no fresh thinking," but pointed to a change in attitude and policy of his Department "in the direction of cutting out particular controls, of generalizing sanctions and of freeing local authorities to operate within reasonably wide limits of autonomy." The job of the Department would increasingly be that of general planning and advice; the relationship "will not be of leader and led, still less of controller and controlled, but a partnership."[4] As yet, however, the system is still to a great extent one of detailed control and central supervision, and if "partnership" ever does become a reality, there will nevertheless be no doubt who is the senior partner.

Central government control extends to supervision not only of performance but of personnel. This takes two forms—selection on a na-

[4] J. L. Garvin, "Local Government and Its Problems," *Administration*, XI (1963), 226.

tional basis of administrative and professional officers, and control by the Department of Local Government of personnel matters generally.

Even before independence, Sinn Féin had indicated its intention of reforming the local government system, which was, in truth, not a single service at all. Local officials were chosen and appointed by the local authorities themselves, and, "as might be expected in such circumstances, recruitment on considerations other than merit was only too frequent."[5] Moreover, authorities being separate jurisdictions, many very small, the promotion opportunities were inadequate and, consequently, morale and incentive were low. Condemning these weaknesses, Sinn Féin promised a national service, appointment by open competition, and mobility.

Such a system was duly instituted, notably by the creation in 1926 of an independent Local Appointments Commission to select and nominate to all administrative and professional posts, and in the creation of a local service code administered by the Department of Local Government. In its annual report for 1950–51, the Department of Local Government could point out that "over a long period the law has vested in the central authority a tight control over local authorities in staff matters. The purpose of this was to ensure that staffs are properly recruited and fairly treated. Generally that position has been reached." The Department was now, the report said, seeking ways of maintaining the advantages without the referral of detail to the center. This it proceeded to do in the years that followed. Once again, however, efficiency had been achieved at the cost of local autonomy, a cost that in this instance few would regard as heavy. Today, the filling of those few appointments that still, anomalously, remain in the hands of the elected representatives—notably the positions of rate collectors—frequently bears witness to the undesirability of such a procedure.

Whereas central control has diminished the discretion of both local councilors and local officials, the creation of a managerial system has increased the local official's role at the local councilor's expense. The manager was intended to replace committee administration, and, thus, in intention and result the arrangement was an important modification of the British inheritance. It was the outcome of a combination of growing dissatisfaction with the operation of local government before independence, the austere idealism of Sinn Féin, and the influence of urban businessmen who wanted to see business methods and procedures applied to city administration, as they thought had been the case in the United States.

5 D. Turpin, "The Local Government Service," *Administration*, II (1954–55), 83.

By the end of the First World War, both Cork and Dublin were being badly governed, a situation made worse by the disruption caused by the war of independence and the subsequent civil war. A combination of administration by elected representatives who were mainly interested in their own wards (city electoral areas) and by staffs who were, taken as a whole, not very efficient or professional had contributed to a situation where Cork was, in the words of one of its distinguished citizens, J. J. Horgan, "in a condition of dirt which would disgrace a native village in central Africa" and Dublin was "notorious as being one of the dirtiest cities in Europe."[6] It became necessary in 1922 and 1923 to suspend the ordinary processes of local government in both these cities and in some counties whose councils had simply ceased to function, replacing the elected authorities by centrally appointed "commissioners." The advantages were immediately apparent and a strong sentiment in favor of retaining them grew quickly in business circles. Governmental commissions and departmental inquiries alike reported in favor of a managerial system "so that there could be brought to the solution of many urgent local problems an absolute impartiality and an understanding of modern developments in city management."[7]

Because the most insistent pressure came from Cork, where a group of professional men and businessmen calling themselves "The Progressives" drafted proposals for a scheme, and because Cork posed a less complicated problem than the much larger Dublin, it was in the Cork City Management Act, 1929, that management was first introduced to Ireland. The Cork pattern was followed with minor variations when it was extended to Dublin in 1930, to Limerick in 1934, to Waterford in 1939, and, finally, to the counties in 1942. As county managers also became managers for each urban authority in their county, all the major local authorities now operate under this system.

IV

The basic principle of the management system, as it was expressed in the Management Acts of 1929 to 1940, is "a legal dichotomy of reserved powers of councils and executive functions of managers."[8] That legislation prescribes the functions of the council, the "reserved functions," and the functions of the manager, the "executive functions." Elected members are to concern themselves with two main types of business:

[6] Quoted in *Studies*, XII (1923), 357, 359.

[7] *Fourth Report of the Department of Local Government and Public Health, 1928–29* (Stationery Office, Dublin, 1930), p. 17.

[8] A. W. Bromage, "Irish Councilmen at Work," *Administration*, II (1954), 93.

first, general policy matters such as the adoption of the budget, the striking of the rate, borrowing, the disposal of council property, the making of local laws (called bylaws) and important planning decisions; and, second, what might be called representational matters, such as the control of elections, the selection of persons to be members of other bodies, the appointment of committees, the salary of the mayor (in towns and cities), etc. All the functions and duties of the council that are not specified as reserved functions are executive or managerial functions. These managerial functions explicitly include the appointment and control of staff insofar as these matters are not centrally controlled, the making of contracts including the letting of houses, the administration of health services, and the determination of entitlement to health and other social benefits. Thus, functions that involved decisions open to personal and political influence and that increasingly, as the welfare state developed, required a mass of detailed administration and decisions unsuited to committee procedures were removed from the elected representatives and from committee decision. Since there was no longer any need for a full-blown committee system, councils were made smaller in size.

The manager is an officer of the council or councils that he serves; he is required to keep them informed about business and to aid and advise them in the performance of their duties. He must attend council meetings, and as their chief executive officer he is responsible for the work necessary to implement their decisions. In his own sphere, he must act by formal "Order" in matters that, had they been council decisions, would have required a resolution of the council, and a register of these orders must be available for council inspection.

Though an officer of the council, the manager is not chosen by the council, being nominated to it by the Local Appointments Commission. Nor can he be dismissed by his council, which has the power (never so far used) only to suspend him and to request the Minister for Local Government to remove him. Thus, clearly, the manager, who has statutory functions and powers and who is neither hired nor fired by his employers, is far removed in conception from the managers of the typical United States system, "where the manager is so clearly the servant of the elected council."[9]

The principle of a rigid division of functions and powers as envisaged in the Management Acts up to 1940 was, however, as little likely to operate in practice as the principle of the dichotomy of politics and ad-

[9] *Ibid.*, p. 94.

ministration propounded by the contemporary public administration theorists, to whom the concept perhaps owed something. Inevitably, in the words of the present Dublin City manager:

The original intention of the legislators to draw a clear line, both in law and in practice, between the Council's reserved functions and the Manager's executive functions has been lost sight of in some degree in the evolution of the system. Managers find themselves involved in business reserved to the Councils. . . . On the other hand Councillors have gained over the years considerable influence in relation to the Manager's functions.[10]

The blurring in practice of the legal distinction between reserved and executive functions was hastened by tensions that arose with the coming of county management in the early 1940's. County councilors had become accustomed to administering their own services, which on the whole they did badly, and resented the new system, the more so since it was applied to them willy-nilly. Furthermore, many saw the new managers as agents of the Department of Local Government. Perhaps, also, some of the first county managers were rigid and pedantic in interpreting their powers according to the letter of the Management Act. A series of circulars were issued from the Department through the 1940's pointing out that, though there was a legal distinction between reserved and executive functions, this did not imply that managers should carry out their duties independently of the councils, and exhorting closer collaboration. Under the pressure of public opinion, the Department increasingly insisted on "the predominant position of the elected body," as a circular put it.

Subsequent legislation, and particularly the City and County Management (Amendment) Act, 1955, has formally invested the elected representatives with more power. Under that act the manager is required to inform his council before he undertakes new works, other than maintenance and repair work, and the council may, if it chooses, prohibit these works, provided that they are not required by law to be done. Also, members may by resolution require the manager to do any act that is lawful and for which money has been provided, notwithstanding that the act is within the area of the manager's discretion. Thus, though, for example, the letting of houses is a managerial function, a council may require a manager to let a house to a particular person. Such an order may not extend to any function in relation to staff or to the entitlement of persons to health services. Again, the Act provides that, though the control of staff is still a managerial function, council sanction is needed

10 M. Macken, "City and County Management and Planning Administration," *Léargas*, No. 10 (June–July 1967), pp. 2–3.

to vary the numbers and rates of remuneration of staff. Finally, the Act gives councils the right, if they wish, to set up estimates committees to take over (formally, at least) the preparation of the annual budget, and some councils have appointed such committees.

It is clear that, from the early 1940's, there has been a conscious attempt to turn back the tide of managerial bureaucracy and to give the elected members the last say, even in the managers' own area of competence. On the other hand, the growth of public services and the need to plan and organize complex schemes has meant that the manager is increasingly the major source of initiative in a local authority. The springs of new policy are here, as elsewhere, often to be found in the administration of existing services. Although it is true that the council must still approve the estimates and vote the rates, the manager prepares the budget, and it is to him that councilors look to propose and prepare schemes of improvement. Even the use of estimates committees has not affected the initiating role of the manager, though it does at least give a few members of the council a more intimate part in planning future activity.

Other factors have contributed to the rise of the manager to the key

TABLE 11.5
Careers of 24 City and County Managers, 1966

Qualification	Number	Qualification	Number
Educational qualifications:		Age at first appointment as manager:	
University degree	10	30–34	2
Accountancy	5	35–39	6
Accountancy and degree	2	40–44	8
Accountancy & Institute of		45–49	3
Secretaries	2	50–54	4
Institute of Secretaries	2	55–59	1
Secondary education	3		
Experience other than in local		Point of entry to local service:	
government:		Clerical Officer	7
Business	3	Staff Officer (or equivalent)	3
Law	1	Town Clerk	5
Journalism	1	County Accountant (or	
Civil Service	4	equivalent)	6
State-sponsored bodies	5	County Secretary (or equivalent)	2
Teaching	2	Manager	1
Accountancy	2		
None, i.e. whole career in the			
local service	6		

Source: D. Roche, *Management in Local Government: The Irish Experience* (forthcoming).

position that he holds in local administration. The absence to a great extent of committees, the fact that the manager is necessarily in close touch with central departments, the existence of a county managers' association, which meets, significantly, in the Department of Local Government, all combine to make the manager the powerhouse of local government. Also there is the fact that these top posts in the local service, being filled by competition open to all, attract men of considerable ability and varied experience at the height of their powers (see Table 11.5 for details).

If the managers have in general become the main source of initiative in local government, the councilors on their side have considerable opportunities to influence the managers' decisions, big and small, within the rather narrow limits that local authorities have for maneuver. Managers are likely to consult councilors about matters involving their own districts or their own constituents, for example in formulating their road programs or when letting houses; and councilors expect them to receive representations on matters within their executive powers. Managers may even promote the setting up of advisory committees of the council, and the use of committees in this way is in fact on the increase. Thus the roles of councilor and manager have evolved differently from those that were at first envisaged and that the original statutes spelled out. These roles are now well understood and accepted.

v

If the tide of bureaucracy that seemed to threaten local government after independence has receded somewhat, it is nevertheless obvious that the role of the councilor is a long way from the Victorian ideal of local representatives deciding and administering neighborhood affairs in the workshops of local government, the committees of the council. As is the case at national level with TD's, the elected member is a consumer representative and more of a factor in the administration of services than a policy maker or legislator. Of course, local government as a whole is to a large extent administration in any case, in the sense that it is concerned with the provision of services decided upon elsewhere; but even within the area of a local authority's discretion, it is the manager who tends to be the architect of community services.

As is the case at national level also, councilors to a great extent accept this role. Once the friction that accompanied the introduction of the manager system to the counties was removed, most councilors have been far more conscious of being frustrated by some action or lack of action

288   *Local Government and Politics*

in a central department than by the manager or the managerial system. Yet again as at the national level, councilors are quite well suited to their role and are, in any case, bound to play it since their chances of reelection depend upon doing so and since, for many, this is the first step in a political career and the only route to national office.

Local representatives, who are overwhelmingly male, are of course people who belong in the districts they represent. The counties are divided for local government purposes into county electoral areas, and a very strong local patriotism, reinforced by a firm belief that it pays to have a councilor in one's own district, ensures that only people belonging to an area will represent it. Even in the cities, which are divided into wards for local electoral purposes, the neighborhood appeal is a strong one.

As far as socioeconomic status is concerned, it is clear from Table 11.6 that county councils are largely composed, on the one hand, of farmers (41 per cent in 1960, 38 per cent in 1967) and, on the other, of shopkeepers, publicans, and small businessmen (33 per cent in 1960, 30 per cent in 1967). Farmers are of course a very numerous occupational group

TABLE 11.6

Socioeconomic Status of Local Authority Representatives Elected in 1960 and 1967

Socioeconomic group[a]	County councils		County borough councils		Urban district councils		Town commissioners	
	1960	1967	1960	1967	1960	1967	1960	1967
Farming and fishing (mainly farmers and farmers' relatives)	41.4%	37.6%	—	—	4.3%	3.0%	3.9%	4.2%
Professional (higher and lower)	7.6	9.8	16.3%	17.6%	8.0	10.4	7.2	5.8
Trade union officials	1.3	1.1	8.2	6.5	1.6	1.7	—	0.5
Employers and managers (mainly small shopkeepers, publicans, family businesses, "contractors")	32.5	30.4	31.6	35.2	42.4	41.0	35.9	42.3
Nonmanual	7.0	10.7	15.3	24.1	18.4	18.8	19.0	15.9
Skilled manual	3.5	2.5	5.1	4.6	11.8	13.4	17.7	12.7
Semiskilled and unskilled manual	2.6	1.8	7.2	3.7	9.2	5.2	11.8	11.2
Unclassified[b]	4.1	6.1	16.3	8.3	4.3	6.5	4.5	7.4
TOTAL	100%	100%	100%	100%	100%	100%	100%	100%

Source: Compiled from notices of poll and local newspapers.
 [a] Groupings adapted from *Census of Population*, III (1961).
 [b] Includes councilors who gave their occupation as "housewife."

in the country areas, though councilors are likely to be from among the more prosperous minority of them. There are, on the contrary, comparatively few shopkeepers in the community, and, thus, as a group they are grossly overrepresented on the councils. In the cities and towns also, this same group dominates, with over 40 per cent of all urban seats. Self-employed as they are, shopkeepers and small businessmen have the opportunity to engage in local government and, given the nature of local services and activities, often have the most to gain by doing so.

Members of lower socioeconomic groups on the other hand do not figure prominently. On the county councils farm laborers are not represented in those districts where they are to be found in some numbers, i.e. in the east and southeast, and the same is true of manual workers generally. Nor, strangely, are there many working-class councilors on the city councils. It is only in the smaller urban authorities that they are present in some numbers. Here, the working class (manual and non-manual) have about 40 per cent of the seats, and it is to these councils also that manual workers get elected. Only in the small towns, then, is politics other than a middle-class or prosperous farmer activity. But these are the minor authorities. In the major authorities, as in national politics, the better-off predominate.

From the point of view of most citizens, however, the predominance of certain occupational groups on local councils probably does not seem important and certainly is not seen as a threat to the proper consideration of citizens' interests. To the citizen the councilor is a neighborhood contact man whose duty it is to help him over problems such as housing, planning permission, and getting grants of one sort or another, and also to secure a good share of new amenities for the district. From his point of view, it is as well that his councilor should be a man of some social standing and active as a local notable. Such a man is thought more likely to have influence than a less well-placed one. What is more, the citizen is in a position to impose this role, for his vote is at issue here. "Service" is an important *quid pro quo* for political support in local as in national politics. Here the TD is as concerned as the councilor—and at the same level of public business, for it is primarily local authority matters that most often and most intimately concern the ordinary person.

This constraint upon representatives has important consequences. It forces the councilor to concentrate upon relative trivia, and it establishes a relationship between the representatives and the manager and his staff which is rather more that of importunate—though important—clients seeking favors than that of a board of directors and their top management. In the council chamber things are different, but many of the matters with which councilors are concerned, being detail, are not effected there. It is possible also for an element of deception to enter into this activity. Sometimes—too often, say some local officials—councilors make requests that they know are impossible to grant, merely in order to appear to be doing a service for a constituent. Similar electoral considerations can also color their speeches in public debate in the council chamber. Local newspapers give much space and prominence to the monthly meetings of the councils, and councilors sometimes strike public attitudes that are unrealistic and even two-faced, but newsworthy and, they hope, vote-catching.

Most councilors are, however, not only local contact men but party representatives, and, as at national level, the public undoubtedly sees them in both roles. Local government is in fact dominated by the national political parties on the electoral plane and to a considerable extent also in the council chamber. This has been the case ever since the state came into existence. From the democratization of local government in 1898, councils were involved in national issues and became foci of nationalism. Subsequently, the civil war split and the deep political divisions that ensued were carried into local government. The tradition established in those days still lingers on in the propensity that councils have to this day to pass resolutions on matters in which they have no competence. Such resolutions are often nationalistic in content and largely ritualistic.

Because the cleavage in the community over the civil war was so deep, local elections were from the beginning fought on national party lines. That does not mean to say that candidates always call themselves Fianna Fáil, Fine Gael, etc.; and, in fact, members of Fine Gael have tended to deplore what they call the "introduction of politics" into local government. However, a candidate's party affiliation, whether formally declared or not, is always well enough known, and until the 1950's at least, most people were unwilling to cross from one side to the other of the chasm that divided De Valera from his opponents. The fact that the election system is the single transferable vote in multimember constituencies has always meant that, for most, a choice of candidates within one's party is available, and thus it is possible to give weight to local and other considerations without going outside the party. Nor has the domination of national parties at local level meant that genuinely independent candidates have been totally absent or that councilors have invariably followed the party line. Some councils have prided themselves on sinking party differences, and it has been common to find working arrangements for filling the post of chairman or mayor, or in electing to other bodies, which have ignored party affiliations.

Progressively, however, parties have tended to strengthen their formal hold on local government, Fianna Fáil most obviously and openly, and Fine Gael with some show of reluctance. The three major parties nominate official candidates and mount official campaigns. All expect council members to abide by party policy and accept party directives. Fianna Fáil and the Labour Party exact signed pledges of loyalty from candidates put forward under the party name.

This politicization of local government combined with the single transferable vote system usually produces quite a high turnout at local elections—high at least compared with the United Kingdom, where low polls and a large number of uncontested seats produce a poor example of local democracy in practice. Table 11.7 shows the turnout at elections since 1950. In interpreting this and the following table, it should be remembered that electors in the four county boroughs and in the countryside vote to fill seats on a single authority, the city or county council, but those who live in towns with "urban district" or "town" status have two votes, one for the county council and one for the town authority. There was a sharp rise in turnout in 1967, when the political parties for the first time fought the elections with their full strength as though they were engaged in a general election. Thus, it looks as though the politicizing of local government tends to increase voter participation, and certainly the 1967 result is striking evidence of the role of parties in getting the vote out.

Table 11.7 reveals also a marked contrast in voter turnout between Dublin—the only big city, which (with 569,000 inhabitants in 1966) is five times bigger than Cork, the second city—and the rest of the country,

TABLE 11.7

Turnout at Local Elections, 1950–67; Total Valid Poll as Percentage of Electorate Entitled to Vote

Authority	Election			
	1950	1955	1960	1967[a]
Urban authorities:				
Dublin County Borough Council	39%	39%	29%	51%
Other county borough councils	57	65	55	66
Urban district councils (including boroughs)	62	62	59	67
Town commissioners	67	68	60	71
County councils	62	65	60	70
Average total valid poll	58	60	54	67

Source: Information made available by Department of Local Government.
Note: The proportion of spoiled votes is, on average, between 1 and 2 per cent.
[a] Elections for local authorities are usually held every five years. The elections of 1965 were delayed because of the general election in 1965 and the presidential election in 1966.

TABLE 11.8

Party Support at Central and Local Government Levels, 1960–67; Percentage of First-Preference Votes Won by Each Party

Election	Fianna Fáil	Fine Gael	Labour	Independents and others
General election, 1961	43.8%	32.0%	11.6%	12.6%
Local elections, 1960[a]	38.4	26.5	10.2	24.9
General election, 1965	47.8	33.9	15.4	2.9
Local elections, 1967[a]	39.8	32.9	14.6	12.7

Source: Official returns and newspapers.
[a] Counties and county boroughs.

TABLE 11.9

Percentage of First-Preference Votes Won by Each Party at Local Elections, 1967

Type of authority	Fianna Fáil	Fine Gael	Labour	Independents and others
County councils	41.3%	35.4%	12.3%	11.0%
County borough councils	34.2	23.6	23.6	18.6
Urban district councils (including boroughs)	29.2	25.3	17.4	28.1
Towns	34.6	29.9	12.4	23.1

Source: Compiled from official returns made available by Department of Local Government and from newspapers.

whether urban or rural. This contrast is to be seen also at general elections.[11] Comparatively, the towns of Ireland other than Dublin are small and have a considerable sense of community, and the rural population is also strongly oriented to local communities. It is probably this sense of identity that explains the higher turnout there than in the big city. It can be seen from Table 11.7, too, that the figures show some correspondence between size of town and turnout—the smaller the town, the higher the proportion who vote.

The support given to the political parties at local elections confirms the strong party orientation of Irish people, to which reference was made in earlier chapters. Table 11.8 shows in a rough way the correspondence between the support a party gets at a general election and that at the local elections held nearest in time to it. It also shows that Independents and candidates of small parties attract more support at local than at national level, though this support was whittled away considerably in 1967, when, significantly, the main parties campaigned particularly strenuously and on national issues.

[11] See p. 156 above and Table B.2 (p. 332 below).

TABLE 11.10

*Election Labels and Party Affiliations in Bray and Wicklow
Urban District Councils, 1960*

Candidates	Fianna Fáil	Fine Gael	Labour	Independents and others
Bray:				
Election label	1	–	1	10
Party affiliation	4	4	3	1
Wicklow:				
Election label	1	–	3	5
Party affiliation	3	2	3	1

Source: Local newspapers and author's inquiries.

Note: "Election label" is the declared affiliation of the elected candidate when he was up for election. "Party affiliation" is the party to which he was said locally to belong.

This attraction of the voters to Independents and small-party candidates is notably stronger in the towns than in the rural areas and stronger in the smaller towns than in the larger, as Table 11.9 shows. This is almost certainly due in part to the fact that it is less difficult for an urban candidate on his own to reach the electors and to the fact that the quotas necessary for election are lower in the small towns. However, it may be also that the small-town voters are particularly susceptible to the appeal of a neighbor, are more aware of local issues, and feel more immediately concerned with them than are the voters of the cities or of the comparatively large county electoral areas.

It is necessary to approach the figures in Tables 11.8 and 11.9 with caution, however. There is much evidence that in the past many so-called Independent candidates and others with labels such as "Ratepayers Candidate" or "Civic Association" have in fact been known members or steady camp-followers of one or other of the main parties. Two examples from County Wicklow are given in Table 11.10. The extent to which the percentages in the "Independents and others" columns of these tables really represent nonparty votes is, therefore, doubtful. Yet the very fact that party men have chosen to go forward calling themselves by other titles suggests that party politicization is by no means complete at local level and that votes may be given more readily than at national elections for reasons other than party affiliation.

VI

Most Irish people almost certainly approve of the idea of local democracy, though they do not feel very strongly about it and may well have only a very hazy notion of what is involved. Yet the trend to bigger units, considerable bureaucratization, and reduction of the councilor to the role of a consumer representative all suggest that local government is in practice not much more than the decentralized administration of certain centrally ordained and controlled services. And, insofar as it is not, the intervention and growing domination of national parties seems inevitable and perhaps, indeed, necessary for the working of democracy at the local level.

However, there is evidence in recent years of self-conscious efforts to stave off the full rigors of bureaucratic administration or to mitigate them—efforts seen in the modification of the management system and the self-declared new role of the Department of Local Government. Furthermore, strong local community feeling and the belief that representatives exist to "service" their constituents are sufficient, given the continuance of the present election system, to prevent the complete monopoly of the national parties and the party machines, though party domination is undoubtedly greater than it was.

TWELVE

The Citizen and the Administration

The primary object of this book is to investigate the institutions and procedures through which the needs and aspirations of persons and groups in the community are expressed as political demands, processed into policy and law, and acted upon. The openness, accessibility, and responsiveness of these institutions and the sensitivity of these procedures are the measures of democracy. In no way can these qualities be better assessed than by examining the machinery for checking the administration, particularly in its dealings with individuals, and for the redress of grievances. The existence of effective procedures for these purposes contributes as much as elections and adequate consultation to the citizen's belief that he lives in a free and—as important—a just community. Feelings of impotence in the face of officialdom lead ordinary men and women to doubt the value and perhaps the existence of democracy and breed indifference, cynicism, and even hostility to government. Furthermore, an administration not subject to scrutiny of its dealings with individuals is likely to become progressively less effective, less sensitive, and less just.

Although no attempt will be made to draw hard and fast lines, we are here concerned primarily with the surveillance of the application of policies and laws to particular cases and individual persons, and not with the general oversight and control of the performance of the administration, i.e. of the quality of its policy decisions, the cost-effectiveness of its programs, etc. These, which are subject to political control by the Oireachtas, have already been dealt with (pp. 195–200). That is not to say that parliamentary and political procedures are not used to control the administration's detailed application of policy and legislation. Far from it: political control by parliamentary representatives and parliamentary procedures is one of the two main forms of control operating to check the administration. The other is the control effected by the courts and the legal system. Behind them both are the mass media with their great ability to throw light into dark corners and to bring to public attention in a compelling way matters that, once noticed, call for investigation and remedy. The place of the mass media in the political process in general was the subject of Chapter 5. Here, the concern will be only with their willingness and ability to publicize and comment on administrative action.

II

The forms of control over administrative action in Ireland derive from the British tradition, involving principles and practices beginning in the seventeenth century. Their pattern and the way in which they have operated reveal a wholesale acceptance of British constitutional and legal theory and practice as these existed in the early part of this century, and to a considerable extent continue to exist today.

From the seventeenth century on, it was thought that governments could and should be controlled as to the legality of their actions by the courts, which were emerging to considerable independence, and politically by Parliament. As J. D. B. Mitchell points out, it is essential to realize that the basic shape and limits of each of these forms of control, legal and political, were established and settled by the latter years of the nineteenth century, *before* the great increase in state functions resulted in a mass of detailed administration and the creation of a myriad of small individual rights and obligations.[1]

Legal control was effected through the ordinary courts, whose main concern was the enforcement of legal rights and obligations and not the fulfillment of public policy. Political control operated through the machinery of ministerial responsibility to Parliament. Belief in this system can be seen in "the steady rise in the popularity of Parliamentary Questions, a rise which reflects both this reliance on parliamentary controls, and the need for a mechanism for dealing with individual grievances."[2] The operations of the emerging welfare state brought the system into difficulties. Its deficiencies as a check on administrative action and for securing redress became increasingly obvious as social and economic legislation began to pour out of Parliament.

By this time, however, strong and seemingly almost unbreakable traditions had been established. On the one hand, the doctrine of ministerial responsibility commanded great respect, a respect that continued

1 See J. D. B. Mitchell, "The Causes and Effects of the Absence of a System of Public Law in the United Kingdom," *Public Law*, 1965, pp. 95–118.
2 *Ibid.*, p. 99.

to be accorded although parliamentary practice failed to develop effectively to deal with the emergence of strong rule by party leaders that followed the coming of the mass parties and machine politics. In the form assiduously fostered by party leaders, especially those in power, it came down to two propositions: first, that ministers had to have considerable power and discretion to act and to protect their servants and their sources of information and advice; and, second, that they were only answerable in the House of Commons, and more narrowly "on the floor of the House," i.e. in full session, and by the traditional (though increasingly archaic) procedure of the debating hall—which the House of Commons essentially was, and is. Even wide-ranging parliamentary committee investigation and discussion were, and are, held to derogate from "the principle of ministerial responsibility."

On the other hand, for their part, the legal profession had developed an unshakable belief in the efficiency of private law procedures and nursed an insular and myopic suspicion of the development in France and elsewhere of "administrative law," i.e. that branch of public law "relating to the organization and working of the public services and the relations of those services with private persons."[3] At the same time, the courts in their judgments showed a great respect for political controls and a consequent reluctance to interfere with administrative action. This extended to "the refusal of courts to examine the realities of parliamentary life and, hence, their inevitable tendency to build the law upon the fictions rather than the realities of that life."[4] Though legislation grew in volume and complexity and ministers acquired rule-making powers to an increasing degree, both without corresponding developments in parliamentary procedures to effect adequate scrutiny, the courts continued to give decisions based on the fiction that Parliament did in fact control. Likewise, as the volume of administration increased, a similar myth continued to be accepted in relation to the growing number of disputes in which ministers assumed the role of arbitrators or judges. A judge in an important case decided during the First World War put it thus: "My Lords, how can the judiciary be blind to the well known facts applicable not only to the Constitution but to the working of such branches of the executive? The department is represented in Parliament by its responsible head."[5] It followed from this, went the argument, that "the individual was not entitled to know or see the individual official who decided (this being, it was considered, immaterial,

[3] L. Rolland, *Précis de droit administratif* (11th ed., Paris, 1957), p. 1.
[4] Mitchell, p. 101.
[5] *Local Government Board* v. *Arlidge* 1915 A.C.120, quoted in Mitchell, p. 101.

since the Minister was responsible) and that decisions need not be reasoned."[6]

The Irish state adopted *in toto* these constitutional and legal principles, myths and all, and the procedures and inhibitions to which they gave rise. And just as in Great Britain there has been no fundamental change in the situation, so too in Ireland. In one respect, indeed, the Irish case is worse. For, whereas the British Parliament has made some, as yet comparatively minor, changes involving the use of committees, and a new office has been created called the Parliamentary Commissioner for Administration (Ombudsman), the parliamentary procedures of independent Ireland have remained unchanged.

In the sections that follow, these controls, legal and political, will be examined and their deficiencies exposed. And because control implies scrutiny and scrutiny is impossible without access to information, it will be necessary finally to inquire whether here, as in the evaluation of governmental policy in general, the community is well enough informed or has access to adequate information to which, one might think, it has a fundamental right.

III

Judicial control over government derives from the Constitution, which provides for courts, including courts empowered with jurisdiction extending "to the question of the validity of any law having regard to the Constitution." The Constitution also ensures, so far as it can, that the judges shall be independent. Since, in addition, it contains statements of the fundamental rights of the citizen and of the functions and powers of the various organs of government, Ireland is formally at least provided with both a reference point for judging governmental action and establishing authoritatively the rights and duties of the citizens, and also procedures by which such judgments may be made.

The Constitution is not sacrosanct, for it can, of course, be amended. To do so, however, requires the approval both of the Oireachtas and of a majority at a referendum, provisions that have the effect of giving a final say to the political rather than the legal authority. Nor of course, at bottom, does a citizen's protection from the state or the rights he actually enjoys depend merely upon their being written down in a constitution. The very foundations of legal control over the government lie in a widespread belief on the part of the community, a belief shared with many Western peoples, that the law should be obeyed, not least by public officials; that it is the duty of courts fearlessly to say what the law is, even if this involves restraining the government itself; and that these

6 Mitchell, p. 102.

TABLE 12.1

*Political Offices Held by Judges of the Supreme Court and
the High Court Before Appointment, 1924–63*

Office	Number
Attorney General (before 1922)	1
Attorney General (after 1922)	10[a]
Candidate for, or member of, British Parliament (before 1922)	1[b]
Candidate for, or member of, Dáil or Seanad	6[c]
No known political office	13
TOTAL	31

Source: Stein U. Larsen (University of Bergen), "Law and Politics in Ireland" (unpublished ms.).
[a] Five of these had also held other political offices.
[b] This judge had also held another political office.
[c] One of these had also held another political office.

courts should be independent in their performance of this duty, and to this purpose need to be insulated from politics and political pressure.

The Common Law of England and British legal institutions have been present in Ireland from the twelfth century, while from the seventeenth century up to independence, the law, the courts, and legal institutions and training generally were very similar in the two countries. It is inevitable, therefore, that ideas of what constitutes justice, what should be the status of judges, and what conditions are necessary to ensure their independence are very similar. The Constitution provides for justice normally to be dispensed in public, in courts established by law, by judges who "shall be independent in the exercise of their judicial functions and subject only to this Constitution and the law." Their independence is ensured by a judge not being subject to dismissal "except for stated misbehaviour or incapacity and then only upon resolutions passed by Dáil Eireann and by Seanad Eireann calling for his removal" and by the safeguard that a judge's remuneration "shall not be reduced during his continuance in office."[7]

It may be found surprising, therefore, that the appointment of judges is in the hands of the government and that by custom the Attorney General, who is the government's legal adviser and state prosecutor, and a political appointee, is always offered any vacancy to the High Court that occurs during his term of office. (Places on the Supreme Court are usually filled by promotion by seniority from the High Court.) The results are not surprising. Appointments have usually been of men openly identified with the government, and the majority of all appointees up to the middle 1960's at least had held political office (see Table 12.1). Because

[7] Bunreacht na hEireann, Art. 35.

Fianna Fáil has been in power for all but six years since 1932, the Bench is largely filled with its nominees. By 1960, eleven out of twelve of the judges of the High Court and Supreme Court had been appointed by Fianna Fáil leaders.

It does not follow, of course, that judges appointed by politicians, even judges with overt political affiliations, are politically biased in their professional activities, and, in fact, there are few in Ireland and none in the law profession who think for one moment that they are. Nevertheless, the practice seems inappropriate to a system that is otherwise self-consciously insulated from contact with party politics.

Given a politically independent judiciary, what matters to the citizen facing his government is, first, the accessibility of the courts and, second, the extent of the courts' powers to review the actions of public authorities. The first is a matter of fact, easily determined; to answer the second fully would necessitate a considerable review and evaluation of the powers and immunities of the state in law and in the decided cases. Only a summary of the position is attempted here.[8]

To be accessible, courts must be physically near at hand; they must be expeditious in their handling of cases; they must not be so expensive that the poor are at a handicap; and they must not be barred to the citizen by laws that give immunity to any person or, particularly, the state. The Irish courts are geographically reasonably convenient and though there are delays in the hearing of some types of cases, they are much less than in many countries. On the other hand, the expenses of litigation can be heavy when counsel is employed, the more so since conventions about the employment of more than one counsel in certain types of case and the appearance of senior counsel attended by a junior result in heavier expenditure than might strictly be necessary. The division of the profession into two groups, barristers and solicitors, while advantageous from some points of view, might well also add to the cost of litigation. But, above all, what weighs the scales against the poor is the absence of a fully developed system of legal aid. Not until 1962 was general provision made for giving free legal aid at criminal proceedings. This does not apply, however, in civil actions or indeed in some matters often connected with criminal proceedings, e.g. an application for an order of habeas corpus.

Whatever doubts may have existed until recently about the legal right

8 On this subject, see J. M. Kelly, *Fundamental Rights in the Irish Law and Constitution*, 2d ed. (Dublin, 1967); Loren P. Beth, *The Development of Judicial Review in Ireland, 1937–1966* (Dublin, 1967); J. M. Kelly, "Administrative Discretion and the Courts," *Irish Jurist*, N.S. I (Winter 1966), 209–21.

of the citizen to access to the courts have been largely dispelled as a result of recent cases. In the case of *The State (Quinn)* v. *Ryan and others* the action of the Garda Síochána in arresting a person wanted on a British warrant and spiriting him out of the jurisdiction was seen as a conspiracy to prevent him from appealing to the courts for relief and was roundly condemned.[9] In the case of *Macauley* v. *Minister for Posts and Telegraphs*, the High Court ruled unconstitutional the statutory requirement that the *fiat* (i.e. leave) of the Attorney General was needed before an action could be brought against a minister.[10] This was a procedure originating in the British principle of the immunity of the Crown which had been carried over into the new state at independence. Though this important privilege no longer remains, the state is still in many other ways favored in its activities and in its dealings with the citizen (see pp. 304–6).

Ireland possesses an all-important combination of institutions for making governments behave and for safeguarding the citizen, namely, a written constitution and independent courts with the legal power to examine and pronounce upon the constitutionality of any measures or actions. To what extent are they effective in practice?

The tabulation below shows the number of cases involving constitutional interpretation from 1938 (the inception of Bunreacht na hEireann) to 1966 and the number of decisions of unconstitutionality.[11]

Cases involving constitutional interpretation	69
Cases involving constitutionality of law, governmental acts, or pre-existing law	56
Decisions of unconstitutionality	23

Analyzing these, Loren Beth commented:

The reader may be surprised that as many as twenty-three cases have involved judgements of unconstitutionality. However, it should be noted again how many of these have involved old laws or rules of common law, in many cases archaic, and certainly developed without any regard to questions of constitutional validity. Nevertheless, eight cases remain, and for a small country in only thirty years, without a tradition of judicial review, this is not a low frequency rate.[12]

However, whether these decisions have overturned rules that were archaic or not is not important from the citizen's point of view. What matters to him is that the court has declared his right and given him a

[9] 1965, I.R. 70.
[10] 1966, I.R. 345.
[11] Taken from Beth, summary of Table 1 in Appendix.
[12] Beth, p. 19.

TABLE 12.2

23 Court Decisions of Unconstitutionality, 1938–66

Cases involving	Number	Cases involving	Number
Freedom of the person	3	Exercise of judicial functions by bodies other than courts	3
Right of association	1		
Property rights	3	Right of access to courts	3
Rights of family, parents, marriage, divorce	7	Other	3

Source: Compiled from data in L. P. Beth, *The Development of Judicial Review in Ireland, 1937–1966* (Dublin, 1967), Appendix, Table 2.

remedy. As Table 12.2 shows, decisions of unconstitutionality have been given in many of the most vital areas of citizens' rights. Thus the importance of this procedure can hardly be overemphasized.

It was argued in Chapter 2 that in their content the constitutional rights of the citizen are a mixture of liberal democratic principles common to Western democracies and Roman Catholic social teaching as enunciated in the Papal encyclicals of the years up to the middle 1930's. In their wording they provide a number of examples of a basic and almost insoluble problem that faces those who draft constitutions. K. C. Wheare puts it thus: "If a government is to be effective, few rights of its citizens can be stated in absolute form."[13] On the other hand, the attempt to qualify them leads to phrases that create doubts and cause legal difficulties, such as "save in accordance with law," "subject to public order and morality," or "when the public good requires it." Rights qualified with such phrases are, more than the other articles in the Constitution, susceptible to governmental abuse on the one hand and to judicial interpretation on the other.

At first, the Irish courts were inclined to interpret such phrases—and indeed the Constitution as a whole—in a manner that appeared to allow the government and the Oireachtas wide scope. For example, in a judgment in 1940, the Chief Justice interpreted the words "in accordance with law" to mean in accordance with the law, whatever it is, as it exists at the time. Furthermore, he did not regard the power of committing a person to indefinite internment as a judicial power at all because, as he thought, it is not a punishment but only "preventive justice" and "a precautionary measure."[14]

More recently, however, the courts have tended to take a bolder and

[13] *Modern Constitutions* (2d ed., London, 1966), p. 38.
[14] Chief Justice Sullivan, in *In re Article 26 and the Offences Against the State (Amendment) Bill, 1940*, 1940, I.R. 470.

more imaginative line. In a case in 1965, the judge went so far as to argue, in John Kelly's words, that "there exists an undefined residue of personal rights, guaranteed by the Constitution though not specifically enumerated in it" and therefore depending on the courts for interpretation.[15] There is now a growing disposition on the part of the Bench and the Bar to look more widely—to natural law, to the encyclicals, and to international declarations and conventions of human rights. This is in effect to give the courts a more important and creative role in declaring the law.

There are probably two reasons for this change. First, it reflects a growing tendency of lawyers to free themselves of the shackles of British traditions, in this case the principle of the supremacy of Parliament. This was a principle that was the more difficult to shrug off since it was strongly held by De Valera, who believed that government emanated from the people and that the Oireachtas represented them, subject only to periodic election, and consequently had an absolute right to decide everything. The rights articles in the Constitution, he argued in 1937, were "headlines with regard to the things the Legislature should aim at. . . . I think the Legislature ought to be enabled in its own judgement to decide, and not the Courts. . . . What we want to see is that in future the Legislature will not be so restricted that it will not be able to function properly."[16] This was, of course, the attitude of the revolutionary republican in a new state that was still—as he saw it—in the process of evolution. Today, times have changed.

They have changed in another way too. The state evolved not only as the outcome of a war of independence but out of civil war. The legacy of that division was the IRA and the fear of civil strife and border incidents that occasionally erupted up to as late as the early 1960's. Because of this, emergency powers involving laws empowering the government to arrest without warrant, to detain without trial, and to try in "special courts" not necessarily using normal judicial processes have been a feature of Irish life and remain on the statute book, notably in the Offences Against the State Acts. Such powers and such courts operated not only in the turbulent 1930's and during "the Emergency," i.e. the Second World War, but also as recently as 1961–62 in order to deal with the IRA and what the Taoiseach at the time called "this armed conspiracy of violence." Because, legally, the state of national emergency declared in 1939 still exists (in 1969), the Oireachtas can under Article 28 of the

15 J. M. Kelly, *Fundamental Rights in the Irish Law and Constitution*, 2d ed. (Dublin, 1967), p. 37.
16 *Dáil Debates*, vol. 67, cols. 1784–86.

Constitution enact any law it wishes, however repugnant to the Constitution, provided that such law is expressed as for the purpose of securing the public safety. There is, however, no such emergency legislation at the moment. Besides, the inhibitions engendered by the fear of civil strife have been removed and it is probable that, if any cases came before them, the courts would take an attitude more favorable to a citizen, even a dissident citizen, than hitherto.

When it comes to the rights and powers of the courts to question and control administrative authorities and to the position of the citizen facing the state, the situation is far from satisfactory. The ease with which a citizen can get a review of a decision or resulting action of a public authority depends upon how the courts characterize it. The courts draw an all-important distinction between a decision that is "judicial" or "quasi-judicial" and one that is "administrative." If it is judicial, certain conditions must be observed in the process of coming to the decision; if it is administrative, this situation does not apply. But the criteria on which a decision is categorized seem (to the layman at least—and apparently to some lawyers as well) to be illogical and unclear, having been evolved to a great extent before the modern welfare state had evolved.

True, an administrative act is not wholly immune:

No administrative act whatever (even though a statute may declare it "final and conclusive for all purposes") can be completely withdrawn from the purview of the courts. Every administrative power depends on law . . . and if an act, order or decision of an administrative authority cannot be justified, whether in form or substance, under the relevant statute, it is liable to be annulled as *ultra vires* . . . *but* [author's italics] . . . provided an authority entrusted with administrative discretion keeps inside its *vires* and (where appropriate) commits no open breach of natural justice, it may act as foolishly, unreasonably or even unfairly as it likes, and the courts cannot (or at least will not) interfere.[17]

This situation arises largely because no system of administrative law or courts has been evolved, the result of inheriting and continuing the British tradition. Ireland has no procedure such as, for example, that in France, where courts exist to review administrative action from the point of view of *détournement de pouvoir*, i.e. abuse of discretion.

What this means in practice can only be explained here in summary form and in general terms. It means that, in dealing with the claims of citizens, administrators are not bound to follow any given procedures unless the law specifically requires them to, provided that, where appropriate, they act judicially and in accordance with the principles of natural justice. It means also that the development of administrative

17 Kelly, "Administrative Discretion," *Irish Jurist*, I, 209–10.

adjudication by civil servants or by tribunals, which is quite inevitable in the modern welfare state, has been unsystematic. Such persons and bodies have no uniform procedures, nor, in many cases, are their decisions subject to the review of the courts. Until recently such adjudication was almost invariably in the hands of civil servants. Increasingly, decisions in matters such as planning appeals (under physical planning and development acts) have been entrusted to departments, i.e. civil servants headed by politicians, with limited rights or perhaps no right at all to further appeal to the courts. Even where statutory duties and powers to adjudicate have been laid on civil servants personally, as in the case of officers appointed to decide disputed cases arising under the Social Welfare Acts, the officers themselves apparently thought that they must obey ministerial directions until the Supreme Court disabused them and their political chiefs in 1958. The attitude of the Appeals Officer in this case was, said the court, "an abdication . . . from his duty. . . . That duty is laid upon him by the Oireachtas and he is required to perform it as between the parties that appear before him freely and fairly as becomes anyone who is called upon to decide on matters of right and obligation."[18]

In litigation involving the citizen and the state, the citizen is also at considerable disadvantage. First, the state has privileges in matters such as the giving of information in the preliminary stages of a process or the withholding of documents "in the public interest," an interest that is interpreted by the state itself. This obviously might make it more difficult for a citizen to prove his case. Second, it is not possible to get the courts to restrain the state or oblige it to carry out a duty to the same extent as they would a private person. The court orders evolved to serve the purposes of justice between private parties are subject to all sorts of limitations and procedural difficulties which unfit them for use between the state and a private party.

Third, the state has legal immunity for some of its activities. Departments of state, and sometimes other public authorities, are not bound by statute unless the statute says so or clearly intends so. They may even be explicitly exempted, as are public authorities from the provisions of the 1963 Planning Act.[19] In respect of breach of contractual obligations or "tort,"[20] the position is summarized by Kelly as follows:

[18] See *McLoughlin* v. *Minister for Social Welfare*, 1958, I.R. 1.

[19] Local Government (Planning and Development) Act, No. 28 of 1963, Section 4.

[20] A "tort" is "a wrong independent of contract where there is a breach of duty fixed by law; the duty is towards persons generally and its breach is redressable by an action for . . . damages." (*Winfield on Torts*, 6th ed., by T. Ellis Lewis, p. 5.)

A private citizen contracting with the State is not, in theory, in as strong a position to have grievances arising from the contract redressed at law as if he had contracted with another citizen. . . . The position of the citizen with a claim against the Irish State founded in tort is, at least according to the notion at present generally received, even less favourable. This notion is that the State, apart from an important but exceptional statutory liability [where injury is caused by the negligent driving of a state vehicle], is absolutely immune from actions founded in tort, and that a person aggrieved by a tortious act committed in the course of his employment by a public servant has no right of action against the State. . . . The public servant himself is, of course, not in any way protected, nor is his superior officer, nor even the Minister in charge of his department, if these have personally authorised the commission of the wrongful act; but a judgement against a minor public servant may be of no value, since he may very well not have the means to satisfy it. Thus the only real prospect which the citizen is thought to have in [such] cases . . . is the possibility that the State will compensate him by means of an *ex gratia* payment.[21]

It will readily be seen that the state of affairs described above, which to a great extent derives from the British doctrine of the favored position of the Crown combined with the absence of an organized system of administrative law and adjudication, might leave an aggrieved or injured citizen at a considerable disadvantage as far as the law and legal remedies are concerned. However, citizens might seek to redress their grievances against the administration by other means. Moreover, disagreements and discontent at the actions of administrators may extend beyond legal wrongs. In these cases another road lies open—political action.

IV

In theory, the political responsibility of ministers brings them to account in the Dáil. However, it is abundantly clear that the operation of the system under conditions of strict party loyalty and discipline makes responsibility mean something different in practice from what constitutional theory suggests. Ordinarily governments simply are not likely to be ousted by a vote of no confidence: at most they have been threatened, though this in itself is an effective enough procedure. Theoretically, also, the government is *collectively* responsible, but collective responsibility has in practice the effect of protecting individual ministers in most circumstances. Apart from disagreements over policy, it is only in a case where there is scandal or personal indiscretion that a minister is almost certainly going to have to resign. Otherwise, however culpable or inefficient his activities or those of his departmental officers, he will only resign in the unlikely event that his colleagues deem it more ad-

21 Kelly, *Fundamental Rights*, pp. 338–45.

vantageous to the government or party as a whole to part with him, or if he himself insists. Dismissal is not a sanction that is normally likely to bother an Irish minister.[22]

What responsibility does mean, however, is the obligation to answer questions asked by representatives and to deal with matters raised in debate. Both for maintaining public confidence in the honesty and efficiency of the public service and for securing to the individual citizen an opportunity to get a review of administrative decisions and perhaps redress, this obligation, as it is honored and carried out in practice, is of the greatest operational importance. The practice of responsibility, i.e. the obligation to answer, "helps to maintain an environment of criticism, probing and controversial argument which is accepted as normal and legitimate."[23] Again, even if it is not likely to involve the removal of a minister from office, it does at least "rub home the subordination of the Civil Service."[24] Both an environment of criticism and the subordination of the Civil Service are important ingredients of democracy. Where they do not exist, the quality of public life is very different indeed.

From the point of view of the public representative and the citizen as his client, the obligation on ministers to answer in the Dáil or Seanad, though a valuable political procedure in its own right, is important because of what it leads to. Because of it, deputies and Senators can communicate directly with officials in departments and obtain information about individual cases and transactions; following on, in some cases, they can get action, or quicker action, force a review, secure the mitigation of a penalty by the minister, or perhaps obtain redress for harm done. Much the same procedure operates at local government level, where councilors and officials are in something like the same relationship. Very occasionally, this type of activity uncovers a serious injustice or an administrative mess.

Because the public expects such a service from its representatives and because the operation of the election system obliges representatives to perform it, the volume of such transactions is very large. Because Ireland is a small country with a comparatively large number of public representatives—one member of the Oireachtas for every 14,000 and one local councilor for every 1,900—and because most of them live among their constituents, who expect them to "do a turn" if asked and act accord-

---

[22] On the practice of individual responsibility, see pp. 185–87 above.

[23] Nevil Johnson, "Answerability and the Civil Service," paper read to the Political Studies Association, 1967.

[24] *Ibid.*

ingly, this procedure is in practice fairly accessible to the public generally and comparatively effective. Individuals can in fact get information,
action, and a review of their cases. No doubt the accessibility of representatives and the effectiveness of their interventions vary between individuals and, perhaps, from area to area, but the procedure is universal
enough for a Minister to be able to declare with justice, in 1966, that
"there is hardly anyone without a direct personal link with someone, be
he Minister, T.D., clergyman, county or borough councillor or trade
union official, who will interest himself in helping a citizen to have a
grievance examined and, if possible, remedied."[25]

This does not mean, as the Minister argued, that an official like an
Ombudsman is not needed in Ireland. Indeed, in saying, as he did, that
"the basic reason . . . why we do not need an Ombudsman is because we
have so many unofficial but nevertheless effective ones," he was ignoring
aspects of the Ombudsman's job that would be of particular importance
in Ireland. The Ombudsman could fill the lacuna in the courts' powers
to review administrative acts left by the absence of a system of administrative law: he could, also, be endowed with the right to demand production of files and to require civil servants to give evidence. Nevertheless,
the Minister was right to draw attention to the ability in practice of the
representative to get a review of an administrative decision.

The inclusion of both official representative and unofficial "public
persons" in the Minister's list of unofficial ombudsmen is significant, reflecting as it does the propensity of the Irishman to seek a personal intermediary to forward his cause, whatever it may be. The political procedure we are examining here is thoroughly congruent with the social
habits of the community. However, while few would deny the facts on
which the Minister based his argument, some would deplore his acceptance of this role for the deputy. Increasing awareness of the inadequacy
of the performance of the Oireachtas has led to mounting criticism of
this aspect of the activities of the TD's by journalists, academics, other
intellectuals, and even some politicians themselves.

No doubt some representatives do abuse the system. No doubt also
there is an element of the "glorified social welfare officer" about some of
the representatives, but as Bernard Crick argues (in a British context),
this kind of criticism "creates as well as reflects a sense of alienation
between the public and its parliament. . . . At times people feel the *need*
(whether rightly or wrongly in administrative terms is *not* the question)
to put their troubles, administrative and personal, before their member."[26] Is it not, he asks, a good thing that people should think of their

25 J. Lynch, then Minister for Finance, quoted in *The Irish Times*, Nov. 12, 1966.
26 B. Crick, *The Reform of Parliament* (London, 1964), p. 71.

representative as a person to turn to? There are few enough links of a personal kind between government and the public. At the very least, one might argue that this practice is justified until alternative procedures are evolved. There are signs in many countries, indeed, that this type of activity by representatives is increasing as public services and benefits increase in number and complexity.

Effective though this "contact man" system is, and useful as it may be for dealing with routine matters like housing and grants of one sort or another, it has obvious limitations when it comes to matters in which the adequacy, propriety, or justice of an official action is called seriously into question. In the words of Mitchell:

There is . . . the remedy which may result. The answer, even when it is followed by a rectification of an administrative error, lacks the quality of a judgement in two respects. It lacks the enduring and formative quality of a judgement which enters into a system of jurisprudence, and it lacks the ability of a judgement to decree compensation.[27]

Also, there are inevitable deficiencies arising from the fact that this is a political procedure, for "the forum for political debate may often not be the appropriate place to argue a question of maladministration."[28] Nor is this forum one in which the contestants are anything like equal in resources. A system by which a questioner faces a minister who is backed by a majority, armed with the shield of constitutional principles, and well able to insulate his civil servants and their files is clearly not designed to facilitate serious questioning or the revelation of awkward or incriminating facts.

It is clear from this review that it is particularly where a matter involves ministerial *discretion* that the problems of scrutiny and control are intractable. Given the limitations of political control and the absence of a fully developed system of public law under which discretionary acts might be subject to legal scrutiny, it cannot be said that either legal or political controls operate effectively. Yet the number and range of matters in which ministers do have such discretion increase continually. Whole areas of official action might be involved, e.g. naturalization, the issue of passports, deportation, indeed, the handling of aliens generally; the tapping of telephones and the interception of mail; licensing of various sorts; and physical planning, which is of ever-increasing importance.

v

One theme has recurred throughout this chapter, as also elsewhere in this study—the disadvantages that the public suffers through lack of

[27] Mitchell, p. 99.
[28] *Ibid.*

information, a deficiency that neither public representatives nor, in some cases, the courts are able to repair. It is evident, as it was in our inquiry in Chapter 8 into the performance of the Oireachtas, that Ireland suffers from the combination of a bureaucracy with a near-monopoly of information and a governmental and parliamentary system based on conventions that inhibit the Oireachtas from extracting it.

Undoubtedly, discussion and criticism of broad policy and the systematic appraisal of the administration suffer most from this comparative lack of openness. Sometimes the person with a serious wrong to be righted might be handicapped. The citizen looking for a house or the district for a new health center is hardly handicapped at all. These contrasts reflect accurately the availability of information and of channels of communication needed to get satisfaction.

To some extent, of course, lack of official information is compensated for by the fact that the country is small and homogeneous. The number of politicians, administrators, newsmen, and commentators involved is small enough for them to be known to each other and for "horizontal" communications to be easy. Furthermore, the press is both responsible and alert, though radio and television are to some extent inhibited from exposing the shortcomings of public authorities or seeking out public scandals (see pp. 137–38). Only the libel laws and the prohibition from mentioning matters that are *sub judice* operate to some extent to inhibit the press from exposing scandals and administrative messes. What the journalists do not have access to, however, is the type of material that an efficient parliamentary system would cause to be produced and published; nor do they face public servants accustomed to comparatively free discussion of matters of public concern. In fact, not only are public servants not accustomed to engage in it, they are not permitted to do so. In respect of public affairs, civil servants have to seek permission to publish or appear on radio or television and, in practice, have often found it quite hard to get it, even for innocuous material. Such activities have not been encouraged, to say the least.

The traditional attitude has been to present as narrow a front as possible towards the public, since from that direction there is little to be expected except mud and brickbats. Consequently information is strictly controlled or channelled—sometimes to the point of ceasing to flow at all. It requires an effort to change so well established a position, which has on the whole been advantageous to the defenders.[29]

Of course, there must be some limits to the disclosure and discussion of public business, but the limits that obtain in any country owe almost as

[29] D. Roche, "The Civil Servant and Public Relations," *Administration*, XI (1963), 108.

much to the development of a particular environment and the acceptance of certain practices—which, strictly, need not have been accepted —as they do to constitutional rules or the law. The Irish environment is, comparatively, one of considerable reticence, even secrecy, which it is sought to justify, like so much else in the governmental system, by reference to the principle of ministerial responsibility.

VI

This review suggests that the citizen seeking redress suffers from the absence of a developed system of administrative law and from the continued existence of an anomalous view of the position of the state vis-à-vis the individual in legal proceedings. It suggests, too, that both he and the citizen seeking information generally are handicapped by the deficiencies of the Oireachtas and, more generally, by supposed constitutional impediments to the flow of information. However, most citizens will never suffer in practice from these limitations and are unaware of them because they have little or no business with public authorities that is not of a purely routine nature. Nevertheless, what little evidence there is of their expectations of their treatment by officials is not wholly reassuring. Table 12.3 shows a comparison of Dubliners' expectations and those of the citizens of some other democracies in respect of how they would be treated and what consideration they would get from public officials and the police. These data should be used with great caution, if only because

TABLE 12.3

Citizens' Expectations of Treatment by Government Officials and the Police

Expectation	Dublin	U.S.	U.K.	Germany	Italy	Mexico
TREATMENT BY PUBLIC OFFICIALS						
They expect equal treatment	55%	83%	83%	65%	53%	42%
They don't expect equal treatment	35	9	7	9	13	50
They expect serious consideration for point of view	37	48	59	53	35	14
They expect a little attention	35	31	22	18	15	48
They expect to be ignored	17	6	5	5	11	27
TREATMENT BY POLICE						
They expect equal treatment	75	85	89	72	56	32
They don't expect equal treatment	20	8	6	5	10	57
They expect serious consideration for point of view	62	56	74	59	35	12
They expect a little attention	23	22	13	11	13	46
They expect to be ignored	10	11	5	4	12	29

Source: Dublin—Munger Survey, unpublished (see p. 144 above). U.S., etc.—G. Almond and S. Verba, *The Civic Culture* (Princeton, N.J., 1963), pp. 108–9.

the Irish figures apply to Dubliners alone. The countryman, as in many countries, may be—and probably is—more suspicious of officials altogether than the town dweller. But, for what it is worth, Dubliners feel markedly less sure of their treatment by officials than the citizens of the United States, the United Kingdom, and Germany, and though the percentages that expect equal treatment and consideration from the police are higher, one-fifth do *not* expect to get equal treatment from them.

Nevertheless, the handicaps, real or imagined, of the citizen must not be overestimated. Though undoubtedly some citizens seeking the redress of particular kinds of grievances are handicapped at the level of the everyday minutiae of administration, most citizens, though not as many as one would hope, may well be content enough with the situation. In any case, the representatives' "contact man" activities provide an important channel of communication and review. At the same time, they soften the administration of certain services and lubricate the abrasive edge of government where it bears upon the *administré*.

THIRTEEN

A Small Island

"Ireland is an independent, sovereign, democratic state"—so says the Constitution. If the essence of democracy is the participation of people in making or influencing the decisions that affect their lives, any assessment of the extent of democracy in a country must be concerned both with the range of matters that fall to be decided within the community itself and with the extent to which decision-making processes allow for the participation of the public and are sensitive to the wishes and feelings of the public. British influence has been the most persistent theme of this study. Given Ireland's size, geographical position, and history, it might be expected—in an age of mass production, large markets, and mass communications—that for all its formal sovereignty, Ireland would in practice be not much more than a detached province of Great Britain. Moreover, Great Britain has been a large exporter of democracy, and the Irish political culture has absorbed a great deal of the British democratic tradition. Consequently, Irish governmental institutions are in form largely British. Yet Ireland is a state whose population is only one-twentieth the size of that of the United Kingdom, and a largely rural country, as opposed to a highly industrialized and urban one. Small size and more intimate communities ought, in theory at least, to give opportunities for greater public participation in public affairs and to make it easier for citizens to comprehend and identify with their government. It is with these topics, which might be called the "external" and "internal" aspects of democracy, that this chapter is concerned.

II

The British influence on Ireland arises from the small size of Ireland in the geographical context of nearness, the historical context of political dominion and social and economic dominance, and the intellectual context of similarity of language and cultural blanketing.

The values and expectations of Irish people to a considerable extent resemble those of the British. Nor is this all only a matter of inheriting a legacy. Since the country could not be a closed society, British influences have continued to operate since independence. They are the stronger because the two countries have a shared language and literature and because of emigration and much going and coming. Thus, the absorption of British liberal democratic ideas, the adoption of British institutions, and the acquisition and retention of similar patterns of public services are among the dominant features of Irish politics. Thus, also, the Irish political culture, with its high potential for democracy of a markedly British variety fully realized, continues to absorb British information and British values. We have noted a similarity not only of formal political and administrative organizations but of procedures, conventions, standards, and style. Cabinet government, parliamentary processes, minister–civil servant relationships, the Civil Service, local government, the courts, and the law—all have a British stamp on them. The continuing influence that arises from the propensity, by reason of convenience and narrow horizons, to look for models to British ways of handling public issues and problems tends to mean that changes both in the form of political institutions and in the content of policies have flowed in the same direction.

To all this must be added also the constraints that flow from the fact that Ireland has been and is partly dependent economically and wholly dependent strategically. True, during the Second World War, Ireland maintained neutrality and remained inviolate, but only because on balance it suited the Anglo-American alliance to have it so and on condition that it was a benevolent neutrality from their point of view. This dependence is constantly brought home by the inability of the Irish government to prevent decisions that affect the country being taken with no reference to it, e.g. the imposition of British import restrictions in 1964 and 1968, and, conversely, by its having little or no option in matters such as policy toward entry to the European Economic Community, the link with the pound sterling, or the adoption of the metric system.

Moreover, Great Britain not only has influenced Ireland but has insulated it from continental Europe, effectively blocking off the social, cultural, and economic influences that might otherwise have affected the life of the country and the policy of the state. Even as a sovereign state, Ireland remained for long comparatively isolated not only from the Continent but from the world in general. This insulation has shown itself not merely in a great ignorance of Europe and the rest of the outside world generally, which is widespread in the community, but in unconcern. Until recently at least, Ireland has simply not been involved, and with one or two exceptions has not felt involved, in what has gone on in Europe. Because of the communications filter interposed by the barrier of language and the dominance of British publishing, even continental Catholic currents of thought and speculation did not permeate to any extent until after the Second Vatican Council.

Strong British influence and insulation from the rest of the world, it could be argued, were to be expected on geopolitical grounds alone. They have, however, been the more marked because the inability of the Irish independence movement to win a complete victory in 1921 led to an obsession with the border and constitutional issues, and with the United Kingdom as the author and possible righter of a number of wrongs that Irish people believed they had suffered.

Since Britain filled the new Ireland's horizon, Irish people had no European perspectives and the Irish government practically no foreign policy. Only a few of the original leaders had European horizons, and when they were gone, Ireland virtually lost sight of Europe. De Valera made a mark in the League of Nations in the 1930's, but this had little effect on the country; no more than had Seán MacBride's activities as Minister for External Affairs from 1948 to 1951. In the Second World War, hostility to Britain and preoccupation with the border—*the* problem as politicians and people alike saw it—led to neutrality, which in turn led to exclusion from the new international groupings of postwar years or unwillingness to join them.

This isolation—political, social, economic, and cultural—meant that the great changes in postwar Europe made little impact upon Ireland. Not until the late 1950's was there a change. In 1956 Ireland was admitted to the UN, where its participation in peace-keeping operations and its position as an ex-colonial and impeccably noncolonial country, which was equally impeccably anti-Communist, made it *persona grata* with Western and emerging countries alike and gave it some scope for diplomatic activity. At the same time, the prospect that the United Kingdom would join the EEC, and, therefore, that Ireland would have to follow suit, led to a serious appraisal of the dangers and opportunities of membership. The country's horizons lifted somewhat. Even so, the European horizon is a limited one—limited to Europe as an economic menace, challenge, and opportunity; and limited to a few leading politicians, a few civil servants, and a very few of the more cosmopolitan TD's. If Ireland now has a more wide-ranging foreign policy, it is a policy formulated and conducted largely without benefit of public commentary or public interest.

If the ability to scan all one's neighbors and not to be oriented on one alone is a sign of a truly independent people, and if the recognition and pursuit of a wide range of international interests is the mark of a truly sovereign state, there are some grounds for speculating on whether, for all her formal sovereignty, Ireland should be thought of as in practice no more than a detached province of the United Kingdom. Some Europeans do see her thus. It would, however, be mistaken to conclude that this is so. Ireland cannot be viewed as simply the most advanced stage of decentralization achieved by the communities peripheral to England, the most distant stop on a line whose intermediate halts are Wales, Scotland, and Northern Ireland. Ireland is a "smaller European democracy" and not a larger British province because, unlike the peoples of the other peripheral areas of the British Isles, her people were not culturally absorbed to the extent necessary to bank down the fires of national self-consciousness and, hence, were not successfully subsumed into the British political system.

Political independence not only reflected the need to recognize differences, but, once granted, bred them. Its practice becomes a habit that cannot be eradicated except by suppression. First, and obviously, it makes a vast political difference. However inevitable political decisions may be for a small country, it makes a very great difference that it takes them itself. For Ireland to be able to decide to remain neutral in the Second World War—however much the inviolability of the country depended on the grace of the United Kingdom and the United States—convinced more Irishmen that their country was really independent after all than almost any other single decision from 1921 on. To have different tax rates, to operate a customs barrier, to make a consular agreement, to receive a foreign head of state, to abstain in a vote at the UN when Britain is committed—to be able to do these things and more like them, however limited the elbowroom for maneuver, is to greatly increase the range of decisions that a community has to take for itself and can feel responsible for. That a state is very small does make it more vulnerable to decisions made by a larger state without considering or consulting its neighbor; it does narrow the range of options in many matters, sometimes to one; it does mean that certain policies cannot be followed which, if the state were larger, it might take up, although, conversely, it gives exemption from having some items on the national agenda at all. What small size does not affect is the importance to a people of the range of decisions which come to be taken at home.

Autonomy is important not only politically in greatly extending the range of political questions for domestic decision, but also because it has the effect of increasing the number and range of matters generally that are dealt with within the community exclusively. The existence of a state boundary, however permeable, produces discontinuities of a different order from other boundaries. The contrast between the equivocal provincialism of Wales, Scotland, and even Northern Ireland and the sense of national identity of Ireland is marked. Dublin is not just a southern Belfast, let alone a western Cardiff. Just as the comparative stability of some states of Western Europe from medieval times led to the growth of separate nations within their borders, so independence in the case of the Republic and Westminster control in the case of Northern Ireland have created different foci of interest and decision. The Republic is Dublin-oriented; Northern Ireland is London-oriented. Because the full range of public affairs in the Republic are dealt with in Dublin, those who wish to influence their course must pursue their activities there also. After 1921, finance and industry, trade associations, unions (with a few exceptions), and the professions all reoriented themselves at varying speeds, but inevitably, upon Dublin.

Being independent and sovereign, then, makes a vital difference. Autonomy is important not only for a sense of national identity and self-respect—a justification in itself—but also politically. No amount of economic, social, or cultural blanketing can obviate the differences that arise as a consequence of having the right to make a decision, even an inevitable one, and not having that right. Further, autonomy not only increases the scope for democracy to operate, but alters the whole community context within which it will operate.

III

For all the similarity between Great Britain and Ireland so far as political institutions are concerned, there is one obvious contrast that might seem to lead to striking differences in practice. The population of Ireland is 2.9 million, of the United Kingdom 54 million. When it comes to participation in politics, to getting consensus, or to the likelihood of citizens identifying with their government or being alienated from it, a system with less than 3 million inhabitants and an electorate of 1.8 million, as the Irish is, might seem to offer greater possibilities for the practice of democracy than a system of 54 million with an electorate of 35 million. Again, it seems to be the case that the larger the political system, the more asymmetrical the pattern of communications between leaders and led. The larger the numbers in the unit, the less directly can citizens communicate with leaders and the greater the leaders' dependence on intermediary subleaders for information about public demands and reactions. If so, then Ireland enjoys conditions more favorable to the generation of mutual understanding and hence genuine and higher-quality democracy. What has been the Irish experience in fact?

Ireland has a ratio of one deputy to 20,000 inhabitants, and if one counts Senators, the ratio of national representatives to people is one to 14,000. (In the United Kingdom it is one to 87,000.) In Ireland, also, there is one local councilor to 1,873 persons, and because of the small total numbers involved, this ratio is possible without the difficulties and loss of contact that arise from having too many layers of authorities from bottom to top or too many units of government. The connection between local and national government is direct and close, and there is considerable overlap. The linkage is remarkably close in fact—from citizen to local representative (often a personal and certainly a local connection)—and in turn from local representative to TD or Senator and thence to minister or department, or, where the local councilor is himself a parliamentary representative, direct. Thus the channels of communication are short and have few intermediary links.

It would be wrong, however, to conclude that this state of affairs leads to the Irish citizen participating more positively in policy making or to his having a greater influence than the citizen of a larger democracy. Clearly, a ratio of 1 : 20,000 is as impossibly large for the consideration of personal views on policy as 1 : 200,000 or, for that matter, as 1 : 2,000 would be. In any case, the vast majority of citizens do not desire a more active role in government, nor are they equipped for it, and Irish representatives do not do much to educate even those who would be educated politically. On the contrary, they are poor communicators of general political information to their constituents. (Never was this more clearly shown than in the early 1960's, when the country faced, it was thought, an imminent entrance into the European Community.) The ignorance of Irish people about issues of foreign or economic policy and of the facts of their economic situation reflects a failure not only of the government but of representatives to communicate them. The truth is that small numbers permit representatives to busy themselves with more homely matters, and other factors such as the electoral system force them to. There is communication, all right, but it is not concerned with general policy. This weakness of the representative does not arise simply because of small scale, however; other factors in the system play their part. Rather, it might be said that small scale, and especially smallness allied to the rural nature of the country, exacerbates it.

The stress on the role of the representative as a contact man—and indeed the intimacy that small numbers in general allow—particularly

in a rural setting and in a locally oriented community, have consequences that are not helpful to representative government. A system like
the Irish tends to produce representatives who are parochial in character
and outlook and who, for all their virtues in some respects, are not well
fitted for the tasks of a national legislator as those are conceived of in
many countries. However, to a great extent the poor showing of the
parliamentary representative is a function of the strong Cabinet government system in which he operates and has little to do with size. What
this study has attempted to show above all is how, in such a system, it is
the general election that is the decisive political battleground; how victory there gives the government its dominating role and hegemonic
position; and how attenuated the role of Parliament tends to be as compared with systems where Parliament makes the laws. That is not to say
that there are not opportunities that exist unexploited under the present system or that the Oireachtas could not be a more effective critic of
policy and a more constructive force in government than it is. And
doubtless small size and parochial attitudes contribute to this state of
affairs. What British and Irish experience taken together suggests, however, is that the decline of Parliament has occurred for reasons other
than size.

If Cabinet government (British style) belittles the role of the elected
representative, so, more generally, does the general acceptance by Western democracies of what Theodore Lowi has called the ideology of "interest-group liberalism."[1] As this study has revealed, policy is made and
public affairs decided by ministers and their Civil Service advisers after
consultation with the spokesmen of the organized interest groups appropriate to the matter under review. These all-important meetings
take place in the minister's room, the civil servant's office, the department's conference room; at this or that council, committee, and advisory
or consultative body meeting. The spokesmen concerned are no doubt
in some senses representative, but all this is a long way from the people's
elected representatives and from the representative assembly. In this system, the contribution of the elected representative to the crucial stages
of decision making may well be at best his expression of the symptoms
of unease (where the shoe pinches) or his negative influence based on an
instinct for political survival (what *they* won't put up with "down the
country"); at worst, it is peripheral.

The whole drift of Irish government may indeed be, as it seems to be

[1] T. Lowi, "The Public Philosophy: Interest-Group Liberalism," *American Political
Science Review*, LXI (1967), 5–24.

in many Western countries, toward Robert Dahl's "democratic Leviathan."[2]

> By the democratic Leviathan I mean the kind of political system which is a product of long evolution and hard struggle, welfare-oriented, centralized, bureaucratic, tamed and controlled by competition among highly organized elites, and, in the perspectives of the ordinary citizen, somewhat remote, distant and impersonal even in small countries like Norway and Sweden. The politics of this new democratic Leviathan are above all the politics of compromise, adjustment, negotiation, bargaining; a politics carried on among professional and quasi-professional leaders who constitute only a small part of the total citizen body; a politics that reflects a commitment to the virtues of pragmatism, moderation and incremental change; a politics that is un-ideological and even anti-ideological.

If this is the general trend, then the effects of small scale and a rural setting are but marginal either way. The locally oriented rural deputy is slightly less well fitted to play even his inevitably small part; on the other hand, small scale and a rural setting help to counter the citizen's feeling of remoteness.

While, on the whole, these most prominent tendencies in Irish government and politics seem to be more related to the system, procedures, and functions of government than to numbers, and small size may only exacerbate them or soften them, in two respects at least scale does seem to be more obviously influential.

First, as we have seen, small numbers and the consequential low ratio of representatives to people and direct local-central linkage make possible administrative procedures that could hardly operate in a large system except for a favored few. The business of individual citizens and local interests can be the subject of direct representations to the appropriate administrator, local or central; a review of a decision already made can be more easily obtained; and the righting of a wrong more easily effected. In fact, our study of representatives shows that this possibility has been exploited to the full, the more so since the political culture of the people favors such procedures and the election system makes them politically profitable.

Again, insofar as the shortcomings of representatives arise from a shortage in their ranks of qualified personnel, i.e. men who are by training, by profession, and by inclination fitted to consider and appraise large-scale public business, this is part of a more general danger of smallness, the danger of a lack of sufficient talent to man governmental and

2 R. A. Dahl, "Reflections on Opposition in Western Democracies," *Government and Opposition*, I (1965), 19–20.

political posts. It would be difficult to quantify the amounts of certain kinds of talents and expertise needed to man a political system and to measure their availability in Ireland today. Besides, this is not simply a matter of numbers in a community, but, as the experience of underdeveloped countries has shown, a matter of levels of education and training, particularly in the social sciences, and of experience, especially in large-scale operations. While there can be no doubt that Ireland is viable, i.e. above the minimum size and the minimum education and experience levels, there are some signs that it is not very far above. The Committee on the Constitution, 1967, reported that one of the arguments it had heard in favor of increasing the number of deputies was to provide an adequate pool from which to select enough ministers.

On the basis of present Dáil membership, the Deputies supporting the Government are likely to number 70 or so. As many of these would, for one good reason or another, be unable to take up Ministerial office, the Taoiseach is, in effect, left with some 35–40 Deputies out of whom he must find about 20 Ministers and Parliamentary Secretaries. This imbalance ought to be rectified, and there is a strong case for an immediate increase in the total membership of the Dáil.[3]

Industry and commerce; the trade associations, the unions and interest organizations generally; the public services; the parties—all are short of the right kinds of experts and, perhaps, of enough talent too. In all too many of the places where government comes into contact with the spokesmen of the community, or needs a chairman for a commission, a board member, or a nominee, a few names recur again and again. Civil servants will tell you that it is not easy to find well-qualified people to serve or to employ for this or that job; conversely, leading businessmen will say that there are all too few really able men in politics or the public service. Both may be exaggerating, and this is all very imprecise. The same is said in communities far larger than Ireland. It may well be, however, that at some level of population not too far below that of Ireland, shortages of talented manpower occur in government and politics, and especially democratic government and politics.

Finally, it may be asked: what if any are the effects of the small size of the Irish state upon community attitudes and cohesion? At elections on the local government level, the smaller communities have a slightly higher turnout rate than the larger ones; politicians are not at all remote from the people, rather the reverse; the shortness of the links between government and people, to which attention has been drawn, does lead to a sense of personal intimacy that may not be possible in bigger

[3] *Report of the Committee on the Constitution, December 1967* (Stationery Office, Dublin, 1968), para. 48.

countries. More important, however, is the fact of mass communications. It is as easy to reach the many with television as the few, and the television appearance can make as direct an impact and almost as direct a link as a personal encounter. Yet, it is a one-way link and increases the inevitable asymmetry of communications between leaders and people in the modern state. The differences of scale between the biggest and the smallest states are not critical in this respect. Where, once again, the critical difference between large and small does arise is in the greater possibility of direct and immediate links being forged by elected representatives and the greater potential for communication that these open up. It is on the use made of this vital political channel that what advantages there are in small numbers might be exploited. Yet, small scale might itself contribute to the failure of Irish parliamentary representatives to act as channels of political communications of certain types rather than as adjuncts of the administration. What is not clear is whether this paradoxical situation is an inevitable one, or simply very Irish.

Appendixes

Basic Social and Economic Data

TABLE A.1

Population, 1821–1966

Area	1821	1841	1861	1881
Republic of Ireland (26 counties):				
Dublin County and County				
Borough	335,892	372,773	410,252	418,910
Rest of Leinster	1,421,600	1,600,950	1,047,383	860,079
Munster	1,935,612	2,396,161	1,513,558	1,331,115
Connacht	1,110,229	1,418,859	913,135	821,657
Ulster (part)[a]	618,043	740,048	517,783	438,259
TOTAL	5,421,376	6,528,799	4,402,111	3,870,020
Northern Ireland (6 counties)	1,380,451	1,648,945	1,396,453	1,304,816
GRAND TOTAL	6,801,827	8,177,744	5,798,564	5,174,836

Area	1901	1926	1946	1966
Republic of Ireland (26 counties):				
Dublin County and County				
Borough	448,206	505,654	636,193	795,047
Rest of Leinster	704,623	643,438	644,924	619,368
Munster	1,076,188	969,902	917,306	859,334
Connacht	646,932	552,907	492,797	401,950
Ulster (part)[a]	345,874	300,091	263,887	208,303
TOTAL	3,221,823	2,971,992	2,955,107	2,884,002
Northern Ireland (6 counties)	1,236,952	1,256,561	—	1,484,775
GRAND TOTAL	4,458,775	4,228,553	—	4,368,777

Source: For Republic of Ireland, 1821–61, Saorstát Eireann, *Census of Population, 1926*, I; 1871–1966, *Census of Population of Ireland, 1966*, I. For Northern Ireland, 1821–1966, *Census of Population, 1966*.

[a] County Cavan, County Donegal, County Monaghan.

TABLE A.2
Estimated Net Emigration, 1926–66
(Annual average rate per 1,000 of population)

Area	1926–36	1936–46	1946–51	1951–56	1956–61	1961–66
Ireland	5.6	6.3	8.2	13.4	14.8	5.7
Leinster	0.4	2.9	2.1	11.4	13.1	1.5
Munster	8.1	7.7	11.7	12.8	14.2	6.4
Connacht	10.2	10.3	15.1	17.4	18.3	13.6
Ulster (part)	10.3	9.7	14.6	19.6	20.7	14.2

Source: 1926–46, *Commission on Emigration Report, 1948–54*, p. 326; 1946–66, *Census of Population of Ireland, 1966*, I, xx.

TABLE A.3
Population Changes in Town and Rural Areas, 1841–1966

Population	1841	1861	1881	1901	1926	1946	1966
Town population (*thousands*)[a]	1,100	986	932	911	959	1,161	1,419
Rural population (*thousands*)	5,429	3,416	2,938	2,311	2,013	1,794	1,465
TOTAL POPULATION (*thousands*)	6,529	4,402	3,870	3,222	2,972	2,955	2,884
Percentage of total:							
In towns	16.8%	22.4%	24.1%	28.3%	32.3%	39.3%	49.2%
In rural areas	83.2	77.6	75.9	71.7	67.7	60.7	50.8
Percentage of total:							
In Dublin	4.1%	7.2%	8.4%	11.1%	13.6%	18.0%	22.5%
In Dun Laoghaire	0.3	0.7	0.9	1.0	1.2	1.8	2.9
In Cork	1.2	1.8	2.1	2.4	2.6	3.7	4.3
In Limerick	0.7	1.0	1.0	1.2	1.3	1.5	2.0
In Waterford	0.4	0.6	0.7	0.8	0.9	1.0	1.0
TOTAL	6.7%	11.3%	13.1%	16.5%	19.6%	26.0%	32.7%

Source: 1841, *Census of Population of Ireland, 1946*, General Reports, Tables 1 and 4; 1861, *Statistical Abstract of Ireland, 1939*, Table 9; 1881–1946; *Statistical Abstract of Ireland, 1964*, Table 9; 1966, *Census of Population of Ireland, 1966*, Volume 1.
 [a] The "town" population is defined as all those persons living in towns with a population of 1,500 or more.

TABLE A.4
Population Density of Ireland and Certain European Countries in 1960–61

Country	Total population per sq. km. of	
	Total area	Agricultural area
Netherlands (1961)	356	498
United Kingdom (1960)	221	234
Ireland (1961)	40	61
Sweden (1960)	17	185
Norway (1960)	11	351

Source: Derived from *UN Statistical Yearbook, 1966*, and *FAO Yearbook*, 1965.

TABLE A.5
Occupational Structure, 1926–66

Sector of economic activity	1926	1936	1946	1951	1961	1966
Agriculture, forestry, and fishing (primary sector)	53.4%	49.6%	46.8%	40.6%	36.0%	31.3%
Mining, manufacturing, etc. (secondary sector)	13.0	16.3	17.0	23.7	24.6	27.6
Services (tertiary sector)	33.6	34.1	36.2	35.7	39.4	41.2
Total at work as percentage of total population	41.1	41.6	41.5	41.2	37.3	37.0

Source: Calculated from *Censuses of Population*, 1926, 1936, 1946, 1951, 1961, and 1966.
Note: For 1926–61, sectors (primary, secondary, tertiary) are as defined by Colin Clark, *The Conditions of Economic Progress*. Data for 1966 are taken directly from *Census of Population, 1966*, III. Information on occupations was not collected by the census before 1926. These data relate only to those "at work" (excluding those out of work at the time of the census) aged 14 years and over.

TABLE A.6
Occupational Structure by Region, 1966

Area	Agriculture and fishing	Other production industries	Service-type industries
Dublin County and County Borough	1.6%	40.5%	40.2%
Rest of Leinster	24.8	20.5	18.5
Munster	33.8	27.5	26.5
Connacht and Ulster (part)	39.7	11.5	14.8

Source: *Census of Population of Ireland, 1966*, III.

TABLE A.7
Employment Classes, 1926–66

Class	1926	1946	1951	1961	1966
Employer	6%	6%	5%	3%	2%
Self-employed and relatives assisting	44	38	36	34	30
Employees and unemployed	50	56	59	63	68

Source: *Censuses of Population of Ireland*.

TABLE A.8
Size of Farms, 1965

Area	Ireland	Leinster	Munster	Connacht	Ulster (part)	Total
Up to 15 acres	24.0%	26.7%	24.8%	28.7%	19.8%	100.0%
16–50 acres	45.9	20.6	25.1	39.1	15.2	100.0
51–100 acres	19.4	26.8	42.7	20.0	10.5	100.0
Over 100 acres	10.7	38.5	44.1	9.6	7.8	100.0

Source: *Statistical Abstract of Ireland, 1967*.

TABLE A.9
Percentage of Irish Speakers, 1851–1961

Area	1851	1871	1891	1911	1926	1946	1961
Ireland	29.1%	19.8%	19.2%	17.6%	19.3%	21.2%	27.2%
Dublin City and County	1.2	0.4	0.8	3.7	8.3	15.5	21.1
Rest of Leinster	4.3	1.6	1.3	3.3	10.2	17.2	23.4
Munster	43.9	27.7	26.2	22.1	21.6	22.0	28.7
Connacht	50.8	39.0	37.9	35.5	33.3	33.2	37.6
Ulster (part)	17.0	15.1	17.8	20.4	23.9	26.0	31.4

Source: 1851–1926, Saorstát Eireann, *Census of Population, 1936*, VIII; 1946, *Census of Population of Ireland, 1946*, VIII; 1961, *Census of Population of Ireland, 1961*, IX.

Note: The category "Irish speakers" includes all those who speak Irish only or who can speak Irish and English. It excludes those who can read, but cannot speak, Irish. The number of "Irish speakers" is far less susceptible of exact measurement than any of the other matters in the census.

TABLE A.10
Membership of the Main Religious Denominations, 1861–1961

Area	1861	1911	1926	1946	1961
Ireland (26 counties):					
Roman Catholics	89.4%	89.6%	92.6%	94.3%	94.9%
Church of Ireland	8.5	7.9	5.5	4.2	3.7
Other	2.1	2.5	1.9	1.5	1.4
Dublin City and County:					
Roman Catholics	75.5	78.7	85.8	90.3	92.4
Church of Ireland	20.9	16.5	10.7	7.1	5.3
Other	3.6	4.8	3.5	2.6	2.3
Rest of Leinster:					
Roman Catholics	90.0	89.7	93.1	94.7	95.0
Church of Ireland	9.1	9.0	6.1	4.7	4.3
Other	0.9	1.3	0.8	0.6	0.7
Munster:					
Roman Catholics	93.8	94.0	96.4	97.3	97.3
Church of Ireland	5.3	4.9	3.0	2.2	2.1
Other	0.9	1.1	0.6	0.5	0.6
Connacht:					
Roman Catholics	94.8	96.2	97.4	98.0	98.1
Church of Ireland	4.4	3.1	2.2	1.7	1.6
Other	0.8	0.7	0.4	0.3	0.3
Ulster (part):					
Roman Catholics	76.3	78.7	81.8	85.3	86.7
Church of Ireland	13.7	12.0	10.1	8.1	7.0
Other	10.0	9.3	8.1	6.6	6.3

Source: 1861, Saorstát Eireann, *Census of Population, 1926*, III, part 1; 1911–61, *Census of Population of Ireland, 1961*, VII, part 1.

TABLE A.11
The Non-Catholic Element, 1926–61

Percentage of non-Catholics in	1926	1946	1961
Population	7.4%	5.7%	5.1%
Agriculture:	6.0	5.2	5.5
Farmers on up to 15 acres	3.3	2.9	2.9
Farmers on 16–30 acres	5.5	4.2	3.7
Farmers on over 200 acres	21.8	23.0	22.7
Farm laborers	2.9	2.1	2.6
Commerce and professions:	14.5	10.9	8.8
Commerce, insurance, finance	14.0	10.6	*a*
Professions	14.6	10.2	8.2
Employers and managers in industry	18.7	20.2	*a*

Source: *Census of Population, 1926*, III; *Census of Population, 1946*, II; *Census of Population, 1961*, VII.
a Owing to changes in the classification of occupations, it is not possible to give figures comparable with those for 1926 and 1946.

TABLE A.12
Comparative Living Standards in Ireland and Certain European Countries, 1950–67

Country	Personal consumption per head of population, Irish £'s 1967			1958–1967 growth	
	1950	1958	1967	National output	Personal consumption
Ireland	163	170	215	39½%	35%
Italy	127	170	260	63	61
Netherlands	202	233	343	50½	59
Belgium	250	276	366	42	35
United Kingdom	290	327	396	32½	30
France	221	298	411	51	53½
Germany (Federal Republic)	185	303	419	53½	52½

Source: From G. FitzGerald, "Comparative Living Standards," *Irish Times*, January 24, 1968.

TABLE A.13
Indexes of Gross National Product and Sectoral Contributions to Output, 1947–66
(1947 = 100)

Index	1947	1951	1956	1961	1966
Index of GNP	100	114	119	137	159
Sectoral contributions to output:					
Industry	21%	25%	24%	27%	33%
Agriculture	27	26	26	22	20
Other	52	49	50	51	47

Source: *National Income and Expenditure* (annual, Stationery Office, Dublin).

Table A.14

Distribution of Trade by Areas, 1938 and 1948
I = Imports (origin); E = Exports (destination)

Area	1938 I	1938 E	1948 I	1948 E
United Kingdom	50.5%	92.7%	53.9%	87.3%
USA	11.4	0.5	8.3	0.8
Germany[a]	3.6	3.8	0.1	0.1
France	1.3	0.5	0.8	0.4
Belgium	2.5	0.5	1.9	3.0
Netherlands	1.1	0.5	1.6	3.6
Italy	0.5	—	—	0.4
All other areas and temporary transactions	29.1	1.5	33.4	4.4
TOTAL	100.0%	100.0%	100.0%	100.0%

Source: *Trade and Shipping Statistics, 1938* (Stationery Office, Dublin); *Trade Statistics of Ireland, December 1948* (Stationery Office, Dublin). [a] In 1938 figures for Austria are included.

Table A.15

Distribution of Trade by Areas, 1958–65
I = Imports (origin); E = Exports (destination)

Area	1958 I	1958 E	1960 I	1960 E	1962 I	1962 E	1964 I	1964 E	1965 I	1965 E
United Kingdom	56.3%	76.9%	49.6%	73.8%	49.9%	73.1%	50.7%	71.5%	50.6%	69.6%
Other EFTA countries[a]	2.9	0.8	3.3	1.2	3.2	0.7	3.8	1.4	3.7	1.5
Member countries of EEC	11.1	4.6	13.0	5.7	15.8	6.2	15.6	11.4	15.3	12.9
USA[b]	7.1	5.7	8.2	8.2	7.6	8.3	7.6	5.0	8.0	4.1
Canada	3.0	0.7	2.1	0.8	2.2	0.9	2.2	0.8	2.6	1.1
All other areas	16.1	5.5	20.6	4.9	18.5	5.6	17.6	5.9	17.6	5.9
Re-imports and temporary domestic exports	3.5	5.8	3.2	5.4	2.8	5.2	2.5	4.0	2.2	3.9
TOTAL	100.0%	100.0%	100.0%	100.0%	100.0%	100.0%	100.0%	100.0%	100.0%	100.0%

Source: *Statistical Abstract of Ireland* (Stationery Office, Dublin). [a] Austria, Denmark, Norway, Sweden, Switzerland, Portugal. [b] Includes U.S. Forces overseas.

The Electorate and Elections

TABLE B.1

The Electorate, 1832–1966

Position after	Population (of 26 counties)	Adult population (21 and over)	Electors	Electors as % of population Adult	Total
Representation of the People (Ireland) Act, 1832	6,193,397 (1831)	3,040,958 (1831)	68,427 (1832)	2.3%	1.1%
The Qualification and Registration of Parliamentary Electors Amendment Act (Ireland), 1850	5,111,557 (1851)	2,535,150 (1851)	119,411 (1852)	4.7	2.3
Representation of the People (Ireland) Act, 1868	4,402,111 (1861)	2,360,324 (1861)	153,979 (1868)	6.5	3.5
Representation of the People Act, 1885	3,870,020 (1881)	2,010,751 (1881)	541,422 (1885)	26.9	14.0
Representation of the People Act, 1918	3,139,688 (1911)	1,861,956 (1911)	1,372,182 (1918)	73.7	43.7
Constitution of the Irish Free State, 1922, and Electoral Act, 1923	2,971,992 (1926)	1,769,880 (1926)	1,725,423 (1927)	97.5	58.1
The position in 1966	2,884,002 (1966)	1,680,526 (1966)	1,709,161 (1966)	101.7[a]	59.3

Source: *Censuses of Population; Statistical Abstract of Ireland; Thom's Irish Almanac and Official Directory; Dod's Parliamentary Companion.*

[a] The fact that the number of electors on the Register is larger than the number of population aged 21 and over is due to (1) the inclusion in the Register, which is compiled in the late autumn and winter, of temporary emigrants who were not in the country on the night of the census; (2) the inclusion in the Register of people who had in fact left the country and who should not have been registered; (3) other errors in the Register (people who are dead, people who have moved and are included twice, etc.).

TABLE B.2
Turnout at General Elections, 1923–65

Year	Total turnout	Turnout in Dublin and environs[a]	Turnout in Donegal, Mayo, Galway W., and Kerry[b]	Turnout in rest of Ireland
1923	61%	55.6%	61.5%[c]	65.0%
1927(1)	68	65.5	61.6[c]	67.2
1927(2)	69	67.5	63.7[c]	69.1
1932	77	70.3	74.3[c]	76.6
1933	81.3	76.6	79.8[c]	82.7
1937	76.2	70.8	70.9	79.3
1938	79.0	68.5	72.7	80.1
1943	74.2	69.0	69.8	77.1
1944	67.7	64.6	65.4	71.6
1948	74.2	70.5	71.0	76.3
1951	75.3	68.9	73.2	78.1
1954	76.4	68.9	73.8	79.9
1957	71.3	61.3	70.5	75.3
1961	70.6	61.0	68.6	75.0
1965	75.1	70.3	72.7	77.7

Source: 1923–32, Flynn's *Oireachtas Companion* and *Parliamentary Handbooks*; 1933–65, Department of Local Government Reports.
[a] Dublin City, Dublin County, and Dun Laoghaire and Rathdown.
[b] In these constituencies the mountainous terrain and the scattered nature of the communities make communications difficult.
[c] These figures include the whole of County Galway, the constituency being not then divided.

TABLE B.3
Percentage of Invalid Votes at General Elections, 1922–65

Election	Invalid	Election	Invalid
1922	3.08%	1943	1.20%
1923	3.66	1944	1.04
1927(1)	2.60	1948	0.98
1927(2)	1.86	1951	0.89
1932	1.60	1954	0.94
1933	1.05	1957	0.93
1937	2.10[a]	1961	0.96
1938	1.20	1965	0.91

Source: *Report of the Committee on the Constitution*, December 1967 (Stationery Office, Dublin, 1967), Annex 13.
[a] On this occasion a referendum on the Constitution was held at the same time as the election.

TABLE B.4

Candidates and Members Elected at General Elections, 1922–65

C = Candidates; E = Elected

Party	1922 C	E	1923 C	E	1927(1) C	E	1927(2) C	E	1932 C	E	1933 C	E	1937 C	E	1938 C	E
Cumann na nGaedheal (Pro-Treaty)	65	58	109	63	97	47	88	62	101	57	85	48	—	—	—	—
Fine Gael	—	—	—	—	—	—	—	—	—	—	—	—	95	48	74	45
Republican (Anti-Treaty)	57	35	85	44	—	—	—	—	—	—	—	—	—	—	—	—
Sinn Féin	—	—	—	—	15	5	—	—	—	—	—	—	—	—	—	—
Fianna Fáil	—	—	—	—	87	44	88	57	104	72	103	77	100	69	92	77
Labour	18	17	44	14	50	22	28	13	31	7	19	8	23	13	30	9
National Labour	—	—	—	—	—	—	—	—	—	—	—	—	—	—	—	—
Farmers	12	7	64	15	38	11	20	6	9	4	—	—	—	—	—	—
Clann na Talmhan	—	—	—	—	—	—	—	—	—	—	—	—	—	—	—	—
National League	—	—	—	—	30	8	6	2	—	—	—	—	—	—	—	—
Clann Eireann	—	—	—	—	7	0	—	—	—	—	—	—	—	—	—	—
Centre Party	—	—	—	—	—	—	—	—	—	—	26	11	—	—	—	—
Clann na Poblachta	—	—	—	—	—	—	—	—	—	—	—	—	—	—	—	—
National Progressive Democratic Party	—	—	—	—	—	—	—	—	—	—	—	—	—	—	—	—
Independents, etc.	21	11	75	17	59	16	32	13	34	13	13	9	36	8	11	7
TOTAL	173	128	377	153	383	153	262	153	279	153	246	153	254	138	207	138

Party	1943 C	E	1944 C	E	1948 C	E	1951 C	E	1954 C	E	1957 C	E	1961 C	E	1965 C	E
Cumann na nGaedheal (Pro-Treaty)	—	—	—	—	—	—	—	—	—	—	—	—	—	—	—	—
Fine Gael	87	32	57	30	82	31	77	40	89	50	82	40	96	47	102	47
Republican (Anti-Treaty)	—	—	—	—	—	—	—	—	—	—	—	—	—	—	—	—
Sinn Féin	—	—	—	—	—	—	—	—	—	—	19	4	20	0	—	—
Fianna Fáil	105	67	100	76	118	68	118	69	112	65	112	78	107	70	111	72
Labour	71	17	29	8	43	14	37	16	42	19	30	12	35	16	43	22
National Labour	—	—	9	4	16	5	—	—	—	—	—	—	—	—	—	—
Farmers	—	—	—	—	—	—	—	—	—	—	—	—	—	—	—	—
Clann na Talmhan	44	14	31	11	17	7	7	6	10	5	7	3	6	2	—	—
National League	—	—	—	—	—	—	—	—	—	—	—	—	—	—	—	—
Clann Eireann	—	—	—	—	—	—	—	—	—	—	—	—	—	—	—	—
Centre Party	—	—	—	—	—	—	—	—	—	—	—	—	—	—	—	—
Clann na Poblachta	—	—	—	—	92	10	26	2	20	3	12	1	5	1	4	1
National Progressive Democratic Party	—	—	—	—	—	—	—	—	—	—	—	—	3	2	—	—
Independents, etc.	47	8	25	9	28	12	31	14	29	5	26	9	28	6	20	2
TOTAL	354	138	351	138	406	147	296	147	302	147	288	147	300	144	280	144

TABLE B.5

Electoral Strength of the Major Parties, 1922–65

Year	Cumann na nGaedheal (later Fine Gael)			Anti-Treaty Party (later Fianna Fáil)			Labour Party			Others		
	Votes	% of valid poll	% of electorate	Votes	% of valid poll	% of electorate	Votes	% of valid poll	% of electorate	Votes	% of valid poll	% of electorate
1922	134,939	21.5%	13.1%	245,401	39.1%	23.9%	132,428	21.1%	12.9%	114,855	18.3%	11.2%
1923	409,421	38.9	22.9[a]	290,489	27.6	16.3[a]	130,509	12.4	7.3[a]	222,076	21.1	12.4[a]
1927(1)	315,277	27.5	18.2	299,226	26.1	17.3	158,211	13.8	9.1	373,746	32.6	21.6
1927(2)	453,121	38.7	26.2[a]	412,141	35.2	23.8[a]	111,231	9.5	6.4[a]	194,363	16.6	11.2[a]
1932	449,506	35.3	26.6[a]	566,498	44.5	33.5[a]	98,286	7.7	5.8[a]	159,736	12.5	9.4[a]
1933	422,495	30.5	24.5[a]	689,054	49.7	40.0[a]	79,221	5.7	4.6[a]	195,788	14.1	11.4[a]
1937	461,171	34.8	26.0	599,040	45.2	33.7	135,758	10.3	7.6	128,480	9.7	7.2
1938	428,633	33.3	25.2[a]	667,996	51.9	39.3[a]	128,945	10.0	7.6[a]	60,685	4.8	3.6[a]
1943	307,490	23.1	16.9	557,525	41.9	30.7	208,812	15.7	11.5	257,882	19.3	14.2
1944	249,329	20.5	14.0[a]	595,259	48.9	33.5[a]	139,499	11.5	7.9[ab]	233,262	19.1	13.1[a]
1948	262,393	19.8	14.5	553,914	41.9	30.8	149,088	11.3	8.3[ab]	358,048	27.0	19.9
1951	342,922	25.7	19.2	616,212	46.3	34.5	151,828	11.4	8.5	220,611	16.6	12.4
1954	427,037	32.0	24.3	578,960	43.4	32.8	161,034	12.0	9.1	167,996	12.6	9.5
1957	326,699	26.6	18.8	592,994	48.3	34.1	111,747	9.1	6.4	195,579	16.0	11.3
1961	374,099	32.0	22.4	512,073	43.8	30.6	136,111	11.6	8.1	146,121	12.6	8.7
1965	427,081	33.9	25.4	597,414	47.8	35.5	192,740	15.4	11.5	35,887	2.9	2.1

[a] Excluding constituencies in which there were no contests.
[b] Including "National Labour," the Labour Party being at that time split.

TABLE B.6

Regional Variations in Party Strength at the General Elections of 1923, 1932, 1948, 1957, and 1965

Region and parties	1923			1932			1948			1957			1965		
	Borough[b]	County	Total	Borough[b]	County	Total	Borough[b]	County	Total	Borough[b]	County	Total	Borough[b]	County	Total
Dublin and environs:[a]															
Fine Gael (formerly Cumann na nGaedheal)	51.6%	48.3%	50.4%	35.1%	44.7%	38.9%	24.7%	23.5%	24.6%	26.6%	25.7%	26.5%	29.2%	27.3%	28.9%
Fianna Fáil (formerly Sinn Féin)	19.2	13.6	17.2	37.6	28.6	34.1	38.4	43.3	38.9	44.1	61.5	46.8	47.9	54.0	48.9
Labour	2.6	8.2	4.6	5.4	7.6	6.3	9.8	15.9	10.4	7.3	12.8	8.1	18.5	18.7	18.5
Others	26.6	29.9	27.8	21.9	19.1	20.7	27.1	17.3	26.1	22.0	—	18.6	4.4	—	3.7
Rest of Leinster:															
Fine Gael	—	33.0		—	34.7		—	21.6		—	29.6		—	33.3	
Fianna Fáil	—	25.1		—	44.0		—	41.3		—	50.2		—	45.4	
Labour	—	19.1		—	14.0		—	16.8		—	14.3		—	19.2	
Others	—	22.8		—	7.3		—	20.3		—	5.9		—	2.1	
Munster:															
Fine Gael	46.1	32.3	33.9	44.0	33.0	34.3	22.6	18.6	19.0	26.0	25.1	25.2	26.5	31.5	30.9
Fianna Fáil	19.8	32.2	30.7	35.9	47.5	46.1	38.0	42.8	42.3	48.8	49.7	49.6	51.5	47.5	47.9
Labour	12.4	12.5	12.5	10.3	8.0	8.3	18.8	14.4	14.9	14.1	12.4	12.6	16.9	18.7	18.5
Others	21.7	23.0	22.9	9.8	11.5	11.3	20.6	24.2	23.8	11.1	12.8	12.6	5.1	2.3	2.7
Connacht:															
Fine Gael	—	47.6		—	38.9		—	17.0		—	25.9		—	44.4	
Fianna Fáil	—	35.9		—	53.1		—	43.5		—	45.8		—	47.9	
Labour	—	4.3		—	3.4		—	3.3		—	1.2		—	5.5	
Others	—	12.2		—	4.6		—	36.2		—	27.1		—	2.2	
Ulster (part):															
Fine Gael	—	37.3		—	27.3		—	13.4		—	26.1		—	42.8	
Fianna Fáil	—	22.3		—	41.7		—	45.2		—	47.1		—	50.8	
Labour	—	8.1		—	2.5		—	1.4		—	—		—	2.1	
Others	—	32.3		—	28.5		—	40.0		—	26.8		—	4.3	

[a] This includes the Dublin City constituencies, the constituency of Dun Laoghaire and Rathdown and Dublin County.

[b] This includes the Dáil constituency of Dun Laoghaire and Rathdown. This constituency is legally a county constituency, but because of the urban nature of the area it has been included with the borough constituencies.

TABLE B.7
Constitutional Referendum, 1959

Proposal to alter Article 16 of the Constitution by substituting a simple majority system for the system of proportional representation by the single transferable vote.

Total poll	Invalid	Total valid poll	In favor	Against
979,678	39,367	940,311	453,322	486,989
(58.4%)	(4%)	(56.1%)	(48.2%)	(51.8%)

Source: Iris Oifigiúil, June 23, 1959.

TABLE B.8
Constitutional Referendum, 1968

(*a*) Proposal that in forming Dáil constituencies, the population per deputy in any case may not be greater or less than the national average by more than one-sixth and that regard must be given to the extent and accessibility of constituencies, the need for having convenient areas of representation, and the desirability of avoiding the overlapping of county boundaries.

Total poll	Invalid	Total valid poll	In favor	Against
1,129,477	48,489	1,080,988	424,185	656,803
(65.8%)	(4.2%)	(62.9%)	(39.2%)	(60.8%)

(*b*) Proposal (1) to substitute for the present system of voting at Dáil elections the "straight vote" system in single-member constituencies; (2) to establish a commission to determine constituencies, subject to the right of the Dáil to amend the constituencies as so determined; and (3) to provide that whenever the Dáil is dissolved, the outgoing Ceann Comhairle (chairman) may be returned without a contest, as a second deputy for a constituency chosen by him, which consists of, or includes a part of, the constituency he represented before the dissolution.

Total poll	Invalid	Total valid poll	In favor	Against
1,129,606	48,212	1,081,394	423,496	657,898
(65.8%)	(4.2%)	(63%)	(39.2%)	(60.8%)

Source: Information made available by the Department of Local Government.

Ministers, 1919-1968

In the following table, names of ministers not in the Cabinet are printed in italics. Ministers holding more than one post have been so recorded. The total of names is not, therefore, necessarily equal to the number of members of the government at any particular time. In the body of the table, dates are given by month followed by day and year, e.g. June 29, 1920, is shown as 6/29/20.

APPENDIX C. *Ministers, January 1919–September 1922*

Office	FIRST DÁIL		SECOND DÁIL		PROVISIONAL GOVERNMENT	
	Jan 1919–Apr 1919	Apr 1919a–Aug 1921	Aug 1921–Jan 1922	Jan 1922–Sept 1922	Jan 1922–Aug 1922	Aug 1922–Sept 1922
President	C. Brugha	E. de Valera	E. de Valera	A. Griffith	M. Collins (Chairman)	W. T. Cosgrave
Finance	E. MacNeill	M. Collins	M. Collins	M. Collins	M. Collins	W. T. Cosgrave
Home Affairs	M. Collins	A. Griffith	A. Stack	E. Duggan	E. Duggan	K. O'Higgins
Foreign Affairs	Count Plunkett	Count Plunkett	A. Griffith	G. Gavan Duffy (7/25–8/12); A. Griffith (7/25–8/12); M. Hayes (from 8/12)		D. FitzGerald
National Defence	R. Mulcahy	C. Brugha	C. Brugha	R. Mulcahy		R. Mulcahy
Local Government		W. T. Cosgrave	W. T. Cosgrave (Asst. Minister K. O'Higgins)	W. T. Cosgrave	W. T. Cosgrave	E. Blythe
Labour		C. Markievicz	*C. Markievicz*	*J. McGrath*	J. McGrath	J. McGrath (incl. Ind. and Commerce & Econ. Affairs)
Industries		E. MacNeill				
Trade & Commerce		E. Blythe	*E. Blythe*	*E. Blythe*		
Economic Affairs			*R. C. Barton*	K. O'Higgins	K. O'Higgins	
Irish (from June 1920)		S. O Ceallaigh (from 6/29/20)				
Fisheries		S. Etchingham (from 6/29/20)	*S. Etchingham*			
Education			*J. J. O'Kelly*	*M. Hayes*	F. Lynch	E. MacNeill
Agriculture		R. C. Barton	*A. O'Connor*	*P. Hogan*	P. Hogan	P. Hogan
Publicity		L. Ginnell	*Count Plunkett*	*D. FitzGerald*		
Fine Arts						
Director of the Belfast Boycott (Jan–Feb 1922)				*M. Staines*		
Postmaster General					J. J. Walsh (from 4/22/22); E. MacNeill	J. J. Walsh
Ministers without Portfolio						
Law Officer				*H. Kennedy*	H. Kennedy	H. Kennedy

a Throughout the period until the truce "substitute ministers" or "substitute directors" were appointed to act for ministers (or directors) who were imprisoned or for some other reason could not act. For example, Desmond FitzGerald was Substitute Director of Publicity from April 1919 until he was imprisoned in February 1921, when he was replaced by Erskine Childers.

Office	Sept 1922–Sept 1923 COSGRAVE (Cumann na nGaedheal)	Sept 1923–June 1927 COSGRAVE (Cumann na nGaedheal)	June 1927–Oct 1927 COSGRAVE (Cumann na nGaedheal)	Oct 1927–Mar 1932 COSGRAVE (Cumann na nGaedheal)
President of Executive Council (called Chairman of Provisional Government until December 1922)	W. T. Cosgrave	W. T. Cosgrave	W. T. Cosgrave	W. T. Cosgrave
Justice (called Home Affairs until 1924)	K. O'Higgins	K. O'Higgins (Vice-President)	K. O'Higgins (Vice-President to 7/10) W. T. Cosgrave	J. Fitzgerald Kenny
Defence	R. Mulcahy	R. Mulcahy (to 3/19/24) W. T. Cosgrave (to 11/20/24) P. Hughes	D. FitzGerald	D. FitzGerald
External Affairs	D. FitzGerald	D. FitzGerald	K. O'Higgins (to 7/10)	P. McGilligan
Finance	W. T. Cosgrave	E. Blythe	E. Blythe (Vice-President from 7/10)	E. Blythe (Vice-President)
Industry and Commerce	J. McGrath	J. McGrath (to 3/7/24) P. McGilligan	P. McGilligan	P. McGilligan
Posts and Telegraphs (called Postmaster General until 1924)	*J. J. Walsh*	*J. J. Walsh*	J. J. Walsh	E. Blythe
Agriculture (called Lands and Agriculture from 1924 to 1928)	*P. Hogan*	*P. Hogan*	P. Hogan	P. Hogan
Fisheries (from 1928 called Lands and Fisheries)	*F. Lynch* (from 12/14/22)	*F. Lynch*	F. Lynch	F. Lynch
Education	E. MacNeill	E. MacNeill (to 11/24/25) J. M. O'Sullivan	J. M. O'Sullivan	J. M. O'Sullivan
Local Government and Public Health (called Local Government until 1924)	E. Blythe	*J. A. Burke*	R. Mulcahy	R. Mulcahy
Ministers without Portfolio	E. Duggan F. Lynch (to 12/14/22)			
Attorney General	*H. Kennedy*	*H. Kennedy* (to 6/5/24) *J. O'Byrne* (to 1/9/26) *J. A. Costello*	*J. A. Costello*	*J. A. Costello*

339

APPENDIX C *(cont.)*. *Ministers, March 1932–February 1948*

Office	Mar 1932–Feb 1933 DE VALERA (Fianna Fáil)	Feb 1933–July 1937 DE VALERA (Fianna Fáil)	July 1937–June 1938 DE VALERA (Fianna Fáil)	June 1938–July 1943 DE VALERA (Fianna Fáil)	July 1943–May 1944 DE VALERA (Fianna Fáil)	May 1944–Feb 1948 DE VALERA (Fianna Fáil)
President of Executive Council (called Taoiseach from Dec. 1937)	E. de Valera	E. de Valera	E. de Valera	E. de Valera	E. de Valera	E. de Valera
Justice	J. Geoghegan	P. J. Ruttledge	P. J. Ruttledge	P. J. Ruttledge (to 9/8/39) G. Boland	G. Boland	G. Boland
Defence	F. Aiken	F. Aiken	F. Aiken	F. Aiken (to 9/8/39) O. Traynor	O. Traynor	O. Traynor
Minister for Coordination of Defensive Measures (1939–45)				F. Aiken (from 9/8/39)	F. Aiken	F. Aiken (to 6/19/45)
External Affairs	E. de Valera	E. de Valera	E. de Valera	E. de Valera	E. de Valera	E. de Valera
Finance	S. MacEntee	S. MacEntee	S. MacEntee	S. MacEntee (to 9/16/39) S. T. O Ceallaigh (Tánaiste)	S. T. O Ceallaigh (Tánaiste)	S. T. O Ceallaigh (Tánaiste to 6/14/45) F. Aiken
Industry and Commerce	S. Lemass	S. Lemass	S. Lemass	S. Lemass (to 9/16/39) S. MacEntee (to 8/18/41) S. Lemass	S. Lemass	S. Lemass (Tánaiste from 6/14/45)
Supplies (1939–45)				S. Lemass (from 9/16/39)	S. Lemass	S. Lemass (to 7/31/45)
Posts and Telegraphs	J. Connolly	G. Boland (to 11/11/36) O. Traynor	O. Traynor	O. Traynor (to 9/8/39) T. Derrig (to 9/27/39) P. J. Little	P. J. Little	P. J. Little

Agriculture	J. Ryan	J. Ryan	J. Ryan	J. Ryan	J. Ryan	J. Ryan (to 1/21/47) P. Smith S. Moylan
Lands (called Lands and Fisheries until 1934)	P. J. Ruttledge	J. Connolly (to 5/29/36) F. Aiken (to 11/11/36) G. Boland	G. Boland	G. Boland (to 9/8/39) T. Derrig	S. Moylan	
Education	T. Derrig	T. Derrig	T. Derrig	T. Derrig (to 9/8/39) S. T. O Ceallaigh (to 9/27/39) E. de Valera (to 6/18/40) T. Derrig	T. Derrig	T. Derrig
Local Government and Public Health (after 1947 called Local Government)	S. T. O Ceallaigh (Vice-President)	S. T. O Ceallaigh (Vice-President)	S. T. O Ceallaigh (Vice-President, called Tánaiste from Dec. 1937)	S. T. O Ceallaigh (to 9/8/39) P. Ruttledge (to 8/14/41) S. MacEntee	S. MacEntee	S. MacEntee
Health (from 1947)						J. Ryan (from 1/21/47)
Social Welfare (from 1947)						J. Ryan (from 1/21/47)
Attorney General	*C. A. Maguire*	*C. A. Maguire (to 11/2/36) J. Geoghegan (to 12/22/36) P. Lynch*	*P. Lynch*	*P. Lynch (to 3/1/40) K. Haugh (to 10/10/42) K. Dixon*	*K. Dixon*	*K. Dixon (to 4/30/46) C. O Dálaigh*

APPENDIX C (*cont.*). *Ministers, February 1948–June 1959*

Office	Feb 1948–June 1951 COSTELLO (Inter-Party)	June 1951–June 1954 DE VALERA (Fianna Fáil)	June 1954–March 1957 COSTELLO (Inter-Party)	March 1957–June 1959 DE VALERA (Fianna Fáil)
Taoiseach	J. A. Costello	E. de Valera	J. A. Costello	E. de Valera
Justice	S. MacEoin (to 3/7/51) D. Morrissey	G. Boland	J. Everett	O. Traynor
Defence	T. F. O'Higgins (to 3/7/51) S. MacEoin	O. Traynor	S. MacEoin	K. Boland
External Affairs	S. MacBride	F. Aiken	L. Cosgrave	F. Aiken
Finance	P. McGilligan	S. MacEntee	G. Sweetman	J. Ryan
Industry and Commerce	D. Morrissey (to 3/7/51) T. F. O'Higgins	S. Lemass (Tánaiste)	W. Norton (Tánaiste)	S. Lemass (Tánaiste)
Posts and Telegraphs	J. Everett	E. Childers	M. Keyes	N. Blaney (to 12/4/57) J. Ormonde
Agriculture	J. Dillon	T. Walsh	J. Dillon	F. Aiken (to 5/16/57) S. Moylan (to 11/16/57) P. Smith
Lands	J. Blowick	T. Derrig	J. Blowick	E. Childers
Gaeltacht (from July 1956)			R. Mulcahy (from 7/2/56 to 10/24/56) P. J. Lindsay	J. Lynch (to 6/26/57) M. O Móráin
Education	R. Mulcahy	S. Moylan	R. Mulcahy	J. Lynch
Local Government	T. J. Murphy (to 4/29/49) M. Keyes	P. Smith	P. O'Donnell	P. Smith (to 11/27/57) N. Blaney
Health	N. C. Browne (to 4/11/51) J. A. Costello	J. Ryan	T. F. O'Higgins	S. MacEntee
Social Welfare	W. Norton (Tánaiste)	J. Ryan	B. Corish	P. Smith (to 11/27/57) S. MacEntee
Attorney General	C. Lavery (to 4/21/50) C. F. Casey	C. O Dálaigh (to 7/11/53) T. Teevan	P. McGilligan	A. O Caoimh

342

Office	June 1959–Oct 1961 LEMASS (Fianna Fáil)	Oct 1961–April 1965 LEMASS (Fianna Fáil)	April 1965–Nov 1966 LEMASS (Fianna Fáil)	Nov 1966–Dec 1968 LYNCH (Fianna Fáil)
Taoiseach	S. Lemass	S. Lemass	S. Lemass	J. Lynch
Justice	O. Traynor	C. Haughey (to 10/8/64) S. Lemass (to 11/3/64) B. Lenihan	B. Lenihan	B. Lenihan (to 3/26/68) M. O Móráin
Defence	K. Boland	G. Bartley	M. Hilliard	M. Hilliard
External Affairs	F. Aiken	F. Aiken	F. Aiken (Tánaiste)	F. Aiken (Tánaiste)
Finance	J. Ryan	J. Ryan	J. Lynch	C. Haughey
Industry and Commerce	J. Lynch	J. Lynch	P. Hillery (to 7/13/66) G. Colley	G. Colley
Transport and Power (from July 1959)	E. Childers (from 7/27/59)	E. Childers	E. Childers	E. Childers
Posts and Telegraphs	M. Hilliard	M. Hilliard	J. Brennan	E. Childers
Agriculture (called Agriculture and Fisheries from July 1965)	P. Smith	P. Smith (to 10/8/64) C. Haughey	C. Haughey	N. Blaney
Lands	E. Childers (to 7/23/59) M. O Móráin	M. O Móráin	M. O Móráin	M. O Móráin (to 3/26/68) P. Faulkner
Gaeltacht	M. O Móráin (to 7/23/59) G. Bartley	M. O Móráin	M. O Móráin	M. O Móráin (to 3/26/68) P. Faulkner
Education	P. J. Hillery	P. J. Hillery	G. Colley (to 7/13/66) D. B. O'Malley	D. B. O'Malley (to 3/10/68) J. Lynch (to 3/26/68) B. Lenihan
Local Government	N. Blaney	N. Blaney	N. Blaney	K. Boland
Health	S. MacEntee (Tánaiste)	S. MacEntee (Tánaiste)	D. B. O'Malley (to 7/13/66) S. Flanagan	S. Flanagan
Social Welfare	S. MacEntee	K. Boland	K. Boland	J. Brennan
Labour (from July 1966)			P. Hillery (from 7/13/66)	P. Hillery
Attorney General	*A. O Caoimh*	*A. O Caoimh (to 3/16/65) C. Condon*	*C. Condon*	*C. Condon*

343

State-sponsored Bodies in 1968

The following abbreviations are used in this appendix:

St. corp.	Statutory corporation	Pub. co.	Public company
HCB	A corporate body established	Pri. co.	Private company
	by ministerial order under	Co. guar.	Company limited
	the Health (Corporate Bodies)		by guarantee
	Act, 1961	Uninc.	Unincorporated body

Name	Form of organi- zation	Principal activity	Sponsor Minister
BODIES ENGAGED MAINLY IN ADMINISTRATIVE, REGULATORY, OR SOCIAL SERVICE ACTIVITIES			
1. The government of professions:			
An Bord Altranais (Nursing Board)	St. corp.	Control of nursing profession	Health
Bord na Radharcmhastóirí (Opticians' Board)	St. corp.	Control of opticians	Health
Dental Board	St. corp.	Control of dental profession	Health
Medical Registration Council	St. corp.	Control of medical profession	Health
Veterinary Council	St. corp.	Control of veterinary profession	Agric. and Fisheries
2. The control of economic activities:			
Bord na gCon (Greyhound Racing Board)	St. corp.	Control of greyhound racing	Agric. and Fisheries
Cork District Milk Board	St. corp.	Regulates milk supply	Agric. and Fisheries
Dublin District Milk Board	St. corp.	Regulates milk supply	Agric. and Fisheries
Foyle Fisheries Commission	St. corp.	Control of Foyle Estuary Fisheries	Agric. and Fisheries
Racing Board	St. corp.	Manages totalizator, betting levies	Finance
3. The administration or provision of social services:			
Bord Seirbhise Fuilaestriu- cháin (Blood Transfusion Service Board)	HCB	Operates national blood service	Health
Board for the Employment of the Blind	Uninc.	Manufacture of cane prod- ucts, etc.	Social Welfare
Bord Uchtála (Adoption Board)	St. corp.	Arranges and supervises adoption	Justice
Arts Council	St. corp.	Promotion of the arts	Finance
Dublin Dental Hospital Board	HCB	Owns and manages a dental hospital	Health

Name	Form of organi-zation	Principal activity	Sponsor Minister
Dublin Institute for Advanced Studies	St. corp.	Academic research	Education
Dublin Rheumatism Clinic	Co. guar.	Manages rheumatism clinic	Health
Hospitals Commission	St. corp.	Disposal, subject to minister-ial control, of sweepstake funds	Health
Hospitals Joint Services Board	HCB	Provides central services such as sterile supplies and laundry	Health
Hospitals Library Council	Uninc.	Library service for hospital patients	Health
Hospitals Trust Board	St. corp.	Trustees of funds raised by sweepstakes	Health
Irish Red Cross Society	St. corp.	Provides Red Cross services	Defence
Slua-Raideagrafaíochta (Mass Radiography Board)	HCB	Provides radiography services	Health
Medical Research Council	Co. guar.	Promotes medical research	Health
Bord Taighde Pobal Liachta (Medico-Social Research Board)	HCB	Promotes socio-medical research	Health
National Rehabilitation Board	HCB	Organizes and operates re-habilitation services	Health
National Theatre Society Ltd.	Pri. co.	Manages the national theater (The Abbey Theatre)	Finance
St. Laurence's Hospital Board	St. corp.	Owns and manages a general hospital	Health
St. Luke's Hospital	HCB	Cancer hospital	Health
Voluntary Health Insurance Board	St. corp.	Manages health insurance scheme	Health

BODIES ENGAGED MAINLY IN TRADING, MARKETING, RESEARCH, OR DEVELOPMENT ACTIVITIES

1. *Trading—Production of goods:*

Arramara Teo.	Pri. co.	Seaweed processing	Gaeltacht
Bord na Móna	St. corp.	Production and processing of peat	Transport and power
Ceimicí Teo.	Pub. co.	Production of alcohol from potatoes	Finance
Colucht Groighe Náisiúnta na hEireann Teo. (Irish National Stud Co. Ltd.)	Pri. co.	Bloodstock breeding	Finance
Comhlucht Siúicre Eireann (Irish Sugar Company)	Pub. co.	Production of sugar, etc.	Finance
Subsidiary: Erin Foods	Pub. co.	Production of processed foods	
Dairy Disposal Co.	Pri. co.	Dairy and other farm pro-duce	Agric. and Fisheries
Subsidiaries:			
(a) Cleeves Confectionery (Limerick) Ltd.	Pri. co.	Toffee production	
(b) Condensed Milk Co. of Ireland (1928) Ltd.	Pri. co.	Dairy products	
(c) Newmarket Dairy Co.	Pri. co.	Butter production	

Name	Form of organization	Principal activity	Sponsor Minister
Electricity Supply Board	St. corp.	Production & distribution of electricity	Transport and Power
Gaeltarra Eireann	St. corp.	Production of tweed, toys, etc. in Gaeltacht	Gaeltacht
Irish Steel Holdings Ltd.	Pri. co.	Steel production	Industry and Commerce
Min Fheir (1959) Teo. (Grass-meal Ltd.)	Pub. co.	Grass-meal production	Industry and Commerce
Nitrigin Eireann Teo.	Pri. co.	Production of nitrogenous fertilizer	Industry and Commerce

2. Trading—Transport:[a]

Name	Form of organization	Principal activity	Sponsor Minister
Aer Lingus Teo.	Pri. co.	Air transport	Transport and Power
Aerlinte Eireann Teo.	Pri. co.	Air transport	Transport and Power
Aer Rianta Teo.	Pub. co.	Airports management	Transport and Power
British and Irish Steam Packet Co. Ltd.	Pri. co.	Cross-channel transport	Transport and Power
Córas Iompair Eireann	St. corp.	Rail, road, and water transport	Transport and Power
Subsidiary: Ostlanna Iompair Teo.	Pri. co.	Hotel management, railway catering	
Irish Shipping Ltd.	Pri. co.	Ocean freight	Finance

3. Trading—Communications:

Name	Form of organization	Principal activity	Sponsor Minister
Radio Telefís Eireann	St. corp.	Television and radio	Posts and Telegraphs

4. Trading—Finance:

Name	Form of organization	Principal activity	Sponsor Minister
Agricultural Credit Corp.	Pub. co.	Credit for farming enterprises	Finance
Central Bank of Ireland	St. corp.	National banking	Finance
Industrial Credit Co. Ltd.	Pub. co.	Industrial financing	Finance
Subsidiaries: (a) Irish Film Finance Co. Ltd.	Pri. co.	Financing Irish-made films	
(b) Shipping Finance Corp. Ltd.	Pri. co.	Financing Irish shipbuilding	
Irish Life Assurance Co. Ltd.	Pub. co.	Life insurance	Finance
Subsidiaries: (a) Ilasco Subsidiary Ltd.	Pri. co.	Manages investment of insurance funds	
(b) Irish Estates Ltd.	Pri. co.	Property ownership and development	

5. Marketing, research, and development:

Name	Form of organization	Principal activity	Sponsor Minister
Bord Bainne (Milk Marketing Board)	St. corp.	Markets dairy produce	Agric. and Fisheries

Name	Form of organization	Principal activity	Sponsor Minister
Bord Fáilte Eireann (Irish Tourist Board)[b]	St. corp.	Development of tourism	Transport and Power
Bord Gráin (Grain Marketing Board)	St. corp.	Markets surplus grain	Agric. and Fisheries
Bord Iascaigh Mhara (Sea Fisheries Board)	St. corp.	Development of sea fishing industry	Agric. and Fisheries
Comhairle Oiliúna	St. corp.	Industrial training	Labour
Córas Tráchtála (Irish Export Board)	St. corp.	Promotes exports	Industry and Commerce
Subsidiaries:[c]			
(a) Kilkenny Design Workshops Ltd.	Pri. co.	Design and marketing of high-quality pottery, metal ware, and fabrics	
(b) Ireland House Shop Ltd.	Pri. co.	Management of an exhibition center and shop	
Foras Forbartha Teo.	Pri. co.	Physical planning and research	Local Gov.
Inland Fisheries Trust Inc.	Co. guar.	Development of angling facilities	Agric. and Fisheries
Institute for Industrial Research and Standards	St. corp.	Industrial scientific testing and standards	Industry and Commerce
Irish Potato Marketing Co. Ltd.	Pri. co.	Markets potatoes	Agric. and Fisheries
National Building Agency	Co. guar.	Housebuilding	Local Gov.
Pigs and Bacon Commission	St. corp.	Markets bacon products	Agric. and Fisheries
Salmon Research Trust of Ireland Inc.	Pri. co.	Salmon research	Agric. and Fisheries
Shannon Free Airport Development Co. Ltd.	Pri. co.	Development and management of industrial estate	Transport and Power
Taisci Stáit Teo.	Pub. co.	Financing of industrial enterprises	Finance
Industrial Development Authority[d]	St. corp.	Stimulation of industry in Ireland	Industry and Commerce

Source: Adapted and developed from G. FitzGerald, *State-sponsored Bodies* (2d ed., 1963).

[a] The Dublin Port and Docks Board, though not strictly a state-sponsored body as here defined, should be noticed. It is a harbor authority, somewhat similar to those to be found in the United Kingdom, in the form of a statutory corporation composed of representatives of the Dublin Corporation and elected representatives of users of the port and other interested parties.

[b] Eight Regional Tourist Companies were set up by Bord Fáilte. They are companies limited by guarantee. Private persons and organizations and local authorities subscribe to become shareholders. Bord Fáilte appoints one director of each company and has some powers of control.

[c] Shipping Services Ltd. is a public company set up to expedite the exports of goods through Liverpool. It is owned by exporters, with Córas Tráchtála holding one share and with the right to nominate three directors. It is effectively a subsidiary of Córas Tráchtála, which set it up and administers it. SSL Distributors Ltd. is a wholly-owned subsidiary of Shipping Services Ltd. It provides warehousing facilities in Liverpool.

[d] Until 1968 the Industrial Development Authority (and a related organization, An Foras Tionscal) was a statutory body under the aegis of the Department of Industry and Commerce. Its staff were civil servants and so were two out of five of the members of the Board. Legislation to change its status to that of a state-sponsored body is pending.

The Dáil Electoral System as It Stood in 1969

For general election purposes the country is divided into forty-two constituencies. Two of them return five members each; fourteen return four members each; and twenty-six return three members each.

Every citizen who has reached the age of twenty-one and who is not placed under a legal disability has the right to vote. To do so, he must, however, be registered as a Dáil elector, which involves him only in filling in a form. Registers are prepared annually by the County Councils and County Borough Corporations, and to be registered in a constituency a person must be over twenty-one, a citizen of Ireland, and ordinarily resident in the constituency.

Similarly, every citizen who has reached the age of twenty-one and is not placed under a disability or incapacity by the Constitution or by the law is eligible for membership in the Dáil (or the Seanad). The following are barred by the Constitution or statute from being elected to or sitting in either House: the President of Ireland, the Comptroller and Auditor General (the parliamentary auditor of the public accounts), the judges, any person undergoing a prison sentence of six months or more of "hard labour" or of any period of "penal servitude," people of unsound mind, undischarged bankrupts, persons found guilty of corrupt practices or other election offenses, members of the defense forces and of the Garda Síochána (police), civil servants, and members of the boards of state-owned companies or corporations.

A candidate for election is not by law required to reside in the constituency he is contesting, though almost all do. He must, however, be proposed and seconded by two electors of the constituency, and he must get the signatures on his nomination papers of eight more constituents (called "assentors"). He must deposit £100, which sum is returned to him "provided that the number of votes credited to him at any time during the counting of the votes exceeds one-third of the quota." In 1957, 45 out of 289 lost their deposits; in 1961, 61 out of 300, and in 1965, 53 out of 280.

The conduct of elections in each constituency is in the hands of a Returning Officer, who is a local government official on whom statutory functions are placed. The Returning Officer accepts nominations, arranges polling places, election machinery, and personnel, presides over the poll, and conducts the count. Polling takes place on a day fixed by the Minister for Local Government between two statutory limits and must take place on the same day in every constituency except in the case of islands, where, because of the possibility of delay due to the weather, the Returning Officer has it in his discretion to fix a day before the general polling day. Voters cast their ballots in polling places, often national schoolhouses, near their homes, and they may vote only in the polling places described for them and of which they are notified by post. Only in the case of members of the defense forces and the Garda Síochána is postal voting permitted. The ballot paper lists the names of the candidates, who in a five-member constituency may number as many as fifteen, in alphabetical order. The surname of each candidate and the name of his political party, if any, are printed in large typeface, and his full name, address, and occupation in small typeface. All or part of this may be in Irish or in English. Candidates do not, however, have complete freedom to designate their own party affiliations. The law provides for the establishment and maintenance of a Register of Political Parties. To be registered a party must be a genuine political party and must be organized to contest elections. Certain criteria to establish these facts are laid down by law, and the Clerk of Dáil Eireann is designated Registrar with an appeal to a judicial tribunal. The name of a party will not be registered if it is identical with the name of any party already registered or may be confused with one such. Some organizations have in fact been refused registration. A candidate is entitled to have the name of his party included on the ballot paper if the party is registered and if he has been accepted officially as a party candidate by the party officers. When a candidate is not a party candidate, he is entitled, if he wishes, to have the term "Non-party" inserted after his name on the paper.

To vote, the elector enters his appointed polling place, identifies himself, and is checked on the register by the Presiding Officer and the personation agents appointed by the parties. The Presiding Officer puts an official mark on a ballot paper and gives it to the voter. The voter goes to a booth, where he marks the paper. He must then, the law says, show the Presiding Officer the official mark on the paper but not the side of the paper on which he has marked his choice, and he must drop the paper in the sealed box provided for the purpose.

The elector casts a single transferable vote, that is, a vote which, in the words of the statute, is "capable of being given so as to indicate the voter's preference for the candidates in order," and "capable of being transferred to the next choice when the vote is not required to give a prior choice the necessary quota of votes, or when, owing to the deficiency in the number of votes given for a prior choice, that choice is eliminated from the list of candidates." The voter must put the figure 1 opposite the name of the candidate of his first choice. He may then put the figure 2 opposite the name of his second choice, 3 opposite his third choice, and so on. If he does not put the figure 1 opposite the name of a candidate, his paper is invalid; if he omits a choice, e.g. numbers his choices 1, 2, 4, 5, his paper becomes invalid where the gap occurs (in this case after the second choice). He is not obliged to indicate more than one choice and he may indicate as many choices as he pleases.

The procedures for counting the votes and ascertaining who has been elected are laid down in a precise and detailed way in the legislation. All the ballot boxes in a constituency are brought to an appointed place. The Returning Officer and his staff inspect them, open them, count the number of ballot papers, and verify the ballot paper account accompanying each box. They then mix all the papers from the various boxes together.

The first stage in the count is to scrutinize all papers and to reject invalid votes. A vote is invalid if it does not bear the official mark, if it does not bear the figure 1 standing alone when only one choice is made (though some Returning Officers do in practice accept an X), if it contains 1 more than once, or if the voter has written anything on the paper by which he may be identified. The valid papers are sorted into "parcels" according to the first preferences recorded for each candidate, and the parcels are counted. Each candidate is credited with the number of votes in his parcel and the total of the valid votes is ascertained. At this point the Returning Officer is able to calculate and declare the "quota." The quota is the number of votes necessary to secure the election of a candidate. The quota used in Irish elections is the "Droop quota," the smallest number of votes that suffices to elect the requisite number of candidates while being just big enough to prevent any more being elected. It is expressed in the formula:

$$\text{Quota} = \frac{\text{The number of valid votes}}{\text{The number of seats} + 1} + 1.$$

Any candidate who obtains a quota or more is now declared elected. If the number elected is less than the number of places to be filled, the counters begin to transfer votes from first to later preferences according to detailed rules. First, any "surplus" votes of the candidates declared elected at the first count are transferred to other candidates, the biggest "surplus" first, and so on. A "surplus" is "the number of votes by which the total number of votes credited to a candidate exceeds the quota." To distribute the surplus of an elected candidate, all his votes are re-sorted and arranged in parcels in order of the next available preferences, if any, shown on them—"available preferences" because a preference for a candidate already elected is ignored and account is taken of the next preference. Candidates who receive such preferences have transferred to them a proportionate number of the appropriate parcel. The number is calculated by using the formula

$$
\begin{array}{c}
\text{No. of Candidate A's} \\
\text{votes to be transferred} \\
\text{to Candidate B}
\end{array}
=
\frac{
\begin{array}{c}
\text{No. of Candidate A's} \\
\text{surplus votes}
\end{array}
}{
\begin{array}{c}
\text{No. of votes transferable} \\
\text{from Candidate A to all} \\
\text{other candidates}
\end{array}
}
\times
\begin{array}{c}
\text{No. of papers in} \\
\text{Candidate B's parcel} \\
\text{of votes transferable} \\
\text{from Candidate A}
\end{array}
$$

The transfer is made by physically removing voting papers from the top of the elected candidate's parcel and putting them with the other candidates' parcels. Thus, the elected candidate is left with his quota, and the other candidates have passed on to them appropriate additions to their parcels of votes. Whenever, in the later stages of the count, a candidate is elected with more than the bare quota, this process is repeated, except that, instead of all the votes credited to the elected candidate throughout the count being re-sorted, only the last parcel he received is taken and re-sorted.

When, in the course of a count, there are no surpluses to be transferred and seats still remain to be filled, the candidate with the lowest number of votes credited to him is declared eliminated from the contest and his votes are transferred to the next available preferences shown on the ballot papers. When there is no indication on a ballot paper of the voter's next preference, the vote is declared "non-transferable," and is put on one side and not used. This process of transferring surpluses and the votes of eliminated candidates goes on until either the necessary number of seats is filled or, as often happens, only two candidates are left, neither with a quota. In this case the candidate with the highest number of votes credited to him is declared elected "without reaching the quota." In practice, a number of candidates are so elected: in 1961, there were 30; in 1965, 29.

In the case of a by-election, the single seat is filled in the same way. The election is thus by the single transferable vote in a single-member constituency, and the quota needed by a candidate to win a seat is an absolute majority.

Further Reading

GENERAL WORKS

Chubb, B., ed. A Source Book of Irish Government. Dublin, 1964.
Donaldson, A. G. Some Comparative Aspects of Irish Law. Durham, N.C., 1957.
Freeman, T. W. Ireland, a General and Regional Geography. 3d ed. London, 1965.
Kohn, L. The Constitution of the Irish Free State. London, 1932.
Mansergh, N. The Irish Free State, Its Government and Politics. London, 1934.
"Survey of Public Administration and Administrative Law in Ireland," *International Review of Administrative Sciences*, XXXIV, i, ii (1968), 1–87.

HISTORICAL BACKGROUND

Beaslai, P. Michael Collins and the Making of the New Ireland. Dublin, 1937.
Beckett, J. C. The Making of Modern Ireland, 1603–1923. London, 1966.
Bromage, M. C. De Valera and the March of a Nation. London, 1956.
Curtis, E. A History of Ireland. London, 1950.
Hancock, W. K. Survey of British Commonwealth Affairs. I, Problems of Nationality, 1918–1936. London, 1937, chaps. 3, 6.
Inglis, B. The Story of Ireland. 2d ed. London, 1966.
Macardle, D. The Irish Republic. 4th ed. Dublin, 1951.
McManus, F., ed. The Years of the Great Test, 1926–39. Cork, 1967.
Mansergh, N. The Irish Question, 1840–1921. Rev. ed. London, 1965.
O'Brien, G. The Four Green Fields, Irish Nationalism from the Union to the Present. Dublin, 1936.
O'Hegarty, P. S. A History of Ireland under the Union, 1801–1922. London, 1952.
Williams, T. D., ed. The Irish Struggle, 1916–26. London, 1966.

SOCIAL STRUCTURE AND POLITICAL CULTURE

Arensberg, C. M. The Irish Countryman. London, 1937.
Arensberg, C. M., and S. T. Kimball. Family and Community in Ireland. 2d ed. Cambridge, Mass., 1968.

Blanchard, J.   Le droit ecclésiastique contemporain d'Irlande. Paris, 1958. English translation under title *The Church in Contemporary Ireland*. Dublin, 1964.

Connery, Donald.   The Irish. London, 1968.

Coogan, T. P.   Ireland since the Rising. London, 1966.

Farrell, B.   "The New State and Irish Political Culture," *Administration*, XVI (1968), 238–46.

Fennell, D., ed.   The Changing Face of Catholic Ireland. London, 1968.

Gray, Tony.   The Irish Answer: An Anatomy of Ireland. London, 1966.

Healy, J.   The Death of an Irish Town. Cork, 1968.

McCarthy, C.   The Distasteful Challenge. Dublin, 1968.

Rumpf, E.   Nationalismus und Sozialismus in Irland. Meisenheim am Glan, 1959.

Sheehy, Michael.   Is Ireland Dying?: Culture and the Church in Modern Ireland. London, 1968.

Thornley, D. A.   "Ireland, The End of an Era," *Studies*, LIII (1964), 1–17.

Viney, M.   The Five Per Cent. Dublin, 1965.

THE CONSTITUTION

Chubb, B.   The Constitution of Ireland. 2d ed. Dublin, 1966.

Costello, D.   "The Natural Law and the Constitution," *Studies*, XLV (1956), 403–14.

Grogan, V.   "The Constitution and the Natural Law," *Christus Rex*, VIII (1954), 201–18.

Hancock, W. K.   Survey of British Commonwealth Affairs. I, Problems of Nationality, 1918–1936. London, 1937, chaps. 3, 6.

Kelly, J. M.   Fundamental Rights in the Irish Law and Constitution. 2d ed. Dublin, 1967.

McDonagh, E.   "Church and State in the Constitution of Ireland," *The Irish Theological Quarterly*, XXVIII (1961), 131–44.

Mansergh, N.   Survey of British Commonwealth Affairs. Problems of External Policy, 1931–1939. London, 1952, chap. 8.

———   Survey of British Commonwealth Affairs. Problems of Wartime Co-operation and Post-War Change, 1939–1952. London, 1958, chap. 6.

PARTIES, INTEREST GROUPS, AND THE MASS MEDIA

Blanshard, P.   The Irish and Catholic Power. London, 1954.

Kelly, J. M.   "The Constitutional Position of R.T.E.," *Administration*, XV (1967), 205–16.

Moss, W.   Political Parties in the Irish Free State. New York, 1933.

Murphy, C.   "Party Organization," articles in *Leargas*, Nos. 12, 13, 14 (Institute of Public Administration, Dublin, 1968).

Thornley, D. A.   "Development of the Irish Labour Movement," *Christus Rex*, XVIII (1964), 7–21.

———   "Television and Politics," *Administration*, XV (1967), 217–25.

Business Representation in Irish National Affairs: The Report of a Study for the '66 Business Conference. Harbridge House Europe. Dublin, 1967.

ELECTIONS

Chubb, B. "Ireland, 1957," in D. E. Butler, ed., *Elections Abroad* (London, 1959). Chap. 3.

Hogan, J. Election and Representation. Cork, 1945.

Lawless, M. "The Dáil Electoral System," *Administration*, V (1957), 57–74.

O'Leary, C. The Irish Republic and Its Experiment with Proportional Representation. South Bend, Indiana, 1961.

Ross, J. F. S. The Irish Election System: What It Is and How It Works. London, 1959.

THE GOVERNMENT AND THE OIREACHTAS

Chubb, B. "Vocational Representation and the Irish Senate," *Political Studies*, II (1954), 97–111.

——— "The Independent Member in Ireland," *Political Studies*, V (1957), 131–39.

——— "Going about Persecuting Civil Servants: The Role of the Irish Parliamentary Representative," *Political Studies*, XI (1963), 272–86.

McCracken, J. L. Representative Government in Ireland: A Study of Dáil Eireann, 1919–48. London, 1957.

O'Sullivan, D. The Irish Free State and Its Senate. London, 1940.

Smyth, J. C. The Houses of the Oireachtas. 2d ed. Dublin, 1964.

——— "Seanad Eireann," three articles in *Administration*, XV (1967), and XVI (1968).

Whyte, J. Dáil Deputies: Their Work, Its Difficulties, Possible Remedies. Tuairim Pamphlet No. 15. Dublin, 1966.

THE ADMINISTRATION OF PUBLIC SERVICES

Barrington, T. J. "Elaborate Contrivance," *Administration*, III, ii–iii (1955), 94–108.

Bristow, J. A., and A. A. Tait, eds. Economic Policy in Ireland. Dublin, 1968.

Bromage, A. W. "Irish Councilmen at Work," *Administration*, II (1954), 87–98.

——— "Council-Manager Plan in Ireland," *Administration*, IX (1961–62), 309–17.

Chubb, B. "Fifty Years of Irish Administration," in O. Dudley Edwards and F. Pyle, eds., *1916, The Easter Rising* (London, 1968).

Collins, J. Local Government. 2d ed. by D. Roche. Dublin, 1963.

Farley, D. Social Insurance and Social Assistance in Ireland. Dublin, 1964.

Finlay, I. The Civil Service. Dublin, 1966.

FitzGerald, G. Planning in Ireland. Dublin, 1968.

——— State-sponsored Bodies. 2d ed. Dublin, 1964.

Garvin, J. "Local Government and Its Problems," *Administration*, XI (1963), 224–41.

Hensey, B. The Health Services of Ireland. Dublin, 1959.

Kaim-Caudle, P. R. Social Policy in the Irish Republic. London, 1967.

Lemass, S. F. The Role of the State-sponsored Bodies in the Economy. Dublin, 1959.

McElligott, T. J.   Education in Ireland. Dublin, 1966.
Meghen, P. J.   A Short History of the Public Service in Ireland. Dublin, 1962.
"The Role and Function of the Councillor," three articles by N. T. Blaney,
    J. F. Gill, and G. A. Meagher in *Administration*, XIII (1965), 73–89.

In addition, the volumes of *Administration*, the journal of the Institute of
Public Administration, contain many articles dealing with the organization and
working not only of the Civil Service but also of public authorities generally.

THE CITIZEN AND ADMINISTRATION

Beth, L. P.   The Development of Judicial Review in Ireland, 1937–1966. Dub-
    lin, 1967.
Delany, V. T. H.   The Administration of Justice in Ireland. Dublin, 1962.
Grogan, V.   Administrative Tribunals in the Public Service. Dublin, n.d.
Kelly, J. M.   Fundamental Rights in the Irish Law and Constitution. 2d ed.
    Dublin, 1967.

Index

tion, 33; split, 59, 60, 70, 71; support for, 86, 88–89, 157; and the Civil Service, 241; and local government, 282, 278
Smith, Patrick, 182
Smyth, J. C., 201
Special courts, 303–4
State-sponsored bodies, 246–68; growth, 222, 241–42, 252–54, 256–59; number employed in, 222, 251–52; definition, 246–49; number of, 247, 345–48; and the Civil Service, 249, 257, 261, 263–65; forms of, 249–51, 254–55; investment in, 251–52; ministerial control of, 258, 259–66; Oireachtas control of, 259–60, 266–68; types of organizations and activities and sponsor ministers, 345–48
State (Quinn) v. *Ryan and others*, 1965, I.R.70, 301
Stephens, James, 27
Stuarts, 11
Supremacy, Act of, 10
Supreme Court, 188, 299, 305

Tánaiste, 169, 191
Taoiseach: powers, 66, 168, 186, 191; appointment of, 167; role, 174, 179, 189–92; resignation, 179; in Bunreacht na hEireann, 187–88, 191; in Irish Free State Constitution, 190–91
Teachta Dála, *see* Dáil deputies
Television, *see* Radio Telefís Eireann
Tenant League, 26
Thornley, David, 17, 47, 53–54, 81, 83, 138
Tone, T. Wolfe, 15, 16
Town commissioners: functions, 272–73; establishment of, 276; decline of, 279; occupations of members, 288–89; and the political parties, 290–91; elections, 291–93. *See also* Local authorities
Towns Improvement (Ireland) Act, 1854, 275
Trade unions: growth of, 36–37; membership in Labour Party, 90, 92; and the Catholic Church, 99; membership of, 107, 109
Transport and General Workers' Union,

see Irish Transport and General Workers' Union
Transport and Power: Department, 228; Minister, 261–62, 263
Treaty (The), 1921: signing, 41; effects, 42, 63, 71, 72, 171, 204; split over, 50, 59–60, 73, 171; and the Civil Service, 233
Troy, T., 196
Tudors, 7, 8, 9, 10, 11
Turpin, D., 282

Ulster: plantation of, 9f; rebellion in, 14; tenant right in, 21, 22; and Home Rule, 32, 34, 39; and trade unionism, 37; and partition, 39, 40, 42. *See also* Northern Ireland
Uniformity, Act of, 10
Union, Act of, 12, 14, 24
Unionist Party, 58, 59, 82, 147
United Irishman, 33
United Irish Society, 13
United Nations, 48, 203, 242, 315
Universities, 19–20, 55, 208
Urban district councils: functions, 272–73; establishment, 276; occupations of members, 288–89; and political parties, 290–91; elections, 291–93. *See also* Local authorities

Vatican Council II, 54, 57, 315
Vikings, 5
Vocational Organization, Commission on, 103, 118–19
Vocational Representation, 205
Volunteers (The Irish), 34, 37–40 *passim*

Wahlke, J. C., 215
Wallas, G., 218
Weber, Max, 280
Wheare, K. C., 166, 194, 197, 200, 302
Whitaker, T. K., 243
Workers' Union of Ireland, 107
Wyndham, G., 23, 218
Wyse, Sir Thomas, 19

Yeats, W. B., 4, 33, 42
Young Ireland Movement, 25, 27, 28